2006

SOCIAL WELFARE IN TODAY'S WORLD

SOCIAL WELFARE IN TODAY'S WORLD

SECOND EDITION

William H. Whitaker
University of Maine

Ronald C. Federico
Late Professor of Social Work
Iona College

This text was originally developed for The McGraw-Hill Companies
by Irving Rockwood & Associates, Inc.

Boston, Massachusetts   Burr Ridge, Illinois   Dubuque, Iowa
Madison, Wisconsin   New York, New York   San Francisco, California   St. Louis, Missouri

WCB/McGraw-Hill

A Division of The **McGraw·Hill** *Companies*

This book was set in Times Roman by The Clarinda Company.
The editor was Nancy Blaine;
the production supervisor was Louise Karam.
The cover was designed by Katherine Urban.
Cover illustration by Jane Sterritt.
The photo editor was Elyse Rieder.
Project supervision was done by Spectrum Publisher Services, Inc.

SOCIAL WELFARE IN TODAY'S WORLD

This book is printed on acid-free paper.

4 5 6 7 8 9   BKM BKM   9 0 9 8 7 6 5 4 3 2 1 0

ISBN 0-07-069624-1

Library of Congress Cataloging-in-Publication Data

Whitaker, William H.
    Social welfare in today's world / William H. Whitaker, Ronald C.
Federico. —2nd ed.
        p.   cm.
    ISBN 0-07-069624-1
    1. Human services—Cross-cultural studies.   I. Federico, Ronald
C. II. Title.
HV91.W495   1997
361.973—dc20   96-22609

CHAPTER-OPENING PHOTOS
Introduction: © Suzie Fitzhugh. Chapter 1: © Suzie Fitzhugh. Chapter 2: Lauren Chelec/courtesy
Catholic Charities. Chapter 3: Lauren Chelec/courtesy Catholic Charities. Chapter 4: Futran
Photography. Chapter 5: Futran Photography. Chapter 6: *Bangor Daily News*. Chapter 7: © Suzie
Fitzhugh. Chapter 8: Futran Photography. Chapter 9: Lauren Chelec/courtesy Catholic Charities.
Chapter 10: Futran Photography.

ABOUT THE AUTHORS

RONALD C. FEDERICO was Professor of Social Work at Iona College in New Rochelle, New York. He held a bachelor's degree from Yale (where he graduated magna cum laude in 1962), a master of social work degree from the University of Michigan, and a Ph.D. in sociology from Northwestern University. Professor Federico was a leader in baccalaureate social work education. He was an active member of the Council on Social Work Education and the Association of Baccalaureate Social Work Program Directors and served as director or program chair of three undergraduate-level social work programs. In addition, he was the author of numerous scholarly studies, the coauthor (with Betty L. Baer) of the highly influential two-volume study, *Educating the Baccalaureate Social Worker* (published by Ballinger, 1978 and 1979), and the author or coauthor of several successful undergraduate-level texts. After being diagnosed HIV positive in 1987, Ron traveled to Poland, Sweden, and Mexico to research and then to author the first edition of *Social Welfare in Today's World.* Ron died from AIDS in 1992. His life and many contributions are celebrated by his students and colleagues throughout the United States and the world.

WILLIAM H. WHITAKER is Professor and Baccalaureate Program Coordinator at the University of Maine School of Social Work. He earned bachelor's and master's degrees in sociology from Ohio State University, a master of social work degree in community organization from Atlanta University, and a Ph.D. in social welfare planning from Brandeis University. Since working in community organizing and administration for 10 years in an interracial settlement house in Columbus, Ohio, Bill has taught undergraduate social work since 1978. He has been elected to the boards of directors of the Council on Social Work Education and the Association of Baccalaureate Social Work Program Directors. As a scholar/activist working on issues of domestic and international hunger, Bill has served as a member of the national planning committees for the Campaign to End Childhood Hunger and the Medford Declaration to End Hunger in the United States, as founder and president of the Maine Coalition for Food Security, as a national board member of Bread for the World, and as principal investigator for the Maine Community Childhood Hunger Identification Project. He is author of numerous scholarly publications and the second edition of *Social Welfare in Today's World.*

To K. J. W. and our future
and to
those undergraduate social work
educators who have done so much
for so many.

Ron Federico

To Fannie and Morris Eisenstein
and to
all those persons
throughout the world
who struggle for social
and economic justice.

Bill Whitaker

THE PROGRESS OF NATIONS

The day will come
when the progress of nations will be
judged not by their military or economic
strength, nor by the splendor of
their capital cities and public buildings,
but by the well-being of their peoples:
by their levels of health, nutrition and education;
by their opportunities to earn a fair reward for their
labours; by their ability to participate in the
decisions that affect their lives; by the respect that is
shown for their civil and political liberties;
by the provision that is made for those who are
vulnerable and disadvantaged; and by
the protection that is afforded to the growing minds
and bodies of their children.

The United Nations Children's Fund, 1993

In the final analysis, however, we must realize that social injustice and unjust social structures exist only because individuals and groups of individuals deliberately maintain or tolerate them. It is these personal choices, operating through structures, that breed and propagate situations of poverty, oppression, and misery.

Pope John Paul II
San Antonio, Texas
September 13, 1987

CONTENTS

ILLUSTRATIONS, TABLES, AND BOXES

Tables

"On the Street" Boxes

"The Human Face of Social Welfare" Boxes

Additional Boxes

PREFACE

PREFACE TO THE FIRST EDITION

The following encounter was reported in a large United States city. [A man sat on the steps of a church, surrounded by his belongings.] "In his outstretched hand he held a paper cup; his plea—'Change. Spare change?'—was addressed to all passers-by, among them a boy of about 8 or 9.

When he heard the elderly man's request, the boy bounced off his skateboard, placed it under his arm and approached the man with concern. 'I don't have any money, but I've got some baseball cards,' the boy said. 'Would you want some of those?'

The man looked at him for a long moment. The squint into the sun turned into a smile. 'Yeah, let's see what you've got,' he said.

The boy knelt on the sidewalk, pulled some cards out of his knapsack and handed over a few. The man held them with great care, turning them over and over as if they were precious objects. When at last he spoke, he said: 'Thanks. Thanks a lot. I could use these.'

Satisfied, the boy hopped back up on his skateboard. The elderly man watched him speed off into the distance."[1]

This book is about encounters of this kind between people. It explores why people are in need, and why others choose to help—or not to help—them. It also examines what makes things valuable to people, and the formal and informal strategies through which people are linked to the resources they need. The helping impulse that leads people to share with others is at the core of this book. What is shared may be love, money, housing, counseling, or even baseball cards. Whatever it is, the quality of social life is affected by how it is shared, either informally (as between the vagrant and the skateboarder) or formally through highly structured social welfare programs.

The book approaches these topics by posing a series of questions, each of which then becomes the focal point of a chapter. These questions move systematically from a concern with the nature of social welfare and why is it needed in today's world to more technical questions about how helping programs are designed and structured. The focus throughout the book is on social welfare in the

---

[1]Sidney Weinberg, "Metropolitan Diary," *The New York Times,* July 6, 1988, p. B2.

United States, but comparative material from three other societies—Mexico, Poland, and Sweden—also is included. This material highlights major issues in the relationship between helping efforts and the political, economic, educational, and family structures of society. It also should serve to expand our thinking about alternative ways of conceptualizing and delivering help to people in need. Using a comparative perspective has the additional benefit of linking the United States with social processes and social issues that seem to be common to all Western industrialized societies.

Learning about organized helping in the United States can be challenging and frustrating. Its mixture of public tax-supported and private non-profit and for-profit services is unique and creative, but also complex. The very controversy over whether providing economic support to the poor and the disadvantaged actually helps or hurts them is symptomatic of the difficult decisions involved in social welfare. To study the limits and nature of our responsibilities to those who are especially vulnerable or disadvantaged brings us close to the heart of the problem. This book seeks to enable its readers to understand these issues better so that they can participate in decision making about them, either in the voting booth or through a career choice.

Acknowledgments

Writing this book has been a wonderful personal experience. I have met many valued colleagues in other societies, and I have had the opportunity to learn much that I value. This project would not have come to fruition without the help of many people, only a few of whom I can cite here.

Iona College granted me the sabbatical leave that made the intensive work possible that was necessary to complete the book. In addition, Iona's commitment to basic human values and to internationalizing its curriculum as a way of helping students understand the common human enterprise in which we are all involved, stimulated and focused my own thinking.

My developmental editor, Irving Rockwood of Irving Rockwood & Associates, was a tremendous support during the formulation and execution of this book. He understood my goals, and he helped me to formulate them so that they could be made real in a book format. He also provided invaluable editorial assistance.

Many colleagues went out of their way to help me obtain data and learn more about social welfare in the United States and elsewhere. In Mexico, I would especially like to thank Lidia Proal, Rosa Maria de Castro Valle, and Jesus Ferreiros Lopez for their help, along with the social work faculty at the Universitaria Nacional Autonoma de Mexico. My work in Poland was made possible by Janet Schwartz, a valued colleague in this country, and Professor Jan Rosner and Professor Ewa Leś, who live in Poland. Professors Rosner and Leś were tireless translators, helpful colleagues, and extraordinary hosts. To them, and all those with whom they arranged meetings for me, I am deeply grateful.

Studying social welfare in Sweden is greatly facilitated by the helpfulness of the Swedish Information Service in New York and the Swedish Institute in Stockholm. Catharina Mannheimer at the Swedish Institute was a most helpful hostess and coordinator of my study efforts in Sweden. I appreciate the cordial help of the many colleagues who met with me, especially Maria Danielsson and Sten-Ake Stenberg, who shared a good deal of literature with me, and Ulf Wester, Goran Hoglund, and Ingvar Krakau, who were unusually helpful and hospitable. Through my Swedish research, I have come to know Mait Widmark and Siri Andersson who continue to expand my thinking about social welfare.

Closer to home, many of my United States colleagues were helpful and supportive. They include Graciela Castex and Dean Pierce, Alvin Sallee, Kay Hoffman, and Robert Berger. In addition, the following persons who reviewed the manuscript were extremely helpful in guiding and sharpening my thinking and writing: Margaret J. Allen, Eastern Kentucky University; L. Jay Bishop, Ohio University; Eleanor Brubaker, Miami University of Ohio; J. Douglas Burnham, Eastern Kentucky University; Edward W. Davis, University of Nevada—Las Vegas; Morris D. Klass, Memphis State University; Kathleen McInnis, Marquette University; Dorothy C. Miller, University of Maryland—Baltimore County; Rosco Y. Miller, California State University—Northridge; Elizabeth Thompson Ortiz, California State University—Long Beach; Robert P. Scheurell, University of Wisconsin—Milwaukee; and William H. Whitaker, University of Maine. I thank everyone who made this a better book because of their time, interest, and expertise. Any errors that remain in spite of their help are my own responsibility.

Finally, my friends and family have played an important role. Without their interest and support, projects like this are impossible, and I am grateful to them.

I wish that I could convey the many wonderful experiences that I have had in writing this book. I will always remember the residents of a geriatric day care center in Poland who proudly showed me their scrapbook, the loving interaction between parents and children in Mexico City's Chapultepec Park, and the father wheeling his baby in a carriage down special ramps provided in Stockholm so that families can have access to the subway. It is indeed a rich and wonderful world, and I am so grateful to have had a chance to learn more of it. I hope you share some of my joy and learning as you read further.

Ronald C. Federico
October 15, 1988

PREFACE TO THE SECOND EDITION

When I was asked to consider preparing the second edition of *Social Welfare in Today's World,* I was delighted to agree to do so. I had the highest regard for Ron Federico and had used his texts in my teaching for a number of years. Like Ron, I believe that students and social workers in the United States need greater understanding of social welfare responses to social needs in countries outside our own. Like Ron, I am strongly committed to baccalaureate education. I believe that BSW social workers have crucial contributions to make to the social welfare of the people of the United States and the world. I hope that our book will encourage its readers to think about, question, and challenge the ways in which we choose to respond to human need.

The importance of the ways in which we choose to respond to human need is reflected in major policy changes that are being enacted by Congress and signed into law by President Clinton as this book is in press (late summer 1996). Having campaigned for the presidency promising to "end welfare as we know it," the President signed "welfare reform" which will reduce the benefits received by more than one-fifth of the families with children in the United States. The new law ends the 61-year-old guarantee of cash assistance to the nation's poorest children, cuts welfare spending by more than $55 billion over six years, requires welfare recipients to work within two years, limits lifetime benefits to five years, and denies food stamps to legal immigrants. While the full human impact of the law remains to be seen, it will push at least 1 million more children into poverty. On a somewhat brighter note, Congress has raised the minimum wage by 90 cents, an important increase but one still insufficient to bring a family of four with one full-time worker above the poverty line.

Acknowledgments

Writing this book has been an adventure that has taken me on brief visits (May 1993) to Sweden and Poland and has provided opportunity for longer but still far too short visits to Mexico in 1993 and 1994.

As a 20-year-old in 1960, I participated in a seminar in Warsaw for students from Poland, Great Britain, the Soviet Union, and the United States. Warsaw's Old Town, lovingly reconstructed after World War II, had impressed me with the indomitable will of the Polish people to survive. A visit to the Nazi death camp at Auschwitz, with its museum rooms filled with baby shoes, shaving brushes, eyeglasses, and suitcases from throughout Europe—a powerful reminder of the Holocaust—became a major influence in my eventual decision to become a social worker and a social justice activist. My return to Poland in 1993 brought new appreciation for Polish people struggling to meet the needs of a changing society. In Warsaw, Mirosław Księżopolski graciously answered my questions.

The 1993 trip also took me to Sweden. In Stockholm, social workers Agneta Heiroth, Maria Mannerholm, and Christina Lundmark, and social work educators Maria Abrahamson, Mait Widmark, and Kenneth Sundh introduced me to the caring and comprehensive Swedish approach to social welfare. I saw for the first time how public housing—appropriately designed and maintained, and available on a nearly universal basis—could function with excellence and without stigma.

In the summer of 1993, I visited Mexico for the first time. Under the auspices of the Fulbright-Hays Seminars Abroad Probram, I spent the five most educationally exciting weeks I have yet experienced. Daily lectures on Mexican history, anthropology, culture, economics, and politics by outstanding experts, combined with field trips to public and private social agencies, archeological sites, and cultural events, opened my eyes and heart to the people of Mexico. Program facilitator Carmen Hernandez and Luz Maria Chapela (who taught me how making books could empower as well as teach people to read) opened their homes and became my friends.

With the support of the University of Maine, I was able to spend the fall semester of 1995 on sabbatical leave in Mexico City at the National School of Social Work of the National Autonomous University of Mexico. The administration, faculty, staff, and students welcomed me and did everything possible to ensure a pleasant and productive visit. I wish to thank especially Lic. Bertha Mary Rodríguez Villa, Lic. Nelia E. Tello Peón, Efrain E. Reyes Romero, Dulce Maria Rivera Ojedo, and Guadalupe Jardon Solis. Lic. Carmen Jonas Medina and Lic. Roberto Garcia Cabrera graciously hosted a memorable visit to the National Autonomous University of Aguascalientes.

In the United States, many colleagues and friends have encouraged and supported me and contributed ideas that have improved the second edition of this book. I especially would like to thank Grace Braley, Don Pilcher, Bill Rau and Susan Roche, Naurine Lennox, Derek Bessey, Phyllis Day, Harper Dean, Cheryl Simpson, Dan and Vivian Weisman, the members of the Council on Social Work Education International Commission, and my baccalaureate social work students at the University of Maine.

Helpful critiques and comments were provided by Stephen Aigner, Iowa State University; Ken Huang, St. Cloud State University; Waldo E. Johnson, Loyola University; Nancy Kelly, University of Maine; Patricia Joseph, Lincoln University; and Marjorie Steinberg, Western Connecticut State University. Virginia Whitaker and Jay Wilson contributed many editorial improvements to my writing. Jean Adamson, Michelle Alexander, Eileen Boardman, Barbara Bragg, Sarah Lowden, Carol Michaud, Jennifer Moulton, and Sherri Thomas served as student research assistants, with their work made possible through governmental Work Study and Work Merit subsidies. Nancy Blaine, my editor at McGraw-Hill, has been both patient and cheerfully encouraging. Irv Rockwood, Jill Gordon, and Phillip Butcher also played supportive roles. I want to thank everyone who has contributed so generously to the improvement of our book, and, as is customary, to absolve them of responsibility for such shortcomings as may still exist.

William H. Whitaker

INTRODUCTION

AN INVITATION TO THE READER

If you have just acquired this book, it is quite likely you have done so because it has been assigned in one of your classes. You may have mixed feelings about reading it: Will it be interesting and informative? Or will it be difficult to understand? Will the class be one you enjoy?

As you begin to read, we believe it might be helpful to talk to you about what you can expect. We want to say we are very happy you will be reading our book. Naturally we are proud of it, but we also know that you will find it very useful.

The major purpose of this book is to describe and explain the *social welfare system* in the United States, but what makes this book unique is that you will see how different countries address social welfare needs in different ways. It discusses our society's basic views about helping people, the resources that we allocate to helping efforts, whom we help and how we help them, the major programs through which help is provided, what it is like to be helped, and what it is like to be involved in helping others.

Learning about the social welfare system is well worth your time and effort. If you choose a career such as social work, mental health, or politics, you will find it essential to have a working knowledge of the social welfare system. Together, the programs that comprise this system supply the assistance needed to help people meet their financial, emotional, nutritional, housing, medical, educational, and community needs on a daily basis. As a social welfare professional, you will need to be able to work with people to help them identify what services they need and want, to know what services are available, and to know how to help people gain access to those services.

There are many times during most people's lives when it is useful to know what social welfare resources are available and how to make use of them. You and your family may experience needs that can be met with the help of social welfare programs. In planning for retirement, for example, most of us rely, at least in part, on Social Security payments in order to provide a decent retirement income. All of us, too, occasionally need medical care; and if we experience emotional stress, we may benefit from counseling.

A working knowledge of social welfare is also an important part of our obligations as responsible citizens in a democratic society. Which helping services should be provided, to whom, and how are major issues of our day. A knowledge of social welfare is important to making informed choices about these and related questions. We hope that this book will help you be a more informed and active participant in the political process.

There is a final way in which an understanding of social welfare is valuable. This book should help you clarify your own personal beliefs and commitments. Part of being an educated person is having the capacity to reflect on one's own beliefs in a systematic way. Social welfare raises some of the most fundamental human issues—freedom and dependence, basic human needs, personal and social responsibility, the rights of citizenship, and so on. We hope that our book will stimulate your thinking about these issues.

As you read *Social Welfare in Today's World,* three points should emerge. First, social welfare as subject matter is endlessly fascinating, challenging your ability to think and reason, your emotions, and your values. Second, social welfare is tightly woven into societal ways of thinking about and organizing daily life. Third, as likely will become apparent, we have tried to create a book that itself exemplifies the goals of social welfare. As a learning tool, this book will help you by providing support, stimulation, and encouragement, and by strengthening your ability to grow and develop.

APPROACHING SOCIAL WELFARE

In discussing the existing social welfare system in the United States, the approach we have adopted is one we call **active choice.** By this, we mean that *social welfare systems result from a society's choices about what the functions and structure of social welfare ought to be.* These choices reflect prevailing values, needs, resources, power relationships, and decision-making structures and processes. In other words, the social welfare system about which you will learn is neither inevitable nor unchangeable; rather, it is the product of thousands of human choices made over many years. You will soon see that choices about social welfare are made by individuals, families, communities, agencies, legislatures, courts,

PLAN OF THIS BOOK

Each of the chapters following this introduction addresses a basic question about social welfare. These are taken up in logical order as follows:

- What is social welfare?
- Why do we need social welfare?
- Why is social welfare controversial?
- How has social welfare developed over time?
- How has social welfare been shaped by social reformers?
- How is social welfare organized?
- What are the major services that social welfare provides?
- How does social welfare relate to the rest of society?
- Who delivers social welfare services?
- What does social welfare have to contribute to our society's future?

If, after reading this book, you are able to answer these questions, you will have acquired a sound basic understanding of social welfare.

Each chapter of the book contains a number of features designed to make it as easy as possible to master.

1 Chapter Overview. Each chapter begins with a brief statement of purpose and a description of the chapter's central topic.

2 Learning Objectives. Following the chapter overview is a list of specific learning objectives to be mastered by the time you have completed the chapter. As much as possible, these are stated in behavioral terms—that is, they are statements of what you will be able to do as a result of your reading and study.

3 Comparative Approach. Perhaps the single most distinctive feature of this book is that each chapter includes examples and illustrations from other nations—principally Mexico, Sweden, and Poland—in addition the United States. The purpose of these examples is to help you better understand social welfare in the United States by placing our nation's experience and practice in a larger context.

4 Illustrations. A variety of illustrative material is included in each chapter. Charts and tables provide statistical and empirical data that are not included in the text. Diagrams and other schematics help clarify relationships between ideas or structures. Photo essays on each of the four countries discussed in the text convey something of the flavor of these four different societies.

5 Case Studies and Examples. Throughout the text, under the heading "The Human Face of Social Welfare," you will find a series of case vignettes. Focusing on real people and real situations, they convey a sense of the human dimensions of social welfare issues and programs. Finally, a series of mini-essays titled "On the Street" describes our impressions of people, places, and programs discussed in the text.

6 Chapter Summaries. A brief summary appears at the conclusion of each chapter. Entitled "Let's Review," these summaries highlight points of particular importance and provide transitions between chapters.

7 Study Questions. Questions at the end of each chapter will help you review, integrate, and apply the material you have read. These questions focus on you and your own life experience, emphasizing the day-to-day relevance of social welfare.

8 Key Terms and Concepts. A list of key terms that appear in the chapter follows the chapter summary. Definitions of these terms appear in the text and in the glossary at the end of the book.

9 Suggested Readings. A short annotated list of suggested readings also appears at the end of each chapter. You will find these sources especially useful for pursuing ideas in depth or for obtaining additional information needed for special projects.

10 References. Each chapter ends with a list of sources cited in the chapter. This list will enable you to refer to the actual works cited in the event that you want more information.

11 Glossary. A glossary containing definitions of the most important technical terms used throughout the text appears at the end of the book, where you can easily refer to it as needed. The glossary also provides a convenient tool for reviewing major concepts whenever you wish.

THE HUMAN FACE OF SOCIAL WELFARE 1

CHOICES

Toy Santiago decided she had an important story to tell. She had lost a drug-addicted daughter to AIDS and was raising two grandchildren who were infected [with the AIDS virus]. All around her she saw young people using needles and dying, and having babies born dying, and she was desperate to sound an alarm: look what is happening to our children. . . .

Across the street from where the family lives is a once fine wooded park that is now . . . rotten with drugs and violence. . . . Nearly all the windows in the entranceway of the brick apartment building in which the family lives are broken. The front doors hang open. . . . A fire in the building in March forced the family to move out for a while, and in the months they were gone, Toy says, some dealers moved into the apartment, set up a crack store and then stole everything—couches, dishes, refrigerator—right down to the faucets. . . .

Toy continued looking for another place and grew hopeful when the housing authority granted her an interview. But 200,000 others . . . were also in line for a project apartment; the wait is about 20 years. The best that the city's Human Resources Administration could offer her was a welfare hotel. . . . Toy feared the drugs and prostitution—I'm raising six girls, she protested—and declined.

In the heat of July, after imposing on various friends and relations for too long, she finally went back to her former place, to the smoked-out apartment with no electricity. . . . It is a home of donated and borrowed scraps held together by Toy's fierce desire to steer this family clear of the "vice" that destroyed her daughter and doomed two of her grandchildren. On about $890 a month—from combined social-security benefits—she has to pay $372 in rent and feed eight. Hard as she tries to make the best of it, she is overcome by grief and worry when she contemplates the disease and the impending deaths and the drugs and the money problems. "I never lived like this," she says, weeping.

Fifteen years ago she had a job at a coat manufacturer and a husband who was a foreman at . . . [a] toy factory. They owned some property in a good . . . neighborhood. They had three children. Then Ed Carrion showed up, a drug user since he was 12, Toy says, "the man who'd come to ruin my daughter's life." Margarita, 17, was a "gal with no

and others. Although none of us can predict what social welfare will be like in the future, we can be certain that we, as a society, will continue to make choices about social welfare on an ongoing basis. We can be sure, too, that the choices made will continue to reflect changing values, needs, resources, and the views of all, including you and us, who have influence in decision-making structures and processes.

A COMPARATIVE VIEW: FOUR NATIONS

In keeping with the active choice approach, this book also employs a **cross-cultural comparative perspective,** drawing on social welfare examples from other countries. Throughout the book, social welfare in the United States will be compared with the social welfare systems of Mexico, Poland, and Sweden. These three systems were chosen because each of the societies involved is of a type that is significantly different from the United States. Mexico is a developing nation in the midst of significant political, economic, and demographic changes. Poland until 1989 was a socialist nation influenced by communist political and economic practices that came from the Soviet Union. Today, Poland is in transition to a neoliberal capitalist economy and, like Mexico, is experiencing significant prob-

vices," Toy recalls, "who stayed home and studied."

The match proved deadly and had the added effect of helping to ruin Toy's own marriage. Her husband, an ambitious man, loathed Ed and his street jive. . . . When [Margarita and Ed] would come to visit, Toy's husband would get angry, she says, and he and Toy would fight. As Toy views it now, she was pushed into making a choice between holding on to her brooding husband and trying to save her daughter from a bad marriage. Eleven years ago, when she was in her early 40s, her husband divorced her and moved back to Puerto Rico. . . .

In the spring of '83 Margarita was ill with AIDS. When she died later in August, ravaged by lymphoma and tuberculosis, Toy experienced the first of many shameful encounters with the disgust and stigma associated with AIDS: until Toy threatened to sue, funeral-home attendants refused to dress her daughter's body for burial.

Mrs. Santiago's story illustrates the many levels at which social welfare choices are made. She has chosen to care for her children and grandchildren despite many obstacles. The city in which she lives has chosen not to provide certain kinds of services needed by people like Mrs. Santiago and her family. And choices made by the larger society have created conditions that people seek to escape through drugs—stresses such as racial and ethnic discrimination, chronic unemployment, inadequate housing, and the like. The combination of stressful living conditions and inadequate social programs create problems like those faced by Mrs. Santiago.

The fact that *Newsweek* magazine chose to publicize the plight of this family is an example of organizational choice. By making their readers aware of such conditions, perhaps *Newsweek* is trying to influence future decisions about social welfare.

Mrs. Santiago's struggle illustrates why people need help, and introduces some of the good and bad aspects of our current social welfare system. It also raises many issues. How do you feel about Mrs. Santiago's situation, the reasons for it, the decisions she has made, the help that she is getting, and her unmet needs? As you consider these issues, think also about the kinds of choices you make.

Excerpt from Terence Monmaney "Kids with AIDS," *Newsweek,* September 7, 1987, pp. 51–59, © 1987, Newsweek, Inc. All rights reserved. Reprinted by permission.

lems of economic structural adjustment. Sweden is an advanced social democracy with a unique commitment to social planning to meet social welfare needs.

It is important to keep in mind that these four nations do not represent the entire world. Each is a Western nation with an economy and a formal social welfare system more extensive than those of many Third World countries. Each of the countries discussed in this book has created its own approach to social welfare. By comparing them, we will see that decision making about similar social issues occurs in different social environments. Sometimes the results are similar; sometimes they are not. As you compare the four countries with each other, you will see that each seeks to integrate social welfare into its basic social fabric. In the process, you will come to a better understanding of your own country and its social welfare system.

As you read this book, it will become apparent that there are both met and unmet needs in each of these countries—including the United States. A little background about each country will provide a helpful context for understanding why this is so. As you learn about each, notice that there are substantial similarities and differences among them in factors such as history, geography, population, the capacity of the economy to generate goods and services, the form of government,

TABLE I-1 FOUR COUNTRIES: AN OVERVIEW

	Mexico	Poland	Sweden	United States
Geographic area				
Square miles	761,604	120,727	173,731	3,618,770
Relative size	3 times size of Texas	A little smaller than New Mexico	A little bigger than California	5 times Mexico 20 times Sweden 30 times Poland
Population (1992)	92,380,000	10,448,000	8,602,000	256,561,000
Percent urban	72 (1990)	62 (1992)	85 (1985)	76 (1990)
Ethnicity (%)	Mestizo (60%) Indigenous (29%) Caucasian (9%)	Polish (98%) Germans, Ukrainians, Byelorussians	Swedish (91%) Finnish (3%) Lapps, European immigrants	Caucasian (83.6%) Black (12.4%) Asian (3.2%) Native American (0.8%) Hispanic (9.3%)
Religion (%)	Catholic (97%)	Catholic (94%)	Lutheran (95%)	Protestant (56%) Catholic (25%) Jewish (2%) No Pref. (11%)
Form of government	Limited democracy with one dominant party	Multiparty democracy	Multiparty democracy with limited monarch	Two-party democracy
Economic stage	Developing	Industrialized	Industrialized	Industrialized
Economic system	Transition to neoliberal capitalist	Transition to neoliberal capitalist	Democratic socialist with strong governmental regulation of business	Capitalist with limited governmental regulation of business
Gross national product/person (1992, $US)	$3,470	$1,960	$26,780	$23,120
Consumer prices (% change 1992)	15.5%	43.0%	2.3%	3.0%

Sources: Per-capita GNP: *The World Bank Atlas 1994.* Washington, DC: World Bank. Other data: *The World Almanac and Book of Facts: 1994.* Mahway, NJ: Funk & Wagnalls.

the level of industrialization, and so forth. Some of these characteristics are summarized in Table I-1. Such factors form part of the social environment in which policy choices are made that affect the lives of the citizens of each country.

Mexico

Geographic Area Mexico, which is three times the size of Texas, is part of Central America. It touches the United States (Texas, New Mexico, Arizona, and

California) on the north and Guatemala and Belize on the south. To its east lies the Gulf of Mexico and the Caribbean Sea, and to its west lies the Pacific Ocean. Much of Mexico is mountainous and high, dry plateau. Rugged topography and insufficient rainfall present obstacles to farming. Coastal lowlands are tropical (Famighetti, 1994).

Texas, California, Nevada, Arizona, New Mexico, Utah, and part of Colorado were once part of Mexico. Texas seceded from Mexico in 1834, and was annexed by the United States in 1845. Following an invasion by U.S. troops in 1848, Mexico was forced to sign the Treaty of Guadalupe Hildago. For $15 million, Mexico ceded claims to Texas, California, Nevada, and Utah, and parts of Arizona, New Mexico, and Colorado. In 1853, the Gadsen Purchase added southern New Mexico and Arizona to the United States. In less than 10 years, Mexico lost more than half of its original territory (Barry, 1992).

The Land at a Glance—Mexico

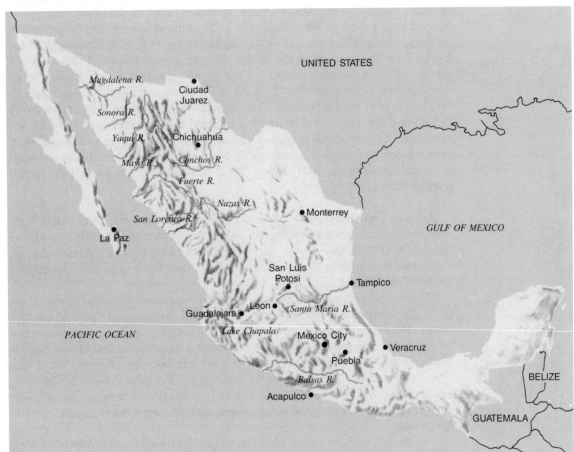

Once, most Mexicans were farmers, but the percentage of Mexicans living in urban areas has increased dramatically—from 40 percent in 1950 to about 72 percent in 1990. As was the case in the United States in the early twentieth century, many Mexicans moved to cities in search of economic opportunities and somewhat better living conditions. Mexico City, the capital, is now the second largest city in the world, with a 1992 population of 21.6 million people (U.S. Department of Commerce, 1993a). In addition to the cities in the south-central part of the country, there are several rapidly growing cities along Mexico's northern border with the United States. Here, growth has been spurred by industrial development and the need for housing the 2 to 4 million Mexicans who live in Mexico but work in the United States (Rudolph, 1985).

Major Cultural Groups The area now known as Mexico—the name comes from *Mexicas,* the name by which the Aztecs called themselves—has been home to major civilizations for at least 3,500 years. More than 1,000 major pyramid sites, many of which rival those of Egypt, are part of the Mexican heritage. Mayan, Olmec, Huastec, Toltec, Aztec, and many other civilizations flourished in Mexico before the Spanish conquest in 1521 initiated large-scale European colonization. Nearly 100 years before the settling of the U.S. eastern seaboard, Mexico City was the thriving capital of the colonial Spanish empire. Today nearly 30 percent of the population consists of indigenous people who speak as their first language one of the more than 50 surviving indigenous languages. Spanish is the first language of the 60 percent of the population that is *mestizo* (descended from Indians and Europeans who intermarried). Spanish is also spoken by most of the 9 percent of the population classified as caucasian. Ninety-seven percent of Mexicans are Roman Catholic, a faith that in Mexico often includes a blend of indigenous traditions (Tagle, 1991; Barry, 1992; Brosnahan et al., 1992; U.S. Department of State, 1992).

Political Characteristics Mexico's current political structure is based on the constitution established following the Mexican Revolution (1910–1917). Mexico has a federal government with thirty-one states and a Federal District—Mexico City—that is similar to Washington, DC. Each state has a popularly elected governor and legislature.

Mexico is a multiparty democratic state. For more than 65 years, however, one party, the Institutional Revolutionary Party (PRI, pronounced "pree"), has held power. The PRI has been in power since 1929, dominating the country's economics and politics, co-opting or crushing opposition movements, and channeling virtually all political activity through the party bureaucracy (Barry, 1992). Ward (1986) characterizes Mexico as an "inclusionary-authoritarian" state that is willing to use repression when necessary, but that "generally prefers to accommodate competing interest groups to some extent and to offer concessions to popular movements."

Two major events in recent Mexican history spurred the development of popular movements. First, when President Díaz Ordáz (1964–1970) was elected on a platform that supported business and deemphasized social programs, massive student protest resulted. On October 2, 1968, government riot police killed several hundred people at a protest rally in Tlatelolco, Mexico City. Subsequent community-based organizing efforts throughout Mexico resulted in urban and peasant movements, independent labor organizations, Christian "base communities," and guerrilla forces. Second, a major earthquake in 1985 caused massive damage in Mexico City. An entire network of grass-roots organizations sprang up when governmental responses were ineffective and dishonest. After the disaster, several of these organizations helped spearhead a growing movement for monitoring and challenging human rights violations by the government (Barry, 1992; Brosnahan et al., 1992).

A significant electoral challenge to PRI hegemony occurred in 1988, when Cuauhtémoc Cárdenas, son of the popular reform president Lázaro Cárdenas, broke with the PRI to run an insurgent campaign. President Carlos Salinas de Gortari was declared the victor in an election that was widely viewed as fraudulent. Massive protests followed. Significant numbers of national and state legislative seats were won by the center-right National Action Party (PAN) and the center-left Cárdenas coalition, which 1 year later became the Party of the Democratic Revolution (PRD).

The PRI responded to the challenge to its control with both stick and carrot. During the first 5 years of the Salinas administration, some 250 PRD local activists were murdered, and more than 200 newspaper reporters "disappeared" or were murdered, presumably by PRI forces (Cazes, 1993; Orosco, 1993).

The "carrot" is rather interesting. In authoritarian states such as Mexico, efficient, well-managed social welfare programs play an important role "in keeping the populace passive" (Ward, 1986). The PRI's power has been maintained through a vast patronage system (Eckstein, 1988). *Pronasol,* the National Solidarity Program, was created by the Salinas administration to channel millions of pesos into community development projects proposed by grass-roots organizations in areas in which the PRD challenge to PRI was strongest. The success of Pronasol in co-opting the grass-roots opposition became evident in the midterm elections of 1991, in which the PRI officially recaptured much of the voter support it had lost to Cárdenas in 1988 (Barry, 1992). The dominance of the PRI suggests that Mexican politics, while democratic in form, generally reflect the priorities and policies of a powerful national elite.

A keystone in the neoliberal economic policies of the Salinas administration was commitment to the enactment of the North American Free Trade Agreement (NAFTA). During a 15-year period, NAFTA will eliminate trade barriers between Mexico, the United States, and Canada. When NAFTA was passed in 1994, critics expected it to further disadvantage Mexico's poor. Projections suggested that as many as several hundred thousand small farmers who grow maize for a living would be forced off their land because they would not be able to compete against cheaply sold, imported U.S. corn (Conroy and Glasmeier, 1993).

NAFTA went into effect on January 1, 1994. In protest against NAFTA, poverty, and years of PRI's broken promises, Mayan peasants organized as the

ON THE STREET IN MEXICO CITY

México—the word "City" is usually dropped from its name or replaced by *D.F. (Distrito Federal)*—is the second largest city in the world. Only metropolitan Tokyo-Yokohama is larger. From a 1930 population of 1 million, it grew to 21,615,000 in 1992. Births and a permanent influx of poor people from surrounding rural states add more than 1 million new faces each year. México is expected to reach 27,872,000 residents by the year 2000, nearly twice the projected size of New York City. Population density in the city center is believed to exceed 51,800 persons per square mile. At an altitude of 7,220 feet in a basin surrounded by mountains, Mexico suffers severe air pollution for much of the year. Temperature inversions trap cloying blankets of smog, which harm health and obscure the views of *Popo* and *Izta*, magnificent volcanoes only 40 miles to the southeast.

México—a city of contrasts, a city of diversity. Built on the ruins of the Aztec capital *Tenochtitlán*, the city today is a dynamic blend of old and new. There are beautiful boulevards and narrow side streets, modern high-rise buildings and many examples of elegant colonial architecture, a wide variety of restaurants and shops. Many buildings are adorned by massive murals by Rivera, Orozco, Siguieros—celebrating pre-Conquest civilizations, resistance, revolution; protesting terror and suffering; offering hope for the future. At the heart of the city is the *Zócalo*, national marketplace and livingroom. The vast open square is bordered by the National Palace, the Cathedral, the excavated ruins of the Aztec *Templo Mayor*. Along the edges of the *Zócalo*, Mayan vendors offer up their wares. Its center is often home to tent and cardboard encampments of protesters—oil workers, fishermen, *campesinos*—seeking an audience with the president, hoping in vain for redress of their grievances; in early 1994, thousands rallied here night and day in support of the Zapatistas. A huge green-white-red Mexican flag flies proudly, greeting president and protestor alike.

Throughout the city, ornate churches both grand and modest welcome parishioners to celebrations of life and death—masses, saints' days, *quinceaños* (a girl's fifteenth birthday celebration), marriages, and funerals. A penitent slowly climbs on her knees the many flights of stone steps rising to the chapel of the Virgin of Guadalupe, patroness and protector of México. Dried aloe and braids of garlic hang unobtrusively in many shops, "for health"; black candles, red beads, and herbs offer themselves for sale in the "witches market." At night in Garibaldi Square, *Mariachi* bands sing of tradition, romance, and loss to throngs of joyful people. Posters announce football matches and bullfights. UNAM, the National Autonomous University of Mexico, is a city within the city. More than 250,000 students study here—learning, challenging, organizing, and preparing for Mexico's future.

Zapatista Army of National Liberation (EZLN) occupied several towns in Chiapas, one of Mexico's poorest states. The EZLN declared war on the Mexican state and called on Mexicans to support its struggles "for work, land, housing, food, health care, education, independence, freedom, democracy, justice and peace" (EZLN, 1993:13). Subcommander Marcos, a Zapatista leader, became a popular symbol of resistance to the PRI, and the example of the Zapatistas inspired many peasants and indigenous people to occupy land, to challenge oppressive authorities, and to assert their rights. By early 1996, negotiations between the Zapatistas and the Mexican government had failed to resolve the conflict.

Economic Characteristics   Mexico's major industries include steel, chemicals, electronic goods, textiles, rubber, petroleum, and tourism. Its chief crops are cotton, coffee, wheat, rice, sugar cane, vegetables, and maize (Famighetti, 1994).

Trade imbalances in the 1980s led to a huge foreign debt, as well as a national debt that is among the highest in the developing world. Unemployment in 1991 was estimated at about 18 percent, although government statistics report urban

Neighborhoods reflect opulence and poverty: quiet, walled streets in Coyoacán and San Angel, concealing colonial mansions; chic, expensive shops for *Zona Rosa* yuppies; partly planned, partly out of control slum-like neighborhoods of the *ciudades perdidas* (lost cities), spontaneous settlements, and shantytowns where more than half of México's population lives, working class and poor.

Dreams and dreams denied in its markets, parks, streets, the *Zócalo:* many people full of energy, working hard to make their living; fewer people, ground down by their daily struggle to survive, listlessly begging out of doorways. Mexicans are teachers, workers, politicians, and more. Masters of the art of survival, Mexicans are street musicians; windshield washers; indigenous *marias* in embroidered blouses and bright-ribbon-braided hair, selling plastic toys to traffic-slowed cars; vendors of baskets, bark cloth, T-shirts, pottery, bead-work, masks, sparkplugs, combs, hand-made silver jewelry, Kleenex, lottery tickets, pinwheels and Mickey Mouse balloons, flowers and fruit of every sort, and cotton candy. Long lines of vendors' tables filling streets, rerouting traffic one day, disappearing the next because, one hears, the right bribes were not paid. Great blocks of ice melting slowly on the sidewalks; bicycle carts delivering *agua pura* bottled water or piled high with fresh-baked breads. Restaurants, sidewalk cafes, vendors of food tempt every palate; bustling stalls with *tacos, tortas, tamales, atole, sopes, birria, pozole,* and ice creams flavored with tropical fruits unknown in *el Norte* delight the senses.

A city of people on the move. A city of pedestrians; a city of passengers. In buses; microbuses; swarms of VW beetle taxicabs—red and white taxis, green "eco-logical" taxis, perhaps using unleaded gas, which charge a little more; its efficient, crowded Metro, with special cars for rush hour protecting women's dignity from *machismo;* nondriving days for private cars attempt to cut pollution.

A city with children everywhere—children selling trinkets, chewing gum; children reduced to begging; children carrying younger children; children laughing, hungry, cherished and worried over by their parents.

A city facing change. Twenty-six McDonalds now (and even Taco Bell!); near the *Zócalo* motorcycles wait to deliver Shakey's Pizza; the Hotel Gran, with its spectacular stained-glass atrium, belongs to Howard Johnson's.

Sources: Personal observations of Bill Whitaker, July–August 1994; U.S. Department of Commerce, Bureau of the Census. *Statistical Abstract of the United States, 1993.* Washington, DC: U.S. Government Printing Office; Jutta Schuetz, ed. *Insight City Guides: Mexico City.* Hong Kong: APA Publications, 1991.

unemployment of less than 3 percent by considering a person employed who works even 1 hour per week. In rural areas nearly half of the workforce is unemployed or underemployed. Inflation cut the purchasing power of wages in half between 1980 and 1991 and then again in half during 1995. In addition, costs of basic necessities increased faster than the general cost of living (Barry, 1992; Beachy, 1995).

Under President Salinas, Mexico followed a neoliberal economic policy; by 1992, inflation seemed to be under control, budget deficits were reduced, social services were cut, subsidies for public utilities and basic goods were reduced, and hundreds of government-owned companies were sold to private investors (Barry, 1992). There was, however, considerable pressure on the Mexican peso. In 1994, the newly elected PRI President, Ernesto Ponce de Leon Zedillo, "floated" the peso, which quickly lost more than half of its purchasing power. Inflation soared, more than 1 million Mexicans lost their jobs, and Mexico appeared to be once again on the verge of defaulting on its international debt. According to the General Coordinator of the Mexican Association of Social Workers, the cost of the basic working-class market basket of eggs, milk, tortillas, meat, and beans increased 400 percent in 4 years (Maria Nanut Hernández, April 1995, personal communication).

Many Mexicans survive by selling goods and services on the street. These people frequently lead a marginal existence in shantytowns on the outskirts of the major cities. They have little economic or job security and no work-related social welfare benefits (Eckstein, 1988). Along the U.S.–Mexican border, approximately 500,000 people, mostly women, are employed in *maquiladoras,* mostly U.S.-owned assembly plants that produce auto parts, clothing, furniture, machinery, and electronic goods (Lovaas, 1993).

Poland

Geographic Area   Poland, which is slightly smaller than New Mexico, is located on fertile lowland in the northern European plain. The Carpathian Mountains rise to more than 8,000 feet on Poland's southern border with the Czech

The Land at a Glance—Poland

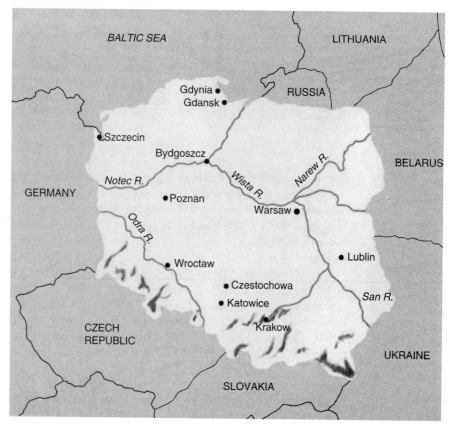

Republic and Slovakia. Poland is bounded by the Baltic Sea on the north; Ukraine, Belarus, and Lithuania on the east; and Germany on the west.

Major Cultural Groups Poland was founded as a nation more than 1,000 years ago. In 966, Christianity was adopted as the official state religion. Cracow University was founded in 1364. The geographic borders of Poland have fluctuated greatly throughout its history. From the fourteenth through the seventeenth centuries, Poland was a great power. From 1772–1918, Poland was partitioned by Austria, Prussia, and Russia. Numerous nationalist uprisings were mounted against such foreign rule. Following World War I, Poland was again an independent state until it was invaded by both Germany and the Soviet Union in World War II, ending the war under Soviet control. The treaties that ended the war shifted Poland's prewar boundaries approximately 150 miles to the west, adding territory from Germany and ceding territory to the Soviet Union. Subsequently, 4.4 million Poles were resettled and 3.5 million Germans deported (Economist Intelligence Unit, 1992). Poland sustained the heaviest human and economic losses of any country in the war, and its postwar recovery was extremely difficult. More than 6 million Poles, 20 percent of its population, died in Nazi death camps, in battle, or as civilian casualties of the fighting. Following the defeat of the Warsaw uprising, the Nazis systematically destroyed much of Warsaw, Poland's capital (Horn and Pietras, 1992).

Poland today is a homogeneous society: 98 percent of its people are of Polish descent. German, Ukrainian, and Byelorussian minorities comprise 2 percent of the population. Before World War II there were 3.5 million Jews in Poland. The postwar Polish government was hostile to the 250,000 Polish Jews who survived the Holocaust, often preventing them from rebuilding their communities. Pogroms, in which survivors of the Holocaust were killed, fueled emigration. Today there are only 5,000 Jews in Poland. Nearly 94 percent of the population is Roman Catholic (Horn and Pietras, 1992; Famighetti, 1994).

Political Characteristics Poland is divided into 49 administrative jurisdictions called *voivodships,* which are made up of smaller, autonomous local government units called *gminas.* There is a bicameral parliament consisting of a lower house, the Sejm, and an upper house, the Senate. Twenty-nine political parties are represented in the Sejm. The nine largest parties control 90 percent of the seats (Organisation for Economic Co-Operation and Development, 1992; World Bank, 1993).

In 1980, following 2 months of crippling strikes, the communist government conceded the right to form independent unions and to strike, both unprecedented developments in the Soviet bloc. By 1981 the independent trade union Solidarity had grown to 10 million members. Fearing Soviet intervention, the government declared martial law, arrested Solidarity leaders and activists, and outlawed the union (Famighetti, 1994). After the imposition of economic sanctions by Western nations and a visit by the Pope, martial law was lifted and political prisoners were granted amnesty. Solidarity reemerged and, with the support of the Roman

ON THE STREET IN WARSAW

Warsaw, the 700-year-old capital of Poland, is located on the Vistula River in the country's heartland. It is a major industrial, trade, and cultural center; home of the Polish Academy of Sciences and the International Chopin Competition; scene of the Warsaw Ghetto uprising of 1943; former battleground of the Polish resistance. Most of Warsaw was razed and 700,000 of its citizens killed during World War II. Rising Phoenix-like from the ashes of Nazi occupation, the city has been reborn.

The business area of Warsaw, with its many high-rise office buildings, hotels, and apartment blocks, congested traffic, bus and streetcar and commuter rail lines, looks much like the downtown of any contemporary European city. Great expanses of Soviet-style apartment buildings on the city's outskirts are home to most of its 1.7 million people. Window boxes of bright geraniums bring an individual touch to apartment balconies. Housing remains in short supply.

The meticulous reconstruction of the *Stare Miastro* (Old Town) and Royal Castle, now looking exactly as it did before the Nazi occupation, testifies to pride in Polish history and culture. The *Stare Miastro* is the living heart of Warsaw. Charming cafés and shops are set in elegant townhouses, many with beautiful and elaborate paintings on their stucco façades. In good weather people throng its cobbled streets, enjoy coffee or Polish beer with their friends. Artists and crafters display their paintings, carvings, and amber jewelry. Sidewalk coffee houses unfurl bright umbrellas revealing advertising for Western cigarettes. Con men offer unwary tourists impossible exchange rates for their dollars. Medical students test blood pressures at sidewalk cardtables. Lines of schoolchildren on holiday cross streets hand in hand.

After many years of communism with goods in short supply, Polish people are hungry for modern consumer goods and technology. Two thousand Western investors are doing business in joint ventures with Polish nationals. The free-market economy is booming. The long lines of former days have disappeared. Goods of all kinds are now available—for those who can afford them.

In Warsaw Square, Poles practice the arts of survival. Goods for sale—from bananas to women's underwear—displayed on blankets, pavement, hoods of cars, offered from cardboard boxes—the booty of weekend trading in Berlin or Turkey. Many would-be entrepreneurs seek their fortunes. For some the enterprise is modest—a few bars of chocolate or bottles of detergent; farmers offer meat from dusty trucks. Watches, TVs, computers, refrigerators—if the price is right, they will appear. Free enterprise is making millionaires . . . and paupers.

Prices rise while wages fall behind; jobs are lost; social benefits are cut. Homelessness appears. Robberies, burglaries, and muggings increase. Grandmothers sell flowers on the street—and beg in church doorways. A man sits on the sidewalk, his cardboard sign reading, "I need money for an operation. This is the truth." Higher prices hit those on fixed incomes hardest. Pensioners and persons with disabilities struggle to survive. In a simple neighborhood restaurant an old woman creeps in, seeking food. A stranger buys her soup and bread, with which she disappears.

And in the square, children . . . beloved and pampered, clothed and fed far better than their parents, eat ice cream and hold plastic pinwheels to the breeze.

Sources: Personal observations of Bill Whitaker, May 1994; Stanislaw Baranczak, "Warsaw Postcard: Point of no Return," *The New Republic*, August 13, 1990; Alfred Horn and Bozena Pietras, eds. *Insight Guides: Windows on the World, Poland.* Hong Kong: APA Publications, 1992.

Catholic Church, forced the government to hold elections, in which the communists were defeated. Solidarity leader Lech Walesa was elected president.

The new Solidarity government was faced with the need to control accelerating inflation while putting together a structural adjustment package acceptable to the International Monetary Fund (IMF) (Economist Intelligence Unit, 1992). In 1993, arguing that the Polish social welfare system was excessively generous, a report of the World Bank proposed lowering family allowance and sick-pay benefit levels, limiting access to benefit programs, and shortening the duration of benefits in order to fund a social safety net during the transition to capitalism (World Bank, 1993). The structural adjustment program designed to transform Poland's economy into a free-market system resulted in inflation and unemployment and was resisted by unions, farmers, and miners. In September 1993, widespread discontent resulted in the election of former communists and other leftist parties to a majority in the Sejm (Famighetti, 1994).

Economic Characteristics Poland's major industries are shipbuilding, chemicals, metals, automobiles, and food processing. Chief crops include grains, potatoes, sugar beets, tobacco, and flax (Famighetti, 1994). Before the electoral defeat of the communist government in 1989, Poland's road to socialism had been more pragmatic than that taken in other Eastern European countries. Agricultural collectivization had been abandoned; workers' councils within enterprises had moderated central economic planning. In a turn toward the West, Poland had entered into joint economic ventures with transnational capitalist enterprises (Economist Intelligence Unit, 1992).

Under communism, about three-quarters of the Polish workforce was employed by government-run businesses and, because the government guaranteed a job to all Polish citizens who wanted one, less than 1 percent of the workforce was unemployed. Today, unemployment has increased dramatically. By the end of 1991, 11.8 percent of all Poles were unemployed, and rates as high as 17 percent have been reported in some provinces (United Nations, 1993).

The transition to neoliberal capitalism has had a negative impact on social welfare in Poland. Under communism, access to important social benefits such as housing, cafeterias, child care, health clinics, and vacation resorts was tied to the workplace. With increasing numbers of people out of work, access to such benefits has diminished. Polish society has paid a high price for the "shock therapy" of transition to a capitalist system. "Unemployment, dismantling the welfare system and sharp increases in the cost of living have bred disappointment, insecurity, and fear of the future" (United Nations, 1993). In June 1992, a participant in the Fourth Congress of Solidarity in Gdansk put it this way: "We were not jailed to be unable to get enough food for our children" (United Nations, 1993).

Sweden

Geographic Area Sweden, which is a little larger than California, is a long, narrow Western European country that stretches nearly 1,000 miles from north of the Arctic Circle to its border with Denmark in the south. Mountains cover approximately 25 percent of Sweden along its northwest border with Norway. Central and southern Sweden is flat or rolling and includes several large lakes. Sweden is bordered by Finland and the Baltic Sea on the east. Although it is on about the same latitude as Alaska, its climate is moderated by the Gulf Stream (Taylor, 1990; Famighetti, 1994).

Major Cultural Groups Swedes are descendants of the Vikings and other indigenous groups. During the sixteenth and seventeenth centuries, Sweden was a

The Land at a Glance—Sweden

major power in Europe and controlled huge territories in the Baltics and south as far as Poland. Sweden was an armed neutral in both world wars. Its population today is relatively homogeneous, about 91 percent of Swedish descent (Famighetti, 1994). The two largest minority groups are those of Finnish descent, and Lapps—indigenous people who live mostly in northern Sweden. Following World War II, refugees from central Europe and the Baltic states made new homes in Sweden, and "guest workers" from Italy, the United Kingdom, West Germany, Greece, Poland, Yugoslavia, and Turkey were invited to work in Sweden's expanding factories. As economic conditions deteriorated in the 1970s, Sweden restricted economic immigration but continued to accept political refugees from Chile, Syria, Iran, and Lebanon. These non-European immigrants have seemed too many and too different to some Swedes. In response, "skinheads" and other racists have appeared in Sweden, a country which for many years served as a liberal conscience for the world (Taylor, 1990). Until 1996, the Evangelical-Lutheran Church was the official state church, and all Swedes were automatically considered members unless they declared otherwise.

Political Characteristics　Sweden is a constitutional monarchy with a parliamentary form of government. The current king, who exerts no political power and takes no part in politics, is Carl XVI Gustav. As in any parliamentary system, government policy making is carried out largely by a cabinet headed by a prime minister. The leader of the party that wins a majority of seats in the popularly elected Parliament becomes the prime minister. The prime minister then selects the other cabinet members—invariably from among the ranks of party colleagues. In 1991, beset by a severe economic recession, the Social Democratic Labor Party, which had been in power for 49 of the previous 55 years, lost its majority. The new conservative coalition government eliminated many public-sector jobs, reduced housing subsidies and sickness benefits, increased fees for medicines, introduced vouchers for schools and child-care services, and increased the retirement age from 65 to 67. The antiwelfare measures apparently angered the electorate. The Social Democrats were returned to power faced with growing budget deficits and unemployment. Provincial and local levels of government are important in Sweden, and elections at these levels are also democratic (Mayne, 1986; Swedish Institute, 1986; Economist, 1993; Facts on File, 1994).

Economic Characteristics　Major industries in Sweden include steel, machinery, instruments, automobiles, shipbuilding, shipping, and paper. Chief crops are grains, potatoes, and sugar beets (Famighetti, 1994). Industrial production makes up approximately 31 percent of the economy and is shared between private and government-controlled firms. Agriculture, forestry, and fishing comprise 3 percent of the economy. The remaining 66 percent of the economy is generated by the service sector (Mayne, 1986).

In the late 1800s, Sweden had a rigid class system in which the upper class lived in opulence while poverty, overcrowding, sickness, and starvation were the lot of working people. Today slums are nonexistent and cases of individual hard-

ON THE STREET IN GOTHENBURG

Gothenburg is Sweden's second-largest city after Stockholm, the capital. It is a major port city and is also the site of a good deal of industry. A North American feels right at home on a street in Gothenburg. At first glance, it seems very similar to a mid-size U.S. city, complete with a large indoor shopping mall at the edge of the downtown area.

Gradually, though, differences emerge. Like most of Sweden, the streets are generally clean and the buildings well kept. Although there is a good deal of new construction, the older buildings are in excellent condition and continue in use. Although there is much activity in the downtown area, it is relatively quiet and calm. Park areas are plentiful and well cared for. Housing tends toward small apartment buildings rather than private homes, and public transportation—in the form of buses and streetcars—is modern, plentiful, and clean.

Many Swedes, unlike their U.S. stereotype, are dark-haired rather than blonde. They tend to be tall and robust, healthy in appearance, and generally well dressed in contemporary styles. Some of the young people sport the latest international hairstyles, clothing,

and jewelry. Husbands and wives are often seen together taking their baby or young child for a stroll. There is a sense of living in a calm, clean, orderly, and well-managed environment, with little street begging and no evidence of homelessness.

Walking along the street in Gothenburg, one is impressed with the abundance in the stores. Products of all kinds are available, ranging from the most practical and basic to the most luxurious and stylish. Restaurants, too, are numerous, including small cafés, specialty restaurants, and popular eating places from fast-food chains to coffee shops. Even the port area seems clean and orderly. Gothenburg gives the impression of being part of a highly productive and affluent society.

In spite of the numerous merits of life in Sweden, there is also a downside evident in Gothenberg. Many Gothenberg youths spend hours drinking beer in the pubs, roaming the streets beyond midnight, picking fights, and showing signs of drunkenness.

Sources: Personal observations of Ron Federico, 1987; Comments of an anonymous reviewer, 1995.

ship are considered so unusual that they are widely reported in the media. Sweden is a social democracy. Instead of socializing the means of production through government ownership—90 percent of the economy is in private hands—Sweden has followed a policy of "socialism in everyday life," which attempts to ensure that the products of private production are shared equitably and that equal opportunity is available to all (Taylor, 1990).

Swedish commitment to egalitarianism has resulted in a family-centered, "cradle to grave" social welfare system that includes free health care, free education from kindergarten through high school, and generous retirement pensions. Sweden's approach to meeting the needs of its citizens is sometimes referred to as a "third way" between communism and capitalism. Private firms are given free rein, earnings are taxed heavily, and comprehensive social welfare benefits are provided universally by the state (Bilski, 1991; Famighetti, 1994).

Official family policy encourages men and women to share responsibilities for child raising. Affordable, neighborhood-based child-care centers enable 82 percent of Swedish women of working age to be employed. Substantial progress has been made in ensuring universal access to adequate housing and education.

Today most Swedes identify themselves as middle class. In a quest for higher status, many persons are even changing their names—replacing rural, working-class family names ending in "son" with the Latinized names of the eighteenth-century elite. For example, Karlsson would become Karnsun (Taylor, 1990). A reduction in middle-class commitment to egalitarianism is leading to demands for lower taxes, although desire for public benefits remains strong. In the early 1990s, Sweden experienced a severe recession in which gross domestic product fell and the rate of unemployment, traditionally less than 2 percent, reached 5.4 percent by late 1992. Nearly 9 percent of the workforce was unemployed, engaged in public relief workfare, or being retrained (U.S. Department of Commerce, 1993b). At the same time, tax reforms reduced the ability of the government to fund parts of the social welfare system (Taylor, 1992). Unemployment increased to 14 percent in 1993 and, together with tax cuts, resulted in an annual deficit exceeding 13 percent of gross national product (Facts on File, 1994).

The United States Of America

Geographic Area The United States is by far the largest of the four countries discussed in this book. With a surface area of more than 3,600,000 square miles, it is thirty times larger than Poland, twenty times larger than Sweden, and nearly five times larger than Mexico. Its topography is varied, including a vast central plain bordered by high mountains on the west and rolling hills and low mountains in the east. Geography ranges from tropical rain forests in Hawaii and Puerto Rico to southwestern deserts, Alaskan glaciers, and fertile midwestern farmlands. The mainland is bordered by Canada on the north, Mexico and the Gulf of Mexico on the south, the Atlantic Ocean on the east, and the Pacific Ocean on the west.

Major Cultural Groups The United States was born out of the struggle of English, French, Dutch, and Spanish colonial powers for the control and exploitation of North America. With colonization of the Atlantic coast beginning less than 400 years ago, the United States is the youngest of the four countries compared in this book. After winning its revolution for independence from England (1776–1783), the new nation expanded west, pursuing a policy of "Manifest Destiny"—the idea that Euro-Americans had a divinely ordained right to possess all the land and resources of North America, regardless of the presence of indigenous nations. Under this doctrine, the U.S. government used armed force to expropriate Native American lands, and carried out a policy of assimilating or using the U.S. Army to exterminate indigenous native peoples. More than 200 years of Native American armed warfare ended in 1890 with the massacre of 200 Native American men, women, and children at Wounded Knee, South Dakota. Congress passed a law in 1924 giving citizenship to Native Americans. Resistance continues today through Native American social movement organizations and the courts. The 1990 U.S. Census reported that there were 1,878,285 Native Americans in the United States. There are ninety-one major federally recognized Native American nations located on 299 reservations in thirty-four states. Many Native Americans do not live on reservations and they can be found in every state. Native Americans today own 82,754 square miles of land in the United States, only 2.3 percent of their pre-colonial holdings (Churchill, 1994; Famighetti, 1994).

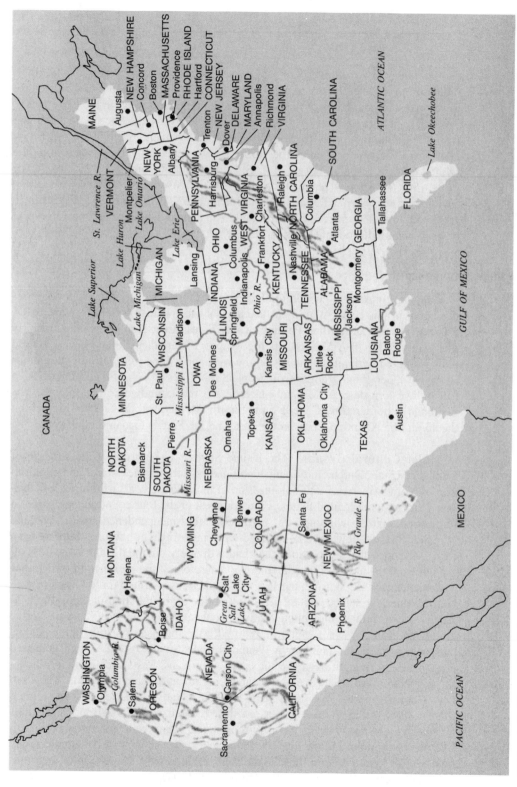

The Land at a Glance—The United States

African Americans comprise about one-eighth of the U.S. population. The majority are descendants of slaves brought to the American colonies and the United States prior to the Civil War (1861–1865). Like Native Americans, African Americans have a long history of resistance and rebellion. The first major slave revolt in the United States occurred in New York in 1712. One hundred fifty-one years later, in 1863, President Abraham Lincoln signed the Emancipation Proclamation, which freed southern slaves. A major social movement for civil rights began with lunch counter sit-ins by black college students in 1960. In 1963, more than 200,000 persons participated in the March on Washington in support of equal rights. Federal legislation banning discrimination in voting, jobs, and public accommodations was enacted in 1964, and the Voting Rights Act was passed in 1965.

Although the United States began as a nation of immigrants, throughout much of its history there has been significant WASP (white, Anglo-Saxon, protestant) sentiment against immigrants who differed from the majority in race or religion. Asians and other people of color were targeted for exclusion. In 1921, Congress sharply curtailed immigration and established a national quota system that favored northern Europeans. During World War II, 110,000 Japanese Americans, including 75,000 American citizens, were removed by force from their homes and held for 3 years in detention camps.

The last blatant racial and ethnic barriers to naturalized citizenship were removed in 1952. The national origins quota system was abolished in 1965, and in 1988, nearly 1.4 million illegal aliens (about three-quarters of whom had entered from Mexico) were given amnesty (all data from Famighetti, 1994).

Illegal immigration remains a significant issue today. As the longest border in the world between a wealthy industrialized nation and a developing nation, the U.S.–Mexican border is the site of much legal and illegal migration. In 1994, passage of California's Proposition 187, denying education, health, and social services to undocumented immigrants and their children, demonstrated the extent to which racism and economic competition continue to enflame emotions around immigration policy. Similarly, large numbers of "boat people," political and economic refugees from Haiti, were turned away from the United States on the orders of both President George Bush and President Bill Clinton. Critics contend that they were rejected because of their African ancestry.

The U.S. 1992 population of approximately 256 million is more than two and a half times that of Mexico, twenty-four times that of Poland, and nearly thirty times that of Sweden. Indeed, the New York metropolitan area contains almost twice as many people as live in all of Sweden.

The United States is ethnically heterogeneous. African Americans, Native Americans, Inuit and Aleuts, Chinese, Filipino, Japanese, Indian, Korean, Vietnamese, and other people of color comprise approximately 16 percent of the population. About 9 percent are of Hispanic origin, coming primarily from Central and South America, and from Cuba. The remainder of the population has European roots, especially in Great Britain, Ireland, Germany, Italy, and Scandinavia. The United States is also religiously diverse. Protestants (56 percent), Roman

---

ON THE STREET IN CINCINNATI, OHIO

Like many large American cities, downtown Cincinnati has experienced an economic rebirth. Sleek new high-rise office buildings and hotels have replaced decayed buildings, and many of the older buildings that remain have been restored or refurbished. A central square is surrounded by places to eat and to shop and by stores selling a wide variety of products. During the day, the downtown is congested with cars, buses, and pedestrians, but it becomes rather quiet after working hours.

During working hours, people on the street tend to wear business clothes and to be a mixture of black and white. In the evening, more adolescents are visible, as are more black people. This reflects residential patterns in the city. Downtown is ringed by an old residential area with decayed housing that is now inhabited by poor people, many of whom are black. The more affluent residents, most of whom are white, live in areas farther from downtown. They can most easily enjoy the beautiful parks for which Cincinnati is famous, set among the scenic bluffs along the Ohio River that separates the city from Covington, Kentucky.

Cincinnati was settled by Germans, and their cultural influence is still evident. German restaurants continue to be popular, as is a massive brick architecture that epitomizes what successful German businesspeople preferred in the 1800s. The city's German cultural roots are also evident in its love of music and the arts. Cincinnati has a world-class symphony orchestra, a fine art museum, and a professional ballet company.

The fine old symphony hall testifies to the changes that have occurred in the city. Once located in a prosperous residential area adjacent to downtown, it now brings white residents of suburbia into an area of run-down housing inhabited by the poor.

The downtown area and the poverty-ridden residential area that surrounds it is home to panhandlers and homeless people. They are black and white, men and women, with some touched by alcoholism, drug use, or mental illness. Favorite haunts are the downtown central square, the bus terminal, and doorways. These residents of the city are not as numerous as in some other American cities, but they are easily noticed even so.

Cincinnati seems a microcosm of contemporary United States. Economic vitality is evident in new construction, busy shops, and abundant traffic. But the limits of prosperity are also in view. Slum neighborhoods are riddled with crime and deteriorated housing. People damaged by social and personal problems and in need of help too seldom receive it. Further, the ongoing exclusion of many people of color from the economic mainstream continues to take a heavy toll.

Source: Personal observations of Ron Federico, 1987.

Catholics (25 percent), and Jews (2 percent) are the major religions. Muslims, Buddhists, and other smaller religious communities also are part of the American mosaic. About 11 percent of the U.S. population expresses no religious preference (U.S. Department of Commerce, 1993a). As we will see later, the heterogeneity of the United States has significant implications for its provision of social welfare.

Political Characteristics   The United States is a federal republic with a strong democratic tradition. It has a presidential form of government with a popularly elected President and Congress. Political power is shared by national, state, and local governments. There are fifty states, each with a democratically elected governor and legislature. Two major political parties, the Democrats and the Republicans, dominate electoral politics at the national and state levels. Increasing numbers of people, however, are dissatisfied with either of the major parties.

Economic Characteristics   Although it suffers from a variety of ailments, the U.S. economy, with a gross national product of about $6 trillion, is the world's largest. The U.S. 1992 per-capita income of $23,120 is one of the highest in the world. Sweden's per-capita income is somewhat higher, and Mexico's and Poland's are much lower. In 1992, the inflation rate in the United States was 3 percent—a little higher than inflation in Sweden, but appreciably lower than inflation in Mexico or Poland. The United States has a mixed economy based on transportation and commerce (42 percent), manufacturing (25 percent), services (19 percent), government (12 percent), and agriculture (2 percent). Private industry generates 88 percent of the U.S. economy. According to government statistics, 6.8 percent of U.S. workers were unemployed in 1993. Thus, at least 8,743,000 U.S. workers could not find jobs. Government statistics are conservative, failing to count discouraged workers who have quit looking for work and failing to take into account large numbers of underemployed workers forced to accept less than full-time work or lower-paying jobs that do not fully utilize their skills (U.S. Department of Commerce, 1993; Famighetti, 1994; U.S. Department of Labor, 1994; World Bank, 1994).

LET'S REVIEW

This chapter offers a sense of what you can learn from reading this book and introduces you to the four countries we compare. We have begun to look at Mexico, a developing nation; Poland, a former socialist society in transition to capitalism; and Sweden, a social democracy. Throughout the book, these countries and their social welfare institutions are compared and contrasted with social welfare in the United States.

We are now ready to consider the first of our questions: *What is social welfare?* From time to time, you may find it useful to refer back to the material in this chapter. Reviewing the book's objectives and its structure can help you to focus your study efforts. Refreshing your memory about particular characteristics of the four countries covered in the book may also be useful when examining the effects of the social environment on social welfare decision making. For now, though, let's move ahead.

STUDY QUESTIONS

1 Write a paragraph describing your understanding of the goals of this book. Try to be as specific as you can. Then write a second paragraph discussing how these goals apply to you—why you are reading the book and what you hope to get out of it. Save your response in your notebook, and reread it from time to time. When you do, you may wish to expand your essay in light of new impressions.

2 Select one of the four societies considered in this book, and write a brief description of your impressions of everyday life in that society. Then compare those impressions with information obtained from one or more reference sources to see which, if any, of those impressions seem to be incorrect.

3 Locate in your local newspaper an article or two that is concerned with social welfare issues affecting an individual or family. Read each article carefully and try to identify the key choices made by the major participants. Consider, for example, decisions about whether people were eligible for help, the kinds of benefits that

were provided or denied, budgetary decisions, and so on. Then think about what effect each of these choices had on the people involved. What alternative outcomes would you have preferred?

KEY TERMS AND CONCEPTS

active choice
cross-cultural comparative perspective

SUGGESTED READINGS

Horn, Alfred, and Bozena Pietras, eds. 1992. *Insight Guides: Windows on the World, Poland.* Hong Kong: APA Publications. The *Insight Guides* provide excellent introductions to history, culture, and contemporary life. This book is written as a collection of brief essays and contains maps and many beautiful color photographs.

Scheutz, Jutta, ed. 1991. *Insight City Guides: Mexico City.* Hong Kong: APA Publications.

Taylor, Doreen, ed. 1990. *Insight Guides: Windows on the World, Sweden.* Hong Kong: APA Publications.

Zinn, Howard. 1980. *A People's History of the United States.* New York: Harper & Row. Detailing the underside of U.S. history with scholarly indignation, Zinn records the struggles of African Americans, Native Americans, women, and other working people to resist oppression.

REFERENCES

Barry, Tom, ed. 1992. *Mexico: A Country Guide.* Albuquerque, NM: Inter-Hemispheric Education Resource Center.

Beachy, Debra. 1995. NAFTA put on hold by peso crisis. *Houston Chronicle* August 11:1C.

Bilski, Andrew. 1991. Sweden: Taxed to the limit, angry voters reject the Social Democrats. *Macleans* September 30:36.

Brosnahan, Tom, John Noble, Nancy Keller, Mark Balla, and Scott Wayne. 1992. *Mexico: A Travel Survival Kit.* Berkeley, CA: Lonely Planet Publications.

Cazes, Daniel. 1993. *University and Citizen Movements of the Past Decade.* Fulbright-Hays Summer Seminar Abroad lecture, Mexico City, Mexico, July 29.

Churchill, Ward. 1994. *Indians Are Us? Culture and Genocide in Native North America.* Monroe, ME: Common Courage Press.

Conroy, Michael E. and Amy K. Glasmeier. 1993. Unprecedented disparities, unparalleled adjustment needs: Winners and losers on the NAFTA 'fast track'. *Journal of InterAmerican Studies and World Affairs* Winter 1993:1–35.

Eckstein, Susan. 1988. *The Poverty of Revolution.* Princeton, NJ: Princeton University Press.

Economist. 1993. Nordic countries: Farewell, welfare. *The Economist* 10(23):67–68.

Economist Intelligence Unit. 1992. *Poland: Country Profile, 1992–93.* New York: The Economist Intelligence Unit, Business International.

EZLN, General Command. (1994). Today we say enough is enough! Original declaration from the Lacandon jungle by the Zapatistas. In *Zapatistas Spreading Hope for*

Grassroots Change Starting from Chiapas, Mexico, ed. Marc Cooper. Westfield, NJ: Open Magazine Pamphlet Series.

Facts on File. 1994. *Sweden's Social Democrats Returned to Power.* 9(22):687–688.

Famighetti, Robert, ed. 1994. *The World Almanac and Book of Facts: 1994.* Mahway, NJ: Funk & Wagnalls.

Horn, Alfred, and Bozena Pietras, eds. 1992. *Insight Guides: Windows on the World, Poland.* Hong Kong: APA Publications.

Lovaas, Scott. 1993. The 700 Club: Observations on the North American Free Trade Agreement. *Social Development Issues* 15(2):77–87.

Mayne, Richard, ed. 1986. *Western Europe.* New York: Facts on File Publications.

Organisation for Economic Co-operation and Development (OECD). 1992. *OECD Economic Surveys: Poland 1992.* Paris: Centre for Co-operation with European Economies in Transition.

Orosco, Guillermo. 1993. *Mass Media in Mexico.* Fulbright-Hays Summer Seminar Abroad lecture, Mexico City, Mexico, July 12.

Rudolph, James D., ed. 1985. *Mexico: A Country Study.* Washington, DC: U.S. Government Printing Office.

Swedish Institute. 1986. *Fact Sheets on Sweden.* Stockholm: The Swedish Institute.

Tagle, Sylvia G. 1991. *National Museum of Anthropology, Mexico.* Mexico City, Mexico: GV Editores.

Taylor, Doreen, ed. 1990. *Insight Guides: Windows on the World, Sweden.* Hong Kong: APA Publications.

United Nations. 1993. *Report on the World Social Situation 1993.* New York: United Nations Publication (Sales No.: E.93.IV.2).

U.S. Department of Commerce, Bureau of the Census. 1993a. *Statistical Abstract of the United States 1993, 113th edition.* Washington, DC: U.S. Government Printing Office.

U.S. Department of Commerce, International Trade Commission. 1993b. *Market Research Report. Sweden: Economic Statistics—IM1930104.* Washington, DC: National Trade Data Bank.

U.S. Department of State, Bureau of Public Affairs, Office of Public Communication. 1992. *Background Notes: Mexico.* Washington, DC: U.S. Government Printing Office.

Ward, Peter. 1986. *Welfare Politics in Mexico.* London: Allen and Unwin.

World Bank. 1993. *Poland: Income Support and the Social Safety Net during the Transition.* Washington, DC: World Bank.

———. 1994. *The World Bank Atlas 1994.* Washington, DC: World Bank.

1

WHAT IS SOCIAL WELFARE?

WHAT TO EXPECT FROM THIS CHAPTER
LEARNING OBJECTIVES
A FRAMEWORK FOR UNDERSTANDING SOCIAL WELFARE
SOCIAL WELFARE REPORT CARD: A FOUR-COUNTRY
COMPARISON
LET'S REVIEW

WHAT TO EXPECT FROM THIS CHAPTER

Social welfare is concerned with empowering people to live more satisfying lives. At first glance, this seems a readily understandable goal: We all believe we know what people need to live decently. In practice, however, there is often considerable disagreement over such questions as what constitutes a satisfying life, whether everyone is entitled to one, and who is responsible for making sure that people are satisfied.

This chapter has two purposes. First, we define a set of concepts that, taken together, constitute the framework we use for discussion throughout the book. These ideas are essential building blocks for understanding social welfare, as a student and as a citizen. The definitions are those used by international organizations such as the United Nations Children's Fund (UNICEF), augmented by standard definitions in the discipline of social work.

Second, we discuss a set of measurements of social welfare progress. These are applied to Mexico, Sweden, Poland, and the United States as benchmarks in a social welfare "report card" for each country.

LEARNING OBJECTIVES

When you have finished studying this chapter, you should be able to:

1 Define social welfare accurately using your own words.

2 Identify and use a set of terms from the reading to describe a framework for understanding the social welfare institution of any country.

3 Identify and use a set of terms from the reading to outline a social welfare "report card" applicable to any country.

4 Use your social welfare report card to compare our four nations in terms of societal capacity to meet social need, the status of children, the status of women, and the status of the general population.

A FRAMEWORK FOR UNDERSTANDING SOCIAL WELFARE

Social welfare may be thought of as a condition of community or societal well-being. In this sense, social welfare is the *result* of a society's ongoing efforts to define a vision of what the quality of human life can and should be, and then to translate that vision into reality. Different countries approach this task in various ways, influenced by their differing histories, cultural traditions, configurations of power, and values.

Social welfare also may be thought of as the sum of a country's programs that contribute to community and societal well-being. In this book we use the definition proposed by Barker (1991:221). **Social welfare** is *"a nation's system of programs, benefits, and services that help people meet those social, economic, educational, and health needs that are fundamental to the maintenance of society."*

Pause here. Think for a minute about what might be meant by "maintaining" a society. Why is it important to work, for example? How are societal values and practices transmitted from one generation to the next? What happens to a society when some of its children don't have enough food?

Naturally, there is considerable variation among societies in the definition of what needs are fundamental and who should be helped. As a result, there are differences in the kind of help offered, the circumstances under which it is provided, and how and by whom it is provided. For example, in Poland under communism, work was believed to be both a basic need and a right. The government guaranteed a job to all able-bodied citizens. Work is also highly valued in the United States, but our government does not assume a similar responsibility for providing a job for everyone who wishes to work.

As you learn more about social welfare, you will see that there is a range of opinion about its nature and goals. We take the position that an important goal of social welfare is to help people function effectively in their social environment. This means not only that they obtain the resources to provide for their basic survival needs (adequate nutritious food, clothing, shelter, medical care, clean air and water), but that they are able to meet all those needs necessary for them to be psychologically well and socially productive. In addition to basic needs, this view of social welfare encompasses, for example, education adequate for successful participation in the economic system, counseling to understand and address personal crises when they occur, and access to employment and other social activities.

Underlying this approach to social welfare is the notion of social cost. When people's needs are not met, they do not function well. Social costs are incurred. Examples of these costs are those associated with building and maintaining prisons and mental-health facilities, with the low economic productivity of a poorly educated workforce, and with expensive hospitalization for babies born underweight or with birth defects as the result of inadequate prenatal care.

The concept of community is central to the idea of social welfare. As we shall see in Chapter 2, community cohesion generates willingness to meet members' social welfare needs, and meeting those needs increases members' solidarity with the community. Social welfare is an important community-strengthening "glue."

Social welfare systems today act "not only to support and enhance the well-being of needy individuals and groups, but also to improve community conditions and help prevent and solve social problems affecting all citizens." Social welfare plays both a **residual** (remedial) role and an **institutional** (preventative) role in society (Trattner, 1994:xxxii). In the residual view the proper role of social welfare is seen as that of responding to breakdowns in the normal functioning of the economy, the family, or the individual. The institutional view emphasizes the preventative role of social welfare in modern industrial societies. Often, of course, a combination of remediation and prevention is required. It is appropriate, for instance, to offer financial assistance or job retraining to unemployed workers. However, if their unemployment is the result of nationwide economic problems, or changes in the way work is done—replacing assembly-line workers with automated machinery, for example—broader action will also be appropriate. By focusing simultaneously on individuals and on their social environment, we can see more clearly the importance of the relationship between the two, and help develop more effective responses to need.

Throughout this book we focus most of our attention on **formal social welfare programs** (i.e., *programs that are organized, structured responses to need*). As we shall see, formal social welfare programs are carried out under either public or private auspices, and provide a wide variety of income maintenance and social service programs. **Informal helping networks** also play a role in social welfare. Informal helping includes activities of *family, friends, neighbors, local churches, synagogues, and mosques, service organizations, and others who provide either spontaneous charity or mutual support in times of need.*

A social welfare system consists of a broad range of programs that provide or support the provision of income, and programs that provide a variety of social services. We look first at income maintenance programs.

Income Maintenance Programs in Social Welfare

Money is a basic resource needed to purchase life's necessities. Many social welfare programs provide financial assistance so that people can purchase what they need in the marketplace. *Services that attempt to ensure adequate financial*

THE HUMAN FACE OF SOCIAL WELFARE 2

CHARITY

The line outside the door moved forward slowly as each person was handed a meal on a paper plate so thin that both hands were needed to keep the food from spilling.

On this day, lunch was corned beef and hash and meatballs, baked beans, macaroni and cheese, two crackers and a cup of sugary iced tea, all that Emma Blake had managed to scrape together. . . .

Every Wednesday afternoon for the last two years, from a sliver of a kitchen just to the left of a storefront church on a Harlem block of boarded-up buildings and crumbling front stoops, this woman of meager means has been feeding the poor.

In the beginning, she paid for almost everything herself, spending as much as $70 a week. But now, there are often small contributions, and Mrs. Blake, a retired practical nurse who lives on Social Security benefits, has been able to cut back her share to about $30.

Some might be daunted . . . by the children who grab eagerly at the plates tucking them close to their chests like something precious, and the adults, some with bloodshot eyes and filthy clothes, who seem not quite conscious of what they are doing.

But Mrs. Blake . . . does not see it that way. "You can alleviate some of the suffering," she said. "You're not going to solve it."

Mrs. Blake, 67 years old, spends most of her week preparing for Wednesday. She hunts for bargains, obtains food from the surplus food bank . . . and tries to use the donations to create a balanced meal. . . .

Cooking often takes up all of Tuesday and keeps Mrs. Blake busy until 1 pm on Wednesday, when she pulls back the metal gates from in front of the kitchen door.

"I couldn't give them canned this and canned that all the time," Mrs. Blake said. "I wouldn't want it, so I'm not going to give it to them.". . .

The people who come to the soup kitchen, more than 200 lately, arrive early and might wait up to two hours for a meal in a quick, often wordless exchange. . . .

A sense of responsibility for others manifests itself in many ways. For Emma Blake, it means running a soup kitchen one day a week in a church in a poor inner-city neighborhood. Emma Blake's soup kitchen is an example of one woman's effort to help people in a personal and direct way. For one meal each week, Mrs. Blake feeds all who come to her for help. How do you think the diners feel about eating in the soup kitchen? Where do they eat during the rest of the week?

At the beginning of the 1980s there were few soup kitchens, food pantries, and shelters for the homeless in the United States. Today some 50,000 private agencies and organizations disburse food to hungry Americans. In a 1992 poll of registered voters, 79 percent reported that "they personally had contributed food or participated in some volunteer antihunger activity" (Beckman and Hoehn, 1992:15–18).

Yet hunger persists, and disenchantment with charity is increasing. Robert Wuthnow (1991) reports that "while 82 percent of the respondents in a survey of volunteers 'thought the need for charities was increasing,' 57 percent believed that charities provide bandaids 'instead of really solving our problems'" (Beckman and Hoehn, 1992:27–28).

What can be done to move from charity to social justice and empowerment of the poor? Bread for the World, a 44,000-member Christian antihunger lobby based in Washington, DC, believes the answer lies in encouraging charity volunteers and the poor to influence public policy by writing letters to elected officials and participating actively in the political process. Information is available from Bread for the World, 1100 Wayne Ave., Suite 1000, Silver Spring, MD 20910; (301) 608-2400.

Excerpted from Suzanne Daley, "Keeping Faith: Emma Blake Feeds the Hungry in Harlem," *The New York Times,* September 1, 1987, p. B1ff. Copyright © 1987 by The New York Times Company. Reprinted by permission.

resources are called **income maintenance programs.** In the United States, some of the best-known income maintenance programs are the ones that issue Social Security payments to retired workers, welfare payments to single mothers, and pensions to disabled veterans. As a general rule, income maintenance payments are relatively small. Their purpose is to enable people to meet their basic needs while encouraging them to be as self-reliant as possible. The examples listed above are publicly funded, but there are private income maintenance programs as well. These include corporate pension plans, medical and disability insurance, and grants from private agencies for food, clothing, or housing.

Cornia and Sipos (1991:xv–xviii) provide definitions of terms related to social welfare income maintenance programs based on United Nations and UNICEF usage. Unless noted otherwise, the definitions that follow are from that source. The social welfare institution is a consequence of the many choices that make up a nation's social policy. **Social policy** is a *"set of measures which aim to achieve a certain level of social welfare or security either for the whole population or for certain population groups.* Social policy usually affects income distribution and the system of social security."

Social security, as the term is used in most countries, consists of *programs of "social insurance and social assistance aimed at providing existential security to the population."* There are five "pillars" of social security: (1) old age, disability, and death benefits; (2) health-care, sickness, and maternity benefits; (3) work-injury compensation; (4) unemployment support; and (5) family allowances (U.S. Department of Health and Human Services, 1993). The five pillars are discussed in detail in Chapters 6 and 7.

In most industrialized countries, the major component of social security is **social insurance.** Social insurance includes pensions, health-care, and unemployment compensation programs, *programs "which depend on previous employment history and, in general, are independent of a claimant's personal or family income."* Social insurance programs are financed by a combination of worker, employer, and/or state payments. Although individual beneficiaries often believe that they have "paid" for their benefits, frequently benefit levels exceed the value of the premiums that have been paid. Old Age, Survivors, Disability, and Health Insurance (OASDHI), commonly referred to as Social Security, is the largest social insurance program in the United States.

Social insurance programs are not "means tested." **Means-tested programs** are *"benefits granted to people if their assessed income does not exceed a given income threshold (which is normally fairly low).* Usually these benefits are targeted to the needy." The "means" in means tested refers to applicants' financial capacity. Often, however, means-tested programs are also mean spirited, inadequately funded, and demeaning. Professor Alvin Schorr once put it this way: "Programs which are only for the poor often end up being poor programs." Income testing embarrasses many people by labeling them as poor and may discourage them from applying for benefits for which they are eligible.

Social assistance programs are *government-financed "means tested public transfers provided to people in need who meet certain eligibility conditions for*

THE HUMAN FACE OF SOCIAL WELFARE 3

LIFE IN A SHELTER FOR THE HOMELESS

It is 2 a.m. Quiet has finally settled on the Salvation Army Emergency Lodge. Three red exit lights glow in the dark. The daytime cacophony of running, screaming children has dwindled to one sick baby's cry. For 11 families, this place is a refuge of last resort. Their new "homes," small, impersonal cubicles, ring the first floor of the four-story brick building. [T]he night staffer plays host to residents of the shelter who cannot sleep. Jim Brand, 37, is one of the wee-hour regulars. "To come here is one step ahead of blowing your damn head off," he says. "You don't want to admit you're a failure. You don't want anybody else to see how bad off you are. . . We fought this for a long time."

For Brand, his wife, Peggy, 38, and their four children, age 5 to 11, the fight ended last fall; they were evicted for the second time in eight months. The Brands' were out of work and there were bills to pay. The emergency shelter was their only option. "If it was only me, I'd sleep in the car. I'm a survivor," says Brand, who was wounded three times in Vietnam. "But I wanted something better for my family."

When the shelter is packed, more than 60 people of all ages can jam the building. Each family is supposed to keep a constant eye on its own children. But Jim complains that some of the other parents "let the kids run wild." The families must share the combination television room and playroom near the office with a transient group of single men, who sleep downstairs, and with the single women, who sleep in a room on the first floor. It is not always the best place for children. When everyone does assigned chores, the rooms are clean. But there's always someone who doesn't do his share. Peggy, a meticulous housekeeper, gets annoyed when she has to clean up someone else's mess. The worst place, she says, is the women's shower and bathtub. Not only is there often a line to get in, but the drain has been clogged since the Brands arrived. There's no shower curtain; privacy is but a memory.

Still, the family tries to keep up appearances. Every morning 10-year-old Jaime and her two sisters wait just inside the entrance for the school buses to stop at the shelter's front door. Despite her girlish bangs and giggles, Jaime plays the role of the wise elder, explaining to her younger sisters the ways of the their new world. Rule number one: you can't let it bother you when

regular or occasional income support." Aid to Families with Dependent Children (AFDC), often referred to as "welfare," and Food Stamps are examples of social assistance programs in the United States.

Universal benefits are *social resources made available to a nation's citizens or residents as rights of membership independent of employment record or income.* They may be cash benefits, such as Sweden's child allowances, or in-kind benefits, such as public education in the United States.

The concept of *entitlement* is closely related to that of universal benefits. **Entitlement programs** are *government-funded benefits of cash, goods, or services that are guaranteed to all people who meet eligibility requirements* (Barker, 1991:75). Examples include Medicare in the United States and health services in Sweden.

Social welfare programs may be funded either publicly or privately, or with a combination of public and private resources. **Public social welfare programs** *are funded by tax monies.* **Private social welfare programs** *are funded by vol-*

kids make fun of you and call you "Salvation Army Girl." Rule number two: you can't go visiting friends after school. The shelter is in a tough neighborhood and it's dangerous to walk home alone after dark.

Sometimes, Peggy says, she thinks that she must have done something very bad, and God is punishing her. How else can she explain her family's fate? Jim isn't the type to agonize about the reasons why his family has fallen on hard times. But he's determined to pass the work ethic on to his kids. "I've taught my kids work is a privilege," Jim says.

The Brands do more than the assigned tasks. "I don't believe in a free lunch," says Jim. Peggy did such a good job in the kitchen that she's now getting paid on the weekends. Jim has become the resident handyman and the nightly driver for the mobile kitchen that brings food to Kansas City's poor. He says that pouring steaming coffee for the street people, some of whom sleep in cardboard boxes under the Missouri River bridges, has made him realize that "there are people worse off than me." That knowledge is small comfort to the Brands' oldest child, 11-year-old Dusty. The boy hates the shelter and its restrictions—especially the 8:30 p.m. curfew for chil-

dren. "Baby hours," he calls it. Even on Friday night he is not supposed to be out of the Brands' 14-foot-by-16-foot shelter room after curfew.

The strict rules that Dusty hates so much are the price the family pays for a safe, clean place to sleep.

The plight of the Brand family is a vivid illustration of the interaction of individual needs and the smooth functioning of society. The Brands are struggling for physical survival, psychological well-being, and a toehold in the larger society—the workplace and school, for example. Their success or failure will have an impact on society. Their children will grow up to be either productive citizens or emotionally scarred and dependent adults. Their parents may stick it out together or separate. If the Brands make it, they will contribute to society. If they sink under the weight of their problems, society will continue to bear the costs of supporting them. This is the challenge of social welfare: How can we build upon the strengths of families like the Brands by providing services they need and by making the environment in which they live more supportive of their needs?

untary charitable contributions of individuals and private organizations, by fees people pay for the services they receive, or by funds spent by corporations to provide social welfare services to their employees. The public/private distinction in the United States has become increasingly blurred as government grants are used to purchase services from "private" agencies, and government tax breaks are made available to corporations to offset the costs of their "private" welfare expenditures.

Social insurance, social assistance, and universal benefits—augmented by programs such as minimum wages, earned-income tax credits, child-care allowances, public housing and homeless shelters, and privately funded social welfare programs—are the basis of **safety nets,** *systems of public and private social welfare programs "which aim to prevent the massive impoverishment of the population."* The historical development of the major programs that constitute the United States's safety net are described in Chapter 6, and the programs are elaborated upon in Chapter 7.

Social Service Programs in Social Welfare

Social services consist of the *"activities of social workers and other professionals in promoting the health and well-being of people and in helping people to become more self-sufficient; preventing dependency; strengthening family relationships; and restoring individuals, families, groups, or communities to successful social functioning.* Specific kinds of social services include helping people obtain adequate financial resources for their needs, evaluating the capabilities of people to care for children or other dependents, counseling and psychotherapy, referral and channeling, mediation, advocating for social causes, informing organizations of their obligations to individuals, facilitating health care provision, and linking clients to resources" (Barker, 1991:221).

Social services, then, help people address personal problems common to daily life, provide protection from abuse in interpersonal relationships and contacts with organizations, and offer opportunities to grow and develop in healthy and satisfying ways.

Social welfare can be seen as the product of a three-step progression from the commitment to societal values, to the allocation of resources to operationalize these values, and then to the use of these resources to provide actual services for people. Now let us look more specifically at the types of services that are commonly provided.

In-Kind Services

Income maintenance programs need not necessarily involve giving people money. Some take the form of **in-kind services,** *services that provide a needed commodity itself rather than the funds to purchase it.* The Food Stamp program is a well-known public example. Food stamps can be used to purchase food items at grocery stores, thereby serving as a replacement for money. In-kind services are a vehicle for ensuring that the aid provided will be used for the intended purpose. Money given to someone for rent payments might instead be used to purchase other items, leaving the rent unpaid. Using a rent voucher instead of cash ensures that this will not occur. The use of vouchers raises important issues of freedom and responsibility, trust and dignity, and stigma. These are discussed in Chapter 3.

Personal Social Services

Kahn and Kammerman (1977:3–11) popularized the term **personal social services** to refer to *nonfinancial social welfare programs that enhance people's personal development and functioning.* Education, protection from physical and emotional harm, health care, and personal counseling to help people solve problems, manage interpersonal relationships, and participate more effectively in society are all examples of personal social services.

Kahn and Kammerman divide personal social services into two major categories: public social utilities and case services. **Public social utilities** are *services that are available to all members of society who have a need for them.* For example, public schools are available to all children, and public police protection to anyone who is threatened with bodily harm. Other examples of public social utilities are public parks, public water and sewer systems, highways, and the legal system. **Case services** are meant *to help those with personal maladjustments, problems, illness, or other difficulties.* Psychotherapy and marriage counseling are case services, as are job counseling, medical care, and nursing-home care, all of which may be provided by either the public or private social welfare systems.

Another way that social services are organized is around the specific needs of particular groups. Child welfare services, for example, help children whose parents cannot care for them, who suffer from physical or emotional abuse, or who are living in poverty. Services for the elderly focus on the elderly's special physical, health, housing, and income needs, as well as helping them to prepare for death. Families may need income assistance or counseling, while those in the workplace may be struggling with work-related stress or alcoholism.

While we usually think of social welfare services as being provided to individuals, it is important to remember that such services may also be provided to groups and communities. For example, the Bureau of Indian Affairs of the U.S. Department of Commerce is mandated to respond to the needs of the Native American population in the United States. The Department of Housing and Urban Development is a federal agency responsible for programs intended to improve and develop communities throughout the United States (U.S. Office of the Federal Register, 1993:331,351–352). There are also private agencies that assist communities. These include major charitable foundations that seek to enhance community facilities for education or the arts, and disaster-relief agencies such as the Red Cross.

Social welfare addresses the full range of human needs, from those of individuals to those of the larger society, from before birth to death. When people function better, communities and organizations benefit, and vice versa.

SOCIAL WELFARE REPORT CARD: A FOUR-COUNTRY COMPARISON

As you continue your exploration of social welfare, it is important to think about how to measure the progress being made in your own country and elsewhere throughout the world. Because children are especially vulnerable to social welfare deficits and because people everywhere care about the health and well-being of their children, we place particular emphasis on measurements related to the status of children. We look also at indicators that provide benchmarks for measuring the status of the general population and the status of women.

The first section of Table 1-1 reports measures of the relative ability of our four countries to fund social welfare programs. We begin with **per-capita gross national product** (GNP): *the share of the dollar value of a country's total output of goods and services theoretically available to each resident if everyone received an equal share.* Sweden and the United States are high-income industrialized countries with per-capita GNPs that place them among the world's eight richest countries. Sweden's per-capita GNP of $25,110 was the third highest in the world in 1991. Only Switzerland and Japan had higher levels. With a per-capita GNP of

TABLE 1-1   FOUR COUNTRIES: CAPACITY AND SUPPORT FOR SOCIAL WELFARE

	Mexico	Poland	Sweden	United States
Per-capita gross national product (GNP/c) 1991 ($US)	$3,030	$1,790	$25,110	$22,240
GNP/c world rank from highest 1991	36th	58th	3rd	8th
Real growth rate GNP/c, 1985–1992	1.1%	–1.9%	0.4%	1.1%
Average annual rate of inflation, 1985–1992	58%	124%	7%	4%
Debt service as percent of export earnings, 1980/1991	50%/31%	18%/5%	NA	NA
Interest payments on debt as percent of export earnings, 1980/1991	27%/17%	5%/3%	NA	NA
Percent central government expenditure: defense, 1980/1991	2.3%/2.4%	NA/NA	7.7%/6.3%	21.2%/21.6%
Percent central government expenditure: education, 1980/1991	18.0%/13.9%	NA/NA	10.4%/9.7%	2.6%/1.7%
Percent central government expenditure: health, 1980/1991	2.4%/1.9%	NA/NA	2.2%/0.8%	10.4%/13.8%
Percent central government expenditure: housing social security, welfare, 1980/1991	18.5%/13.0%	NA/NA	51.5%/56.4%	37.8%/28.7%

Sources: GNP/c and world rank, debt service and interest, central government expenditures from *World Development Report 1993: Investing in Health.* Washington, DC: World Bank. Real growth and inflation rates from *The World Bank Atlas 1994.* Washington, DC: World Bank.

$22,240, the United States ranked eighth highest, a little lower than Norway, Finland, Denmark, and Germany. Mexico was thirty-sixth highest in the world, with a per-capita GNP of $2,940, and Poland's $1,790 ranked fifty-eighth.

Since GNP is never shared equally, per-capita GNP says nothing about the actual distribution of a country's resources. But it does provide a means to compare the potential capacity of countries to provide for the social welfare of their people. The World Bank ranks countries according to per-capita GNP. Sweden and the United States are classified "high-income" countries, Mexico is among twenty-two "upper-middle-income" countries, and Poland is among forty-three "lower-middle-income" countries. Thus, none of the countries we are studying falls into the world's poorest group of forty nations, designated "low-income" by the Bank (World Bank, 1993).

Additional economic factors that affect a nation's capacity for supporting social welfare include the rate at which its economy is growing, the rate of inflation, and payments of interest and principal on its external debt. Mexico, Sweden, and the United States experienced modest annual increases in per-capita GNP adjusted for inflation from 1985 to 1992. Although Mexico's real growth rate was equal to that of the United States, from 1985 to 1992, Mexico experienced serious inflation, which was brought under control from 1993 to 1994 but flaired out of control once again following President Zedillo's devaluation of the peso in late 1994. From 1985 to 1995 Poland also experienced serious inflation and faced a decline in per-capita GNP. Inflation affects social welfare by reducing the purchasing power of those on fixed incomes or with incomes that do not increase as rapidly as the cost of living rises.

During the 1980s, Mexico and many other developing countries experienced a debt crisis, which continues to affect the resources that might be available for social welfare programs. Both Poland and Mexico have faced severe debt-servicing difficulties and are classified by the World Bank as "severely indebted middle-income economies" (World Bank, 1993:xi).

Counting on its large oil reserves as its ticket to the future, during the 1970s and early 1980s Mexico borrowed large amounts of foreign funds and spent them for industrial development, public-sector investments, wage increases for public employees, and expanded social services. Falling oil prices in 1982 brought Mexico to the verge of economic collapse. In 1986, as a condition for receiving new credit, Mexico agreed to lower trade barriers, privatize many of its public enterprises, and reduce public spending.

From 1982 to 1991 Mexico paid foreign creditors more than $125 billion in debt service, including about $83 billion in interest. The debt repayment was in large part made at the expense of the Mexican people. Wages were reduced. Many workers lost their jobs. Social services were cut, and the costs of public utilities, food, and shelter increased. Critics argued that the Mexican poor were making foreign creditors rich (Barry, 1992:77–90). Today, debt service continues to equal nearly one-third of the value of Mexico's total earnings from exports.

Any nation's commitment to social welfare is reflected in the ways it spends its money. The second section of Table 1-1 shows changes in central government expenditures for defense, education, and health, and for housing, social security, and welfare, from 1980 to 1991. In the United States, the percentage of the national budget given to military expenditures is three times greater than in Sweden and nine times greater than in Mexico. The military share of our national budget increased slightly from 1980 to 1991. During the same period the share of the U.S. national budget spent for housing, social security, and welfare fell by nearly a quarter. Similar reductions occurred in Mexico. Sweden spends more than one-half of its budget on housing, social security, and welfare—nearly twice as large a budget share as the United States. From 1980 to 1991 Sweden increased its budget share for these purposes. Mexico, the poorest of the three countries for which data are available, allocated a higher proportion of its national budget to education than did Sweden or the United States.

THE HUMAN FACE OF SOCIAL WELFARE 4

SELF-HELP AND DIGNITY

Just a quarter of a century ago, there was little here except barren plains and a salty, swampy lake bed. Today, 2.5 million people live in this sprawling, jerry-rigged settlement just east of Mexico City. . . .

Greater Mexico City is already home to more people than any other metropolis on earth, but even by local standards the growth of this working-class "dormitory city" has been explosive. Yet as Nezahualcóyotl . . . recently marked the 25th anniversary of its incorporation, the local authorities said they hoped that the days of seemingly limitless and uncontrollable growth were gone.

"There's no more space for us to grow physically," Mayor José Salinas Navarro . . . said in an interview. "We hope that the only growth we experience from now on will take place in the provision of basic public services."

. . . Only half of Nezahualcóyotl's 750 miles of streets are paved, leading in the rainy season to extensive flooding to back up the sewer system.

The city authorities boast that every house in Neza, as the city is universally known throughout Mexico, has electricity and running water. But many homeowners complain that because

approximately 1,000 miles of pipes are hooked up to a single, antiquated mainline intended to serve a much smaller population, water pressure is inadequate and they must dig wells in their backyards, or buy water from roaming water trucks.

Overcrowding is another major problem: Neza already has more than 100,000 inhabitants a square mile, and the population has grown by as much as 5 percent a year recently. Two or more homes have been built on many of the city's 160,000 residential lots, straining to the breaking point basic public services Mr. Salinas has pledged to improve.

Then there are the city's 800 youth gangs . . . [which] find abundant prey in the hundreds of thousands of recent immigrants from poor southern states like Oaxaca, Guerrero and Michoacán. Many [newcomers] commute to low-paying jobs in Mexico City and would live elsewhere if they had a choice.

"I'd much rather move back to my home village in Michoacán than be here," said Marta Ochoa de Prado, a 24-year-old housewife who lives in the neighborhood of El Sol, near a garbage dump that residents pick through in search of fuel and resalable goods. "The air is cleaner there, the food is better and cheaper, and the streets are safer, but there's no job for my husband, so here we stay."

One might reasonably expect wealthier countries to provide more and better-quality social welfare services than poorer countries. With per-capita GNP more than ten times as great as either Mexico or Poland, one would expect the social welfare systems of the United States and Sweden to far outperform those of the poorer countries. As we will see when we review the status of children and others, for the United States this is not always the case.

Table 1-2, on page 40, reports measurements related to the health status of children. Unless noted otherwise, these and subsequent definitions of social welfare report card indicators are those used by UNICEF (1994:86). **Infant mortality rate (IMR)** is the *number of deaths of infants under one year of age per 1,000 live births.* More specifically, this is the probability of dying between birth and exactly one year of age." The single most important measure of changes in the level of child well-being used by UNICEF is the **under-five**

Mrs. Prado said her husband, Victor Manuel, spends four hours a day traveling back and forth to his job at a glass and crystal factory in Mexico City. He leaves at 6:30 A.M. and returns at 8:30 P.M., after spending nearly a fifth of his daily wage of $3.86, the legal minimum, on transportation. But like most residents of Neza, the Prados simply cannot afford to live in the capital.

From its earliest days Neza has hardly seemed to be a place propitious to human settlement. Bounded on the East by the Mexico City airport and on the north by a lake that has since been converted into a sewage treatment center, the site "was dusty like a desert during the dry season, and muddy like a swamp during the rainy season," said Mr. Salinas, who first came here in 1960.

But workers dreaming of owning a home of their own were willing to risk their fortunes after Mexico City put restrictions on construction and the parceling of lots into subdivisions. . . .

"When I got here in 1963, the conditions were almost inhuman," said Salomón Alemán Garcia, owner of a fish and poultry stand at an open air market. "There was no water, no electricity, no sewers, no streets, no sidewalks and no schools. Whatever the need, we didn't have."

Soon after building his home, Mr. Alemán discovered that he was not the owner of the plot of land he thought he had purchased from a real estate company. In fact, he learned after further investigation, the company itself did not even have title to the parcels it had sold to him and tens of thousands of other homesteaders.

Along with many of his neighbors, Mr. Alemán began a campaign to convince the Mexican Government to change his status from squatter to homeowner. It was not until 1984, after a 20-year battle, that he received the deed for the piece of land on which his house, where he and his wife have raised 10 children over the years, sits. . . .

"Nothing has come easy for the inhabitants of this city," said Próspero Domínguez Trejo, Neza's official chronicler. "Everything that has been gained here has been achieved on the basis of struggle. The people of Nezahualcóyotl are tenacious, skillful and accustomed to adversity."

The development of Neza exemplifies the process by which government can be compelled to respond, when people are empowered to organize and to struggle for their needs and rights. Even in opposition to powerful, entrenched political interests, organized communities can enhance their social welfare through self-help initiatives.

Excerpted from Larry Rohter, "Nezahualcóyotl Journal: In Plain of Hungry Coyote, Millions Dwell in Hope," *The New York Times,* May 31, 1988, p. A4. Copyright © 1988 by The New York Times Company. Reprinted by permission.

mortality rate (U5MR), *the "number of deaths each year of children under five years of age per 1,000 live births."* The U5MR reflects the probability of a child dying before his or her fifth birthday. U5MR is used by UNICEF and other world organizations for two reasons. (1) It measures end results of social welfare policy instead of inputs such as expenditures for medical programs. (2) It is a consequence of a wide variety of inputs, including "the nutritional health and the health knowledge of mothers; the level of immunization and oral rehydration therapy use; the availability of maternal and child health services (including prenatal care); income and food availability in the family; the availability of clean water and safe sanitation; and the overall safety of the child's environment" (UNICEF, 1994:79).

In each of the four countries reported, there has been steady reduction in the U5MR since 1970. All four are now well below the internationally accepted goal of

TABLE 1-2   FOUR COUNTRIES: HOW HEALTHY ARE THE CHILDREN?

	Mexico	Poland	Sweden	United States
Infant mortality rate (IMR): deaths/1000 under 1 year old, 1960/1992	98/28	62/14	16/6	26/9
Under 5 mortality rate (U5MR): deaths/1,000, 1960/1980/1992	141/81/33	70/24/16	20/9/7	30/15/10
U5MR average, annual reduction rate (%), 1960–1980/1980–1992	2.8%/7.5%	5.3%/3.3%	4.1%/1.6%	3.3%/3.3%
U5MR performance gap (U5MR compared with national capacity)	–3	+26	+3	–3
Life expectancy at birth	70	72	78	76
Percent low-birth-weight births, 1990	12%	NA	5%	7%
Daily per-capita calorie supply as percent of requirements, 1988–1990	131%	131%	111%	138%
Percent children 0–4 yrs underweight, 1980–1992	14%	NA	NA	NA
Percent children 24–59 mos stunted, 1980–1990	22%	NA	NA	2%
Percent children 12–23 mos wasted, 1980–1990	6%	NA	NA	2%
Goiter rate 6–11 years old, 1980–1992 (%)	15%	10%	NA	NA
Percent 1-year-old children fully immunized, 1990–1992 (TB/DPT/polio/measles)	95/91/92/91	94/98/98/94	14/99/99/95	NA/58/74/77
ORT use rate, 1987–1992 (%)	63%	NA	NA	NA

Source: *The State of the World's Children 1994.* New York: United Nations Children's Fund. U5MR performance gap from *The Progress of Nations 1993.* New York: United Nations Children's Fund. Stunting and wasting from *World Development Report 1993: Investing in Health.* Washington, DC: World Bank.

reducing the U5MR for all countries to 70 or less by the year 2000. Progress has been especially dramatic in Mexico and Poland. Nineteen nations, including Spain, Greece, and the Republic of Korea, have U5MR levels lower than that of the United States. The rate of progress in reducing the U5MR is measured as its average annual reduction rate.

The **U5MR performance gap** measures *the difference between the level of U5MR that a country could reasonably be expected to achieve given its per-capita GNP and its actual level of U5MR.* By this measurement Poland is doing much better than would be predicted, Sweden is doing better, and both Mexico and the United States are falling short of their potential.

U5MR rates may vary within a country. While Mexico in 1982 had an average rate of 71, its rate for cities was 32 and its rate for rural areas was 104. In the

United States, the 1990 IMR was 7 in San Francisco—the same as Norway or Switzerland—while Detroit ranked below Cuba, and Washington, DC, was at the same level as the much poorer country Jamaica. White infant mortality in the United States was 8 per 1,000 live births, but black infant mortality was 18 per 1,000—worse than Poland's or Bulgaria's (UNICEF, 1993:13).

Thus U5MR, like per-capita GNP, may be distorted by averages that conceal the privileged position of wealthy minorities. U5MRs within a country will vary for people with different income levels unless choices are made to supplement income with social security benefits.

Life expectancy at birth is *"the number of years newborn children would live if subject to the mortality risks prevailing for the cross-section of the population at the time of their birth."* All four countries have life expectancies longer than the world average of 66 years (World Bank, 1993). **Low birth weight** refers to *births less than 2,500 grams (about 5.5 pounds).* Infants with low birth weights are commonly referred to as being born prematurely. Low birth weight often results from the mother's poor health or malnutrition before or during pregnancy. The lower an infant's birth weight under 5.5 pounds, the greater is the risk of infections, sickness, and death (Cornia and Sipos, 1991:xvi).

Each of our four countries produces more than enough food to meet the nutritional needs of its people. Daily per-capita food supplies are substantially greater than minimum requirements. When hunger is present in these countries, it is a problem of access to food, not a problem of there not being enough food to go around. Policy choices about how societal resources are shared can create or can eliminate hunger.

In the developing world, childhood hunger frequently results in children who are underweight, wasted, or stunted. **Underweight** *measures weight for age against a reference population.* Children who weigh less than normal for their age are considered underweight. **Wasting** *measures weight for height against a reference population and is a possible consequence of severe short-term malnutrition.* Children who weigh less than normal for their height are considered to be wasted. **Stunting** *measures height for age against a reference population and is frequently the outcome of persistent long-term malnutrition.* Children who are shorter than normal for their age are considered stunted.

There is controversy about whether all racial and ethnic groups have an equal genetic potential for size. Mexicans, for example, on the average are shorter than Euro-Americans. How much of the difference is related to genetic potential, and how much reflects nutritional history? To get around the issue, some people advocate using Mexicans as a reference group for Mexicans. This practice may avoid inflating rates of stunting according to standards that are temporarily or permanently unrealistic.

Of our four countries, only Mexico reports substantial incidence of underweight, stunting, and wasting. Childhood hunger is not a problem in Sweden. At least until recently, it has not been a serious problem in Poland. What about the United States? Let's look in detail at childhood hunger in the United States.

**MOMENTS IN AMERICA
FOR CHILDREN**

- Every 9 seconds, a child drops out of school.
- Every 10 seconds, a child is reported abused or neglected.
- Every 14 seconds, a child is arrested.
- Every 25 seconds, a baby is born to an unmarried mother.
- Every 32 seconds, a baby is born into poverty.
- Every 34 seconds, a baby is born to a mother who did not graduate from high school.
- Every 1 minute, a baby is born to a teen mother.
- Every 2 minutes, a baby is born at low birth weight.
- Every 3 minutes, a baby is born to a mother who received late or no prenatal care.
- Every 4 minutes, a child is arrested for an alcohol-related offense.
- Every 4 minutes, a child is arrested for a violent crime.
- Every 4 minutes, a child is arrested for a drug offense.
- Every 10 minutes, a baby is born at very low birth weight.
- Every 15 minutes, a baby dies.
- Every 2 hours, a child is killed by firearms.
- Every 4 hours, a child commits suicide.
- Every 7 hours, a child dies from abuse or neglect.

Source: Reprinted with permission from *The State of America's Children Yearbook 1996.* Washington, DC: Children's Defense Fund, 1996.

In the United States, **hunger** has been defined as *"the mental and physical condition that comes from not eating enough food due to insufficient economic, family, or community resources."* In 1995, the Community Childhood Hunger Identification Project (CCHIP) studies, coordinated in sixteen states and the District of Columbia by the Food Research and Action Center, reported that 4 million U.S. children under 12 experienced hunger sometime during the year, and that another 9.6 million children under 12 lived in households at risk of hunger. Twenty-nine percent of all U.S. children under 12—13.6 million children—were reported living in households with at least one food shortage problem. The CCHIP studies were used to fuel a national Campaign Against Childhood Hunger (FRAC, 1995).

Recent research has found that even moderate undernutrition of the sort commonly experienced in the United States can have lasting negative effects on the cognitive development of children. Even short-term nutritional deficiencies "influence children's behavior, ability to concentrate, and to perform complex tasks. . . . Undernutrition, along with environmental factors associated with poverty, can permanently retard physical growth, brain development, and cognitive functioning." Fortunately, many of these consequences can be reduced or eliminated by improved food intake and remedial programs (Center on Hunger, Poverty and Nutrition Policy, 1993:5–7).

Micronutrient malnutrition is a serious problem in many parts of the developing world. Vitamin A and iodine are two essential micronutrients. Lack of vitamin A results in permanent blindness for 250,000 children every year and "leaves tens of millions more susceptible to the three leading causes of child death—diarrheal disease, measles, and pneumonia." Adding small amounts of fruit or green vegetables to a child's diet, or supplementing it with vitamin A capsules three times a year, solves the problem. Such capsules cost 5 cents each (UNICEF, 1993:15).

In parts of the world where soils lack iodine, iodine deficiency disorders including goiter and cretinism are widespread. **Goiter,** *enlargement of the thyroid gland visible as swelling of the throat,* affects 200 million people. In 30 years as a social worker in the United States, I [Bill Whitaker] have encountered only two cases of goiter. In Mexico, 15 percent of all children between 6 and 11 years of age have goiter, as do 10 percent of Poland's 6- to 11-year-olds. The presence of goiter implies a more devastating consequence of iodine deficiency. Worldwide each year, 120,000 children who lack iodine are born brain-damaged; and millions more grow up "stunted, listless, mentally retarded, and incapable of normal speech or hearing." Iodine deficiency can be eliminated by adding iodine to salt at a cost of about a nickel per person per year (UNICEF, 1993:15).

Immunization against childhood diseases is another key to increasing well-being at modest cost. In Mexico, Poland, and Sweden, more than 90 percent of 1-year-old children are fully immunized against polio, measles, and DPT (diphtheria, whooping cough, and tetanus). In the United States during 1990–1992, only three-quarters of 1-year-olds were fully immunized against polio and measles. Only six out of ten were fully immunized against diphtheria, whooping cough, and tetanus. In 1993, President Clinton began an immunization campaign, declaring immunization to be the right of all children—"like clean water and clean air" (UNICEF, 1993:46).

Throughout the world, 2 million children under 5 die needlessly each year as the result of dehydration related to diarrhea. **Oral rehydration therapy** (ORT) is an inexpensive, effective remedy that is now saving a million lives every year. Dehydration can be prevented with packets of salts that cost about 10 cents each, or with home remedies such as rice water or weak tea. In Mexico (1987–1992), ORT was being used in 63 percent of the cases of diarrhea among children under five. President Salinas launched a campaign to bring ORT to every Mexican child in every Mexican state under the banner, "The best solution" (UNICEF, 1993:6).

In November 1989, the U.N. General Assembly adopted the Convention on the Rights of the Child, which seeks to protect children throughout the world from exploitation, neglect, and abuse. In September 1990, the World Summit for Children was convened at the United Nations. Seventy-one heads of state attended and adopted goals for the year 2000, which would reduce by one-half protein-energy malnutrition in children under 5; reduce the rate of low-birth-weight births to under 10 percent in all countries; reduce levels of iron-deficiency anemia in women by at least one-third; and virtually eliminate iodine and vitamin A deficiencies. By 1993, the Convention on the Rights of the Child had been signed and ratified by 118 countries, including Mexico, Poland, and Sweden. (The United States, commemorating the work of UNICEF director James Grant, signed in 1995, but has not yet ratified the Convention.) By 1995, fifty-eight countries including Mexico, Sweden, and the United States—but not Poland—had finalized and submitted to the U.N. "National Programmes of Action" for achieving year 2000 goals (UNICEF, 1993:15, 46–47).

Education is a major contributor to a nation's social welfare. Education level and literacy, for example, affect people's chances of being employed in jobs that pay enough to support their families. The first section of Table 1-3 reports educa-

TABLE 1-3   FOUR COUNTRIES: HOW AVAILABLE IS EDUCATION?

	Mexico	Poland	Sweden	United States
Gross primary school enrollment ratio				
Male: 1960/1986–1991	80/113	110/99	95/106	NA/105
Female: 1960/1986–1991	75/110	107/98	96/107	NA/104
Percent of grade 1 enrollment reaching final year primary school, 1988	70%	92%	100%	90%
Gross secondary school enrollment ratio				
Male: 1986–1991	52	80	89	92
Female: 1986–1991	53	84	93	91
Percent age group enrolled in tertiary education, total, 1970/1990	14%/14%	18%/22%	31%/33%	56%/75%
Adult literacy rate (15+ yrs)				
Male: 1970/1990	78%/90%	98/NA	NA/NA	99/NA
Female: 1970/1990	69%/85%	97/NA	NA/NA	99/NA
Primary pupil/teacher ratio, 1970/1990	46/31	23/16	20/6	27/NA
Radio sets per 1,000 pop., 1990	243	429	888	2123
TV sets per 1,000 pop., 1990	139	293	474	815

Sources: Age group school enrollments, pupil/teacher ratios from *World Development Report 1993: Investing in Health.* Washington, DC: World Bank. All other data from *The State of the World's Children 1994.* New York: United Nations Children's Fund.

tional participation and achievement in our four countries. Comparisons over time show the progress a nation is making in educating its entire population. Because in many parts of the world women and men have unequal access to education, comparisons are reported by gender when data are available.

Gross primary and secondary school enrollment ratios are *"the total number of children enrolled in a schooling level—whether or not they belong in the relevant age group for that level—expressed as a percentage of the total number of children in the relevant age group for that level."* Percentages may exceed 100 because some students are older or younger than the standard age for their level. Poland, Sweden, and the United States achieved universal primary school enrollment before 1960. Mexico achieved universal primary school enrollment between 1960 and 1991. In Sweden, all children who enter primary school complete that level. In the United States and Poland, one out of ten children, and in Mexico three out of ten children, fail to complete primary school. A little more than 50 percent of all Mexican children begin secondary school, compared with 80 percent of Polish students and about 90 percent of the children of Sweden and the United States. Tertiary enrollment consists of the percent of students ages 20–24 enrolled in colleges and universities, vocational schools, adult education programs, 2-year community colleges, and correspondence programs. In 1990, such postsecondary enrollments were 14 percent in Mexico, 22 percent in Poland, 33 percent in Sweden, and 75 percent in the United States. Only the United States showed a major percentage increase since 1970.

Adult literacy rates report the *"percentage of people aged 15 and over who can read and write."* Poland, Sweden, and the United States report nearly universal literacy among adults. Mexico improved its literacy rates significantly between 1970 and 1990. However, 10 percent of Mexican men and 15 percent of Mexican women cannot yet read and write. No other major gender-based differences in education were reported. Although the United States reports that 99 percent of U.S. adults are literate, there is growing concern about the extent of **functional illiteracy** in the United States. Persons are considered functionally illiterate if their *"reading and writing skills are not of sufficient quality to permit their use in normal socioeconomic relationships"* (Barker, 1991:109).

The second section of Table 1-3 reports primary school teacher/pupil ratios, and ownership of radio and television sets. Although averages may conceal wide differences within a society, the average number of pupils being taught by each teacher has been getting smaller in each of the four countries. In the United States, differences in the ability of local communities to pay for education means that some children have access to better education than others. Indigenous people in Mexico's rural states, such as Chiapas, express similar concerns.

Table 1-4 reports how income is shared between rich and poor, the share of household income spent for food, and several indicators of public health. Describing income distribution by quintiles, each including 20 percent of the nation's population, permits us to think about how fairly income is distributed.

Before discussing income shares, however, it is important to think about the concept of poverty. **Absolute poverty** exists when *people are unable to afford the "least costly satisfaction of a minimum nutritionally adequate diet plus a few other essential non-food requirements."* **Relative poverty** exists when *people are able to satisfy minimum socially accepted needs, but are deprived compared to nonpoor members of their society.* Relative poverty lines are generally set at 40 to 50 percent of a nation's median income (Cornia and Sipos, 1991:xvi–vii).

The U.S. federal poverty line was developed by the Social Security Administration in 1964 as an index for measuring the progress of the Johnson administration's War on Poverty. The measure is based on the cost of the U.S. Department of Agriculture's "Thrifty Food Plan," the least expensive of four food budgets developed by the USDA. Assuming that most families spend one-third of their household budgets on food, the cost of the Thrifty Food Plan was multiplied by 3 to calculate the poverty line. Although serious questions have been raised about the adequacy of the Thrifty Food Plan poverty line, it is adjusted annually to reflect cost-of-living increases, and it continues to be used as the official measure of poverty in the United States.

In 1992, the U.S. poverty line was $14,335 for a family of four. Thirty-six million nine hundred thousand persons were poor, the highest number since 1962, when poor residents of the United States totaled 38.6 million. In 1992, 14.5 percent of the U.S. population had incomes below the poverty line. Poverty rates were higher for African Americans (33.3 percent) and people of Hispanic origin (29.3 percent). Although the rates for Native Americans were not reported separately, they are the highest among people of color in the United States. Over one-

TABLE 1-4   FOUR COUNTRIES: WELL-BEING OF THE GENERAL POPULATION

	Mexico	Poland	Sweden	United States
Income shares by quintile (%): lowest/second/third/fourth/ highest/highest 10%	(1984) 4/8/12/20/ 56/40	(1989) 9/14/18/23/ 36/22	(1981) 8/13/17/25/ 37/21	(1985) 5/11/17/25/ 42/25
Food costs as percent of household consumption, 1980–1985	35%	29%	13%	10%
Percent population with access to safe water, urban/rural, 1988–1991	81%/68%	NA	NA	NA
Percent population with access to adequate sanitation, 1988–1991, urban/rural	70%/17%	NA	NA	NA
Percent population with access to health services, 1985–1992, urban/rural	88%/60%	NA	NA	NA
Deaths from communicable diseases and maternal, perinatal causes per 100,000 people, 1985–1990	168	73	41	54
TB cases/100,000 people, 1990	110	43	7	10
Percent adults who smoke, female/male	44%/47%	29%/63%	30%/26%	24%/30%
Tobacco consumption: kg/yr/ adult, 1974–1976/1990/2000	1.4/1.0/1.1	3.4/3.5/3.7	1.9/1.5/1.3	3.8/2.6/2.2

Sources: Access to water/sanitation/health services from *The State of the World's Children 1994.* New York: United Nations Children's Fund. Adults smoking from *The World's Women 1970–1990: Trends and Statistics.* New York: United Nations, 1991. All other data from *World Development Report 1993: Investing in Health.* Washington, DC: World Bank.

third (34.9 percent) of all U.S. households headed by women were poor (U.S. Bureau of the Census, 1993).

From a global perspective, poor people in a rich nation like the United States might appear to be well off. Some of the worst housing in which they live, for example, might seem "normal" to a rural *campesino* who was not perceived to be poor in Mexico. It is important, of course, to take climate into account when making cross-country comparisons of housing. Housing that is appropriate for a warm climate may be inappropriate in colder places. Each society must respond to poverty within the context of its present economic circumstances.

In addition to being concerned about the needs of their own citizens, social justice demands that rich nations contribute to the development of poorer nations throughout the world. During the 1960s, industrialized nations set a target for annual assistance to developing countries of 0.7 percent of donor country GNP. In 1991, Sweden's aid to developing nations was 1.0 percent of GNP or about $234 per Swede. The United States gave 0.2 percent of GNP, about $44 per person (UNICEF, 1993:44).

ON THE STREET IN THE UNITED STATES—HOMELESSNESS

The United States presents a striking duality in social welfare. On the one hand, it has an elaborate and complicated network of social welfare services and, on the other hand, there are large gaps in the resources that are made available to people. Nowhere is this duality more evident than in the treatment of the homeless.

Every large American city has a population of people living on the street. Popular living areas include grates over exhaust vents, where the escaping air provides life-giving warmth. Others find corners or doorways in which to set down cardboard "beds" on which they sleep and live. Lacking sanitary facilities, it is not unusual to find street people urinating or defecating in a public place.

Other homeless people seek shelter within railroad and bus stations. New York's Grand Central Station has a large population of homeless, who use its waiting room as a dormitory and its corners as bathrooms. Some live in the labyrinth of tracks, and on at least one occasion thousands of commuters were affected by fires started by homeless residents living in unused train cars.

Lacking money and other resources, the homeless are not appealing to be near. They are often dressed in torn rags that may expose open sores. Some are shoeless, walking on gnarled and filthy feet that are sometimes cut and bloody. Others are dressed in many layers of clothing regardless of the season and the temperature. Without basic hygiene facilities, many smell of sweat, dirt, and body wastes.

Estimates of how many homeless exist in the United States vary widely. Dear and Wolch (1987:175) cite figures ranging from the U.S. Department of Housing and Urban Development's estimate of 350,000 per night to the figure of 2.5 million offered by the National Coalition for the Homeless. Included among these people are individuals suffering from some form of mental disability, young unemployed drifters, alcoholics, substance abusers, people squeezed out of the job market, and families too poor to afford escalating rents, especially poor women and their children.

Does the United States have the resources to eliminate homelessness? Yes. Poland, a far poorer society, is close to doing so, although housing there is in short supply and far from luxurious.

Why, then, does homelessness continue to exist and even to increase in the United States? There are many reasons. Many mental hospitals have been closed, forcing their residents onto the street in the absence of other facilities. An increasingly high-tech economic system has few jobs to offer people with little skill, education, and tolerance for stress. Stubborn historical patterns of racism and sexism that continue to exclude members of minority groups from access to adequate education, opportunities for advancement, and economic security also contribute to the problem; and underlying all of these factors are values that deny the homeless the resources they need.

As a result, the homeless survive on their own as best they can. Often they obtain help from a variety of sources, utilizing some parts of the formal welfare system (such as temporary shelters and hospitals), any available semiformal resources (for example, Emma Blake's soup kitchen), and assistance from informal helping structures (begging and seeking help from other homeless people). Only rarely are the homeless poor organized to advocate on their own behalf, as the low-income home owners of Neza are. For a compelling challenge to the common belief that the homeless are incapable of such self-help, see David Wagner (1993), *Checkerboard Square: Culture and Resistance in a Homeless Community*.

Now let's take a look at how income is shared in our four countries. Table 1-4 reports the share of income received by each fifth of the population in each country. Income distribution is most unequal in Mexico, where the richest 20 percent receives 4.5 times as much income as the poorest 40 percent of the population. In the United States the richest 20 percent receives about 2.5 times as much as the poorest 40 percent. In Sweden the top 20 percent receives 1.8 times the income of the bottom 40 percent. Income distribution is least unequal in Poland, where the richest 20 percent gets 1.6 times as much income as the poorest 40 percent.

The proportion of a household budget that must be spent for food is higher in poorer countries than in richer ones. On the average, Mexican families spend three-and-a-half times more income on food than is the case in the United States.

Poor families in each of the four countries would be likely to need to spend higher than average percentages to feed their children. Consequently, poor families have less money with which to meet other needs.

Statistics on access to safe drinking water, sewage disposal, and health services in Poland, the United States, and Sweden are not reported by the United Nations. Although the assumption is that these amenities are available to most people in those countries, there is growing concern about industrial pollution of drinking-water supplies in Poland and the United States. In 1994, lack of health insurance affected access to health care for about 38 million U.S. residents. Universally available health insurance that could not be taken away was proposed by the Clinton administration, but failed to be enacted by Congress. In Mexico, access to safe drinking water, sewage disposal, and health care remains a problem for many, especially in rural areas.

Unsafe water, poor sanitation, and lack of access to health services contribute to deaths from communicable diseases and childbirth-related deaths of mothers and infants. Mortality from these causes was more than four times as high in Mexico as in Sweden, with Poland and the United States falling between the extremes. Incidence of cases of tuberculosis showed a similar pattern. Use of tobacco causes many health problems. The percentage of the population that smokes tobacco was highest in Poland and Mexico and lowest in the United States. Tobacco consumption has been declining in Mexico, Sweden, and the United States, but is increasing in Poland, which already has the highest consumption per capita of our four countries.

The status of women is an important aspect of any assessment of social welfare. Table 1-5 concludes our social welfare report card with a look at health and other indicators of the well-being of women in our four countries. Women live longer than men in each of the four countries. Nearly one-third of all families in Poland, Sweden, and the United States are headed by a woman. Data are unavailable for Mexico. In all four countries today, women are about as likely as men to attend primary or secondary school.

The **total fertility rate,** *"the number of children that would be born per woman, if she were to live to the end of her child-bearing years and bear children at each age in accordance with prevailing age-specific fertility rates,"* is important to both society as a whole and to individual women. For a country, they affect the size of the population that must be provided for by societal resources. Thus, the annual rate of reduction in fertility rates in a society is an important indicator of its potential for future improvements in the general welfare of its people. On a personal level, too, the number of children a woman bears affects her continued health and her physical ability to work and meet the needs of her family. In each of our four countries, fertility rates are declining. Mexico is notable among developing countries in having reduced its fertility rate by half since 1960. In a single decade between 1980 and 1991, Mexican women reduced family size by one child or more (UNICEF, 1993:34).

Maternal mortality rate is *"the number of deaths of women from pregnancy related causes per 100,000 live births."* Among our four countries, maternal death rates are highest by far in Mexico and lowest in Sweden.

TABLE 1-5   FOUR COUNTRIES: WELL-BEING OF WOMEN

	Mexico	Poland	Sweden	United States
Females' life expectancy as percent of males', 1992	110%	113%	108%	109%
Percent female-headed households, 1980s	NA	27%	27%	31%
School enrollment ratio females as percent of males, primary/secondary, 1986–1991	97%/102%	99%/105%	101%/104%	99%/99%
Total fertility rate, 1960/1980/1992/2000	6.8/4.7/3.2/2.4	3.0/2.3/2.1/2.1	2.3/1.6/2.1/1.9	3.5/1.8/2.1/1.9
Annual rate of reduction in fertility rate (%), 1960–1980/1980–1992	1.8/3.2	1.3/0.8	1.8/–2.3	3.3/–1.3
Maternal mortality rate per 100,000 live births, 1980–1991	110	11	5	8
Contraceptive use by married women, 15–49, 1980–1993	53%	75%	78%	74%
Percent pregnant women anemic, 1970s–1980s	41%	16%	NA	17%
Percent pregnant women immunized against tetanus, 1990–1992	42%	NA	NA	NA
Percent births attended by trained health personnel, 1983–1992	77%	100%	100%	99%

Sources: The State of the World's Children 1994. New York: United Nations Children's Fund. Anemia, projected year 2000 fertility rate from *World Development Report 1993: Investing in Health.* Washington, DC: World Bank. Percent female-headed households from *The Progress of Nations 1993.* New York: United Nations Children's Fund.

Women's access to contraception, adequate nutrition, and health services is important to reducing the number of children they bear and to improving the outcome of their pregnancies. It is estimated that "the rate of population growth in the developing world would fall by approximately 30% if women could choose how many children to have." This would mean about 1 billion fewer people in the developing world by the year 2025 (UNICEF, 1993:35). In Sweden, Poland, and the United States, about three-quarters of married women ages 15–49 report using contraceptives. In Mexico, about one-half of married women do so.

Poor nutrition may result in **anemia,** *a condition in which lack of dietary iron causes deficiency in red blood cells or hemoglobin in the blood.* Anemia affects both men and women, and has major consequences for women during pregnancy and lactation. Anemia results in "impaired work performance, body temperature regulation, behavior, and intellectual performance; decreased resistance to infections; and increased susceptibility to lead poisoning" (U.S. Department of Health and Human Services, 1993:47). Anemia is no longer a problem in Sweden. About two-fifths of pregnant women in Mexico, and a little less than one-fifth of pregnant women in Poland and the United States, suffer from anemia. Anemia during pregnancy persists in the United States at least in part because Congress has not fully funded the Special Supplemental Food Program for Women, Infants, and Children (WIC), a cost-effective program that lowers infant mortality and improves the health of women and children who take part.

In the developing world a mother's death during or following childbirth is often related to lack of safe water and sanitation. Under such circumstances, it is especially important to be immunized for tetanus. **Tetanus** is *an acute infectious bacterial disease often introduced through an open wound. An early symptom of tetanus is muscle spasms and inability to open the jaws, hence its colloquial name, "lockjaw"* (Woolf, 1979). Throughout the world, "every minute a newborn dies of tetanus infection. Every ten minutes, the same disease strikes down a new mother. Every year, an estimated 50,000 maternal deaths and nearly 600,000 neonatal tetanus deaths . . . could be prevented by tetanus vaccination and clean birth practices."

Tetanus is a result of "unsafe birth practices which bring tetanus spores into contact with the unhealed umbilical cord or birth canal" (UNICEF, 1994:10). When births are attended by physicians, nurses, midwives, primary health-care workers, or traditional birth attendants trained in the "three cleans"—"clean hands, a clean surface for delivery, and clean cutting and care of the cord"—maternal and infant deaths from tetanus are reduced dramatically (UNICEF, 1994:10). In Mexico, the maternal mortality rate is more than ten times as great as in Poland or the United States, and twenty times as great as in Sweden. Only two-fifths of pregnant Mexican women are immunized against tetanus; only three-quarters of Mexican births are attended by trained health personnel.

LET'S REVIEW

Before we end this chapter, let's review the basics of social welfare. We have seen that an important goal of social welfare is to help people function effectively in their social environment. This means not only providing for people's basic survival needs (adequate nutritious food, clothing, shelter, medical care, clean air and water), but also meeting all requirements for them to be psychologically well and socially productive. Accordingly, we have defined social welfare specifically as a society's governmental and nongovernmental "programs, benefits, and services that help people meet those social, economic, educational, and health needs that are fundamental to the maintenance of society."

Next, we discussed the various types of social welfare programs. These included income maintenance programs, in-kind services, and personal social services of two types, public social utilities and case services.

We then set our understanding of social welfare in an international context. We reviewed indicators of progress, using them to create a social welfare report card comparing needs and progress in Mexico, Poland, the United States, and Sweden.

It is probably clear to you that the study of social welfare can be a mammoth undertaking. In addition to the services provided to people, many other areas of social life are relevant to such a study: the political system in which decisions are made, the economic system that affects resources and their allocation, social welfare organizations that employ and organize the people who deliver actual services, societal values and the ethical behaviors that flow from them, historical factors that have created patterns of inequality. These are topics we address in future chapters.

Social welfare is a social creation. What you learn about it will change as it changes in response to its dynamic environment. During your life you will see many changes, whether as a citizen, a user, or a practitioner. Knowledge of where these changes come from will help you understand and participate in shaping a changing and dynamic social welfare system.

As you complete this chapter, you should have a reasonably clear idea of what social welfare is and the types of programs it involves. You should also understand how progress toward achieving social welfare goals can be measured, and have a good sense of the degree of success of the United States, Mexico, Sweden, and Poland in meeting the social welfare needs of their people.

Now we are ready to move to the next chapter, where we explore some of the major reasons why people need social welfare services. We see that the biological, psychological, cultural, and social structural dimensions of daily life often cause the problems that the social welfare system seeks to address. Other problems arise from the tensions and abuses flowing from the way nations organize interactions between people. Still others result from choices people make for themselves. In response, social welfare is the result of active choices made by people who define a vision of what the quality of human life can and should be, and then attempt to translate that vision into reality.

STUDY QUESTIONS

1 Review the new concepts that were introduced in this chapter. Definitions can be found both in the text and in the glossary. Make sure that you can define each concept in your own words. For each concept, try to give an example based either on your own experience or on something you have read or seen.

2 Why should people who live in industrialized countries be concerned about the well-being of people who live in developing nations? Try to answer this question from the perspective of residents of the United States or Sweden. Then answer from the perspective of Polish and Mexican people.

3 Think about some of the differences in human well-being that exist among our four countries. Try to imagine what it would be like to be a parent in each society. In each country, what concerns would you have for the future of your children?

4 What are some of the obstacles in Poland, Mexico, and the United States that make the achievement of universal social welfare programs such as those in Sweden difficult to attain?

5 Use your library to find out more about the work of UNICEF and the World Summit for Children. What are some of the advantages of operating social welfare programs through an intergovernmental organization such as UNICEF, compared with bilateral efforts such as the United States Peace Corps? What disadvantages might there be?

KEY TERMS AND CONCEPTS

social welfare	social policy
residual approach to social welfare	social security
institutional approach to social welfare	social insurance
formal social welfare programs	means-tested programs
informal helping networks	social assistance programs
income maintenance programs	universal benefits
entitlement programs	underweight
public social welfare programs	wasting
private social welfare programs	stunting
safety nets	hunger
social services	micronutrient malnutrition
in-kind services	goiter
personal social services	oral rehydration therapy
public social utilities	literacy
case services	functional illiteracy
per-capita gross national product	poverty
infant mortality rate (IMR)	fertility rate
under-five mortality rate (U5MR)	maternal mortality rate
U5MR performance gap	anemia
life expectancy at birth	tetanus
low birth weight	

SUGGESTED READINGS

Children's Defense Fund (CDF). 1994. *The State of America's Children Yearbook 1994.* Washington, DC: The Children's Defense Fund. An annual assessment of progress toward meeting the needs of children. Under the leadership of Marian Wright Edelman, the CDF is one of the foremost organizations advocating for children in the United States. The CDF publishes many excellent resources of interest to students of social work and social welfare: 25 E Street, NW, Washington, DC 20001; (202) 628-8787.

UNICEF. 1993. *The Progress of Nations 1993.* New York: United Nations Children's Fund. An annual ranking of the nations of the world according to their achievements in health, nutrition, education, family planning, and progress for women. This inspiring report is beautifully written and illustrated, and contains excellent graphics.

UNICEF. 1994. *The State of the World's Children 1994.* New York: United Nations Children's Fund. An excellent annual publication that provides current data on the well-being of children, identifies work that needs to be done, and provides numerous examples of positive accomplishments throughout the world.

Wagner, David. 1993. *Checkerboard Square: Culture and Resistance in a Homeless Community.* Boulder, CO: Westview Press. A well-written, often dramatic look at homelessness from the inside. Wagner challenges the common idea that poor and homeless people cannot organize and advocate effectively.

REFERENCES

Barker, Robert L. 1991. *The Social Work Dictionary* 2d ed. Silver Spring, MD: National Association of Social Workers.

Barry, Tom, ed. 1992. *Mexico: A Country Guide.* Albuquerque, NM: Inter-Hemispheric Education Resource Center.

Beckman, David, and Richard A. Hoehn. 1992. *Transforming the Politics of Hunger.* Washington, DC: Bread for the World Institute on Hunger and Development.

Center on Hunger, Poverty and Nutrition Policy. 1995. *The Link between Nutrition and Cognitive Development in Children.* Medford, MA: Tufts University School of Nutrition.

Cornia, Giovanni A., and Sandor Sipos. 1991. *Children and the Transition to the Market Economy: Safety Nets and Social Policies in Central and Eastern Europe.* Brookfield, VT: Gower Publishing Company.

Dear, Michael, and Jennifer Wolch. 1987. *Landscapes of Despair: From Deinstitutionalization to Homelessness.* Princeton, NJ: Princeton University Press.

FRAC. 1995. *Community Childhood Hunger Identification Project: A Survey of Childhood Hunger in the United States.* Washington, DC: Food Research and Action Center.

Kahn, Alfred J., and Sheila Kamerman. 1977. *Social Services in International Perspective.* Washington, DC: U.S. Government Printing Office (SRS 76-05704).

Trattner, Walter I. 1994. *From Poor Law to Welfare State: A History of Social Welfare in America,* 5th ed. New York: The Free Press.

UNICEF. 1993. *The Progress of Nations 1993.* New York: United Nations Children's Fund.

————. 1994. *The State of the World's Children 1994.* New York: United Nations Children's Fund.

U.S. Bureau of the Census. 1993. *Poverty in the United States: 1992* (Current Population Reports, Series P60-185). Washington, DC: U.S. Government Printing Office.

U.S. Department of Health and Human Services. 1993. *Nutrition Monitoring in the United States: Chartbook 1: Selected Findings from the National Nutrition Monitoring and Related Research Program.* Washington, DC: U.S. Government Printing Office.

U.S. Office of the Federal Register. 1993. *The United States Government Manual 1993/94.* Washington, DC: U.S. Government Printing Office.

Wagner, David. 1993. *Checkerboard Square: Culture and Resistance in a Homeless Community.* Boulder, CO: Westview Press.

Woolf, Henry B., ed. 1979. *Webster's New Collegiate Dictionary.* Springfield, MA: Merriam-Webster.

World Bank. 1993. *World Development Report 1993: Investing in Health, World Development Indicators.* Washington, DC: World Bank.

Wuthnow, Robert. 1991. *Acts of Compassion.* Princeton, NJ: Princeton University Press.

2

WHY IS SOCIAL
WELFARE NEEDED?

WHAT TO EXPECT FROM THIS CHAPTER
LEARNING OBJECTIVES
PERSONAL NEEDS AND SOCIETAL NEEDS
COMMON HUMAN NEEDS AND HUMAN DIVERSITY
NEEDS THROUGHOUT THE LIFE SPAN
HUMAN NEEDS AND SOCIETAL RESPONSES
SOCIAL WELFARE'S CONTRIBUTION
THE "GLUE" OF SOCIAL WELFARE
LET'S REVIEW

WHAT TO EXPECT FROM THIS CHAPTER

This chapter addresses the question of why we, or any society for that matter, need a social welfare system. You will recall from Chapter 1 that social welfare involves helping people and societies to function more effectively in their environment. In this chapter we explore what it is about human beings and the way we live that makes social welfare a necessary part of our lives.

Social welfare raises issues that many people would rather avoid. Most of us like to think of ourselves as competent and self-sufficient. At some level, of course, we acknowledge that we have needed help at various times in our lives, especially when we were children. Furthermore, we see all around us people who encounter obstacles in their day-to-day activities—frail elderly relatives, friends sick in the hospital, or physically limited people. We are also aware of our own problems, whether they involve success in school, getting or keeping a job, or managing relationships with family members. So we know that many aspects of living can be troublesome.

Still, many of us resist thinking about needing help. It seems as if admitting that we need help compromises our sense of self-worth as adults. It is hard to ask for help without thinking that we have failed in some way or that it is our own fault. We worry that friends or colleagues may think less of us if we cannot "make it on our own." Such thinking is reinforced by stories of self-made millionaires, heroes who have triumphed over incredible adversity, and poor, hard-working folk who accept their lot quietly rather than ask for help. If they can do it, why can't we? Isn't it lazy or selfish to seek help rather than solving our own problems? Shouldn't we be content with what we have, even if it is very little?

LEARNING OBJECTIVES

When you have finished studying this chapter, you should be able to:

1 Describe basic and intermediate personal needs and their relationship to societal needs.

2 Discuss the relationship between common human needs and the needs of diverse groups.

3 List biological, psychological/emotional/cognitive, and social/environmental factors that lead people to need help.

4 Discuss types of mistakes or poor choices that people make, which are likely to create the need for social welfare.

5 Use the concepts of manifest and latent functions to analyze the impact of social welfare programs on individuals and on society.

6 Discuss positive and negative ways in which social welfare functions as societal "glue."

7 Provide your own answer to the question of why social welfare is needed, based on the material in this chapter.

Our discussion of the need for social welfare in this chapter draws on evidence of two quite different types. One type is empirical, consisting of the findings of social scientists and human service professionals concerning the conditions that promote individual well-being and societal functioning. The other is normative, consisting of the values that affect people's perceptions of helping and being helped. Both types of evidence—the empirical and the normative—shape our thinking about social welfare.

PERSONAL NEEDS AND SOCIETAL NEEDS

Needs are *"physical, psychological, economic, cultural, and social requirements for survival, well-being, and fulfillment"* (Barker, 1991:153). Both persons and societies have needs. Let's look first at personal needs.

All human beings are wonderfully complex organisms born with the potential to grow, think, question, learn, and find answers to developmental tasks. We are born into physical and social environments that provide resources that facilitate the realization of our human potential, and that present obstacles to its realization. Throughout our lives we need the help of other people to achieve our maximum potential. Compared with other species, we have large brains. In order to house our large brains, our heads require a major share of the body mass with which we are born. This means that human babies are vulnerable for a longer period of time during infancy than are the young of most other species, and must be nurtured and protected during an extended period of dependence during childhood. Throughout our lives we need to eat and stay warm in order to survive in good health (Doyal and Gough, 1991:37). Some people have physiological deficits that impose limits on their potential for independence. There is, then, a biological context for human needs.

Human life also takes place in a physical context—air, water, vegetation, and other forms of life—that can facilitate or impede people's efforts to realize their genetic potential. The nature of people's interaction with their physical environment is a second factor that gives rise to the need for social welfare.

Another powerful influence on human life is the **social environment:** *the social arrangements created by people that serve to structure their daily behavior.* Other individuals, families, small groups, organizations and communities, and social institutions—including social welfare—are all part of the human social environment. So, too, are our values and beliefs, the norms that guide our behavior, and the roles we play as we interact with others.

When members of groups and organizations within the social environment work together and "follow more or less the same rules concerning what they perceive to be the most significant aspects of their everyday life," they are said to share the same **culture** (Doyal and Gough, 1991:79).

For a culture to persist and flourish over time, four goals must be achieved. First, enough goods and services must be produced and distributed by the society to ensure minimal levels of survival and health for its members. Second, enough children must be reproduced and socialized to replace members of the culture who leave or die. Third, enough members of the society must be taught the skills and values that are required for the production of goods and services and the reproduction and socialization of children. Finally, there must be political authority with the ability to ensure that the culture's rules will be taught, learned, and followed (Doyal and Gough, 1991:88).

Successful achievement of each of these four societal goals is a necessary precondition for the satisfaction of the personal needs of the members of society. Simply put, individual existence is a social condition that depends on the involvement of other individuals who depend on still others. Ultimately, meeting societal needs depends on the presence and involvement of the members of society. People and society depend on each other.

COMMON HUMAN NEEDS AND HUMAN DIVERSITY

Let's think about the concept of *common human needs,* the needs all people have at some point in their lives. The timing of these needs and the ways in which they are expressed vary for members of different groups. Three factors affect how people meet their common human needs: (1) human biological and developmental characteristics; (2) the physical and social environment; and (3) choices that people make that may or may not be in their best interest. The first part of this chapter, then, discusses why people sometimes do not function effectively.

Common human needs are *those personal needs that are shared by all human beings because they are basic to their survival and development* (Towle, 1965:6–11). According to Charlotte Towle, a social worker writing during the 1940s, common human needs include physical well-being, personality development, emotional growth, development of intellectual capacity, relationships with others, and spiritual needs.

Psychologist Abraham Maslow took Towle's list of common human needs one step further, arranging them in a hierarchy (1970:35–46). As shown in Table 2-1, Maslow believed that some human needs were more basic than others and that people must fulfill their needs in a particular order. First, he argued, come the physiological needs basic to physical survival. Higher-level needs for safety, belongingness and love, esteem, and self-actualization follow in ascending order. In Maslow's view, higher-level needs cannot be met until all preceding lower-level needs have been taken care of. Thus, according to Maslow, a person struggling to find safe housing for her family would be unlikely to have time or energy to be concerned about self-actualization—"becoming everything that [she] is capable of becoming." Both Towle and Maslow recognize that some of these common human needs may not be met for everyone. Unmet needs may lead to the necessity for social welfare programs.

Len Doyal and Ian Gough (1991:36, 49–75) argue that Maslow's list of needs is incomplete and that his strict sequencing of need fulfillment is wrong. They contend that humans in all societies have two basic needs: the need for good physical health and the need for autonomy, i.e., the ability to initiate action (see Table 2-2). Autonomy requires good understanding of one's self and one's culture, good mental health, and opportunity for new and significant action.

Satisfaction of each basic need depends on meeting several related intermediate needs. Physical health is dependent on adequate nutritional food and clean water, adequate protective housing, a nonhazardous work environment, a nonhazardous physical environment, and appropriate health care. Because mental health, a major factor in human autonomy, is affected negatively by "an emotionally deprived

TABLE 2-1   MASLOW'S HIERARCHY OF COMMON HUMAN NEEDS

Function	Need	Example
Self-fulfillment	Self-actualization	Graduating from college
Self-respect	Esteem	A promotion at work
Acceptance	Belongingness and love	Committed relationships
Security	Safety	School crossing guards
Survival	Physiological	Food, shelter, health care

TABLE 2-2   BASIC AND INTERMEDIATE COMMON HUMAN NEEDS

Basic needs	Intermediate needs
Physical health	Adequate nutritional food and water
	Adequate protective housing
	A nonhazardous work environment
	A nonhazardous physical environment
	Appropriate health care
Autonomy	Security in childhood
	Significant primary relationships
	Physical security
	Economic security
	Basic education
Women's health and autonomy	Safe birth control and child bearing

Source: Len Doyal and Ian Gough. 1991. *A Theory of Human Need.* New York: Guilford Press.

childhood, the loss or absence of significant others, insecurity and economic deprivation," basic emotional autonomy is related to four additional intermediate needs: security in childhood, significant primary relationships, physical security, and economic security (Doyal and Gough, 1991:191–193). A tenth intermediate need, appropriate education, enhances cognitive autonomy. Finally, for women, the capacity to bear children creates an eleventh intermediate need, the need for safe birth control and safe child bearing.

Intermediate human needs are met through personal efforts together with the formal and informal activities and the public and private programs that make up the social welfare institution. Successful meeting of intermediate human needs results in meeting the basic human needs for good health and autonomy. When the intermediate and basic human needs of its members are met, the goals necessary for the persistence and flourishing of society are likely to be achieved as well.

Helen Harris Perlman, a social worker like Towle, emphasized the holistic nature of common human needs (Perlman, 1957:6–7, language modified to remove gender bias). "People," she suggested,

> are whole in any moment of their living. They operate as physical, psychological, social entities, whether the problem is one of neurotic anxieties or of inadequate income; they are product-in-process, so to speak, of their constitutional makeup, their physical and social environment, their past experience, their present perceptions and reactions, and even their future aspirations. It is this physical-psychological-social past-present-future configuration that they bring to every life-situation they encounter.

This unity of the biological, psychological, and social components of humans has come to be called the *biopsychosocial whole*. A **holistic approach** is *an attempt to understand and treat the whole person or phenomenon by taking into account and integrating all the relevant "social, cultural, psychological, and physical influences"* (Barker, 1991:102). This way of thinking recognizes that, as biological, psychological, and social beings, people seek to meet their needs through interpersonal relationships and the social structures in their environment.

These two concepts—common human needs and the holistic approach—are central to an understanding of how people interact with their social and physical environment as they attempt to realize their full, inherited potential.

While all people seek to meet their needs for growth, development, and survival, the ways they do so vary. Common human needs are expressed and met in marvelously varied ways by different groups of people (Berger and Federico, 1985:88), for diversity is a basic characteristic of our species. **Human diversity** refers to *the biological, psychological, social and cultural differences among people* that affect the way their needs are expressed and satisfied. Some of the most significant types

---

ON THE STREET IN SWEDEN—SUBWAYS FOR EVERYBODY

In Stockholm, subways are for people—all people. The design of the Stockholm subway system illustrates how obstacles in the social environment that could thwart people's efforts to meet their personal needs can be minimized.

Subways in Stockholm, as in most large cities, are a valuable tool in helping people pursue their daily activities. Adults travel to work and students go to school. Parents take their children shopping and elderly citizens go visiting. Although many Swedes have cars, public transportation (buses, suburban trains, ferries, and the subway) is a popular way to move around the city.

Many subway systems around the world have characteristics that discourage the frail and disabled from using them. Stairs (and even escalators) create obstacles for the physically limited, parents with youngsters, and the elderly. In some cities, crime also makes many people reluctant to use subways. Dirty and isolated corridors and subway platforms further limit the appeal of underground travel to many potential users.

Stockholm has taken these problems seriously and created a subway that is accessible to everyone. Elevators and ramps are provided at all stations, so the stations are readily accessible to those in wheelchairs or who are accompanied by grocery carts or baby carriages. Many corridors in the system feature shops that make it possible to combine shopping activities with travel. Crime is minimal, and the subway system is kept clean. Many of the stations have artwork or interesting architectural features that enhance their esthetic appeal.

The result is a public social utility that is accessible to virtually everyone. Neither people's physical safety nor their psychological sense of well-being are threatened when using the system. Their sense of participation in their urban environment is enhanced. They are able to go where they need to when they want to. The Stockholm subway provides a good example of how the physical and social environment can be designed to minimize obstacles to the realization of human potential.

Of course, the Stockholm subway system did not just happen. It is the product of active choice by those responsible for designing and operating the system. Most of all, it is a result of a view in which a physical limitation is seen not as the individual's problem but as a problem in the interaction of the individual and society. In this view, those with physical limitations can meet their common human needs and participate effectively in community life, if their environment provides the resources they need.

Other communities, viewing matters differently, often resist making their public transportation systems accessible to those with limitations, perceiving the added costs involved as "too expensive" in relation to other purposes preferred by the community. Whatever the reasoning, the net effect of such decisions is a public transportation system that represents an obstacle blocking those with limitations from utilizing their abilities to the fullest.

Source: Personal observations of Ron Federico, 1987, and Bill Whitaker, 1993.

of diversity are gender, age, race, ethnicity, physical and mental health, sexual orientation, and socioeconomic class.

There are many possible examples of the impact of human diversity on people's ability to realize their potential. Studies have shown that a child's physical welfare is affected by the socioeconomic status of its caretakers. Poor children are more likely to have birth defects, low birth weight, and illness at birth. They are also more likely to suffer from hunger and malnutrition and to be abused or neglected (National Association of Social Workers, 1987:3). In the United States, African American and Hispanic people are more likely than whites to live below the poverty level (U.S. Department of Commerce, 1993:471). Consequently, their children are more likely to experience physical problems. Gay and Lesbian people, and persons with mental or physical limitations, may also encounter special problems in meeting their needs. Their families and neighbors often withhold the social acceptance and emotional support that they need to meet their needs for love, esteem, and self-actualization (Dane, 1985; Slater and Wikler, 1986; Berger, 1987).

What we see, then, are two distinct sources of human needs. All people have certain common needs that range from physical survival through self-fulfillment. At the same time, the way in which people attempt to meet these needs is influenced by human diversity. Children and old people both must eat to survive, but they differ in what they eat, how they eat it, and how it is obtained. Similarly, adult men and women have a need for psychological security, but the precise form of these needs, and the ways in which they can best be met, may vary.

NEEDS THROUGHOUT THE LIFE SPAN

Human needs are not static: They take on different forms over the course of the human life span. The **life span** is *the period from conception to death* and is *usually discussed as chronological stages,* each of which is associated with a distinctive set of social expectations about how needs will be met (Berger and Federico, 1985:112–113). For example, it is generally expected that many of the psychological, emotional, and social needs of teenagers will be met in the context of their school experience. This extends beyond the classroom to sports, dances, and other interactions with their peers. Adults are more likely to meet these same needs in the workplace, through recreational activities, and via intimate relationships.

The social expectations concerning the expression and fulfillment of needs at each stage of the life span usually reflect the biological capacities associated with, and the resources commonly available to, people at that stage. For example, young children in the United States are not expected to earn a living, because they are socially defined as not yet physically or mentally capable of doing so.

Such definitions vary according to societal context. A hundred years ago in the United States, it was commonplace to find children working in mines, textile mills, and agriculture. Today, it is expected that U.S. children will be nurtured and protected by their families until they are able to be financially independent. These general expectations prevail even though we know that not all families are able or willing to care for and protect their children. We know that poor children—who are disproportionately likely to be members of oppressed racial and ethnic groups—must often find a way to earn a living much earlier than those who are better off. In less affluent countries such as Mexico, many young working-class children must work to help ensure the survival of their families and themselves. It is estimated by Mexican authorities that as many as 1 million Mexican children live on the streets without families—supporting themselves by selling gum, candy, and trinkets; working as acrobats, singers, or clowns; cleaning windshields; etc. (Chimley, 1993, Cruz, 1993).

We can see, then, that each stage of the life span is associated with certain general biological, psychological, and social characteristics. Let's look at these in more detail.

Biological Processes

Human physical, psychological, and social development is a lengthy process, and it is many years after birth before people become relatively self-sufficient. Genetic programming heavily influences the rate and extent of human biological and physical development, but so, too, do disruptive illnesses, accidents, and natural disasters, which may occur at any time. In addition, few people in industrialized societies can grow all their own food, construct their own housing, or make their own clothing. Meeting basic physical needs usually requires collaboration with others. Most people must work to earn an income that enables them to purchase necessities from others. Meeting one's physical needs in today's world involves interaction with a complex social environment.

Periods of biological helplessness can also influence other needs. Children are especially dependent on others for meeting their emotional, intellectual, personality, and social needs, in addition to ensuring their basic physical survival. The elderly may find that their social relationships and their sense of psychological well-being are jeopardized if they become dependent on others. Adults at any age can also experience difficulty in their social relationships, social participation, and sense of well-being, if their independence is lessened through illness, accident, or loss of a steady job.

Table 2-3 illustrates the different ways in which basic physical needs are met throughout the life span. Notice that the same needs persist throughout life; physical survival and well-being. However, the resources available to meet these needs change, as do the obstacles that may be encountered. Keep in mind that the pattern shown here is typical of people in general but not necessarily of any single individual, whose life history will, of course, be shaped in part by human diversity. Note, too, that a similar chart could be made for other types of needs.

Emotional and Cognitive Growth

As people move through the life span, they meet their basic needs in different ways. Emotional tasks, such as managing stress, expressing affection for others, perceiving the environment accurately, and controlling one's feelings, are man-

TABLE 2-3   MEETING PHYSICAL NEEDS THROUGHOUT THE LIFE SPAN

Stage	Strategies for meeting physical needs
Prenatal	Dependent on the mother's nutrition and health
Birth	Influenced by birthing events and the birth environment
Infancy	Dependent on caretakers, usually family members and medical personnel
Childhood	Heavily responsive to caretakers, especially at home and in school; growing importance of friends and own activities
Adolescence	Limited dependence on caretakers; growing importance of own activities and decisions, especially regarding smoking, drinking, nutrition, sexual activity, friends, and so on
Young adulthood	Much less dependent on family; assumption of economic and nurturing roles for self; significant relationships with spouse/lover/friends that include mutual care
Middle adulthood	Maximum autonomy and self-care; continuation of mutual care relationships
Retirement	Continue self-care and mutual care patterns as much as possible; increasing dependence on spouse or lover, family, friends, health-care professionals
Death	Final loss of control over physical self

aged more effectively as people mature emotionally. Intellectual development also brings changes. The ability to reason cognitively grows, and the individual's store-house of knowledge increases. Consequently, new opportunities and new decisions continually emerge. The integration of cognitive capacity with spiritual and moral standards takes place. Personal goals are clarified, and strategies for meeting them are chosen. In short, we increasingly realize our capacity for individual diversity, a capacity we never lose.

As an illustration of the importance of emotional and cognitive development to need-meeting behavior, consider the changing role of women in the United States. In comparison with the past, women today have greater access to education and employment opportunities. Their increased opportunities for cognitive development and functioning that accompany being educated and gainfully employed, in turn, affect the emotional growth of many women, enhancing their sense of autonomy and well-being.

Among the beneficial results of this development is a reduced likelihood that women will be victimized by abusive personal relationships (Finkelhor, 1983:18). A reduction in the incidence of abuse of adult women is likely to spare their children from abuse as well (Straus, 1983:219). Thus, enhancing women's opportunities to grow and develop cognitively and emotionally may help break the generational cycle of child and spouse abuse (Herrenkohl et al., 1983). In this case, as in many others, as individuals become better able to meet their needs effectively, a significant social problem is reduced.

Meeting needs, then, is never a static process. As people move through the life span, they grow and change, using new resources to meet their basic needs and encountering new obstacles at each stage. We can see in this process the holistic nature of human life, particularly the interaction of biological, psychological, and social factors. As one change spawns others, people engage in a process of ongoing adjustments to their perceptions and behaviors.

The Impact of the Environment

Just as people themselves change throughout the life span, so do the physical and social environments in which they live.

The physical environment is subject to short- and long-term changes. Droughts, floods, earthquakes, and other natural catastrophes can quickly change the conditions under which people live. Longer-term changes, such as the gradual destruction of arable land and forests through agricultural mismanagement, urbanization, and industrial pollution, have created major problems in many nations, including Mexico, Poland, and the United States. Throughout the world, it is estimated that "about 26 percent of arable land, permanent pasture and grazing land has been degraded to varying degrees as a result of human mismanagement" (United Nations, 1993:170). Water pollution is becoming increasingly serious. For example, water from less than 4 percent of the total length of Poland's major rivers can now be made drinkable after disinfection. Half of all Polish cities and 15 percent of Poland's factories have no wastewater treatment systems (United Nations, 1993:168).

The nuclear explosion at Ukraine's Chernobyl power plant, and the deadly gas leak at the Union Carbide chemical factory in Bhopal, India, are dramatic examples of the impact of technology on the environment and human welfare. Events of this magnitude that have immediate life-and-death significance for people are relatively rare, but less dramatic developments are all too common. Chlorofluorocarbons, for example, are continuing to be released from refrigerators and air conditioners that have been disposed of improperly. These chemicals deplete the ozone layer in the upper atmosphere, which provides vital protection against skin cancer.

Changes are also increasingly important in the social environment. As developing nations industrialize, as corporate takeovers occur in capitalist societies, and as formerly socialist nations move to free enterprise, conditions of economic survival are significantly altered. Inflation, trade imbalances, and the growth of transnational corporations all affect the availability of jobs and the economic well-being of millions of people. A stock market crisis in the United States has an immediate effect on stock prices around the world. By depressing consumer spending in the United States, it may decrease the volume of U.S. imports and the number of jobs available in those nations that export to the United States.

Economic factors also have an impact on many other aspects of social life. Communities have to respond to issues of poverty, homelessness, and crime. Families are affected when both parents must work in order to meet minimum economic needs. Rural residents of economically depressed areas move to locations where they hope job opportunities will be better. This reduces the tax base of the communities they leave and may at the same time strain the roads, housing stock, and schools of the communities to which they move. Citizens of societies experiencing economic or political problems emigrate—sometimes illegally—to new societies where they may experience—and their presence may aggravate—cultural conflicts, housing shortages, or unemployment.

In an increasingly interdependent world, national responses to such changes may lead to further change. During the 1980s, the United States enacted legislation designed to limit the number of immigrants and control the influx of illegal aliens into the United States. By 1994, proposals were being made to deny social welfare benefits to noncitizens—even to legal residents (Berke, 1994).

Immigrants are especially vulnerable to dislocation as a result of changes in their social environment. In response to economic stress, the most employable members of a family may emigrate to other societies in hopes of eventually earning enough money to reunite the family. Often, however, immigrants are refused permission to become citizens of the new society, and are instead allowed to stay only temporarily to meet short-term employment needs. Turkish and Finnish workers who have emigrated to Sweden have experienced precisely this type of difficulty, as have Mexicans in the United States. People who try to immigrate illegally risk their lives. Recently, a group of Mexicans attempting to enter the United States died when they were locked in a railroad car—without adequate food, water, and ventilation—by people they had paid to smuggle them across the border.

Immigration, one of the most common responses to changes in the social environment, itself creates both problems and opportunities. Members of immigrant groups are encouraged to become educated and to work in the schools, social agencies, and businesses that serve their compatriots. Women from these populations are usually able to enter the workforce, although often in part-time and low-paid positions. Some communities become economically stronger as a result of immigration; others become more ethnically diverse.

Similarly, transnational corporations bring jobs to nations struggling to meet the needs of their workforce, although often under exploitative conditions. At the same time, jobs are lost in unionized, higher-wage areas. As always, change, and the responses it generates, creates both problems and opportunities for people and societies.

Making Choices

So far in this chapter we have examined two factors that affect the need for social welfare: needs based on genetic inheritance, and needs created by changes in the physical and social environments. Now we are ready to turn to a third and final individual factor affecting social welfare: the choices people make.

Everyone begins life with access to certain resources in the form of inherited abilities and opportunities afforded by their environment. Abilities and opportunities vary. Opportunities very often depend on the race, class, and gender into which one is born. Racism, sexism, and other forms of institutional discrimination may create an uneven playing field. In the face of such obstacles, many people make exceptionally good choices and use their resources skillfully to meet their needs. Sometimes, however, people make poor choices.

THE HUMAN FACE OF SOCIAL WELFARE 5

CHILDREN WORKERS

"I still have a limp."

I started working at the block factory when I was 13. Almost a year ago I had an accident at work. The machine was missing a piece. I had told the boss about it, but he didn't pay attention.

That day it was raining. Everything was flooded. I slipped, the machine got me, and a block hit my foot.

The boss wasn't there. Some friends helped me up, took me to the back room, and kept me there for about two hours. I kept telling them my foot hurt a lot, and asked them why they didn't take me to the Red Cross. But the foreman told me to take it like a man, and went to the office. After a long time, he came back and told me that the company's doctor was on his way. I endured the pain until the doctor came almost two hours later. What else could I do?

At last the doctor checked me. Because my foot hurt so much, he couldn't move it. He touched it a little bit and gave me some pills. He said there was just a bruise that would hurt for a few days and then be gone. It was late so they took me home in a car.

The guy who brought me home told my mother "your son had an accident, but don't worry. Our doctor checked him and he just needs to rest." At first, mama trusted him.

I didn't complain because it didn't hurt me— I think it was because of the pills they gave me which I took for several days. On the fourth day my foot started getting purple and the swelling didn't give up. Mama went to talk with my boss. He told her not to worry, that he would send a car the next day to take me for x-rays. But he didn't. Mama called him again, and he didn't answer. His secretary said they would send a car. But they never did.

After 10 days, mama was mighty scared. She and a girl friend of hers helped take me off to the

Red Cross. I held onto both of them since I couldn't put weight on my foot. Everything hurt. Even my good foot. And I had a fever.

When we got there, the doctor said if we'd waited two more days, they would've had to cut off my foot. Mama cried. They gave me who-knows-what injections and sent me to the Civil Hospital. There they put me in, and, after several doctors checked me, they wrapped up my foot and hung my leg from some pieces of iron. I stayed like that for almost 15 days, and then they operated.

I stayed in bed for three months. Doctors came and went, moved my foot, stood me up, laid me down. They all said things and I only looked at them. Mama worried a lot and cried.

They called my boss a number of times since he had to sign some papers, but he never appeared. My father had to do it. When I was dismissed, my folks were told that the fee was 2,800,000 pesos [about US$930]. To let me go they had to pay at least a quarter of that. Then father got mad and went off to look for my boss. He didn't find him that day, but kept watch until he showed up. My father only got the boss to give him 400,000 pesos [about US$130], but that was enough to get me out. But the hospital wouldn't give us my documents or x-rays. Nothing.

When I left, the doctors told my mother that I needed rehabilitation that was going to take several months. They said she should look to my boss for help.

Mama tried to talk to him, but he hid from her. Finally she got him and he promised to send a car to get me every time I had to go to the hospital. He did that two or three times, but only when my mother went all the way to the block factory to get it. Since mama had to confront the boss every time, I used to tell her not to go. She'd answer "he's responsible, so he can't stay out of this." And that's why she went.

One day we were taken to the hospital, but

they didn't pick us up to go back home. My father had to give the taxi driver his watch. Mama was furious. In fact, all of us were, but she was the one who said more.

Since I had to go to rehabilitation every three weeks, mama went to see the wife of the mayor of Santa where we lived. She told mama that they had social workers there and that she would talk to them.

Heaven knows what she did. The fact is a few days later I was given Social Insurance and the rest of the workers at the block factory were too. It seems the boss got scared.

When we went to the Clinic, they told us that the operation on my foot was wrong. They would see how things went, but they were afraid that they might have to operate again.

The clinic doctor told me to do some bicycle riding, that that would be good for my foot. He told me to be careful not to overdo it. And he sent me back to work so I could keep my Social Insurance.

Now, at times it really hurts a lot. When the temperature changes and it gets chilly, it hurts. A lot more now that it is winter. It hurts almost every day. At work I tell them, but they tell me to be patient, to bear up, and to work slowly. Nothing else.

They ask me to stack blocks and I get tired. That's rough. I have to stack them in rows eleven high and fifty across. If I sit down, the foreman makes me get up and says "work slowly, but don't sit down." They also send me on errands on a bicycle, but they rush me.

If I want to go to the Clinic, they don't let me. Or they dock my pay. Even though I get my incapacity papers at the Clinic, they won't make it good at the factory.

Now I am legally on the Clinic patient list. I go there once a month for a check-up. I get x-rays. I get checked to see how my foot is doing. But I still have a limp.

On my part, I don't want to go to work. The job is too much for one person. And now, since my accident, I'm beginning to dislike it.

Luis, 15 years old, works in a concrete block factory. His story is typical of the experiences of many young Mexicans. His employer violated the law by not providing safe working conditions and by not providing Social Insurance for his employees. Legally, Luis is eligible for health care. The Mexican Institute of Social Security (IMSS) is mandated to provide health care for workers like Luis, but in reality many are excluded (Ward, 1986:110–114). So in this case, legal rights are at first denied and then eventually upheld.

Luis has some important advantages. Mexican family ties are strong. His parents were able and determined to fight for him. His mother used the Mexican system of patronage when she appealed to the mayor's wife for help. The intervention of the mayor's wife resulted in insurance coverage for the workers in the block factory. Although his injury never healed properly, Luis was able to get medical care, which is not universally available. Eligibility for Social Insurance in Mexico is tied to employment. Luis has to work or he will lose his health coverage.

Many other young Mexican workers are not as fortunate as Luis. They may not have parents who can fight for them, or they may work in the informal economy or in other jobs that are not usually covered by the Social Insurance system. Not everyone has access to a bicycle on which to exercise an injured foot. Many child workers in Mexico are much younger than Luis. Finally, as the title of the book implies, for Luis and many working-class Mexican children, there is no time for play.

Excerpted from Sandra Arenal, "Me Quedó una Bola," in *No Hay Tiempo para Jugar. . . . Niños Trabajadores (There is No Time for Play Children Workers)*, México, DF: Editorial Nuestro Tiempo, 1991, pp. 14–16. Translated by Luz Maria Chapela. Copyright © 1991 by Editorial Nuestro Tiempo. Used by permission.

There are, of course, many reasons for poor choices, including limiting genetic characteristics and environmental barriers. Choices are made in the context of a person's physical and social environments. Thus we can see once again how the biological, psychological, and social components of human behavior interact. Now let's look in more detail at three types of choices that people must and do make.

Using Available Resources   People do not always use the resources available to them. All of us know youngsters who are bright and capable but who seem unable to mobilize their talents. Similarly, when we examine the social welfare system, we find many people who do not know what programs exist nor how to gain access to them. If the available programs were better advertised or more easily accessible, they might be far more successful in helping people meet their needs.

It is important to note that one reason people often do not use resources is because they are blocked from doing so by personal or environmental barriers. Battered women have frequently noted that they become so psychologically depressed and insecure that they do not believe in the existence of any options to their present plight (Fedders and Elliott, 1987). Fear of being deported is an environmentally generated barrier that may be very effective in preventing illegal residents from seeking the assistance they need.

Avoiding Destructive Behavior   People sometimes engage in behavior that is self-destructive or that injures others. Reckless driving, smoking, abusing alcohol and other drugs, unsafe sex, poor eating habits, using violence to try to solve problems, and similar behaviors are all likely to create more needs than they solve. Once destructive patterns are learned, they become self-reinforcing and are difficult to change. Breaking destructive behavior patterns is itself a need for some people. Finding successful ways to avoid destructive behaviors helps not only the individual, but by eliminating a source of problems for others, it also helps society.

Planning   Most people try to plan to meet their needs. However, planning to meet needs has both a long- and a short-range component. Education is a good example. It not only meets immediate needs for knowledge and personal growth, it also lays the foundation for more advanced studies and improves access to desirable jobs. Many students attend school on a daily basis, yet fail to perceive the connections between this behavior and the larger context of educational, career, and life planning.

Long-range planning is often difficult to do. The impact of what one does today on one's future ability to meet needs is not always clear. Moreover, meeting one's daily needs today may require so much energy that there is little time or inclination to think about the future. Many people never have enough stability and security in their lives to believe that long-range planning is even possible, let alone to carry it out. Young people, especially members of oppressed groups who face bleak employment prospects, may find it difficult to plan for the future. Advanced education, a family, a rewarding career, and preretirement planning are likely to seem at best as only vaguely attainable goals. Without planning, however, need meeting may remain episodic and ineffective.

Although most people are successful in meeting the majority of their needs, many are unable to do so at one time or another. As we have seen, there are several reasons why this is so. Biological factors can limit people's ability to meet their needs, or may create special needs that are especially difficult to fulfill. The environment can create physical or social obstacles that make need attainment problematic, or that generate additional needs. As people grow and develop emotionally and cognitively, their perception of needs and acceptable need-meeting strategies changes. Finally, people do not always use resources effectively, sometimes making choices that create additional needs instead of moving toward need fulfillment.

All of this is to explain why people need help. To be sure, the need for help is sometimes the result of poor choices. However, we have seen that the complex interplay of biological, psychological, and environmental forces puts many people in positions where their ability to meet their own needs on their own is very limited. Neither people nor the conditions under which they live are perfect.

With this as background, we are ready to focus on society's responses to people's needs. We will see first that society has its own needs for structure and order. As a result, society's task becomes one of enabling people to meet their individual needs while at the same time working toward the attainment of societal needs. This reminds us yet again of the holistic nature of human life. We will also see how social welfare must fit into a larger network of societal efforts to organize people's behaviors so that the needs of everyone are met more or less simultaneously.

HUMAN NEEDS AND SOCIETAL RESPONSES

Let's now switch our focus to society's needs. Just as individuals sometimes need help to function more effectively, so does society. People experiencing dysfunctions and dysfunctional social systems are very costly to society. Social welfare supports societal goals by removing barriers to well-being, by building on people's strengths, and by providing resources.

For the most part, the organization of social life facilitates people's efforts to meet their personal needs. Social institutions such as the family, schools, organized religions, and economic and political systems function together to provide some of the resources that people need. However, these institutions are often flawed by prejudice and discrimination of many sorts. Social welfare attempts to support and supplement the efforts of these other social structures.

Expectations concerning differences in human needs at different life-span stages influence the types of resources that society attempts to provide. Public schools, with curricula that focus on developmental needs, are provided for children. Young adults who have children may be able to receive child care and some financial assistance from their parents and other relatives. The elderly often have resources to help them remain active and socially involved, such as senior citizen centers, church programs, reduced admissions fees at museums and theaters, and sometimes even reduced tuition for college courses. These are examples of how social structures are organized so as simultaneously to promote orderly patterns of behavior and to meet the needs of individuals and of society itself.

The Usefulness of Social Order

Social order, the *maintenance of predictable patterns of behavior,* makes it possible for people to live together. Society is essentially an agreement among its members to follow certain rules (Cuzzort and King, 1976:31–36). If that agreement breaks down, organized behavior becomes impossible and society disintegrates into a series of unplanned interactions among individuals and groups. This type of disorganization makes it far more difficult for most people to meet their needs.

The agreements that support society are pervasive. Even social competition and conflict involve agreement on a basic set of rules. Airlines compete with each other for passengers, but all are subject to a variety of governmentally imposed safety regulations. Similarly, in the political arena, there are certain rules of fair play that attempt to govern conflicts between political parties. At the personal level, two individuals may argue, but agree to provide mutual companionship and support.

Society employs two major techniques to maintain the social order. We look briefly at each.

Social Solidarity

Ideally, societies would operate by consensus. If everyone shared the same goals, beliefs, and values, patterns of interaction would be stable. This is often the case in preindustrial societies, where there is little differentiation among people so they tend to act and think similarly (Federico and Schwartz, 1983:12). This can occur in large industrial societies, but it is far less likely in such settings because of the social fragmentation and specialization—in terms of vocation, life style, ethnic and cultural background, and education, to name a few examples—that characterize such societies.

A recent U.S. study illustrates the difficulty of attaining societal consensus in a society like our own. In *Habits of the Heart,* the authors examined why many North Americans find it increasingly difficult to feel close to other family members, their neighbors, and their fellow citizens (Bellah et al., 1985). They concluded that such diverse factors as the growing number of two-wage-earner families—itself the result of economic pressures, geographic mobility, the weakening of traditional family patterns, and an increasing desire for personal gratification—contribute to a sense of estrangement or isolation from others. In such a society, consensus cannot be relied on as the only basis for social order.

Social Control

Of the various strategies used by societies to discourage people from disrupting established behavior patterns, the most common and effective is **socialization,** *"the process whereby individuals learn to behave willingly in accordance with the prevailing standards of their culture"* (Mitchell, 1979:299). Most socialization occurs during infancy and childhood, when behavior patterns and social expectations are learned at home and in school. Much learning occurs through observation, as children copy the behavior of their parents and peers. Socialization continues throughout the life span, although less intensively than during early childhood.

Socialization is effective in most situations for most people. It is an efficient means of controlling behavior because it is built into the operation of many social institutions, especially the family, the school system, and organized religion. Naturally, the diverse cultures in U.S. society socialize their members according to their own distinctive beliefs and behavior patterns. Nevertheless, the values and behaviors imparted are sufficiently similar to contribute to social solidarity.

Other social control mechanisms come into play when established norms of behavior are violated. These range from informal expressions of disapproval, such as a frown, to legal penalties, such as parking tickets, and on to actual physical restraint, such as arrest and imprisonment.

Maintaining order may contribute to helping people meet their needs. It makes it more likely that they will share reasonably common perspectives on needs and the strategies considered appropriate for attaining them. Any form of social control inevitably raises the issue of potential conflicts between the needs of society and the rights of individuals.

There is always the risk that dominant groups in society will use their power to oppress other groups, denying them the right to pursue their needs in accordance with their own beliefs. The historical treatment of Native American and African Americans in the United States illustrates this phenomenon only too well, while Jews in Poland and indigenous peoples in Mexico have experienced similar treatment. A seemingly small, yet significant, example of the clash between the beliefs and needs of dominant and oppressed groups occurs when U.S. Customs officials desecrate or confiscate sacred eagle feathers used by Native Americans for religious and cultural purposes (Banville, 1994). In legislating protection for species deemed in danger of extinction, important cultural needs of indigenous peoples may be denied. Thus, while the maintenance of social order is generally necessary if people are to be able to meet their needs, societal maintenance can also be used oppressively to deny the needs of groups within society.

SOCIAL WELFARE'S CONTRIBUTION

The social welfare system helps meet personal needs in three ways. It reduces obstacles to well-being, strengthens people's ability to overcome obstacles, and provides necessary resources. These activities are major functions of the social welfare system. We look at each in more detail as follows. However, we first need to look at the distinction between *manifest* and *latent* functions. **Manifest functions of social welfare** are the *intended and recognized consequences of social welfare programs.* **Latent functions of social welfare** are *unintended or less recognized consequences of social welfare programs.* While the manifest functions of social welfare generally are described as benefits to users of social welfare programs and to the general welfare of society, latent functions of social welfare may disadvantage users of social welfare programs and serve the special needs of powerful interests. When one thinks about the purposes of social welfare, it is important to consider both manifest and latent functions.

Like all the social institutions, *social welfare focuses on preserving the existing social order by strengthening the linkages between people and the society in which they live.* In most instances, these efforts are beneficial, helping provide most people with access to resources they need to survive and develop—money, education, housing, counseling, and so on. This in turn is usually beneficial for society, for when people function better, the overall quality of life is enhanced. In other words, the manifest function—strengthening individuals—has a latent function—strengthening society.

Difficulties arise when the existing social order hurts people, thus requiring change. In the United States, for example, African American and Hispanic youngsters drop out of school much more often than their white counterparts, because of the disadvantageous social and economic conditions under which they live. The amelioration of such problems requires change at the societal level. In other words, changing society in some way is sometimes one of social welfare's manifest functions. Such efforts will, of course, have the effect (latent function) of helping some individuals.

It is important to remember as you read the rest of this chapter that social welfare may both strengthen the existing social structure and work to change it. The immediate needs of people must be met. Doing so often does not necessitate change at the societal level—although it often does require change in smaller social units, such as a married couple getting a divorce or an employer creating a new job in the workplace. In other situations, individual needs are not being met primarily because of structures or patterns such as discrimination or economic policies that can only be addressed at the societal level. These, too, must be changed if the individuals who are disadvantaged by existing arrangements are to have a better chance to meet their own needs.

Reducing Obstacles

One way that social welfare attempts to help people meet their needs is by reducing the obstacles they face in doing so. Children with physical limitations, for example, are like other children in that they need education to help them develop their intellectual capacity, social skills, and physical abilities. In addition, they may require physical therapy, medical care, and environmental modifications to help them overcome the obstacle of their sometimes obvious physical limitations. One of the social welfare system's functions is to provide precisely such assistance.

However, physically limited children may face many other obstacles as well. The families of many physically limited children do an excellent job of providing for their children. Sometimes, however, they have insufficient understanding of their children's needs or are ashamed of their condition (Konle, 1983:87–95). The family may also be unable to respond to the child's special needs as a result of poverty or discrimination (Wells and Masch, 1986:13–18). In such cases, parental knowledge and values, the structure of the family, and the social conditions that perpetuate the family's poverty each may be an obstacle to meeting the child's needs. Efforts to overcome these obstacles are as important as the provision of physical care, education, and modifications to the child's physical environment.

Almost always, reducing obstacles involves change at the individual, environmental, and social levels. A troubled spouse can learn how to modify disruptive behavior, but others who are directly involved—the spouse, children, in-laws, and friends—may also need to learn new behavior patterns in response to the changed behavior. In some cases, marital tension is in part a result of larger societal factors, as when the merger of two companies results in large-scale layoffs and financial anxiety on the part of those directly affected. Unemployment causes problems for individuals, their families, and their communities. The resulting needs must be addressed at all these levels. When unemployment results from discrimination or structural factors in the economy, these obstacles, too, require attention.

You are probably thinking that there is a big difference between trying to change an individual's behavior and trying to change structural factors in the economy—and you are correct. We see in later chapters that social welfare agencies and providers tend to specialize, with some focusing on the needs of individuals and others addressing larger issues. However, even given this specialization, it is important for all social welfare workers to understand the relationship between individual needs and larger social processes. Only then can they hope to identify and bring to bear on a particular need the entire range of appropriate responses, thus dealing with the need holisticly.

Building on People's Strengths

Another strategy for helping people is to help them improve their ability to meet their own needs and to overcome obstacles. Again, this is part of a two-pronged effort: helping the individual while at the same time reducing obstacles.

Often people lack either information or confidence in their own abilities. They may not know that potentially useful programs exist, nor how to obtain them. They may doubt their ability to solve problems, or feel that no one cares if they do. Thus, some social welfare programs are designed specifically to deal with such problems by providing information and helping people strengthen their ability to act on their own behalf. This assumes that the persons involved are psychologically healthy. If they are not, then the psychological dysfunction becomes an additional obstacle to be overcome.

It may seem odd that people need help in order to mobilize their own resources, but this is surprisingly common. The society in which we live is very complex, and at times even overwhelming. This is especially so for people with little edu-

THE HUMAN FACE OF SOCIAL WELFARE 6

GOING HOME TO DIE

The night before his highschool class reunion, the telephone rang for Dean Lechner.

A classmate he had known since kindergarten was calling on behalf of the reunion organizing committee, she said, to tell him not to come.

"If you come," she warned, "people will leave."

And for the first time since Mr. Lechner had been diagnosed with AIDS, he sat down and cried.

AIDS strikes most often in big cities, but many of [those who have become ill] have come from small towns like Waseca, a quiet place of 8,000 people in the farm country of southern Minnesota.

Often just out of college, many young people had left for New York or Chicago or San Francisco, ambitious and bursting with notions about life in a glamorous metropolis. For gay men, there loomed all this and more: the promise of tolerance in the city, a chance to live out loud a way of life that had been unspeakable back home. . . .

[Dean Lechner] did not know how Waseca would greet its native son, back from a life in San Francisco.

In other small towns around the country, he knew, [persons with] AIDS had been excluded from schools, restaurants, swimming pools. In one case, a house was burned. . . .

Dean Curtis Lechner was born Nov. 10, 1953, in Waseca County Hospital . . . He grew up in a 19th-century white clapboard house on a nameless country road here. . . . He attended Waseca public schools from kindergarten through high school. . . . (His highschool) yearbook gave no clue that classmates called him "queer" behind his back or that his car was scrawled with venomous graffiti.

At a school dance, he was hit over the head with a beer bottle. He picked himself off the floor to leave, only to be followed by his tormentors in a car and a pickup truck that tried to run him off the road. At home that night, he closed the garage door and left the car motor running for a time. And he pondered taking his 17-year-old life.

Years later, when death became no longer a matter of his own choice or timing, he wondered what lay ahead on his road home. . . .

When Mr. Lechner caught a cold in May, . . . he was diagnosed with bronchitis. "Never once did I even imagine it could be AIDS," said Mr. Lechner. "For the past three years, I had either been celibate or practiced 'safe sex.' I thought I was safe." . . .

It was decided that [his] family members would take turns caring for Mr. Lechner. Most of the time he would stay in the house where he grew up, with his mother.

. . . She brings her son coffee every morn-

cation, limited intellectual capacity, who have been deprived or abused, who are members of immigrant or oppressed groups, and who lack experience dealing with large-scale social structures. Such everyday activities as voting, enrolling a child in school, using the emergency room of a hospital, taking public transportation, and knowing how to deal with physical or emotional crises confuse and intimidate many people.

In order to be able to obtain and use information, and to make use of available resources, people need a sense of entitlement and a willingness to advocate for themselves. One objective of many social welfare programs, therefore, is to empower people to develop the skills needed to manage their own lives and to change undesirable social conditions. This involves education, learning how to use organizations, and knowing one's rights. Developing better interpersonal skills is also important. As these abilities grow, people are less helpless when confronted

ing, cooks him hearty meals, and pesters him about not going outside in the chill air. . . .

[Even so, the family has had to adjust to Mr. Lechner's homosexuality.] "I have trouble talking about it, even with my minister," his mother said. "But Dean has my support all the way."

He has known that for a long time. Not long after he moved to San Francisco, she had gone to visit him. At the time, he did not know quite how he would explain his way of life.

When she arrived, she saw that he was living with a man in an apartment with one bedroom.

Not a woman at ease with words, she had stammered a bit in trying to explain her feelings. Her son does not remember precisely what she said that day, but the meaning was clear: "You are my son, and I love you.". . .

[After he moved back to Waseca, and the community learned of his diagnosis] nearly 200 cards of support were mailed to Mr. Lechner. People sent books, poems, prayers, money. . . .

But when the call came from the woman on the reunion committee, he wondered if he had given the town too much credit. . . .

Mr. Lechner attended his high school reunion. And no one left.

At the reunion, Mr. Lechner saw the faces of those who had tormented him in high school. One by one, they came to him and apologized.

Mr. Lechner accepted each apology with a handshake. And later, he turned to the woman who had warned him not to come. He raised a glass of champagne and said, "I understand."

She turned and walked away.

This account of the experiences of a gay man with AIDS illustrates how meeting individual needs may involve social action. Among Dean Lechner's needs are medical care, financial assistance (since he can no longer work), and counseling for himself and his family. All of these needs may be met through the social welfare system.

People like Dean Lechner have other needs, however—needs that can only be addressed by social change. The social discrimination against gay men and lesbians that drives men like Dean Lechner to leave their families and their hometowns often leaves them socially isolated, financially vulnerable, and exposed to drugs and unsafe sex practices. Enduring the pain and humiliation of harassment by peers increases their risk of mental illness, low self-esteem, and suicide. It also subjects them to other forms of physical harm (as when Dean Lechner's car was forced off the road). It is social welfare's unique role to help people meet their needs by focusing directly on those immediate needs and also on the social conditions that have created them.

Excerpted from Dirk Johnson, 1987, "Coming Home, with AIDS, to a Small Town," *The New York Times,* November 2, pp. A1ff. Copyright © 1987 by the New York Times Company. Reprinted by permission.

by an obstacle or problem. They become more effective advocates of their own needs, and more effective participants within their own family, their community, their place of work, and their society. Once again the importance of the interaction between individual and social functioning is clear.

Providing Resources

The most common conception of how social welfare helps people meet their needs is by providing resources, and this is indeed an important function. Social welfare provides money, food, housing, clothing, medical care, counseling, emotional support, legal aid, physical protection, and many other resources for people who need them. In Chapter 7, we look at how some of the specific programs that provide such resources are organized.

Here too, though, there is a need for action at both the individual and social levels. It is important to provide unemployment insurance to individuals who are out of work. But it is also necessary to try to increase the number of jobs available by influencing the economic decisions of communities, corporations, and governments. Advocates seek simultaneously to make more nursing home beds available while lobbying on behalf of a more coherent policy of care for the elderly that will enable more elderly people to remain in their home communities. Low-birth-weight infants of teenage mothers receive the special medical care they need, while community programs are developed to reduce teen pregnancy.

For whom, then, does social welfare provide resources? As you would expect, resources are provided for individuals (a Social Security check) but also for families (health insurance and housing), corporations (alcoholism counseling for employees, tax breaks), communities (recreation centers, senior citizen centers, and shelters for battered women), and society (clinics and schools for a healthy and educated population). Everyone benefits from social welfare because everyone has needs that social welfare helps meet. These needs exist at many levels, and resources must therefore be provided at each level as appropriate, beginning with the individual and extending outward to the society as a whole.

THE "GLUE" OF SOCIAL WELFARE

By now you should be able to understand social welfare as a type of social glue. It helps to heal broken people, broken relationships between people, and broken bonds between people and the social organizations in which they live. It does so by a combination of building on people's strengths, strengthening organizations, reducing obstacles, and providing resources.

This effort gives rise to some interesting manifest and latent functions. At the most obvious level, social welfare performs the manifest function of helping people observe prevailing standards of what is right and decent. This meets society's need for social order and, ideally, the person's need for a satisfying life.

At the same time, there are inequities built into the social order. Thus, as Piven and Cloward and others have pointed out, by helping to maintain the existing order, social welfare actually functions to perpetuate inequality (Piven and Cloward, 1971; Ryan, 1976). For example, in 1991 the average monthly U.S. Social Security payment to individual disabled workers was $609, while the average monthly welfare payment to families receiving Aid to Families with Dependent Children (AFDC) was $390 (U.S. Department of Commerce, 1993:375, 382). AFDC payments are at best large enough to enable those who depend on them to survive. They are extremely unlikely to help them out of poverty. A latent function of these social welfare programs is to "glue" recipients into their existing places in society.

However, some social welfare programs generate change. Legal Aid allows people to fight for their rights, and to challenge laws and behaviors that perpetuate inequality. Public schools make it possible for people to grow and use their abilities to take advantage of opportunities. Teaching people how to be advocates for their own interests allows them to improve their lives. Providing shelter and protection for abused and exploited people may provide an alternative to victimization. This is a different kind of "glue." It bonds people together through common purpose: seeking a decent life and equal opportunity for all.

In an important way, then, social welfare becomes a crucible for change. By confronting the questions who should be helped, how, and by whom—questions that are fundamental to social welfare—society is pushed into more clearly identifying its goals and the means to attain them. Different groups in society compete to have their needs and preferred strategies for meeting those needs included in the dialogue. As long as this competition is conducted within the society's generally accepted rules, social order is likely to be maintained.

Social welfare helps people provide to survive on a day-to-day basis while also trying to help society make the changes needed so that all people can not only survive, but also thrive on their own. It is not too much to say that, in the long run, the survival of society depends in large part on the success of social welfare's efforts.

LET'S REVIEW

This chapter has sought to explain why social welfare is needed. People have common human needs because they require certain basic resources for their biological, psychological, and social development. These needs are linked to life-span stages, and are expressed and fulfilled differently by members of different groups.

All of society's social institutions seek to enable people to function effectively. However, it is the unique role of the social welfare institution to focus exclusively on this task. It does so in three ways: by reducing obstacles to effective functioning and need meeting; by building on people's strengths so that they can better meet their own needs; and by providing resources that are otherwise lacking. In carrying out these tasks, social welfare works both to preserve the social order and to facilitate planned change.

As we have discussed why social welfare is needed, it has probably become clear to you that conflict exists over who should be helped, how and by whom. We consider these and other value conflicts in Chapter 3.

STUDY QUESTIONS

1 Think about your own needs for a moment. At this time in your life, what do you think are your more important physical, emotional, and social needs? List each need and describe its importance in your life in a sentence or two.

2 Review Dean Lechner's story (The Human Face of Social Welfare 5) in this chapter. List his physical, psychological, and social needs as an adult gay man with AIDS. If necessary, do supplemental reading on homosexuality and AIDS. A good place to start is with the overviews on gay men and lesbians in *The Encyclopedia of Social Work,* 19th ed.

3 Select a story from a newspaper or a news magazine that discusses a situation in which people are in need. Identify the needs, remembering that needs can be experienced by individuals, groups, organizations, or society as a whole. Then identify the kinds of social welfare programs that you think would help meet these needs.

Try to identify programs that would do one or more of the following: eliminate obstacles to meeting needs, build on people's strengths, or provide needed resources.

4 In this chapter we have talked a lot about needs. You now have a cognitive framework to use in identifying types of needs and responses to them. However, people also usually have feelings about needs. What are yours? To what degree do you think people should be responsible for meeting their own needs? How many people, in your opinion, are freeloading on society rather than helping themselves? How strict should the social welfare system be when providing help to people? In this exercise, don't worry too much about justifying your ideas. Just try to think honestly about these issues in ways that make sense to you. Share your ideas with your classmates and discuss any differences that emerge.

KEY TERMS AND CONCEPTS

needs

social environment

culture

common human needs

holistic approach

human diversity

life span

social order

socialization

manifest functions of social welfare

latent functions of social welfare

SUGGESTED READINGS

Behar, Ruth. 1993. *Translated Woman: Crossing the Border with Esperanza's Story.* Boston: Beacon Press. A passionate and compassionate sharing of life experiences by a middle-class Cuban American anthropologist and a Mexican street peddler. Esperanza tells in her own words her life story of struggle, strength, creativity, and hope. As Ruth becomes involved in learning Esperanza's story, she reflects on her own life as a Cuban immigrant to the United States.

Clausen, John. 1986. *The Life Course.* Englewood Cliffs, NJ: Prentice Hall. An excellent and concise overview of the life cycle and life-cycle stages. Looks systematically at the biological, psychological, and social needs of people at each point in the life cycle.

Devore, Wynetta, and Elfriede G. Schlesinger. 1987. *Ethnic-Sensitive Social Work Practice,* 2d ed. Columbus, OH: Merrill. This book provides a clear analysis of the impact of human diversity on people's needs and discusses the implications of diversity for the delivery of social welfare services.

Hellman, Judith Adler. 1994. *Mexican Lives.* New York: New Press/W. W. Norton. Shows the interaction between individual, family, and community needs and society's efforts to maintain a social order. Beautifully captures the voices, emotional and pragmatic, of fifteen Mexicans, rich and poor, caught in the vice of economic and political change.

Rank, Mark Robert. 1994. *Living on the Edge: The Realities of Welfare in America.* New York: Columbia University Press. By exploring the lives of a wide range of individuals and families, Rank attempts to answer three questions about welfare in the United States: Why do people turn to welfare? What is it like to survive on these programs? What can be done to improve welfare? The book dispels myths and shows the societal forces which push many people to the edge.

Towle, Charlotte. 1965. *Common Human Needs,* rev. ed. Silver Spring, MD: National Association of Social Workers. This classic work examines people's needs and the responsibility of society and the social welfare professions to meet them. A caring and powerful book that argues on behalf of fundamental human values.

Urrea, Luis Alberto. 1993. *Across the Wire: Life and Hard Times on the Mexican Border.* New York: Doubleday. A graphic, empathetic look at life in the dumps and *barrios* of Tijuana, Mexico. The book focuses on the successful and unsuccessful struggles of human beings to meet their needs, largely in the absence of public social welfare. An uncritical description of private charity dealing with symptoms rather than solutions.

REFERENCES

Arenal, Sandra. 1991. *No hay tiempo para lugar . . . niños trabajadores.* México, DF: Editorial Nuestro Tiempo.

Banville, Beurmond. 1994. Customs confiscates eagle feather: Agents at border in Van Buren detain Indian boy. *Bangor Daily News,* May 9:A1.

Barker, Robert L. 1991. *The Social Work Dictionary,* 2d ed. Silver Spring, MD: National Association of Social Workers.

Behar, Ruth. 1993. *Translated Woman. Crossing the Border with Esperanza's Story.* Boston: Beacon Press.

Bellah, Robert. 1985. *Habits of the Heart.* Berkeley: University of California Press.

Berger, Raymond. 1987. Homosexuality: Gay men. In *Encyclopedia of Social Work.* 18th ed., vol. 1: pp. 795–804. Silver Spring, MD: National Association of Social Workers.

Berger, Robert and Ronald Federico. 1985. *Human Behavior,* 2d ed. White Plains, NY: Longman.

Berke, Richard L. 1994. Politicians discovering an issue: Immigration. *The New York Times,* March 8:A14.

Chimley, Eduardo Chimley. 1993. 17,000 Street children in Guadalajara. *Excelsior* (Mexico City), June 11:2.

Clausen, John. 1986. *The Life Course.* Englewood Cliffs, NJ: Prentice Hall.

Cruz, Rafael Medina. 1993. One million street children in country. *Excelsior* (Mexico City), April 15:4A.

Cuzzort, R. P., and E. W. King. 1976. *Humanity and Modern Sociological Thought.* Hinsdale, IL: Dryden Press.

Dane, Elizabeth. 1985. Professional and lay advocacy in the education of handicapped children. *Social Work,* 30(6):505–510.

Devore, Wynetta, and Elfriede G. Schlesinger. 1987. *Ethnic-Sensitive Social Work Practice,* 2d ed. Columbus, OH: Merrill.

Doyal, Len, and Ian Gough. 1991. *A Theory of Human Need.* New York: Guilford Press.

Fedders, Charlotte, with Laura Elliott. 1987. *Shattered Dreams.* New York: Harper & Row.

Federico, Ronald, and Janet Schwartz. 1983. *Sociology,* 3d ed. New York: Random House.

Finkelhor, David. 1983. Common features of family abuse. In D. Finkelhor et al., eds. *The Dark Side of Families.* Beverly Hills, CA: Sage, pp. 17–28.

Hellman, Judith Adler. 1994. *Mexican Lives.* New York: New Press/W. W. Norton.

Herrenkohl, Ellen, with Roy Herrenkohl and Lori Toedter. 1983. Perspectives on the intergenerational transmission of abuse. In David Finkelhor, ed., *The Dark Side of Families.* Beverly Hills, CA: Sage, pp. 305–316.

Johnson, Dirk. 1987. Coming home, with AIDS, to a small town. *The New York Times,* November 2:A1.

Konle, Carolyn. 1983. *Social Work Day-to-Day.* White Plains, NY: Longman.

Maslow, Abraham. 1970. *Motivation and Personality.* New York: Harper & Row.

Mitchell, Geoffrey D. 1979. *A New Dictionary of the Social Sciences.* New York: Aldine.

National Association of Social Workers. 1987. Public service drive to hit child poverty. *NASW News,* January.

Perlman, Helen Harris. 1957. *Social Casework.* Chicago: University of Chicago Press.

Piven, Francis, and Richard Cloward. 1971. *Regulating the Poor.* New York: Vintage Books.

Ryan, William. 1976. *Blaming the Victim.* New York: Vintage Books.

Slater, Mary, and Lynn Wikler. 1986. "Normalized" family resources for families with a developmentally disabled child. *Social Work,* 31(5):385–390.

Straus, Murray. 1983. Ordinary violence, child abuse, and wife-beating: What do they have in common? In David Finkelhor, ed., *The Dark Side of Families.* Beverly Hills, CA: Sage, pp. 213–234.

Towle, Charlotte. 1965. *Common Human Needs,* rev. ed. Silver Spring, MD: National Association of Social Workers.

United Nations. 1993. *Report on the World Social Situation 1993,* ST/ESA/235 E/1993/50/Rev. 1. New York: United Nations.

U.S. Department of Commerce. Bureau of the Census. 1993. *Statistical Abstract of the United States 1993.* Washington, DC: U.S. Government Printing Office.

Ward, Peter. 1986. *Welfare Politics in Mexico: Papering over the Cracks.* Boston: Allen & Unwin.

Wells, Carolyn C., and M. Kathleen Masch. 1986. *Social Work Ethics Day to Day.* White Plains, NY: Longman.

3

WHY IS SOCIAL WELFARE CONTROVERSIAL?

WHAT TO EXPECT FROM THIS CHAPTER

At first glance, it might seem strange that helping others might be controversial. After all, we learn from the time we are children that we should be nice to others, and that we should be helpful when we can. As we grow older, however, we learn that helping is more complex than we thought. When confronted with a series of people with needs, should we feel an obligation to help them all? What kind of help should we give? Are we certain that giving money will benefit them? Or are we instead contributing to alcoholism, drug use, or just plain laziness? We may even be putting our own safety at risk. Is that hitchhiker standing beside a seemingly disabled car actually in need, or is that person a criminal who will rob us if we stop to offer help?

These are troubling questions not just for individuals but for society. What types of assistance are truly helpful? Are there times when we should refuse to give aid because giving it will actually compound the problem? If we cannot meet need completely, is it worth doing anything at all? Finding answers to these questions is important, hard work. Part of the difficulty is that we lack some of the data that would tell us what kind of programs work well and what kind do not. There is a need for systematic program evaluation to help us decide which social welfare programs to continue, which to modify, and which to replace with more effective interventions.

There is also another difficulty: *The answers to these questions involve values.* Our decisions about when to offer help and what to expect in return are very much reflections of our values. **Values** are *"customs, standards of conduct, and principles considered desirable by a culture, a group of people, or an individual"* (Barker, 1991:246). As we will see, values may differ significantly within a society. Value conflicts are important because values affect how we behave and the choices we make.

Some people, for example, are willing to dispense birth control measures because their goal is to stop out-of-wedlock births. Others agree with the goal, but disagree with the means. Still others believe that people should be free to do whatever they want as long as they are willing to accept the consequences. Yet others focus on the children born out of wedlock and ask whether these children should be the victims of their parents' behavior. As you can see from this example, there are many ways to look at solving a single problem that affects the welfare of society. Conflicting values are the major reason that social welfare is controversial.

This chapter examines some of the major value conflicts that characterize choices about the provision of social welfare. You have probably noticed already that the authors of this book have a point of view about many social welfare issues. While we attempt to be fair in our presentation of data and the way in which we portray perspectives that conflict with our own, we make no claim to dispassionate objectivity. We believe that the study of social science in general, and social welfare in particular, cannot be "value free." We therefore openly share our point of view.

Our primary goal in writing this book, however, is to help students of social welfare understand what we believe are *the issues* essential to the functioning of society, not to insist on specific "right" answers. There are no simple answers to these controversies. There is much room for reasoned difference as to what is right or effective. Social welfare will always be controversial, because most people have strong and often ambivalent feelings about helping and being helped. As you study this chapter, we encourage you to open yourself to viewpoints that differ from those you now hold—regardless of where you begin. By thoughtfully considering alternatives, your understanding of social welfare will be strengthened.

LEARNING OBJECTIVES

When you have finished studying this chapter, you should be able to:

1 Discuss major value conflicts in the United States that affect choices made about the provision of social welfare.

2 Explain in your own words why social welfare is controversial.

3 Discuss the process of *blaming the victim,* and its relationship to social welfare programs.

4 Compare and contrast *universal* and *selective* approaches to social welfare in light of their moral and financial effects on individuals and on society.

5 Discuss the implications of treating people as *supplicants* or as *citizens* for empowerment and social control through the provision of social welfare benefits.

VALUES AND CHOICES

Professor of Social Work Morris Eisenstein often told the story of his army unit entering a small German town toward the end of World War II. On the outskirts of the town was a Nazi death camp in which thousands of prisoners had been murdered and cremated. The smoke from the crematorium was clearly visible from the town. Yet when the villagers were asked about the camp, they replied *"Wir sind die kleine Leute. Wir kennen nichts."* ("We are the little people. We don't know anything.")

Perhaps you saw the 1993 film, *Schindler's List.* At the same time that Oscar Schindler, a businessman, was protecting the lives of Jews working in his war materials factory during the Nazi occupation of Poland (Rafferty, 1993), some social workers in Germany were handing over to the Nazis lists of physically handicapped and mentally ill clients. Those clients were rounded up and sent to the death camps. Reportedly, the social workers believed that by giving up some clients, they could protect others. The behavior of social workers, like that of all of us, may reflect conflicting values (Brandwein, 1994).

Another disheartening example involving social workers occurred in Cuba in 1959. As the revolutionary forces of Fidel Castro swept triumphantly into Havana, the entire faculty of the University of Havana School of Social Work fled the country rather than staying to become part of the struggle for a new society. Ironically, under Castro the health and education of ordinary Cubans improved dramatically.

In *Common Decency* (1986:1), social worker Alvin Schorr cites a song by Jacques Prévert written following an unsuccessful attempt by young offenders to escape from prison in Paris. "Bandits, riff-raff, thieves and scoundrels! The pack that hunts down children is composed of decent people." Schorr identifies the striking paradox "that citizens who are good neighbors and give time to charitable activities . . . can also, in concert, behave brutally." Then, describing how private and public behavior are sometimes compartmentalized, he relates a story about Ronald Reagan in which the President is said to have left an important budget meeting to be photographed with a crippled child for an Easter Seals poster. Moved emotionally, the President said later that he would have done anything to be able to help her. "Mr. President," someone remarked, "you have just cut from the budget $350 million for children like her."

The choices made by these people—to remain unaware of the Nazi death camp, to protect the lives of one's workers, to send one's clients to their deaths, to leave a revolutionary situation rather than remain to struggle for the best possible new society, to be concerned about a single child while failing to consider the many children affected by a policy decision—each is the result of values.

We believe that one of the most important aspects of becoming an educated citizen or social worker is to develop, to articulate, and to try to live one's life according to a coherent personal philosophy. In this sense a **philosophy** is *the set of values, ethics, and principles by which one attempts to understand the world, to develop one's perspective on social and economic justice, and to behave.* Every person has a philosophy. Often, however, that set of values, ethics, and principles is unexamined, contradictory, and incoherent. Lack of clarity about what we believe can cause us to act in ways that we may later regret. Lack of clarity about the *implications* of your values, ethics, and principles may lead you to pursue a profession or employment that is not a good fit, or to behave in ways you later regret.

DEVELOPING YOUR OWN PERSPECTIVE

As you develop a better understanding of why social welfare is controversial, you are likely to realize that some of the value conflicts pose serious problems for you. One objective of this chapter is to help you develop your own informed positions.

Most people are more comfortable when they have taken a position about issues. We encourage you, however, to retain some flexibility and openness about the value conflicts which characterize social welfare. You can, for example, be in favor of certain goals and still disagree with programs designed to achieve them. Believing that social welfare in general is good does not mean that you have to agree with everything that is done in this area.

A second point to consider is that your perspectives are likely to change over time. As you have different kinds of experiences, you may come to understand issues in different ways. After an especially stressful period in your own life, your perceptions of why people sometimes stop trying to be self-reliant may alter. What this all means, of course, is that our experiences and cultural backgrounds affect the ways in which we view human need. Minorities who experience discrimination on a regular basis feel differently about it than people who do not. To some— a woman looking for a desirable job, African American parents seeking a good school for their children, or a gay man considering the risks involved in coming out—the problem of discrimination may loom much larger than it does to those who are less likely to encounter it, and who, consequently, are more in control of their lives.

You can expect yourself to have strong emotional reactions to many social welfare issues because they involve your values as well as your intellect. As an educated person, you will want to use your analytical skills to obtain as much data as you can about issues before making up your mind. But also try to be in touch with your own feelings. Try to understand their origins. Often, we have been socialized to accept values without really thinking much about them. Examine your feelings within the context of the knowledge you possess. Are your feelings consistent with what you know?

Do not avoid taking positions about social welfare controversies. Your positions may sometimes be challenged. Your positions may change. However, unless people become truly involved with these issues and take thoughtfully considered positions, social welfare value conflicts will not receive the attention and action they deserve. Whether in the political arena, the family, church, synagogue, or mosque, school or university, or social welfare agency, the conflicting values raised by your study of social welfare need to be aired, debated, and understood. Controversy can be healthy as long as it leads to socially productive discussion and action.

Finally, try to be clear about the implications of your positions. If you believe that recipients of public assistance typically are cheats and do not deserve what they get, you will probably not want to plan on a career as a social worker. If you feel strongly that society does not spend enough on social welfare programs, you might want to consider working as a legal aid lawyer or running for political office. If you have a commitment to helping people develop their own capacity to become healthy, self-reliant adults, working in education might make sense. In other words, try to align your daily activities with your positions about social welfare issues so that you are not constantly in a position where your values conflict with your behaviors. It may be that a career in social work *is* for you.

There are no easy answers to value conflicts. For each of the issues discussed in this chapter, there are valid opposing viewpoints. Researching the facts can help. But facts alone do not solve the dilemmas. Research tells us that most unemployed people would rather work than receive public assistance. But if people want to work and cannot find jobs, how hard must they search before they have explored every "reasonable" possibility? Do they have to accept physically dangerous or very low-paid work? Ramona Parish, a mother receiving AFDC to help support her three children, speaks eloquently to these concerns. (See The Human Face of Social Welfare 9.) These, you see, are value-related issues for which there are no factual answers.

Many of the choices you make will be informed by the values that make up your philosophy—the framework or paradigm through which you perceive the world.

COMPETING PARADIGMS

Throughout much of U.S. history, political thought and social policy have been shaped by classical economic and political *liberalism,* a philosophy that influences both free-market conservatives and liberal capitalists today. **Classical liberalism** traces its roots to the writings of seventeenth- and eighteenth-century thinkers such as Thomas Hobbes (1839), John Locke (1960), and Jeremy Bentham (1948).[1] Major contemporary champions of liberalism or neoliberalism include Nobel laureate economist Milton Friedman (1962, 1984), George Gilder (1981), Thomas Sowell (1980), and Charles Murray (1984).

[1]These twentieth-century dates are references to recent reprintings of these writers' works; evidence that interest in classical liberal thinking remains a part of contemporary culture.

To a remarkable degree, the policies of U.S. Republican presidents Ronald Reagan and George Bush, and Democrat Bill Clinton, were rooted in classical liberalism. The three Presidents were in basic agreement about the desirability of a capitalist economic system. One way in which they differed is in the degree to which they were willing to soften free-market capitalism's impact on the poor.

Policies that accept the basic premises of classical liberalism—modified only to the extent necessary to give those premises a more "human face"—may be labeled **neoliberal.** Neoliberal policies are so widely accepted by both "conservatives" and "liberals" in the United States today that they tend to be taken for granted as natural truths. The structural adjustment prerequisites for loans from the World Bank and the International Monetary Fund in economically developing countries, such as Mexico, and countries in transition to capitalism, such as Poland, also reflect a neoliberal perspective. In our discussion, the classical liberal perspective is referred to as the *old paradigm.*

Frances Moore Lappé, in *Rediscovering America's Values,* contrasts the old paradigm, which she believes has become outmoded, with an emerging new paradigm that is more compatible with contemporary thinking in social work (Lappé, 1989:1–17). Lappé's premise is challenging to students of social welfare: "Until we as a people are honestly willing to confront the conflicting understandings of the values shaping American life, we cannot overcome the mounting pain of hunger, poverty, fear, and cynicism that divide us from each other. Only by engaging fearlessly in that dialogue can we begin to heal our nation and together build a politics of hope" (Lappé, 1989:270).

Lappé states that the new paradigm dates in part from the eighteenth-century writings of Adam Smith (1982), the same thinker celebrated by contemporary business leaders "for supposedly proving that individual self-interest can drive a productive economic system" (Lappé, 1989:12). In the *Theory of Moral Sentiments* (first published in 1740), Smith presented a compelling case for the importance of the social context of human life. In addition to Lappé, contemporary champions of the new paradigm include social work educators such as Alfred Kahn and Sheila Kamerman (1975) and Alvin Schorr (1986), and scholar-activists such as Michael Harrington (1984), Marcus Raskin (1986), and Marian Wright Edelman (1992).

The old and new paradigms differ significantly in how they understand human nature, morality, compassion, freedom, justice, poverty, government, popular democracy, private property, and the marketplace. Major differences are summarized in Table 3-1. In the old paradigm, people are believed to be basically selfish and to derive their sense of self-worth from individual freedom to speak, to act, and to improve their material well-being. The emerging new paradigm characterizes people as social beings who become fully human only in association with other people.

The old paradigm tends to focus more narrowly on individuals, while the new paradigm looks at individuals in their social environments. The old paradigm tends to limit *morality* to responsible behavior in personal, face-to-face relationships with family, friends, and associates; the new paradigm expands moral concern to

TABLE 3-1 COMPETING PARADIGMS

	Old paradigm	New paradigm
Human nature	People are self-seeking, independent, acquisitive; sense of self-worth is closely identified with individual freedom to speak, act, acquire material possessions; individuality develops as a defense against encroachments of society.	People are social creatures, fully human only in relationships with others, interdependent, empathetic; sense of self-worth is embedded in social relationships; individuality stems from a unique mix of relationships with family, friends, neighbors, colleagues, and others.
Morality	Limited primarily to responsible behavior in personal relationships.	Includes responsibility for economic and political environments.
Compassion	Appropriate private concern of family, church, and community, but not marketplace or government.	Appropriate concern of all levels of human organization including marketplace and government.
Freedom	Unlimited individual autonomy to improve individual circumstances; zero-sum (my freedom can expand only at the expense of yours).	Human development of unique talents and common enterprises through interaction with others; my maximum freedom depends on yours.
Justice	An artificial device to keep interpersonal transgressions in check.	A core value derived from capacity for empathy and need for community; the sense that societal rules are fair and equitably applied.
Poverty	The result of personal failure to work hard enough, thus breaking the work ethic bargain with God, who rewards work with prosperity.	While poverty may be caused in part by individual shortcomings, societal barriers to success are important causes of poverty.
Government	An artificial, necessary evil which must be kept carefully in check.	An expression of our social nature.
Popular democracy	Strong doubt that people can act through government for the common good; politics are suspect, must not interfere with economic lives; attempts to plan social change are negative, will only make things worse.	Affirms that people *can* act through government for the common good; politics are a process for making and remaking social reality in order to better serve human needs; individuals, families, organizations set goals and attempt to reach them—results may go awry, but the process is essential to fulfill human nature.
Private property, marketplace	Almost sanctified as natural rights; because wealth originates from personal and family efforts, all production belongs to individuals and none is left over for social distribution.	Subordinate to socially defined needs because societal health is vital to individual well-being; because wealth is derived from a common pool of knowledge and public works developed over generations, social distribution of accumulation is appropriate.
Major contributions	Concept of innate human worth leading to inalienable human rights and civil liberties.	Concept of "rights of membership" to healthy life and human fellowship.

Source: Frances Moore Lappé. 1989. *Rediscovering America's Values.* New York: Ballantine, pp. 1–17.

include responsibility for the indirect effects of behavior on a wider circle of humanity. Thus, from the new perspective, the health of the economic and social environments is a moral concern.

In the old world view, *compassion* is seen as the private concern of family, church, and community, but not, as the new world view would suggest, an appropriate concern for government or the marketplace.

The concept of *freedom* is understood very differently by the two approaches. From the old perspective, freedom means unfettered autonomy to improve one's individual circumstances; from the new perspective, freedom exists when humans can develop their unique talents to a maximum through interaction with other people and can collaborate with others for the common good.

In the old paradigm, *justice* is deemed an artificial invention to keep control over interpersonal transgressions; the new paradigm considers justice a core value derived from human capacity for empathy and need for community. From this perspective, justice prevails when societal rules are perceived as fair and equitably applied.

According to the old view, *poverty* is an indication that people have not worked hard enough, and have failed to keep their bargain with God, who rewards the work ethic with prosperity; the poor and hungry are merely receiving their just deserts. The new perspective takes into consideration societal as well as individual barriers to success, and attempts to remove both.

Government, in the old paradigm, is a necessary evil that must be kept carefully in check; in the new paradigm, government is an expression of human social nature. The old perspective distrusts *popular democracy,* doubts that people can act through government with positive results, and believes that attempts to intervene for social betterment will likely only make things worse. The new paradigm suggests otherwise. Its proponents contend that we *can* use politics to modify society for the common good. While results may sometimes go awry, our attempts to respond organizationally to human need are essential to the fulfillment of our human potential.

In the old world view, *private property* and the *marketplace* are almost sanctified as natural rights. Because *wealth* is seen as resulting from the efforts of individuals and families, the fruits of production rightly belong to individuals; nothing is left over for social distribution. The new world view understands private property and the marketplace as among the means available for meeting socially defined ends. From this perspective, wealth is derived from a common pool of knowledge and public works developed socially over many generations. Since wealth is created socially, social distribution of some of the accumulation of wealth is appropriate.

The old paradigm has made major contributions to human society, including the concept of the innate worth of the individual and the notion of inalienable human rights and civil liberties. The new paradigm affirms these values and adds the concept that, simply as members of society, all people have "rights of membership" to both healthy life and human fellowship.

We live in a challenging and exciting period of change. Sweden, among our four countries, comes closest to the new paradigm. Within Sweden, slowing economic growth and increasing unemployment rates are refining policy within a framework that strongly supports the new paradigm. As Mexico and Poland adopt neoliberal policies, they seem to be affirming the old paradigm. In the United States, a mixture of the old and the new prevails. The controversies surrounding the 1994 Republican "Contract with America," health insurance, and welfare reform reflect the conflicting values of the old and new paradigms. Conflicts between the values of the two paradigms are the principal reasons that social welfare programs are controversial.

BLAMING THE VICTIM

Saul Alinsky, a radical community organizer during the 1960s, was an articulate opponent of social work and many social welfare programs. From Alinsky's perspective, social work spent too much time applying "bandaids" to social problems instead of dealing with their causes. A favorite Alinsky story described the heroic efforts of a person who, at great personal risk, jumped into a raging torrent to rescue someone being swept down stream. Successful, the heroine was being congratulated by bystanders when a second person floated past helplessly. Once again, the heroine risked her life to make the rescue. But when a third person bobbed past, she made no attempt at rescue. Instead, she started running upstream. "Where are you going?" a bystander challenged. "To find the SOB who's pushing them in!" she responded.

The choice between trying to save individuals in trouble and making it possible for them to stay out of trouble in the first place is a major value conflict in social work and social welfare. That conflict is central to *Blaming the Victim,* a book by William Ryan (1976) that introduced the concept of **blaming the victim**[2] to social welfare discourse in the United States. Blaming the victim is the process by which middle-class liberals and others "justify inequality by finding defects in the victims of inequality." The process enables victim blamers to reconcile their class interests with their humanitarian impulses (Ryan, 1976:xiii, 27).

There are four steps to victim blaming. First, identify a **social problem,** *"a general pattern of human behavior or social condition that is perceived to be a threat to society by significant numbers of the population, powerful groups, or charis-*

---

[2]Ryan has introduced into the vocabulary of social work an important concept. Unfortunately, the concept has a negative side effect. Victim blaming emphasizes the role of oppressed people as *victims* rather than underscoring their often active resistance, their role as *fighters* on their own behalf. Some oppressed people are ground down and victimized; many others, however, are survivors who persevere against great odds. We correctly speak of incest survivors, not victims. Similarly, the efforts of community groups to stop construction of dams and freeways, and to prevent the displacement of viable working-class communities, deserve to be celebrated—even when they are unsuccessful. Ryan's book is most valuable as an exposé of the ideology used by many middle-class people to distance themselves from those who should be their natural allies: the poor and members of oppressed minorities.

matic individuals and that could be resolved or remedied (Maris, 1988:37). "Second, study those affected by the problem and discover in what ways they are different from the rest of us as a consequence of deprivation and injustice. Third, define the differences as the cause of the social problem itself. Finally, . . . invent a government program to correct the differences" (Ryan, 1976:8–9).

The social programs created by victim blamers "are based on the assumption that *individuals* 'have' social problems as a result of some kind of unusual circumstances—accident, illness, personal defect or handicap, character flaw or maladjustment—that exclude them from using the ordinary mechanisms for maintaining and advancing themselves." Victim blaming depends on the language of prejudice, a language in which poor people are seen as "disadvantaged," "socially deprived," or "lacking" in important ways. By focusing on the defects of the individual, victim blamers overlook personal strengths and environmental factors such as "unequal distribution of income, social stratification, political struggle, ethnic and racial group conflict, and inequality of power" (Ryan, 1976:14–15).

Thus, victim blamers ignore the effects of **institutional discrimination,** *"discrimination which, in the hands of people with power, raises to the level of social structure the tendency to use superiority as a solution to discomfort about difference."* Institutional discrimination flows from social structures that exclude oppressed minorities "from resources and power and then blame them for their failures, which are due to lack of access" (Pinderhughes, 1989:89).

Victim blaming has been the dominant strategy in the United States for dealing with the problems of oppressed people. However, there is an alternative, competing strategy, in which defects are sought "in the community and the environment rather than in the individual." In this **public health approach to social welfare,** *the emphasis is on preventing rather than repairing social problems* (Ryan, 1976:16–17).

A public health strategy assumes that all persons experience a series of predictable risks during the course of their lives. Since risks are predictable and universal, it is reasonable to develop universal programs in response. Because all children have predictable developmental needs, programs such as well-baby clinics are made available. Because family size affects need, and because family size is not easily taken into account in the structure of wages, children allowances or earned income tax credits are created as wage supplements. Since all workers face reduced income upon retirement, social security retirement pensions are created. Since all workers run the risk of job loss, unemployment insurance is made universally available, and so on. This is, of course, the strategy generally followed in Sweden.

This alternative to blaming the victim takes a *strengths-based approach* to social welfare. Rather than asking, "What's wrong with people?" a **strengths-based approach to social work** celebrates the resilience of the human spirit, the ability of people to survive and to overcome enormous barriers in their social environment. A strengths-based perspective *asks how the natural abilities of all persons can be nurtured to enable them to realize their maximum potential.*

Victim blaming is a seductive process. It is very easy to slip into its trap of seeking causes of social problems primarily within flawed individuals while overlooking causes within the institutions that constitute the social environment. It is essential to keep in mind that reducing obstacles to meeting human needs involves change in both individuals and their environment.

Social workers must deal with these conflicting values every day as they participate in **social reform,** *"activity designed to rearrange social institutions or the way they are managed in order to achieve greater social justice or other desired change."* As you can imagine, in their efforts to reduce *social inequality* and to enhance *social justice,* social workers and others must grapple with value-based choices. **Social inequality** exists when *"some members of a society receive fewer opportunities or benefits than other members."* **Social justice** is an *"ideal condition in which all members of a society have the same basic rights, protection, opportunities, obligations, and social benefits"* (definitions from Barker, 1991:219–220).

How much social inequality is desirable, necessary, acceptable? Is this definition of social justice a good one? What vision of the good society would contribute to social justice? These are important questions about which we encourage you to think seriously.

Before we turn to look more specifically at conflicting values in the United States, we need one additional definition. In the United States, *conflict* is frequently seen as a negative condition, something to be avoided. We have many aphorisms that make this point—"let sleeping dogs lie," "don't rock the boat," "too many cooks spoil the broth," "you can't fight city hall," for example. However, conflict can also be seen simply as the stuff out of which life is made. For our purposes in this book, **conflict** is simply *a condition in which there exists an opposition of alternatives, a condition in which more than one choice is possible.* From this perspective, life consists of a series of conflicts that concludes only with death. Conflict itself is neither positive nor negative, but its results may be— depending on the values that underlie the choices made during its resolution.

Resolution of value conflicts is more easily obtained in some societies than in others.

The small size and the cultural and religious homogeneity of Sweden make it relatively easy for Swedes to agree on common values. In Poland under communism, and in Mexico under the long rule of the PRI, there was for a time enough centrally controlled power to permit government to act as if there was a value consensus even when there was not. Opposing values survived in Poland and resulted in the independent trade union Solidarity, and the eventual change of governments. In Mexico, the Zapatistas received broad support because they reaffirmed values of the Mexican Revolution that many Mexicans believe had been abandoned as the PRI embraced neoliberalism.

In the United States, by contrast, it is often difficult either to arrive at or to impose a value consensus. The heterogeneous nature of the U.S. population means that there are many different cultural groups, each with its own values. In addition, the U.S. tradition of allowing freedom of expression makes it difficult for religious or political structures to impose any single set of values on the larger society. Instead, a working consensus on values sufficient to guide daily life is negotiated in the political arena, in community interaction, and through personal communication. The nation's cultural history and traditions provide guidelines within which negotiations take place. The process, however, is necessarily slow, complex, and virtually continuous.

The written statement of the philosophy of South Side Settlement, an interracial social agency in Columbus, Ohio, was a consequence of conflicting community values. When Settlement-sponsored organizations advocated for welfare rights, adequate housing, neighborhood-based health clinics, and involvement of students in their own education, the agency's funding was threatened by opponents. One response of the agency's board of directors was to articulate its philosophy as clearly as possible. (See box, p. 95).

Let's look more closely at some of the value conflicts that affect social welfare in the United States by looking at two key questions: Who should be helped? How should help be provided?

WHO SHOULD BE HELPED?

As we will see when we discuss the historical development of social welfare (Chapters 4 and 5), many contemporary social welfare issues in the United States trace their roots to sixteenth- and seventeenth-century English policies. In response to the age-old ethical questions, "Am I my brother's keeper?" and "Who is my neighbor?," the Poor Laws took the position that charity begins—and ends—at home. The **residence requirement,** *ensuring that assistance was provided only to persons who had lived in a community for at least a prescribed time,* was one form of social control.

Another key concept with roots in the Elizabethan Poor Laws is the distinction commonly made between the **worthy poor** and the **unworthy poor.** The Poor Laws articulated differential rights and responsibilities linked closely with work. *Persons with a socially acceptable work history or those who could not be expected to work because of age or infirmity were considered worthy of assistance. The able-bodied unemployed—considered irresponsible, lacking in ambition, and potentially dangerous to society—were deemed unworthy.* The worthy poor were treated better than the unworthy poor, who, considered more at blame for their plight, were subjected to harsher forms of social control.

The practice of categorizing participants in social welfare programs as worthy and less worthy continues today in the United States. The higher level of financial support provided to (worthy) disabled workers compared with (unworthy) recipients of Aid to Families with Dependent Children (see Chapter 2) is one indicator of the continued linkage of work status and worthiness in the United States. Workfare programs are another. Even in Sweden, local welfare agencies are experimenting with demanding work in return for social security benefits (Hallstahammar, 1987).

In addition to being defined as worthy or not based on work connection, worthiness is also often based on race or ethnicity, gender, age, or sexual orientation. People of color, for example, historically have been less well provided for in the United States than Anglo-Europeans. A protest song from the 1930s makes the point: "If you're white, all right; if you're brown, stick around; but if you're black,

THE PHILOSOPHICAL FRAMEWORK OF SOUTH SIDE SETTLEMENT

At South Side Settlement we believe in people's ability to shape their environment and the character of their society. We value the idea that all people should be fully involved in those problems which affect their lives. The creation of a democratic society demands an active, thinking citizenry unafraid of responsibility, actively experimenting with the means to meet the changing needs of its neighbors. At our house we seek to involve the people of our community in defining common problems and encourage maximum participation in developing solutions to those problems.

Inherent in our approach is a value system that encompasses the following concepts:

1 Our objective is the improvement of the quality of human life through the creation of a *community of culture and concern* in a society rooted in economic and social justice. We reject the goal of becoming an island unto ourselves and seek to involve all segments of our society in the fashioning of that community within the real world of human strengths and limitations. In that quest we are committed to lead out of our neighborhood into the larger city, state, nation, and world.

2 The *richness of difference* characterizes the meeting and interaction of human beings of inherently equal worth yet marvelous diversity. We welcome differences of class, race, religion, sex, age, belief and background as sources of cross fertilization and enrichment presenting possibilities of new human achievement through interdependence. The richness of difference implies mutual acceptance and trust, reciprocal respect but not necessarily approval or agreement. We reject both "tolerance" and "separatism" as inferring superior and inferior worth. Discrimination and segregation on the basis of differences are seen as destroyers of people and society.

3 *Freedom and responsibility* are inseparable. Freedom can be extended only through increasing acceptance of social responsibility. We oppose the tendency of many in our society to seek freedom without responsibility, to search for individual satisfaction divorced from social interaction and response. Only through social relationships and social structures can people protect the rights and extend the potential of every human being.

4 *Conflict and struggle* are as central to the task of creating a community of culture and concern as they are to human life itself. Conflict, the state in which there exists the opposition of alternatives, is neither negative nor a breakdown in our society. It exists. Life is the process of resolving an endless series of conflicts. One cannot choose to avoid conflict. One can only choose whether to participate in helping to determine its resolution or to leave that determination to others. Conflict cannot be resolved without struggle, the process of conflict resolution. At South Side Settlement we consciously use conflict in order to create the conditions for learning, movement and change. Our settlement is an arena where ideas are consciously introduced across lines of difference. They are examined, rejected, refined and yet again examined in order to unleash the potential for meaningful social change and the reduction of alienation.

5 An essential complement to the resolution of conflict is *celebration,* the act of sharing with family and friends the whole gamut of human emotion and experience. Celebration includes loving and laughing and sometimes crying together; singing and dancing and reveling in the accomplishments of the moment and in the fantasy of achievements yet to be. Celebration is the joy of living that provides the physical and psychological energy to continue on even in the face of what at times appear to be insurmountable odds.

6 Program at South Side Settlement reflects the *conscious testing of ideas.* We see ourselves as a laboratory for social change and understand that experimentation can result in failure as well as success. We seek the courage to risk ourselves—to try, to fail, and yet to try again and succeed. Critical and constructive self-examination is central to our existence. We strive for excellence and reject perfectionism.

Implicit in this system of values is the recognition that our philosophy must be responsive to the times in which we live and that all facets of our program must be open to challenge and change.

(Approved as a working document—10/28/70)

The South Side Settlement is a community centered group work agency in which people meet and organize to search for solutions to their common problems. We are interracial and nonsectarian. Our goal is to cut across the divisions of race, color, creed, sex, and age which separate people and to welcome the richness of human difference. Through our work we try to enrich the social, cultural, and educational experiences of all people with whom we come in contact. We are financed by the United Way of Franklin County and the National Division of the Board of Global Ministries of the United Methodist Church.

buddy, stay back, stay back, stay back." The public inattention to the AIDS epidemic, as long as it was perceived to relate primarily to (unworthy) gay men, is another example (Kayal, 1993). In spite of laws that attempt to ensure civil rights and more equitable treatment, racism, sexism, ageism, and heterosexism/homophobia continue to affect who is considered deserving of help.

A *sense of responsibility for others* is a value. All the societies discussed in this book accept some responsibility for their citizens. They vary, however, in the degree of responsibility they shoulder. Table 3-2 shows the range of responsibility for helping others, from the most personal to the most general. Responsibility is more likely to be accepted when the reasons for being in need are obvious, when the need seems to be beyond the control of those affected, and when the need is experienced by people who are held in reasonably high esteem.

Consider human infants and homeless adults. Many societies have legal definitions of the responsibilities of parents toward their children. An infant is totally helpless, and so adults offer their care. Homeless people, however, are often seen as being at least partially responsible for their own plight and thus less deserving of help. While extreme conditions may prompt people to provide temporary shelter during periods of below-freezing temperatures, the ongoing ability of the homeless to get food, to have access to a toilet or a bath, to have proper clothing, or to get medical and psychiatric care may be largely ignored. Many people believe that adults should provide such things for themselves, even if they are homeless. These values allow for assistance in meeting basic survival needs but little more, unless the need stems from illness, age, mental impairment, or another socially acceptable cause.

The conflicts between the new and old paradigms are reflected in two fundamentally different responses to the question of *who deserves to be helped.* One response is a **universal approach to social welfare,** in which *benefits are made available to all people as needed, independent of their employment records or income.* The universal approach is consistent with the institutional view that social welfare programs should be a normal aspect of daily living. Such programs are intended to prevent problems rather than trying to remedy them after they occur.

As we noted in Chapter 1, a universal approach to social welfare is closely linked to the concept of **entitlement,** *the belief that government should be responsible for guaranteeing to all eligible persons, as a right of membership, benefits necessary to meet their common needs.* The universal entitlement approach is most consistent with the emergent new paradigm.

A second response is a **selective approach to social welfare,** in which *benefits are focused on the "truly needy," and relatively little assistance is provided to*

TABLE 3-2   THE RANGE OF RESPONSIBILITY TO HELP OTHERS

Most personal ◄---► Most general

Responsible for kin	Responsible for friends	Responsible for members of own community	Responsible for citizens only	Responsible for all in own society	Responsible for humankind

those believed able to care for themselves on their own. The selective approach is consistent with the residual view that social welfare programs should respond to breakdowns in the normal functioning of the marketplace, the family, or the individual. From this perspective, social welfare programs are usually remedial rather than preventative. The selective approach is most consistent with the old paradigm. Let us examine these two positions in terms of their results.

Choices about social welfare provision have both moral and financial impacts. *Moral impacts* are those that alter people's values, thinking, and behavior. The alteration may be either desirable or undesirable. Being responsible for someone else is a commitment that usually involves scarce resources. *Financial impacts* stem from the allocation of scarce dollars. Once spent, those dollars cannot be spent for other, competing purposes. As you read the following, try to think about the impact of choices on both individuals and society.

The Universal Approach to Social Welfare

Among the social welfare systems discussed in this book, Sweden's is the best example of a system based on a universal approach. The Swedish answer to the question of who should be helped is: "Everyone." In Sweden, all citizens are provided with comprehensive entitlements including health insurance, housing and children allowances, unemployment insurance and retraining assistance, child care, retirement pensions, maternity/paternity benefits, and public education. Social insurance payments that replace earnings are high, allowing families to maintain essentially their accustomed living standard (Huber and Stephens, 1993:2). The Swedish system is described in detail in Chapter 7.

The Swedish approach has several goals. One is to improve the overall health and productivity of the population, a goal that has most certainly been met if judged in terms of such commonly used standards as infant mortality, average life span, incidence of poverty, and unemployment rates. (See Social Welfare Report Card in Chapter 1, and On the Street in Stockholm—Maternal and Child Health Care, later in this chapter.)

A second goal in Sweden is to foster an educated and motivated population that can adapt to changes in the workplace and that will ensure Sweden's economic competitiveness. Until the late 1980s, Sweden maintained a very low rate of unemployment together with high rates of productivity (Huber and Stephens, 1993).

The third goal is social cohesion, a general commitment by the members of the society to its existing political and economic structure based on satisfaction with the society's quality of life and a belief that it should be preserved. The political dominance of the Social Democrats for most of the past 60 years offers strong evidence of the existence of such a consensus in Sweden (Esping-Andersen, 1985:106–113). As we noted earlier, there is some evidence that that consensus may be weakening today.

Sweden's approach to social welfare has helped create a society in which people are fundamentally healthy and generally satisfied with the quality of their lives. The result has been a stable and economically productive society. Thus, the financial impact on individuals and on society has been positive in many ways. It is, however, a costly approach when viewed in purely financial terms. Sweden spent about three-fifths of its gross domestic product for public-sector expenditures in 1991 (Swedish Institute, 1991:FS1).

In the past, the cost to individuals through taxes was also high. In 1990, however, Sweden restructured its taxes to lower rates and broaden the tax base. After deduction of the universal child allowance payment, the effective rate of income taxes for a family with two employed adults and two children ranges from 1.6 percent for families with incomes of about $11,000 to 22.6 percent for families with incomes of about $43,000 (Swedish Institute, 1993:FS35). The Swedish tax system is progressive; i.e., tax rates increase according to ability to pay. Lower-income families are kept out of poverty; tax rates have been decreased to more manageable levels for higher-income households.

On the whole, Swedes seem to value their social welfare system, and it does not appear to have substantially reduced people's feelings of personal responsibility or initiative (Heckscher, 1984:102–123). Swedish social planners are nevertheless monitoring carefully several potentially negative effects. One is the possibility that a comprehensive system may reduce the extent to which people care for themselves. Another is a potential reduction in the use of informal natural helping networks, while a third is a possible reduction in the frequency with which people volunteer to help others (Ording, 1987).

An extensive social welfare system depends on a productive economy that in turn is in large part dependent on favorable economic and political conditions, both domestic and international. A nation's economic strength is also affected by social welfare's effectiveness at preparing domestic workers for a changing and increasingly complex workplace.

Given the brevity of our experience with a truly universal approach to social welfare, we do not know how a country with a comprehensive social welfare system would react to a long-term decrease in economic resources. Would everyone's benefits be reduced, or would universal programs be replaced by programs targeted to the poor? It is not clear how durable an experiment the current system in Sweden will prove to be. The significant successes of the Swedish approach may yield the unrealistic expectation that all social problems will be eliminated (Heckscher, 1984:160–180). Future generations who grow up without ever having experienced the human consequences of poverty may become unwilling to continue to pay for universal social welfare programs. However, universal eligibility may generate the social solidarity necessary for ongoing popular support of a comprehensive social welfare institution.

The Selective Approach to Social Welfare

The alternative approach for deciding who should be helped focuses on assisting only the most needy. Programs based on such an approach are usually means-tested.

None of our four countries uses a purely selective approach. Social welfare in the United States is, however, far less comprehensive and much closer to the selec-

ON THE STREET IN STOCKHOLM—MATERNAL AND CHILD HEALTH CARE

The Kronan District Health Care Center serves the residents of a lower-middle-class neighborhood of Stockholm. It is reasonably representative of other similar centers scattered throughout Sweden's capital city.

One center program deals exclusively with the health-care needs of infants and children. Prenatal services begin when nurses from the center visit a pregnant woman in her home. During the course of her pregnancy, nurses check the health of the woman and her fetus, provide brochures on health care and nutrition, and instruct the mother-to-be in infant and child care skills. After the new mother and child come home from the maternity hospital, nurses continue to visit. Later, when she is able to do so, the mother brings her baby to the center once a week to be weighed, measured, and tested.

The center has a cozy, personal feel. Examination rooms are decorated with colorful mobiles and pictures. Mothers and children develop a close relationship with the staff. During my visit to the center, I [Ron Federico] observed one mother chatting easily with the nurse and handling her own baby while it was being weighed and measured. The baby was calm and content, clearly accustomed to the staff and the surroundings.

After 6 months, the mother is asked to bring her child once each month and then, after the child is 2, once or twice a year. When the child begins school, the center forwards its records. In the school the resident nurse takes over the child's health care. Although not all parents make full use of them, pediatric nursing services are available to all Swedes, regardless of income, education, or other characteristics.

Another mother, one with grown children, told me she believed the system worked well and found it a valuable aid in raising her children. She had taken advantage of an option available to all working parents to reduce their work week in order to have more time at home with their children. Sweden's social welfare system provides parents with optional time off from work at reduced salary, so that they can meet their children's health and education needs. This mother worked 6 hours a day instead of 8 until her children were grown.

On the whole, while she wished her taxes were not so high, the mother found her public social welfare services very helpful. Her family received 485 *krona* per month from the government toward the cost of day care for her child. Since the actual cost was about 600 *krona,* her total child care cost was about 115 *krona* out of her monthly salary of about 10,000 *krona.* Her husband, whose salary was higher than hers, was also employed.

Observing the Swedish social welfare system in action, it is evident that it is used by virtually everyone. The services are provided in an appealing way, and they seem to be effective. There is some concern that such a system is so costly. However, when asked directly, the Swedes with whom I talked believed that the system was worth the cost.

In the several years since my visit to the Kronan District Health Center, taxes have been reduced. It is too soon to say what effect fewer governmental resources will have on the provision of public social services in Sweden.

Source: Personal observations of Ron Federico, 1987.

tive approach than is the Swedish system. The U.S. response to the question, "Who should be helped?" is "*sometimes everyone,* but more often only those who are deemed most worthy and most in need." In the United States, a few basic universal services (Social Security retirement pensions, workers' compensation, and Medicare) are combined with a much larger number of residual, means-tested programs (Aid to Families with Dependent Children, Food Stamps, Supplemental Security Income, and Medicaid, for example).

The financial impact of this "mixed" approach, in which some programs are universal entitlements—or almost so—has caused critics to question its efficiency. Expenditures for the relatively few universal programs are four-and-a-half times larger than for those that are means-tested (Domestic Policy Association, 1985:16). The most expensive programs are Medicare and pensions for veterans, neither of which is means-tested, and the Social Security retirement and disability programs, which are partially means-tested. Proponents of targeting services for the most needy decry universal programs as a waste of money, an inefficient way to meet the needs of those who are most in need. Why, they ask, should we give money to wealthy retirees or to wealthy veterans? Why not spend the money on the poor?

It is important to consider *both* moral and financial impacts. Under a selective system the poor might potentially receive increased benefits, but how should it be decided who is, or is likely to become, "truly needy"? And how much reason is there to believe that the savings that would accrue from replacing universal with selective programs would be used for the benefit of the poor? Is it not as likely that they would be used for other, more popular purposes—say, reducing the federal budget deficit or for military spending?

Consider the experience of retirees. Even those with substantial incomes during their working lives may have their savings depleted by illness or nursing-home care. Is it fair to require that they exhaust all resources—that they become poor—before they qualify for help? This is precisely the experience of those who wish to qualify for Medicaid. Many people are economically marginally secure and thus ineligible for most means-tested programs. Often, however, they lack enough money to weather an illness-related economic crisis or to pay for long-term institutional care.

Society, too, gains and loses under a selective system. Social welfare costs are more easily controlled. If the poor receive enough help, some might find it possible to break out of the cycle of poverty and become self-reliant. It is hoped that the number of people in need will gradually shrink, saving money and reducing the waste of human potential. However, means-tested programs involve application procedures that are cumbersome and expensive to operate.

In a selective system, social welfare programs are linked more closely to the poor and needy, stigmatizing of recipients increases, and people's willingness to pay for programs from which they do not benefit directly may decrease. Selectivity can lead to a "we" and "they" mentality, in which those whose taxes pay for programs attribute negative personality and behavioral characteristics to those who use them.

We can see, then, that a selective approach may reduce the financial costs of social welfare while substantially increasing the moral costs. The question is, which of these potential impacts is more important?

Undermining social solidarity and creating a society divided into "haves" and "have nots" is risky. In Mexico's highly stratified society, the wealthy have little contact with the poor, and often use their power to limit social welfare services. Ultimately, the poor may revolt, as in the 1994 Zapatista uprising in Chiapas. Or they may riot, as happened in Los Angeles in 1993 following the acquittal of the police who beat Rodney King, a low-income African American. Polarization may have negative impacts on the poor as well as on society. Increases in social stigma may cause users of means-tested programs to see themselves as less worthy than others, and to lose confidence in their ability to improve their circumstances.

While both political "liberals" and "conservatives" in the United States, i.e., both Democrats and Republicans, often support a selective approach to the provision of social welfare, conservatives tend to draw the boundaries around the "truly needy" more narrowly than do liberals. Conservatives argue that the public social welfare system has become too large and that its programs should be reduced (Murray, 1984).

Conservatives believe that "the welfare state is inherently inefficient, a threat to personal freedom, a strategy that undermines the very sense of community it is supposed to embody" (Domestic Policy Foundation, 1985:9). Although meeting human need may be a worthwhile goal, conservatives argue, the current social welfare system actually hurts people rather than helping them.

Proponents of shrinking the social welfare system by limiting eligibility assert that the system discourages people from working and taking responsibility for themselves. Public assistance, according to these critics, becomes a way of life for too many recipients. However, Ramona Parish, an articulate mother raising her three children with the help of AFDC, demonstrates the determination of many welfare recipients to become self-reliant. (See The Human Face of Social Welfare 7: Messages from a Welfare Mom.)

Conservatives believe that society cannot afford the cost of a universal entitlement system (Domestic Policy Association, 1985:25–26). They argue that costs of universal programs inevitably spiral out of control and contribute to budgetary deficits. In any case, they contend, the resources required for universal social welfare programs could be put to other, more preferred, purposes such as national defense, research and development, or reduction of the federal deficit.

In the moral realm, conservatives believe that reducing public services will increase people's sense of responsibility toward each other. They are concerned that the availability of formal social welfare programs may reduce reliance on informal helping systems. When people know that formal services are available, conservatives argue, they are less likely to make use of their natural helping networks. Conservatives are also concerned that when people believe the needs of others are being met by government, they may assume less personal responsibility for helping.

There is a larger moral concern as well. Conservatives worry about the loss of community that they believe accompanies reliance on large-scale governmental programs. Proponents of a selective approach to social welfare eligibility believe that their approach will enhance the moral strength of the larger society and will increase people's sense of personal responsibility for others as well as for themselves. They see government programs as remote from and poorly understood by ordinary citizens, who are left with the impression that social welfare needs are being met, uneasy as to whether their tax money is being well spent, and with a belief that paying taxes is all that is required of them. Far from developing a sense of community solidarity—one for all, and all for one—conservatives believe that large-scale public programs promote a reluctance to become further involved. The governmental social welfare system, they contend, seems too large, too complicated, and imposed from above (Bellah, 1985; Domestic Policy Association, 1985:29–30).

THE HUMAN FACE OF SOCIAL WELFARE 7

MESSAGES FROM A WELFARE MOM

Like many other single mothers, I [have been] on welfare . . . ever since I divorced my husband six years ago. Living on government aid does several things to people. It destroys their pride and dignity; it makes them dependent on a system that penalizes them for being willing to work. I am not lazy and I want to work. But at this time the best I can hope for is a minimum-wage job that would only undermine my attempts to get ahead. Instead of just being poor, I would become one of the nation's working poor. I cannot survive on $3.35 per hour with three children, without regular child-support payments or health insurance. So I live on AFDC and often feel guilty because I take advantage of this system and its services. But I'm also made to feel ashamed because I cannot pay for things with my own hard-earned money.

To the people behind me on the grocery-store line: You have helped me feel guilty. You chip away at what little pride I have left by snickering to others when I use my food stamps, at the same time commenting loudly about an abuse of taxpayers' dollars.

To all landlords: Some of you believe that because I receive welfare I have no pride in my home or my surroundings. Many times I've called on the phone to ask about a rental and, sight unseen, been turned down when I mention I receive AFDC . . . On the other hand, there are some of you who will rent only to welfare. . . . You don't care what condition your apartment is in because if I complain about needed repairs . . . you tell me [to move out]. Because there are only a few of you who will rent to AFDC, your apartment will not be empty long. . . .

To my children: I did not intend to raise you on welfare. Bear with me a few more years, for I am trying to make a bad situation better. . . . I know how ashamed you must feel when you're singled out in the classroom as a free-luncher, and the hurt caused by whispers among your friends that you're poor and your mother is on welfare. I'm sorry for the things I can't afford. . . .

To all doctors and dentists: Would my hysterectomy which was done three years ago when I was only 28 have been so urgent if I hadn't had Medicaid to pay for it? . . . I wonder if some professionals take advantage of Medicaid recipients because women on AFDC are seen as uneducated. . . . And would that explain why so many AFDC women have lost all their teeth? . . . I'm too embarrassed to tell people that dentists suggest pulling teeth because Medicaid won't pay for root canals and crowns. . . .

To all social-service case workers: When I am willing to help myself and work, why do you take

To summarize, the universal and selective approaches to deciding who should be helped impact differentially on individuals and society. A universal approach is costly but maximizes opportunities for individual and social development. It may also, however, reduce people's self-reliance and willingness to use informal support networks. A selective approach reduces costs but leaves unresolved the issue of deciding who is "truly needy." In addition, many taxpayers rooted in the old paradigm of neoliberalism may resent supporting services that they believe do not benefit them personally. Conservatives would reduce public social welfare expenditures still further in favor of increased public spending on other non-welfare-related activities. Implicit in the conservative perspective is the assumption that informal support networks will be sufficient to meet people's needs. Analyzing the approaches to social welfare eligibility in terms of their moral and finan-

everything away? Can't you at least let me keep the food stamps and medical insurance until I'm above the poverty level? Without these benefits I cannot make it, so I stay on the soaring welfare rolls. I don't want a free ride, but I do need a lift.

To whom it may concern: Do not feel pity for me. I don't want it. . . . Enrolling in college and getting an education is my key to a future without AFDC. Managing a full-time class load, 20 hours a week on a work-study program, and being a mother hasn't been easy, but I've survived. . . . With each passing semester my head lifts a little higher. What I could use is a smile of understanding and words of encouragement and support. With help, not hindrance, I will make it.

Ramona Parish lives in a small town in Michigan. She discusses from the heart her direct experience with many of the issues we have been examining. Some people would question the wisdom of her divorce, saying that, if she could not support herself, she should have stayed married. Others recognize that a bad marriage may be far more damaging than welfare over the long run.

In her efforts to become self-reliant, Ms. Parish has experienced problems with the economic system (employment and housing), the social welfare system (inadequate benefits), and social stigma in her community. Her plea for understanding from her children is moving because they, too, have been stigmatized by welfare. What steps could be taken to reduce the stigma of insufficient income?

In July 1997 the minimum wage will be increased to $5.15 per hour. Is the current minimum wage enough to meet the needs of a family of four?

In her discussion of the problem of finding adequate housing, Ms. Parish has identified a dilemma that confronts many poor people in the United States. Slumlords make excessive profits by renting substandard housing to people with no real choice of place to live. Ironically, in doing so they provide a "social service." Except for access to dilapidated, often dangerous, code-violating slum apartments, many poor people would become homeless. The shortage of decent housing in many parts of the United States makes more difficult the efforts of advocates and grass-roots housing organizations to enforce housing codes. In treating the poor as supplicants, as a society we have failed to make available enough safe and habitable shelter.

Ramona Parish hopes that her enrollment in a program to become a legal secretary will enable her family to break free from welfare. Is this a realistic goal for every mother raising a family on AFDC? What alternatives do these women have?

Excerpted from Ramona Parish, "Messages from a Welfare Mom," *Newsweek,* May 23, 1988, p. 10. Copyright © 1988, Newsweek, Inc. All rights reserved. Reprinted by permission.

cial impact on individuals and society helps to identify the conflicts associated with each.

HOW SHOULD HELP BE PROVIDED?

As you read this section, it is helpful to keep in mind what we mean by social welfare. *Social welfare is "a nation's system of programs, benefits and services that help people meet those social, economic, educational, and health needs that are fundamental to the maintenance of society"* (Barker, 1991:221).

In market-oriented industrial societies, the economic marketplace assumes major importance for meeting needs (Gilbert, 1983). We expect that most people will earn the money to purchase essentials such as food, clothing, and housing; those who cannot, receive assistance from social welfare programs.

As we have seen, both conservatives and liberals share a belief that, at least under some circumstances, it is appropriate to take responsibility for others. While there is disagreement about who should be considered worthy, what needs require a response from others, and under what circumstances help should be offered, few people today would argue that no help at all should be made available to those in need.

Many issues relevant to the provision of social welfare are closely related to the perceived status of the user of social welfare programs. We have already discussed how perceptions of worthiness and unworthiness affect *who* is considered deserving of assistance. Let us now turn to another aspect of status, which affects *how* social welfare is provided.

Consumers of social welfare may be treated as *citizens* or as *supplicants*. Both citizens and supplicants have needs but, as we will see, their needs are responded to very differently as a consequence of their status.

A **citizen** is *a person who, in exchange for allegiance, is entitled to certain rights, privileges, and protections from the government.* A citizen has *rights of membership* to a healthy life and human fellowship. Citizens are included in community life and are provided "resources to earn a living or to thrive even if they cannot work" (Lappé, 1989:14, 95). This concept of citizen is not necessarily limited to those who are native-born or naturalized. Every society makes choices about how broadly or narrowly to define "citizen." Proponents of actions such as California's Proposition 187, which proposed denying health and education benefits to illegal immigrants and their families, define citizen narrowly; others would provide citizen rights of membership to all residents of a given country regardless of their legal status.

A **supplicant** is *a person without rights, a person who must earnestly and humbly beg that his or her needs be met.* Meeting the needs of supplicants depends on acts of charity, benevolence, or kindness to which they have no entitlement. Benefits may or may not be provided to them as a favor.

Whereas citizens can stand tall, seeking aid as a matter of right, supplicants must ask for help "hat in hand." Whereas citizens can expect to be treated with dignity, supplicants are often stigmatized and demeaned. Citizens receive entitlements; supplicants are granted alms, or forced to go on the dole.

Human Liberation and Social Control

Whether social welfare programs will be structured in ways that are liberating or controlling is affected significantly by whether participants are deemed citizens or supplicants. Where programs are delivered, program adequacy, the degree to which participants are trusted, whether or not participants will be involved in decision making, and even requirements for work are affected by this status distinction.

These distinctions are related to the conflicts between the old and the new paradigms. The new paradigm, you will recall, stresses citizen rights of membership; the old paradigm implies charity to supplicants. When people are seen as citizens, programs that enhance human dignity and autonomy and build on strengths follow naturally. The new paradigm, therefore, emphasizes the liberation and empowerment of citizens; the old paradigm emphasizes social control.

One way in which the liberation–control conflict is evident is that efforts are made to include citizens in every aspect of community life; supplicants, in contrast, are often excluded from participation in community affairs. The English Poor Law practice of providing *outdoor relief* for the worthy poor and *indoor relief* for the unworthy poor is a good example of the differential treatment of citizens and supplicants in this regard.

Outdoor relief is *social welfare support provided to persons in their own homes*—outside of institutions. Outdoor relief makes it more likely that the recipient will be able to continue to participate in community life. The provision of community mental health centers that support the possibility of deinstitutionalizing the chronically mentally ill is a contemporary example of outdoor relief. Placement of children in foster homes or with adoptive parents instead of in orphanages is another.

Indoor relief is *social welfare support provided within residential institutions.* When people are institutionalized, their ability to participate actively in community affairs is minimized. Poorhouses, workhouses, houses of corrections, reformatories, juvenile detention centers, prisons, and mental institutions are examples of indoor relief, some historical and some contemporary.

The conflict between liberation and social control is reflected in the tension in social welfare between *punishment* and *compassion.* **Compassion** is *"sympathetic consciousness of other's distress together with a desire to alleviate it"* (Woolf, 1979:227). Compassion is closely related to the social work concept of **empathy,** *"the act of perceiving, experiencing, and responding to the emotional state," ideas, and circumstances of another person* (Barker, 1991:73). Often, people are more likely to have compassion and empathy for those seen as respected citizens and more likely to be punitive toward those perceived as supplicants. The pensioner on Social Security is treated compassionately compared with the parent who must endure the punishment of onerous application procedures and stigma in order to qualify for AFDC (Tropman, 1989:14, 62).

The *amount of assistance* provided to those in need is also affected by whether an applicant is seen as a citizen or a supplicant. Since the Great Depression, the poorest 20 percent of the U.S. population has received about 5 percent of the nation's income. In *Common Decency,* Alvin Schorr (1986) proposes a policy of "fair shares" as part of his proposal to strengthen community. Under Schorr's proposal, the share of national income of the poorest 20 percent of the population would be doubled to about 10 percent. Interestingly, during the Reagan-Bush administration (1980–1988), the magnitude of the redistribution of funds necessary to achieve that goal was exceeded, but in the opposite direction—from the poorest 40 percent of the population to the wealthiest 40 percent (Schorr, 1986:27). When the poor are perceived as citizens, we are more likely to accept fair shares as just than we are if the poor are perceived as beggars with their hands out.

When beneficiaries of social welfare are perceived as supplicants, benefit levels tend to be kept at the lowest possible levels. States commonly establish a minimum standard of need below which it is virtually impossible to maintain "health and decency." AFDC payments are then set at some percentage of that minimum level.

Low levels of benefits, of course, function to force as many persons as possible to accept employment—even at wage levels that are inadequate to support themselves and their dependents. This practice, too, has roots in the English Poor Laws. It is a direct descendent of the concept of **less eligibility,** *the Poor Law principle that no unemployed person should be better off than the lowest-paid worker.*

The liberation–control conflict also influences questions of *trust.* When people are esteemed as citizens, they are more likely to be trusted to be able to make appropriate decisions about how they use their resources. Accordingly, social welfare benefits are more likely to be provided *in cash* when the benefits are perceived as a societal right of membership. Supplicants are apt to be distrusted; they are believed to be incompetent or unwilling to make appropriate choices on their own behalf. Consequently, social welfare benefits to those perceived as supplicants are likely to be *in kind.* A Thanksgiving food basket is an in-kind benefit, as opposed to a check that might (or might not) be spent on a Thanksgiving dinner. Benefits-in-kind limit personal freedom of choice; the recipient is able to use them only for the purpose intended by the provider. Thus, benefits-in-kind may be seen as an aspect of the social control function of social welfare.

Ironically, the goal of liberating people to function with greater autonomy brings with it limits to individual freedom. Deciding how to help people without depriving them of freedom to live their own lives is a very sensitive task. The needs of individuals and societies sometimes conflict. Should the individual have the right to fail or to make choices that have social costs, even though society may then have to expend considerable effort to "rescue" him or her? Should people, for example, be free to refrain from using seatbelts in automobiles or from wearing helmets when riding motorcycles? If an accident occurs, the exercise of personal freedom may result in high costs to society through medical expenditures or social insurance disability or survivors' benefits.

How much control over individuals should society have in order to foster or to protect capacity for self-reliance? (See the Human Face of Social Welfare 8: The Mayor Hits the Streets.)

Dependence and Self-Reliance

When people are perceived as citizens with rights of membership, we are apt to approach the issue of dependency differently than when they are perceived as supplicants. The question regarding persons with rights of membership is likely to be: "What can we do to enable our fellow citizen to achieve independence?" By *independence* we mean maximum personal freedom and self-reliance. This is quite different from the question for supplicants: "What measures are necessary to ensure that she or he cannot persist in dependency?"

Most societies encourage people to be as self-reliant as possible. Individuals are expected to provide for their own needs and those of their families if they can. Certain types of dependence, however, are defined as acceptable by virtually all societies. The very young and the very old are universally thought to deserve help, as are the ill and those with mental or physical limitations. Notice that these

THE HUMAN FACE OF SOCIAL WELFARE 8

THE MAYOR HITS THE STREETS

. . . I asked her how she liked the apartment.

She said, "It's wonderful." And it is. I asked her where she lived before. She said she'd been living in one of the welfare hotels. I asked her how long she had been there. "Five years," she replied.

I was shocked. . . .

I said, "Five years—and we [referring to the city's welfare department] never offered you an apartment?"

She said: "Oh no, Mayor. Of course you did. Your people showed me 19 apartments."

"Why didn't you take one?"

"I didn't like any of them. Either they weren't located in nice buildings or nice neighborhoods, or they weren't in the [part of the city] I wanted to live in."

Again I was shocked. Here was a person who was bringing up her children under difficult, squalid circumstances in a welfare hotel and she'd turned down 19 apartments until she got the one she wanted. I thought to myself, people who are part of the working poor, and who are perhaps either doubled up or living in substandard housing would be furious, if they knew they'd been denied the opportunity to take one of those 19 apartments this woman had turned down.

Something has gone wrong when people on public assistance have more choices than people who are making it on their own. However, when I sought to place restrictions on the number of apartments any recipient could turn down, welfare advocates denounced me. . . .

When rights without responsibilities become the order of the day, we encourage a social breakdown that will harm us in ways yet unimagined. There is a limit to what government can and should do in a democracy. No city or state can be expected to protect adults from themselves. If that is the course we choose for our society, then nothing can protect us from each other.

These words were written by Edward Koch while he was the mayor of New York City. The issues he raises about the moral impact of social welfare on people are important ones. He questions the extent of society's responsibility for human well-being; he challenges the right of the needy to decide what type of help is acceptable. Do you think that this mother's choices indicate that the social welfare system has damaged her moral integrity? Can you suggest other reasons that explain why she acted as she did? Do you agree with Mayor Koch that this woman exercised "rights without responsibilities"?

acceptable varieties of dependence are related to personal attributes over which the individual has little or no control.

There are additional causes of dependency over which the individual also lacks control, but that exist in the social environment rather than the person. These include racism, sexism, homophobia, and ageism. Together, these factors constitute institutional discrimination.

Institutional discrimination is gradually being better understood as a cause of dependency. For example, racial minority groups whose members are denied access to quality schooling are at a disadvantage in the job market and thus are less likely to attain economic self-reliance. Therefore, an important goal of social welfare is to remove institutional discrimination as a social obstacle that prevents people from becoming independent.

The rhetoric of independence is sometimes different from the reality of social arrangements. Sweden, where equality and self-reliance for all is an explicit societal goal, uses many elements of the social welfare system to achieve this goal. Men and women are treated equally in the workplace, and family policy encourages equal participation in childrearing by both parents when two are present. Housing policy provides for the special needs of children, adolescents, the elderly, and those with physical limitations, so that all can develop fully and be as independent as their abilities permit. Even the subway system in Stockholm has ramps and elevators to ensure accessibility to all, from babies in carriages to the elderly and the physically limited. This kind of mobility strongly supports people's efforts to be independent. While the United States also values equality and personal independence, it has yet to find ways to translate this goal into day-to-day reality for many people.

However much self-reliance is stressed, there will always be people who cannot care for themselves. This may be a temporary or permanent condition and may range from near-total incapacity to minimal levels of dependence.

We all know that some people need help over an extended period and that others are only temporarily impaired. For example, we expect children to need help for many years and recognize that those with physical limitations may require aid all their lives. Social welfare services to promote the personal growth and development of infants seek to maximize their later self-reliance. Similarly, rehabilitation programs aim to move those who are dependent toward greater independence.

Those who are unemployed are generally thought to have a temporary problem. As a result, programs designed to help children and the disabled often provide services over relatively long periods, while programs designed to alleviate unemployment provide services for a much shorter time. When problems that "ought" to be resolved relatively quickly persist for a long time, controversy is likely.

Fostering dependency may be an outcome of social services. Most people agree that dependency is undesirable. In fact, much of the controversy surrounding AFDC has to do with precisely this issue.

Underlying the controversy is the sense that the inability to support one's family should be a relatively short-term problem. If a decent-paying job or adequate day care is needed, these needs should be met fairly quickly. Similarly, if job training is the issue, this too should be a relatively short-run problem. When these needs are not met quickly—or simply not met at all—recipients of aid are likely to wonder whether they will ever become self-reliant. The same question is asked pointedly by conservative critics of social welfare.

There is a folk saying that goes something like this: "Give someone a fish and they can eat for a day; teach them to fish, and they can eat for a lifetime." It is a saying that captures part of the essence of the argument over the type of help social welfare should provide. The conflict is not over the ultimate goal of social welfare. Most people would agree that it is better to enable people to care for themselves than simply to meet their immediate needs.

One important factor in promoting self-reliance is job training. Suitable training for employment is a critical need for the potentially employable but unemployed poor. Yet training is costly. Although most people recognize that it is far more economical over the long run to train people for maximum self-reliance—even if this means increased short-term costs—this is not always a politically popular strategy (Hochschild, 1988:177). A particularly distressing prospect in 1995 is the proposal of the Clinton administration and the Republican "Personal Responsibility Act" to limit eligibility for AFDC—and consequently the amount of education or training one can receive through the AFDC JOBS[3] Program—to 2 years. If this proposal becomes law, it will end the 4-year college education option through which, for example, many mothers receiving AFDC have earned college degrees. Throughout the United States, you may be interested to know, there are many women who have used the JOBS program to become first-class baccalaureate-level social workers.

In a democratic system that works on a 2-year cycle as does the U.S. Congress, proposals that involve higher initial costs in order to obtain future savings can be difficult to explain to voters. Negative votes are often classic examples of being "penny wise and pound foolish."

As long as we fear that people who receive assistance are uninterested in fending for themselves, it will be difficult to resolve the "spend more now in order to realize future savings" versus "spend only what you must" dilemma. Providing educational preparation for jobs that pay a living wage takes time. Changing the social and environmental conditions that are impeding people requires a strong and sustained societal commitment. Creating jobs that pay living wages requires time and commitment. Without such commitment, many people will be prevented from becoming full and productive members of society. We will continue to give people enough to survive but not enough to thrive.

At the heart of the controversy over self-reliance is the question of whether recipients should be required to "earn" the benefits they receive: of whether they should be encouraged, or even required, to work. This controversy occurs because, in an industrial society, it is through work that most people earn the money to be self-reliant.

Money, however, is not the only potential obstacle to self-reliance. Many of the poor are in poor health, have limited work skills, or have responsibilities for caring for young children or incapacitated family members. If they are also women or people of color, they must contend with discrimination that limits the number and type of positions open to them (Hochschild, 1988:177–178). More important, there simply are not enough well-paying jobs available. In the final analysis, the issue of unemployment is grounded in societal more than individual shortcomings.

The fundamental question is how to help people on a day-to-day basis while at the same time preparing them to become as independent as possible.

Work and Welfare

The conflict between liberation and social control is especially acute when expectations about work are involved. Many people believe that a person in need should

---

[3]Job Opportunity and Basic Skills Training Program (JOBS).

THE HUMAN FACE OF SOCIAL WELFARE 9

DOWN IN THE VALLEY

The Gonzalez family lives in the lower Rio Grande Valley in a cramped, dark and drafty three-room shack. Their home is in a *colonia* (neighborhood), an unincorporated rural subdivision. They have no heat or sewage system, and when it rains, the *colonia*'s rutted dirt roads and yards flood so badly that children must wade through a stew of water and raw sewage to get to the school buses. . . .

In "the Valley," as it is known, Gonzalez and up to 250,000 other American citizens live in more than 400 rural slums. Unemployment . . . runs as high as 50 percent, water supplies are fouled and chronic diseases are rampant. Schools . . . are hopelessly overcrowded. In short, the conditions in the *colonias* are the worst America has to offer. And the population is increasing so rapidly that studies predict it will double by the year 2000. . . .

Like most of the *colonia* residents, Gonzalez is a first-generation Mexican-American whose parents came to the United States in search of opportunity. . . .

[Another example of life in the *colonia* is provided by the Costilla family.] Gloria Costilla's two-room home in El Dora has dirt floors and wall-to-wall beds—for herself, her husband and eight children. Unable to afford either the $200 meter installation fee or the developer's monthly water-supply bill of $14, she resigned herself to rising each dawn and hauling eight 10-gallon buckets from a neighbor's house. . . .

Doctors in the valley work overtime controlling basic illnesses normally seen only in developing countries. Their patients' lack of education and the high cost of medicine make health care [an almost hopeless] task. Diabetes, for instance, which can be easily controlled [when adequate medical care exists], frequently causes blindness and limb loss in the Valley. . . .

Most of the people who live in the *colonias* do not have health insurance, and there is widespread ignorance about Medicaid. . . .

The fertility rate in the *colonias* is estimated at twice the national average, and infant mortality is high. . . . If pregnant women receive prenatal care, it is usually not until they are well into pregnancy, and often ill mothers give birth to babies with a variety of sicknesses and disorders. . . .

Though school is a haven—most children get their only decent meal of the day there—few make it beyond the ninth grade. Many children of migrant farmhands miss the beginning and end of the school year, and the overall dropout rates are pushing 50 percent. . . .

It was not until three years ago that state officials even acknowledged the desperation in the Valley. . . . According to a recent study by the Texas Water Development Board, it would take 30 years and at least $200 million just to bring clean water and sewage lines to all 400 of the existing *colonias*. . . .

Antonio Gonzalez, who has worked as a migrant laborer since he was 10, has one great hope: "I tell my children, This is not life, you must get an education and get out." But the *colonias* are prisons of poverty from which few have managed to escape.

Limited education, poor housing, low employability, and minority status often accompany poverty. Taken together, these factors make it very difficult for the poor to change their situation. The families described above live in the Rio Grande Valley in Texas, now considered the poorest region in the United States. They need many resources if they are to become healthy and economically self-reliant.

As a result of institutional discrimination, families in the *colonias* are often treated as supplicants rather than citizens. Very often they are blamed for circumstances over which they have at best partial control. What should be done to enable these residents to do more than simply survive at their current levels?

welcome work—any kind of work—if employment is available. Should not, they ask, a parent receiving AFDC be required to apply for a job if, say, a new fast-food restaurant opens nearby?

Many low-income persons, including recipients of AFDC, have strong desires to increase their independence through work, and do work in jobs such as this. There are, however, major barriers to relying exclusively on such employment. First, such jobs simply do not pay enough to make ends meet. Thirty-five percent of all full-time U.S. hourly wage earners in 1992 earned less than the minimum wage of $4.25 per hour. Even if a job pays the minimum wage, a full-time, year-round worker's earnings were insufficient to bring a family of three above the poverty line (U.S. Department of Commerce, 1993:474).

Second, minimum-wage jobs are unlikely to provide health insurance. When a parent leaves AFDC for such employment, she soon becomes ineligible for Medicaid health coverage. If her child becomes involved in an accident or becomes ill, there may be no recourse other than returning to AFDC in order to receive Medicaid.

Third, many minimum-wage jobs are dead ends with few prospects for advancement. Lack of safe and affordable child care is a fourth potential barrier.

Studies consistently show that people prefer to work, if they can support themselves by doing so (Perales, 1983; Morris, 1986:46–53). In the absence of adequate wages, wage supplements, and subsidized support services, however, the parent may have no real choice but to rely on welfare.

Underlying much of the controversy about work and workfare is the widespread belief in the myth of the "welfare Cadillac"; the belief that poor people drive fancy cars that they can afford while hard-working people cannot, that poor people are simply lazy and unwilling to help themselves, expect everything to be handed to them on a platter, and will avoid work if at all possible. The belief that welfare recipients live "high on the hog" and receive excessive benefits contributes to resentment by those who see themselves as supporting unworthy "ne'er-do-wells." When welfare recipients do get money, so the thinking goes, they spend it on things like televisions, fancy clothes, and luxury foods. Many people get angry at "welfare cheats" and believe that they do not deserve help.

Some welfare recipients do lie about their needs and accept money for which they do not qualify. Most do not. However, many otherwise law-abiding citizens cheat on their income taxes, make unauthorized copies of computer software, and defraud insurance companies with bogus claims.

Cheating, whether by the rich or the poor, is wrong. Actually, however, fraud rates among welfare recipients are quite low, in part because states with high rates of errors in determining welfare eligibility lose federal funds. Like most people, welfare recipients want to work and would prefer to be self-reliant. Yet this remains a difficult goal for many.

The cumulative effects of disadvantage may lead to long-term dependence and despair. Instead of driving welfare Cadillacs, most poor people face deprivation and discrimination on a daily basis. In the words of Hochschild (1988:177–178), "Solving the problem of cumulative inequalities . . . would require a coordinated attack on racial discrimination and poverty and political powerlessness. . . ."

Until this occurs, we can anticipate that at least some disadvantaged people will be forced into long-term dependency.

To many, this will seem inappropriate. Citizens whose taxes support such programs may be angry that their money is going to support unemployed adults rather than providing short-term help to poor families with needy children. At the very least, they contend, adult welfare recipients should be required to earn their keep.

Over the years, there has been a recurring controversy—dating back to the days of workhouses and poor farms—over proposals that the poor be required to earn their benefits. The contemporary name given to *plans that require people who receive public assistance to work in return for their benefits* is **workfare** (Gueron and Auspos, 1987).

Workfare has several manifest functions. One is to enhance the self-respect of the recipients of aid. Instead of receiving charity, they can legitimately claim to have earned their way. A second objective is to provide an opportunity to learn useful work skills. A third is to reinforce social cohesion by providing those who receive help with the sense that they are contributing something in return. Finally, workfare is designed to reduce the cost of aid by providing society with tangible goods and services in return for its social welfare expenditures.

As the workfare program has actually been implemented, it is bound by the constraint not to replace existing workers. Several undesirable latent functions have emerged. The jobs involved often are not ones in which marketable skills can be developed. They are likely to be boring jobs that demand little of the worker's intelligence. They usually pay only the minimum wage. Child care is seldom available. By making public assistance as unattractive as possible, workfare discourages eligible persons from applying.

A second latent function of workfare is creation of a pool of low-paid workers who compete in the job market with other workers who are not receiving any financial assistance. This may have the consequence of depressing wages or creating unfair competition. For this reason, Polish cooperatives for the disabled are granted the exclusive right to produce certain types of products and are limited to those products in order to ensure that their output does not compete with that of other workers who must depend exclusively on unsubsidized wages.

Involving People in Decision Making

What should be the role in social welfare decision making of those who receive services? Should consumers of social welfare be seen as supplicants who ought to accept gratefully, without question or choice, whatever they are given? Or should consumers of social welfare have citizen rights of membership? Those with greatest need are often politically inactive. Much of the planning for the services they receive is done by others. When consumers are treated as supplicants, as is very often the case in the United States, they are unlikely to be invited or expected to participate in social welfare policy making. Sometimes, however, there is a shift in public sentiment toward treating consumers as citizens. When this occurs, attempts are made to include consumers in policy making.

AVOIDING DEPENDENCY: THE SWEDISH APPROACH

Sweden's strategy for avoiding long-term dependency is built around education and employment. Other supportive services, including virtually free health care and subsidized housing, help. In Sweden, providing public assistance checks is not a fundamental strategy for meeting need, although assistance is available to those who require it. Instead the Swedish focus is on efforts to prepare people for self-reliance.

Free universal public education is a critical component. Swedish education is highly diversified, with many types of vocational and other specialized programs available full and part-time. Education is valued. Public radio stations air home-study programs.

Swedish high schools make a concerted effort to prepare students for the job market. As part of their studies, students spend time working in positions that provide them with first-hand business experience and a sense of what different types of jobs are like. They are not paid for this; it is considered part of their learning. This helps them to identify possible career options that can then be pursued through appropriate educational programs.

The Swedish political system and Swedish values provide additional help. The goal of equality for all—women and men, immigrants and native Swedes alike—is diligently pursued. Substantial efforts are made to ensure that all types of education and all jobs are accessible to both women and men. The educational system instructs immigrants in their own language; the social welfare system provides services on a similar basis. The goal is to help integrate immigrants into Swedish society as quickly as possible, enabling them to become full-fledged and productive citizens.

Labor unions play a significant, formal role in political decision making; full employment is an articulated societal goal. The Swedish social policy mandate to involve people in productive work that makes self-reliance possible is reflected not only in the substance of policy but in the social and political structures for policy implementation.

While Sweden's aspirations sometimes outstrip its fiscal abilities to achieve them, the Swedish approach to self-reliance offers an interesting model for other societies to consider.

A notable example occurred during the Johnson administration's War on Poverty. The Community Action Programs created as a result of the 1964 Economic Opportunity Act included a requirement for "maximum feasible participation" by the poor (Kramer, 1969). The results, however, were politically controversial. Newly enfranchised community boards came into conflict with established community decision organizations. The heady experience of political involvement sometimes led to confrontation. Eventually, the nation's mayors were able to thwart the implementation of maximum feasible participation and to co-opt the representatives of the poor.

In recent years the pendulum has swung back in the direction of treating the poor as supplicants. There are currently few serious efforts to involve users of services in social welfare decision making. In part, this is because consumers are not well enough organized to demand representation and to be able to choose representatives to speak for them in the policy-making arena. Members of such advisory groups as do exist are usually selected by program administrators. Advisory groups seldom have significant decision-making authority.

Another form of citizen participation allows choice among competing service vendors. Competition among doctors, for example, allows those who are ill to choose a physician whom they believe will provide optimal care. National health insurance is vigorously resisted by some who argue that it might limit freedom to choose one's physician. Similarly, those who support proposals to give parents educational vouchers, which would be good at any public or private school, argue that providing people with choices would improve the quality of education by stimulating competition among school systems.

The right of people to determine their own fate is a deeply held value in the United States. Allowing people to choose the social welfare services they want is consistent with this goal. However, the presumed benefits of being able to choose among vendors can be realized only if two conditions are met. First, potential consumers must have access to several competing vendors. Second, they must be sufficiently knowledgeable to recognize differences in quality of service and to select services of optimal quality.

A third form of citizen participation is *self-help,* involvement in the actual delivery of services. By assuming some responsibility for acknowledging needs and participating in efforts to find solutions along with others with similar needs, people can become more involved in their own care. Organizations such as Alcoholics Anonymous use self-help extensively. However, most types of services can be delivered in ways that encourage people to participate more actively. For example, good health requires people to eat nutritiously and to stop unhealthy behavior such as smoking, as well as to go to the doctor. Consumers of social welfare can be empowered to make choices that enhance their personal well-being.

We can see, then, that people can be involved in social welfare decision making in at least three different ways: through planning and policy making, by choosing among competing vendors, and through self-help efforts. Each type of involvement raises its own set of value conflicts. Whether consumers are enabled and encouraged to participate will depend to a large extent on how they are defined: as citizens or as supplicants.

Competition for Scarce Resources

The importance of resources for social welfare is cogently expressed by Hecksher (1984:105): "welfare states more than others need an economic basis, which can be created only if the economy as a whole is prosperous; and in conditions of today it can remain prosperous only if it proves competitive in an international market where countries with other socioeconomic traditions and aims also attempt to achieve a growing share."

In other words, providing resources and services for people is costly. Those costs can take many forms: money for benefits, trained people to provide services, land and buildings to house programs, and the time spent by planners determining what services are needed. In advanced welfare societies such as Sweden, these costs—among which are large government expenditures, the possibility of reducing people's motivation to work, and possible disincentives for people to save money as part of their planning for remaining self-reliant later in life—are increasingly the subject of debate (Hecksher, 1984:7). Although research shows that most societies continue to believe that the benefits of social welfare outweigh its costs, there is no doubt that these costs are being carefully watched (Alber, 1987).

The availability of resources is an important constraint on social welfare in many developing nations. Even though these nations may want to provide a high level of social welfare services, the lack of resources may make this impossible. Ward (1986:8) describes such a pattern in Mexico, where total expenditures by the central government on social welfare declined 7.7 percent from 1972 to 1981 because of severe economic problems. Sokolowska (1987) describes a similar situation in Poland, where the government's role in the health-care delivery system has been declining due to what she describes as the country's "economic crisis."

These examples illustrate the range of resources that can be allocated to social welfare. The provision of money, services, and trained personnel characterizes highly developed, formal social welfare systems. When these are in short supply, the human networks, caring, and expertise characteristic of informal helping systems become especially important. Formal and informal resources always coexist. What varies is the balance between them, a balance that reflects both the availability of resources and the values of the society. Without resources of some kind, either formal or informal, social welfare cannot exist, for the delivery of services requires tangible resources.

A CHALLENGE TO THE READER

One of your responsibilities as a citizen is to identify social welfare policies or programs where change is needed, and then to work for those changes however you can: by voting for candidates who support your position, participating in relevant community activities, and so on. You want to be sure to have a clear objective in mind—the creation of a specific program or the passage of a particular piece of legislation, for example. The important thing is to have reason to believe that the change sought will help meet the need for which it is intended.

Controversy about social welfare involves fundamental value conflicts about human nature and the proper relationship between society and its members. These conflicts involve competing perspectives that have been argued throughout human history and will continue to provoke argument in the future.

Our challenge to you is to understand these conflicts fully, to form your own informed positions with sensitivity, and ultimately to advocate your beliefs with courage. There is a poem that we believe speaks to this issue. We would like to share it here as a challenge to you as a human being and citizen.

Sonnet

You tell me that nothing that I do avails
to tip the scales where justice
hovers in the balance.
I never thought to guarantee I could.
But I reserve beyond dispute
my right to choose which side shall feel
the stubborn ounces
of my weight.

LET'S REVIEW

Our discussion of why social welfare is controversial in this chapter has been organized around three questions: (1) What are the conflicting values that characterize contemporary social welfare? (2) Who should be helped? (3) How should help be provided? In each case, we have seen that there are conflicting points of view. These perspectives reflect differences in values as well as varying interpretations of data related to the costs and benefits of social welfare.

In examining the controversy over who should be helped, we focused on the moral and financial impact of social welfare on individuals and society. We highlighted the different impacts of major approaches: providing services to all (the universal approach), and providing services to only the most needy (the selective approach). We also highlighted the importance of economic factors in deciding whom to help. Furthermore, we saw that, however well intended, helping sometimes has negative consequences for recipients.

Our discussion of the controversies surrounding what kind of help should be provided centered on differences related to whether consumers of social welfare services are deemed citizens or supplicants. The chapter ended with a discussion of the importance of taking informed positions on these controversial issues.

The roots of social welfare go back into antiquity. However, the services provided and the ways in which they are provided have changed considerably over the years. In the next two chapters we look at some of these changes, showing how they have had an impact on our current thinking about social welfare.

STUDY QUESTIONS

1 In the course of conversation at a party, someone you have just met expresses his opinion that there are too many "welfare cheats." How would you respond? Would you agree? Would you try to steer the conversation to some other topic? Would you present facts? Would you express your own opinion? In general, how do you think you would feel in this situation?

2 Select a social welfare benefit that you have received. (Don't forget such programs as student grants, health care, tax breaks, and so on.) On a piece of paper, make two columns, one headed "financial" and the other "moral." Then list as many of the effects as you can that the program has had on your life, separating them into financial and moral categories. For example, if you were awarded a student grant that made it unnecessary for you to work, what has been the effect on your sense of independence? Or perhaps you received the grant but continued to work so that you could buy the car you have always wanted. How has this affected you? Try to be as thoughtful and honest as you can.

3 Review the philosophy of South Side Settlement. The statement was written in 1970. What revisions might be made if the statement were drafted today?

4 Work is becoming a reality for more and more people. Try to list as many effects of this as you can. For example, as work becomes more necessary, what happens to those who cannot work, or who become unemployed? What about the family? Who will be available to provide care for children or for sick or elderly members? In what ways is work a source of problems as well as a solution to problems?

5 Write a short essay describing your position on the controversial questions, "Who should be helped?" and "How should help be provided?" Think carefully about your positions in light of the distinctions between worthy and unworthy poor, and between citizens and supplicants. Share your essay with a friend. How similar are your views? Why do you think this is the case?

6 Read the short story, "The Town Poor," by Sarah Orne Jewett (in *The Country of the Pointed Firs, and Other Stories,* Doubleday, Garden City, NY, 1956, pp. 278–289). Discuss what happened to the Bray sisters in light of the old and new paradigms, worthy and unworthy poor, and indoor and outdoor relief. Why was Mrs. Trimble upset about the fate of the Brays? In what ways does contemporary social welfare practice in the United States seem similar to or different from that described in this story set in a nineteenth-century small Maine town?

7 Social welfare is controversial both because it helps to maintain the social order and because it encourages planned change. Some people think that disadvantaged groups should be encouraged to rebel rather than to accept their current lives. Others believe that change is unnecessary and that people should be grateful for what they get. What do you think? In your opinion, what should be the role of social welfare in helping people meet their needs?

8 Use the problem of homelessness to consider the issues of societal responsibility and the problem of dependency. Specifically, address the following issues: Who are the homeless? (You can get some actual data from the 19th edition of *The Encyclopedia of Social Work.*) Who is responsible for helping the homeless? (Consider at least the homeless themselves, their families, their communities, society as a whole.) What should the homeless do in return for being helped to find shelter? What problems might result from helping the homeless? Summarize what you have learned about issues of responsibility and dependency in social welfare.

9 What do you think the objectives of social welfare ought to be? Be sure to include manifest and latent functions. Try to identify as many of your own personal values as you can that influence your view of what social welfare ought to be. Finally, think about where your values have come from. Consider your family, your religion, school and university, friends, personal experiences, and so on.

10 Think about a situation in which you helped someone. Now think of a situation in which you were helped. How did it feel to help someone? How did it feel to be helped? Why did you help the person you did? Did you feel that you had any choice? After you were helped, did you feel any sense of obligation? If so, to whom? How does this exercise help you to understand responsibility and self-reliance as a part of social welfare?

KEY TERMS AND CONCEPTS

values
philosophy
classical liberalism
neoliberalism
blaming the victim
social problem
institutional discrimination

public health approach to social welfare
strengths-based approach to social work
social reform
social inequality
social justice
conflict
residence requirement

worthy poor	outdoor relief
unworthy poor	indoor relief
universal approach to social welfare	compassion
entitlement	empathy
selective approach to social welfare	less eligibility
citizen	workfare
supplicant	

SUGGESTED READINGS

Bellah, Robert. 1985. *Habits of the Heart.* Berkeley: University of California Press. This sociological study takes an in-depth look at people's perceptions of their connections with each other and with society as a whole. The authors focus on contemporary values that affect people's willingness to take responsibility for others in their communities and in society.

Block, Fred, Richard A. Cloward, Barbara Ehrenreich, and Frances Fox Piven. 1987. *The Mean Season: The Attack on the Welfare State.* New York: Pantheon Books. A volume of progressive essays that explore the moral and financial impact of cutbacks in social welfare during the Reagan administration. A provocative counterpoint to the conservative point of view expressed by Murray (see below).

Edelman, Marian Wright. 1992. *The Measure of Our Success: A Letter to My Children and Yours.* Boston: Beacon Press. A brief, powerful book on values by the President of the Children's Defense Fund, a leading advocacy organization for children in the United States.

Heckscher, Gunnar. 1984. *The Welfare State and Beyond.* Minneapolis: University of Minnesota Press. The author uses the social welfare system of Sweden and other Scandinavian countries to explore the strengths and limitations of a universal approach to social welfare. Includes a discussion of some of the major reasons why social welfare is controversial, including its cost, impact on tax rates, implications for economic growth, effect on informal helping efforts, and potential impact on self-reliance.

Lappé, Frances Moore. 1989. *Rediscovering America's Values.* New York: Ballantine Books. The author of *Diet for a Small Planet* and several other books on hunger and poverty calls this book "a provocative dialogue for exploring our fundamental beliefs and how they offer hope for America's future." It is.

Moon, J. Donald, ed. 1988. *Responsibility, Rights, and Welfare.* Boulder, CO: Westview Press. An examination of three aspects of social welfare: the reasons for its existence, its origins, and the right to be helped. Moon provides a thoughtful and in-depth analysis of why social welfare is needed by individuals and society.

Murray, Charles. 1984. *Losing Ground: American Social Policy 1950–1980.* New York: Basic Books. A forceful expression of the conservative perspective on social welfare. Murray attempts to show how increased social welfare services are financially irresponsible, ineffective, and morally damaging.

Ryan, William. 1976. *Blaming the Victim,* rev. ed. New York: Vintage Books. A classic exposé of middle-class ideology, this powerful book explores many of the most popular myths about people in need. Ryan argues that society must take responsibility for social problems and the individual crises that they create.

REFERENCES

Alber, Jens. 1987. *The Crisis of the Welfare State.* Paper presented at the annual meeting of the American Sociological Association, Chicago, August 19.

Barker, Robert L. 1991. *The Social Work Dictionary,* 2d ed. Silver Spring, MD: National Association of Social Workers.

Bellah, Robert. 1985. *Habits of the Heart.* Berkeley: University of California Press.

Bentham, Jeremy. 1948. *An Introduction to the Principles of Morals and Legislation.* New York: Hafner.

Block, Fred, Richard A. Cloward, Barbara Ehrenreich, and Frances Fox Piven. 1987. *The Mean Season: The Attack on the Welfare State.* New York: Pantheon Books.

Brandwein, Ruth. 1994. Conversation describing her discussions with social workers from Germany at the Berlin International Conference on Social Welfare, March 5.

Domestic Policy Association. 1985. *Welfare: Who Should Be Entitled to Public Help?* Dayton, OH: The Domestic Policy Association.

Edelman, Marian Wright. 1992. *The Measure of Our Success: A Letter to My Children and Yours.* Boston: Beacon Press.

Esping-Andersen, Gosta. 1985. *Politics against Markets.* Princeton, NJ: Princeton University Press.

Friedman, Milton. 1962. *Capitalism and Freedom.* Chicago: University of Chicago Press.

————, and Rose Friedman. 1984. *Tyranny of the Status Quo.* New York: Avon.

Gilbert, Neil. 1983. *Capitalism and the Welfare State.* New Haven, CT: Yale University Press.

————. 1986. The welfare state adrift. *Social Work,* 31(4):251–256.

Gilder, George. 1981. *Wealth and Poverty.* New York: Basic Books.

Gueron, Judith, and Patricia Auspos. 1987. Workfare. In *Encyclopedia of Social Work,* 18th ed. Silver Spring, MD: National Association of Social Workers, pp. 896–900.

Hallstahammar: Financial support only if you work. 1987. *Socialnytt.* Stockholm: National Board of Health and Welfare.

Harrington, Michael. 1984. *The New American Poverty.* New York: Holt, Rinehart & Winston.

Heckscher, Gunnar. 1984. *The Welfare State and Beyond.* Minneapolis: University of Minnesota Press.

Hobbes, Thomas. 1839–1845. *The English Works of Thomas Hobbes of Malmsbury.* London: J. Bohn.

Hochschild, Jennifer. 1988. Race, class, power, and the American welfare state. In Amy Guttman, ed., *Democracy and Social Welfare.* Princeton, NJ: Princeton University Press, pp. 157–184.

Huber, Evelyn, and John D. Stephens. 1993. The Swedish welfare state at the crossroads. *Current Sweden,* 1/93:394. Stockholm: The Swedish Institute.

Jewett, Sarah Orne. 1955. The town poor. In *The Country of the Pointed Firs, and Other Stories,* Garden City, NY: Doubleday, pp. 278–289.

Kahn, Alfred J., and Sheila Kamerman. 1975. *Not for the Poor Alone.* Philadelphia: Temple University Press.

Kayal, Philip M. 1993. *Bearing Witness: Gay Men's Health Crisis and the Politics of AIDS.* Boulder, CO: Westview Press.

Kramer, Ralph. 1969. *Participation of the Poor.* Englewood Cliffs, NJ: Prentice Hall.

Lappé, Frances Moore. 1989. *Rediscovering America's Values.* New York: Ballantine Books.

Locke, John. 1960. The second treatise on civil government, in Peter Laslett, ed., *Two Treatises of Government.* Cambridge: Cambridge University Press.

Maris, Ronald W. 1988. *Social Problems.* Chicago: Dorsey Press.

Morris, Robert. 1986. *Rethinking Social Welfare.* White Plains, NY: Longman.

Murray, Charles. 1984. *Losing Ground: American Social Policy 1950–1980.* New York: Basic Books.

Ording, Jan. 1987. Interview with Mr. Ording, Head of the Division for Care of the Elderly, Economic Assistance and Social Care for Immigrants, of the National Board of Health and Welfare, February 23.

Perales, Cesar. 1983. Myths about poverty. *The New York Times,* October 26, p. A27.

Pinderhughes, Elaine. 1989. *Understanding Race, Ethnicity, and Power: The Key to Efficacy in Clinical Practice.* New York: The Free Press.

Rafferty, Terrence. 1993. Schindler's List (movie reviews). *The New Yorker,* December 20, p. 129.

Raskin, Marcus. 1986. *The Common Good: Its Politics, Policies and Philosophy.* New York: Routledge and Kegan Paul.

Ryan, William. 1976. *Blaming the Victim,* rev. ed. New York: Vintage Books.

Schorr, Alvin L. 1986. *Common Decency: Domestic Policies after Reagan.* New Haven, CT: Yale University Press.

Smith, Adam. 1982. *The Theory of Moral Sentiments.* Indianapolis, IN: Liberty Classics.

Sokolowska, Magdalena. 1987. The official health system and alternative solutions in Poland of the 80s. Paper delivered at the Annual Meetings of the American Sociological Association, Chicago, August 19.

Sowell, Thomas. 1980. *Knowledge and Decisions.* New York: Basic Books.

Swedish Institute. 1991. FS1. Fact sheets on Sweden: The Swedish Economy. Stockholm: The Swedish Institute.

———. 1993. FS35. Fact sheets on Sweden: Taxes in Sweden. Stockholm: The Swedish Institute.

Tropman, John E. 1989. *American Values and Social Welfare: Cultural Contradictions in the Welfare State.* Englewood Cliffs, NJ: Prentice Hall.

U.S. Department of Commerce, Bureau of the Census. 1993. *Statistical Abstract of the United States, 1993.* Washington, DC: U.S. Government Printing Office.

Ward, Peter. 1986. *Welfare Politics in Mexico: Papering over the Cracks.* London: Allen & Unwin.

Woolf, Henry. 1979. *Webster's New Collegiate Dictionary.* Springfield, MA: G. & C. Merriam.

Zimbalist, Sidney. 1987. A welfare state against the economic current: Sweden and the United States as contrasting cases. *International Social Work,* 30(1):15–29.

4

WHAT ARE THE HISTORICAL FOUNDATIONS OF SOCIAL WELFARE?

WHAT TO EXPECT FROM THIS CHAPTER

This chapter examines the historical development of social welfare. The approach is thematic in that the chapter focuses on four major historical themes that have shaped our thinking about social welfare and its structure: (1) the development of a sense of responsibility for others; (2) the evolution of helping roles; (3) the intellectual traditions that have shaped ideas about social welfare; and (4) the responses of society to categories of the poor. A section of the chapter is devoted to each of these four themes, and the discussion in each section is organized chronologically. In each case the objective is to examine the theme's influence on the development of social welfare.

Chapter 5 continues our historical view by focusing on how social mobilization and social reform movements have affected social welfare in the United States. Taken together, Chapters 4 and 5 give a sense of the thinking, the people, and the events that have helped to shape today's social welfare institution.

In Chapter 3, we discussed how the ideas of classical liberalism are reflected in the "old paradigm" approach to social welfare. The primary goal of this chapter is to introduce additional major ideas that have shaped the Western world's thinking about social welfare. This is an important task because those same ideas continue to influence contemporary social welfare. After reading this chapter, you should have a better understanding of the intellectual origins of the current U.S. social welfare system. This, combined with the discussion in Chapter 5 of social reform movements that have shaped social welfare in the United States, will give you an appreciation for the interplay of ideas and events in shaping the conditions of human life.

LEARNING OBJECTIVES

When you have finished studying this chapter, you should be able to:

1 List at least three social units that promote the development of a sense of responsibility for helping others.

2 Describe four intellectual currents that have influenced social welfare.

3 Identify three categories used to differentiate among the poor in the Elizabethan Poor Law of 1601, and describe the types of services provided for people in each category.

4 Briefly summarize in your own words the relationship between the themes identified in the chapter and the historical development of social welfare in the United States from 1700 until today.

The four themes discussed in this chapter have had an enduring influence on the organization of social welfare. Our concern here is with the historical development of that influence up to the present day. As we examine the first of our major themes—the development of a sense of responsibility for helping others—we trace its origins to four sources: family and kin, relationships among the wealthy and their dependents, religion, and the community.

DEVELOPING A SENSE OF RESPONSIBILITY FOR HELPING OTHERS

Family and Kin

Our first sense of responsibility for others often derives from our family experience. The development and persistence of the human family is deeply rooted in a sense of responsibility toward biologically and legally related others who require our assistance. As we have already noted, infants and children require the assistance of others. Before they can function independently, they must learn many things and perfect the skills necessary for survival. Without physical care, human infants will die, and without nurturing and social stimulation, their psychological and social potential will not be realized.

At birth the human infant has traditionally been linked most directly to its biological parents, receiving milk from its mother, and warmth, nurturing, and protection from its mother, father, and other close relatives and friends. In the structure of the traditional nuclear family unit—mother, father, and children—and in all of the family's more contemporary variations, lies one of the fundamental sources for the development of a sense of responsibility for others. In this book the concept of **family** includes *any grouping of one or more adults sharing affection, resources, residence, and responsibility for any children that may be present.* From this perspective, the adults in a family may or may not differ in gender, and may or may not be united by formal marriage.[1]

The nuclear family that is common in the United States provides a limited base for developing a sense of responsibility for helping others. During most of human history the family was a much larger unit, and in many societies today large families are far more common than they are in the United States. Large families are economically desirable in preindustrial, agricultural societies because they provide the labor necessary for the survival of the family unit. In such societies, family members of almost all age groups can contribute to family well-being—for example, they can plant and harvest, hunt, make clothes, cook, care for children, produce and sell handicrafts, or even beg.

Traditional societies often are made up of extended families, consisting of grandparents, parents, children, and other kin, all of whom often live together or near each other. Such extended family units include large numbers of people who feel some degree of responsibility for each other, and who cooperate in meeting daily needs. The essay, "On the Street in Mexico City" (see "Introduction"), illustrates the important contributions made to their family well-being by young children working as street vendors.

When kin-based groups inhabit a geographic region for a long time, they take on the characteristics of a *community*. They feel bonds toward each other and often share common beliefs, behavior patterns, and even a distinctive language. Native American nations in the United States are examples; so are ethnic neighborhoods in urban communities. These can be seen as larger units of shared responsibility that extend the notion of kin to those who share ethnic and cultural characteristics. Thus, the biologically based bond of the parent–child relationship, extended through larger family, kin, ethnic, and social networks, provides an important basis for fostering a shared sense of responsibility for helping others.

Relationships between the Wealthy and Their Dependents

Reciprocity and exchange as a basis for helping strangers, which is common in many societies, can be traced back at least as far as ancient Greece (Morris, 1986:86–99). When travel was hazardous and life in general was uncertain, aid was extended in part because the giver could imagine being in a similar situation, knowing that life itself might easily depend on being helped by a stranger.

Reciprocity and exchange also came to provide a basis for help extended by the wealthy to those on whom they depended and who were dependent in return,

[1]Traditional conceptionalization distinguished *nuclear families* consisting of married pairs of adults and their children, and *extended families* of one or more nuclear families and a network of persons related by blood or marriage. Extended families often included representatives of more than two generations. Many persons in the United States, Mexico, Sweden, and Poland have in mind the traditional conceptualization when they refer to family.

especially servants and workers. Landowners and others who depended on the efforts of their workers and slaves came to recognize that meeting the basic needs of these individuals was a responsibility, albeit one often rooted in economic and political self-interest.

The Influence of Religion and the Church

The intellectual roots of charity in the Western world can be traced back to the writings of early humanists such as Cicero and Seneca in ancient Rome. However, prescriptions about helping others were also formalized in early Western religious writings. For example, basic ideas derived from the Judeo-Christian tradition expanded the responsibility for helping to include all humanity. These include a belief in (1) the fallibility (weakness) of humans, (2) a responsibility to serve God by serving people, (3) the inability of people to judge their fellow humans appropriately, and (4) the supremacy of love over force (Keith-Lucas, 1972:140–141).

Religious beliefs about responsibility for others are important in two ways. First, they greatly expand the group for whom responsibility is felt. In many faiths, this group theoretically includes all humankind, although reality often limits the effective scope to members of the same religious affirmation. Nevertheless, a faith-based sense of responsibility goes far beyond family and kin (Klein, 1968).

THE CHARITABLE IMPULSE

Some insight into how religious beliefs have motivated people to perform charitable acts is seen in the following excerpt from Reid and Stimpson (1987:546).

[The origins of charity] may be found in the Old Testament. Toward the poor God demanded both justice—they should be given what they had been deprived of—and compassion—they should be given relief with sympathy. In the subsequent teachings of Christ and his disciples, acts of charity became expressions of the selflessness that was to characterize the brotherhood of humanity under God. The virtues of charity were joined with the necessities of survival. The first Jews and the first Christians were members of weak, impoverished, persecuted sects. Mutual assistance was a vital part of their struggle for existence. Although the Judeo-Christian concept of charity was universal and transcendental in character, to be applied to all human relations as evidence of devotion to God, the charitable efforts of Judeo-Christian sects have often reflected the historical function of providing help to those of the faith. Whether the good works were confined to particular sects or offered to the world at large, the values of charity became cornerstones of the Jewish and Christian religions.

A full-page ad entitled "Jews Don't Only Help Jews" by the American Jewish World Service gives contemporary expression to the religious basis of efforts to help others. The ad, which featured a large picture of a starving African, said in part (*The New York Times,* December 14, 1987, p. C24):

As Jews, we have known suffering too deeply, too personally, to turn away from the pain of others.

We do not see a child with eyes wide with need, with limbs shrunk by starvation, and ask the child's faith. We only ask, "How can we help?"

Second, historically religious beliefs led many religious groups to provide social welfare services. Churches and monasteries dispensed food, clothing, shelter, and even money to those in need. Convents and monasteries protected the poor and the orphaned, and provided a vehicle for wealthy people who sought opportunities to serve others. We will see later that organized religion continues today to provide a wide range of social welfare services.

The Community

The community emerged as the focus for an expanded sense of responsibility to help others because it contained many of the groups discussed above: kin, wealthy people and their dependents, and organized religious groups. The community was especially important in agricultural societies, where most people did not move very often. Thus, when England reorganized its social welfare services in the 1500s, local government parishes were given a prominent role. Government officials sought to coordinate helping efforts by religious groups and the wealthy so that the needy would be served effectively (Steinberg, 1963:280).

The community's sense of responsibility was enhanced by the effects of the **Industrial Revolution,** *the period during which machine power replaced human and animal power in the production process.* The Industrial Revolution had a dramatic effect on the sources and distribution of wealth in society. Whereas wealth had previously depended on annual feudal payments from tenants to the aristocratic owners of extensive landholdings, it now became associated with the control and ownership of the means of production, such as machines, factories, and the capital necessary to build them.

The Industrial Revolution began in England in the late 1500s and rapidly grew in importance. The large-scale application of industrial technology in the wool processing industry made the wool trade more profitable than farming (Schenk and Schenk, 1981:44). Small farmers, displaced from their traditional landholdings to make room for sheep, moved into growing industrial cities.

Although the Industrial Revolution created hardships for workers, the migrations to urban areas were advantageous for industrialists, who needed a large, low-wage workforce living near their factories to produce and also purchase their new, mass-produced goods. In the densely populated urban slums that sprang up near the factories, workers encountered problems such as disease and crime. Workers had little control over their new living and working conditions, while those to whom they could earlier have turned for help—landowners and the church—were increasingly powerless (Mencher, 1967:27). Need increased. Thus, as a consequence of the Industrial Revolution, local and later national government had to assume more responsibility for social welfare (Coll, 1969).

These changes resulted in the creation of the **Elizabethan Poor Law of 1601,** which codified a system of national standards for social welfare, and provided for administration at the local parish level. The Poor Law provided for a land tax to generate funds for social welfare services when private charity was insufficient for this purpose. This was the first such use of public funds; the Poor Law was the first formal acknowledgment in England of governmental responsibility for the well-being of its citizens.

Industrialization has been a stimulus for the passage of social welfare legislation in many nations. Two factors help to account for this. One is the growing economic capacity of industrialized nations to support social welfare programs. The second is the increased vulnerability of workers, a majority of whom are dependent on wages and live in small family units, often in urban areas. Most Western industrial societies passed significant social welfare legislation in the early part of the twentieth century, when economic capacity, evidence of human need, and progressive political ideas converged. Later legislation tended to extend earlier benefits. The dates of the major pieces of social welfare legislation in the four countries discussed in this book are listed in Table 4-1.

Today, many developing nations are undergoing their own industrial revolutions. Mexico is an example. Before the Mexican Revolution in 1910, the country was predominantly an agricultural society. The church wielded a great deal of power through its landholdings and its spiritual teachings. Following the revolution, which was in part a response to the beginnings of industrialization, the government assumed ownership of all land (Hellman, 1983). This effectively weakened the power of previous landowners, including the church. Shortly thereafter, the Constitution of 1917 transferred responsibility for many social welfare functions to the government—including the power to set a minimum wage, the

TABLE 4-1 SOCIAL WELFARE LEGISLATION IN COMPARATIVE PERSPECTIVE

Type of benefit	Year legislation enacted			
	Mexico	Poland	Sweden	United States
Old age, disability, death				
First offered	1943	1927, 1933	1913	1935
Current plan	1973, 1991	1982	1962/1976/1988	1935/1984[a]
Sickness, maternity				
First offered	1943	1920[b]	1891/1931[b]	1965/1972
Current plan	1973	1974	1962	Same[c]
Work injury				
First offered	1931	1884	1901	1908/1911
Current plan	1973	1975	1976	by 1920
Unemployment				
First offered	NA[d]	1924	1934	1935
Current plan	NA[d]	1991	1956/1973	1935

[a]Date of the most recent amendment; the 1935 law is still in effect.
[b]Medical care is essentially free; sickness benefit refers to salary payments while ill.
[c]Sickness benefits are determined primarily by employers.
[d]Mexico has a lump-sum compensation for those losing their jobs.
Source: U.S. Department of Health and Human Services. 1992. *Social Security Systems throughout the World—1991.* Washington, DC: U.S. Government Printing Office.

power to regulate working conditions, and the responsibility to provide compensation for work-related injuries.

We have seen in this section how a sense of responsibility for the well-being of others has developed and expanded over time. Starting with the family, it grew into a gradually widening web of social and economic networks responsible for the needs of their members. Thus, acceptance of responsibility for the well-being of others expanded from family to larger kin-based groups, wealthy people and their dependents, communities, and finally government. Of these, the family continues to

---

THE HUMAN FACE OF SOCIAL WELFARE 10

THE GOVERNMENT AND THE WORKPLACE

From outside, the building . . . looked as if it had been abandoned years ago. A layer of grime coated the windows and a rusting metal grate stretched across the store-front. But [the inspector] knew better. He found a battered door on the side and pushed it open.

Inside a small factory buzzed with activity. Along cluttered aisles, dozens of women hovered over sewing machines, chatting in Spanish as they furiously assembled dresses that would later be sold for $80 apiece. Near the entrance, a punch clock read 9:00 AM even though it was only 8:10. . . .

For three months, [the inspector] and seven other members of a new state task force have visited dozens of factories, looking for safety hazards and violations of the labor laws. . . .

Definitions of sweatshops vary. . . . The task force considers them to be factories that "take liberties with every law: safety, minimum wages, child labor, compensation" to "get a competitive edge". . . .

Unlike legitimate garment businesses, many of which are unionized, sweatshops frequently do not pay their workers the [1987] legal minimum wage of $3.35 an hour or overtime after 40 hours of work. The sweatshop owners also do not provide worker's compensation, health insurance or other benefits. . . .

More than 90 percent of the workers [in sweatshops] are women from Asia, the Caribbean, or Latin America. . . .

Potential fire hazards [in one shop] included an inadequate ceiling and blocked exit in the basement, poor ventilation and exposed wires touching fabric.

Laws governing the conditions under which people work are an example of government intervention to protect people from some of the dangerous effects of industrialization. Such efforts have expanded over the years to include regulations concerning the number of hours worked, minimum pay scales, and occupational safety. These laws exist because some employers cannot be trusted to assume responsibility for the welfare of their employees, even though a modern employer's responsibility toward his or her employees is thought by many to be similar to that of the wealthy toward their workers or servants in ancient times.

In 1996, the legal minimum wage was $4.25 per hour. Inflation has eroded its purchasing power. A worker in 1996 would have had to earn $5.75 per hour to equal the average purchasing power of the minimum wage during the 1970s. Full-time work at the minimum wage falls short of bringing a family of three up to the poverty line. In February 1995, President Clinton proposed raising the minimum wage by 90 cents over 2 years—to $5.15 (Shapiro, 1995). In July 1996, Congress increased the minimum wage in two steps to $4.75 initially, and to $5.15 effective July 1997.

Excerpted from Michael Freitag, "New York Is Fighting the Spread of Sweatshops," *The New York Times,* November 16, 1987, p. A1. Copyright © 1987 by The New York Times Company. Reprinted by permission.

be important, while the charity of the wealthy toward their dependents has been largely replaced by employer benefits. Most important, local, state, and national governments have now become a major source of social welfare services. We will see later why the role of government has become so important.

THE EVOLUTION OF HELPING ROLES

Informal Helping

Evolving, as it did, first out of the biological and then out of the social relationships between family and kin members, helping has been first and foremost a function performed by people in the course of their everyday activities. Rarely have those involved, be they family members, neighbors, or friends, had special training in helping others. They have simply done what seemed to be needed as best they could.

Within the family, responsibilities for helping have tended to be divided along gender lines. Broadly speaking, and with some notable exceptions, responsibility for child care and other nurturing activities has been assigned to women (Bernard, 1981:38–94). Traditionally, men have generally been responsible for providing the basic resources needed by family members—food, clothing, shelter—through hunting, fishing, farming, or paid employment in wage-based economies. There are, of course, notable exceptions to such generalizations. In much of Africa, for example, women raise most of the food for their families.

Much help has also been provided through religious groups whose representatives—priests, ministers, rabbis, and others—were trained to meet people's spiritual needs. This was a source of great comfort to many who sought solace for life's problems. However, religious training was generally limited to the use of prayer as a solution. When concrete benefits such as food, housing, and schooling were dispensed by the church, those who provided help often had little to guide them beyond their own sense of responsibility and personal experience.

The fact that early helping efforts were carried out by people with no special social welfare training does not mean that they were ineffective. Indeed, help provided by nonprofessional helpers who are motivated by caring about others is still a widespread form of assistance. Parents care for children, friends and relatives provide emotional and financial support, priests and ministers offer advice and counsel, and neighbors watch out for one another. Many of people's daily needs are met effectively by informal helpers.

Formal Helping

The emergence of formally organized social welfare services with trained workers was the result of two developments. The first was the ever-present struggle to translate limited public and private resources into the most help possible. The second development was the rise of modern science. The 1700s and 1800s saw dramatic developments in the physical sciences. The work of Isaac Newton (1642–1727) in physics, Charles Darwin (1809–1882) in biology, and G. J. Mendel (1822–1884) in genetics led to optimism about science's ability to solve social as well as physical problems. This optimism was reinforced by the successful application of scientific knowledge to industrial techniques, which made the Industrial Revolution possible.

At the heart of science lies the *scientific method,* a method advocated by Francis Bacon (1561–1626) and Newton—among others—as the most effective source of accurate knowledge about the world. The **scientific method** consists of *"principles and procedures for the systematic pursuit of knowledge involving the recognition and formulation of a problem, the collection of data through observation and experiment, and the formulation and testing of hypotheses"* (Woolf, 1979:1026–1027). The scientific method's logical and systematic approach to problem solving contrasted substantially with earlier views derived from abstract philosophical theories and religious theology. During the late 1800s, social reformers "carried forward old ideals of humanitarian reform and social justice, of social progress, but increasingly they aspired to be scientific. By this they meant secular, rational, and empirical as opposed to sectarian, sentimental, and dogmatic" (Lieby, 1978:91).

"Scientific Charity"

The result of this kind of thinking was *scientific charity* or *scientific philanthropy.* **Scientific philanthropy** was *an attempt in the United States during the late 1800s to coordinate the help provided by different social agencies within communities by collecting empirical data about individuals or families receiving assistance* (Lieby, 1978:114–115). The goals of scientific philanthropy were to avoid fostering dependency, to reduce cheating, and to prevent wasteful duplication of services. This new approach was embodied in the work of the **charity organization societies,** which originated in London and were introduced into the United States beginning in 1877.

These societies introduced a number of innovations. People seeking aid were investigated to assess the type and extent of their need. Individualized helping plans were developed based on these assessments. Directories were compiled of all the helping agencies in a community, along with a registry of families receiving aid. These last two actions were intended to reduce duplication of helping efforts (Lieby, 1978:115–116; Brieland, 1987:740). Suddenly charity was no longer based simply on the desire to do good. The charity organization societies sought to attain the scientific philanthropy goal of rational, systematic helping. In doing so, they functioned as important instruments of social control.

At first, *the people who did investigations for the charity organization societies,* called **friendly visitors,** were not given any special training. However, gradually it became clear that serious efforts to understand need and develop useful helping plans required specialized knowledge and skills. This led Mary Richmond (1861–1928), first a worker and later a leader in the charity organization society network, to provide formal training for workers in these agencies (Lieby, 1978:120–122). A summer training program inaugurated in New York in 1898 was converted into a 1-year program in 1904, and to a 2-year program in 1910.

Eventually this program became what is now the Columbia University School of Social Work (Columbia University, 1987:23).

In the process, a new profession—social work[2]—was born. Growing out of the scientific philanthropy movement, the manifest function of social work was to develop trained professionals to provide effective social welfare services to those in need. Social control of the poor was an important latent function.

Efforts to apply the scientific method to human behavior resulted in the emergence of what we now call the social and behavioral sciences. Two of these, psychology and sociology, have been particularly important to the development of social work. Community and group approaches to intervention were stimulated by sociology and social psychology, while clinical practice was heavily influenced by the work of Sigmund Freud in the early 1900s. Ongoing developments in these fields continue to be incorporated into the education and training of social welfare professionals in social work and other fields.

The Interaction of Informal and Formal Helping

While the trend toward greater reliance on formal helping is a worldwide phenomenon, there is considerable variation in the proportion of formal to informal assistance. Poland represents an interesting intermediary position in the use of formal and informal helpers (Rosner, 1976:28–31). In Poland, medical and social work personnel often work together in community health centers. While the doctors and community nurses are full-time professionals, the social workers are a combination of trained professionals and volunteers. The volunteer social workers are responsible for assessing needs in their neighborhood and bringing these to the attention of professional workers, who draw up the plans for delivering services. Even the volunteer workers, however, receive some training and have access to the specialized skills of professional social workers, lawyers, psychologists, teachers, and sociologists, who also supervise their work.

This system seeks to make maximum use of the informal networks that exist in the workplace and the community. Volunteer social workers carry out their assessments where they work and live. They are familiar with people's needs, and in many instances have the trust of those they help. Training programs provide them with a certain amount of expertise in assessing needs and available resources. The actual services are then provided by those who do have specialized expertise. We can see, in such a system, a continuum of assistance ranging from informal help provided by family and friends, to assessments carried out by partially trained volunteers, to service delivery by formally trained professionals.

Under communism, Poland's system made maximum use of limited resources and was shaped by a collective approach to social life (Madison, 1968:107–108).

---

[2]The term *social worker* was coined by Simon Patten in 1900 to include friendly visitors and residents of settlement houses. Patten and Mary Richmond hotly disputed over "whether the major role of social work should be advocacy or the delivery of individualized social services" (Barker, 1991:262).

THE HUMAN FACE OF SOCIAL WELFARE 11

SOCIAL WORKER ADVOCACY

Deciding just how far one's responsibility to clients goes and how to coordinate that responsibility with the work of other professionals is often a problem for conscientious social workers. . . .

Last fall, a young Hispanic worker came to the [out-patient medical] clinic complaining of nausea, stomach pain, and headaches. . . . [D]octors . . . at the clinic began to suspect chemicals at . . . the fabric-coating factory where he worked pouring solvents.

Doctors finally determined that the worker had a noninfectious form of hepatitis. In subsequent weeks, other . . . workers . . . complaining of similar symptoms sought treatment at the clinic . . . [and] tests showed that ten . . . had the same noninfectious hepatitis, and another 20 of the factory's approximately 50 employees showed liver damage.

[The social worker's] part in the early stages of the response to the outbreak was to provide traditional, direct services to workers and their families, helping them apply for benefits and find other employment. . . .

But she grew concerned with the direction of the follow-up with the stricken workers.

[At the factory,] empty chemical drums littered the overgrown, trash-strewn yard. The basement was crowded, poorly ventilated, hot from the ovens, with chemical odors everywhere, making some workers vomit. Workers dipped chemicals from open vats with ladles and did not have protective clothing, gloves, respirators, or training in handling dangerous substances. Some even heated their lunches in the drying ovens.

[Suggestions for improving conditions were made and accepted by the factory. The social worker felt, however] that simply working privately with [the factory] owners was not enough. She told her co-workers that the . . . workers should be informed of their right to contact federal investigators from the Occupational Safety and Health Administration (OSHA). . . .

[The social worker also contacted the union representative, who] involved OSHA officials, state Department of Environment officials, the state attorney general, the . . . mayor, the [city] Health Department, the media, and an organization of neighbors who wanted the factory shut down. . . .

Eventually, investigators found [the factory] had violated air-quality standards and hazardous waste laws, allowed improper food storage and consumption, failed to provide adequate protective equipment for workers, and failed to adequately train workers in safety procedures. [The union became active in negotiations with the firm, which resulted in substantially improved working conditions].

[The social worker] feels strongly that the social work skill of advocacy—especially in occupational social work, but in any field where people are at risk—is vital. "Social workers need to understand that without this skill, their efforts may not lead to where they want to go," she said.

This account demonstrates how professional training prepares people to tackle complex problems that involve multiple systems. First comes direct work with people—counseling, helping workers obtain financial and medical benefits, and so on. But the professional social worker goes further, identifying environmental problems, making use of the legal system, helping workers empower themselves, and working with professional colleagues in other fields. This social worker shares the human concern and desire of many volunteers to help. However, the trained social worker has knowledge and access to resources that make it possible to tackle more complex and difficult problems.

Today, as we have seen, Poland's social welfare system is in transition. Developing nations such as Mexico have limited resources available for public social welfare programs and tend to rely more heavily on informal, family-centered helping than do the more highly industrialized Western welfare states.

In summary, all societies rely on informal helping provided by the family, friendship networks, and the community. In addition, the industrialized societies have developed extensive formal helping networks staffed by social workers, educators, medical personnel, and others. In between are the societies whose resource limitations and values have led them to make maximum use of informal helping as a supplement to their more limited formal social welfare programs.

INTELLECTUAL CURRENTS

As we have seen, social welfare is very much affected by prevailing ideas. An emphasis on helping others has been common to all major religions, for example. Similarly, the rise of science led not only to the Industrial Revolution that altered social life and human needs, but to a scientific approach to solving human problems. Social welfare is influenced by intellectual currents because it is so closely tied to the other institutions of society. Ideas and values that arise in these other institutional areas inevitably affect thinking about social welfare. In Chapter 3 we discussed the origins in classical liberalism of the old paradigm for providing social welfare. Now we summarize some of the other important intellectual currents in Western society that have had a lasting impact on social welfare.

Protestantism

The rise of organized religion and the charitable activities it supported provided a foundation for helping efforts. By the late 1400s, however, the dominant Roman Catholic Church had developed a powerful hierarchical structure that was often rigid, authoritarian, corrupt, and intolerant. This led to two intellectual responses: Protestantism and humanism.

The first response was Martin Luther's (1483–1546) successful theological challenge, which culminated in the **Protestant Reformation.** Protestants objected to Catholic doctrine that placed the clergy in the role of intermediary between God and humankind. They argued, instead, for a direct relationship between the individual and God, thus eliminating the need for much of the ritual and structure of the Roman Catholic Church. Although Protestants favored charity, they also placed great emphasis on the value of work and, in at least some instances, tended to view economic success as an indication of personal salvation (Morris, 1986:123).

This association of economic success with salvation was especially important to two Protestant groups, the Calvinists and the Puritans. Often persecuted in Europe because of their unorthodox religious and political views and their outspoken rejection of many popular forms of pleasure and relaxation, many members of these and other Protestant groups fled to North America during the seventeenth century and established their religious faith here (Macarov, 1978:201–202). Their beliefs helped to create what came to be called the **Protestant ethic,** *the belief, based in Protestant religious values, that work fulfills God's will and that those who do not work are sinners.*

The Protestant ethic was well suited to a developing nation such as the United States. Much hard work was needed to settle and develop the land. Living conditions were not easy, and resources were scarce. A doctrine that urged people to work, and that provided a rationale for denying aid to those who were unwilling to do so, was well suited to the social environment. The ideology of the Protestant ethic, combined with the English roots of many of the original settlers, led to the widespread adoption in the colonies of social welfare legislation derived from the Elizabethan Poor Law of 1601. The principles embodied in those laws—the emphasis on work, and the establishment of categories to determine who should be helped—became the policy of the new nation. In addition, the Protestant work ethic became part of a societal tradition that soon took on a life of its own. Today, the work ethic is no longer linked to a particular set of religious beliefs.

As we noted in Chapter 3, the equating of work with salvation was a restraining influence on social welfare. Early legislation was designed to provide aid primarily to worthy persons whose reasons for needing assistance were obviously beyond their control. The proper balance between work and social welfare remains a major issue in the United States today.

Humanism

The second intellectual reaction against Roman Catholicism was **humanism.** Humanist philosophers *disputed the literal interpretation of the Bible and advocated a more just and equal world based on reason rather than church teachings.* Two of the more influential of these were the English philosopher John Locke (1632–1704) and Jean Jacques Rousseau (1712–1778) of France. Locke, Rousseau, and others argued that society was based on a *social contract,* an implicit agreement to establish a form of government and a social structure designed to serve the common needs of all members of society.

Such an argument challenged the unbridled power of the aristocracy and the church by asserting the equality of all human beings, and the obligation of the leaders of society to protect and enhance the lives of the common people (Locke, 1690; Rousseau, 1762). The views of these "contract philosophers" played an important role in the great democratic revolutions in France and the United States in the eighteenth century and reinforced the belief that government has an obligation to help its citizens.

The humanists had a dual impact on social welfare. First, their thinking was inherently supportive of the idea of helping. The idea that government had an obligation to provide help laid the foundation for what we now call welfare states. The humanist analysis of the social causes of human need provided a basis for aid that to some extent countered the emphasis of the Protestant ethic on work and self-reliance. Both humanism and the Protestant ethic have become part of the intellectual tradition of modern Western society. Much of the controversy over social welfare reflects these dual and inconsistent parts of our culture.

The second way in which humanism influenced social welfare was by laying the groundwork for what we now call scientific thinking. As long as church doctrine could not be questioned, it was impossible for people to promote ideas, even those based on empirical analysis, that contradicted the teachings of the Church. For example, Galileo's view that the earth was not the center of the solar system directly challenged church-approved doctrine. Galileo was condemned by church officials and was prevented from continuing his research (Redondi, 1987). Through their advocacy of empirical study, humanists made possible the scientific study of human and social life, and had a powerful impact on social welfare.

Applications of the Scientific Method

With the new scientific approach to the study of social life came several developments that proved to be especially significant for social welfare.

The first of these came in the emerging field of economics, when a Scottish social philosopher, Adam Smith (1723–1790), advanced the idea that the most efficient and productive system was one based on **laissez faire economics,** *the doctrine that an efficient and productive economy is best achieved by minimizing governmental intervention in economic activities* (Smith, 1776). Smith's views, which in due course became the cornerstone of classical economics, were highly compatible with the Protestant ethic. Both placed a great emphasis on the value of work and economic success. Remember, however, that Smith's theory also contained the seeds of the new paradigm for the provision of social welfare.

In the period following the American Revolution, *laissez faire* provided a basis for an attack on the poor laws. Classical economists argued that taxing the wealthy for the benefit of the poor was immoral—a violation of the "natural right" to accumulate property and wealth. A watershed shift in public attitudes toward the poor occurred. Need was no longer seen as a result of misfortune for which society should assume responsibility; destitution was assumed to be the fault of individuals. The philosophy of victim blaming was alive and well.

Public assistance for the able-bodied was ended. Assistance to all categories of the poor outside institutions was cut indiscriminately. The principle of **less eligibility**, *the belief that those receiving assistance should live less well than the lowest-paid self-supporting laborer,* received broad public support. In short, life for the poor was to be made so miserable that nobody would choose public assistance over work (Trattner, 1994:50–55).

The work of Robert Malthus (1766–1834), another early economist, also called the usefulness of social welfare into question. Using mathematical techniques to estimate world population trends and food production capacity, Malthus concluded that population growth would inevitably outstrip the earth's ability to produce food. Given this, the most important problem facing society, according to Malthus, was finding ways to limit world population. The only alternative was global starvation.

Malthus's ideas were reinforced by the work of Charles Darwin (1809–1882). Darwin, a biologist, popularized the theory of evolution, which held that life, rather than having originated with the creation of Adam and Eve by God, had instead evolved through natural processes. From this perspective, the driving mechanism of evolution was the **survival of the fittest,** *Darwin's label for the mechanism whereby the strongest members of a species are the ones most likely to survive, to breed, and to pass on their genetic traits to future generations.* In this manner, the weaker members of the species, Darwin contended, are gradually replaced by the stronger—those more suited to their environment—thereby strengthening the species as a whole.

Darwin's ideas were based on research with plants and animals, but they were applied to human society by Herbert Spencer (1820–1903), an English philosopher. Spencer popularized what came to be known as **social Darwinism,** *the belief that Darwin's principle of the survival of the fittest applied to humans as well as other species* (Schenk and Schenk, 1981:11–12). Social Darwinists argued against help for the needy. Those in need were seen as weak. Social Darwinists argued that it was right, and natural, that the weak should perish while the strong survived. Helping the weak would only drain society's resources and weaken the human species as a whole. Furthermore, governmental intervention on behalf of the poor could only result in a less efficient economic system. While there had always been controversy about the role of social welfare, the coming together of the Protestant ethic, laissez faire economics, Malthusian ideas about population growth, and social Darwinism provided a formidable intellectual challenge to social welfare. Although these ideas were later modified or rejected as inaccurate, they heavily influenced the thinking of their time and continue even today to fuel criticism of the social welfare institution.

Intellectual support for social welfare, however, also came from a variety of sources. These included religious teachings in opposition to those of the Protestant ethic, socialism, and the developing social sciences.

It is important to note that the emphasis of the Protestant ethic on work and self-reliance is not without contradiction in Christian doctrine. The Christian premise of universal brotherhood under God, Jesus's repeated call to give up one's worldly possessions in order to be his true follower, and parables such as that of the Good Samaritan, represent opposing points of view that support the provision of social welfare to those in need.

Socialism

A third important intellectual current that has had a major impact on the development of social welfare is *socialism.* **Socialism** is *an economic philosophy that advocates "a system of social organization in which private property and the distribution of income are subject to social control, rather than [solely] to determination of individuals pursuing their own interests or by the market forces of capitalism"* (*New Encyclopedia Britannica,* 1992, 10:926). Socialism emerged as a reaction to the injustices, inequalities, and suffering that accompanied capitalism and the free market in the wake of the Industrial Revolution. Although socialism has taken many forms, socialists agree that all citizens should be assured at least "minimum levels of housing, clothing, and nourishment as well as free access to essential services such as education, health, transportation, and recreation" (*New Encyclopedia Britannica,* 1992, 27:442).

The earliest modern-day socialists were romantic idealists who advocated peaceful, gradual transition to socialist society by establishing small, experimental cooperative communities in which people would voluntarily work, share, and live joyfully together (Berki, 1991:19). Numerous utopian communities—Brook Farm; the Oneida Community; New Harmony, Indiana; Shaker communities, for example—were founded in the United States, flourished for varying periods of time, but disappeared without transforming society. Two other varieties of socialism—Marxism and democratic socialism—however, have had lasting effects on contemporary social welfare institutions.

In 1848, the highwater of socialist mass movements in Europe, two Germans, Karl Marx (1818–1883) and Friedrich Engels (1820–1895), published the ***Communist Manifesto,*** a document that claimed to demonstrate through "scientific socialism" the historical inevitability of working-class victory over capitalism. Marx argued that, in order to make a profit, capitalist employers had to extract "surplus value" from their employees, exploiting and reducing them to "wage slavery." The modern state, he argued, exists to meet the needs of the capitalist class. Capitalism would be overthrown when increasing worker "class consciousness" resulted in revolution (Berki, 1991:20; *New Encyclopedia Britannica,* 1992, 10:926; Streeten, 1992).

Marxism, the ideology based on the works of Marx and Engels, inspired revolutionary movements in Russia, China, and many parts of the developing world. Fear of Marxist socialism in the United States contributed to enactment of the social welfare programs of the New Deal as a counter to the appeal of socialism. Following World War II (in which the United States and communist Russia had been allied against fascism), Cold War military expenditures helped limit the expansion of social welfare programs in the United States. The ideas of Marxist socialism played a central role, of course, in the development of the Polish social welfare institution while Poland was a satellite state of the Soviet Union.

Democratic socialism, the belief that the transition to socialism can be achieved peacefully, through legislated reforms, without resorting to revolutionary violence, has played a greater role than Marxist socialism in shaping the modern welfare state. Democratic socialists stress that civil rights must be safeguarded and contend that without freedom there cannot be socialism. Sweden, Denmark, and Great Britain are examples of countries in which democratically elected socialists have shaped the social welfare state and developed universal minimum standards of living. Throughout the world, socialist ideals have influenced the ways in which nations respond to human need (Laidler and Henri, 1992).

It is important to avoid the error of equating specific economic systems with specific political systems. Democracy as a form of political organization is not owned exclusively by capitalist economies. It is equally possible to have either capitalist or socialist economies in political democracies. It is also possible to have totalitarian governments that are either capitalist or socialist. Most countries today have made choices—often influenced by socialist ideas of fairness and justice—to mitigate the impact of unrestrained, free-market capitalism on their people. As we saw in Chapter 3, the choices we make are influenced by our values, the ideas we hold about the kind of world in which we want to live.

The Social Sciences

Socialists are by no means the only thinkers who have attempted to understand society through scientific reasoning. A successful application of scientific methodology to the study of individual and social life came in medicine. Illness, it became clear, was much influenced by the environment. Next, the work of sociologists such as Charles Horton Cooley (1864–1929) and George Herbert Mead (1863–1931) showed how much individuals are affected by their interactions with others. Their findings were supported and extended by the work of other sociologists during the first half of the 1900s, who demonstrated how much social life is influenced by community structures. Subsequent sociological research provided evidence of the magnitude of income differentials within society and the links between the living conditions of the poor and such problems as illness, family breakdown, and crime (Zimbalist, 1977:73–175).

The intellectual work of Sigmund Freud (1856–1939) had a striking effect on social welfare. Freud's theory of psychoanalysis greatly increased people's awareness of the complex factors that influence individual growth and development (Brenner, 1957). Freud also speculated about the nature of organized social life. Although he recognized that social organization is essential to individual well-being, he believed that interaction between social organizations and people results in stresses and limitations on individual behavior that can be harmful to people's psychological health (Freud, 1962). The work of Freud and his successors helped to expand the domain of social welfare to include many levels and areas of psychological functioning that had previously been poorly understood and for which few services were available. The overemphasis of many Freudians on internal, individual roots of human need also contributed in the United States to the ideology of victim blaming.

The use of scientific methods to research fundamental issues about who should be helped and how help should be provided has not resolved the debate between those who believe that society should provide more programs for people in need and those who believe that society's role should be minimized. As we saw in Chapter 3, the major reason for this lack of resolution is the differing values out of which the dialogue grows. Those who believe that social welfare helps people, do research to prove their point, and those who believe the opposite do the same. The results are rarely conclusive. In addition, the social and behavioral sciences most relevant to social welfare—particularly sociology, psychology, and economics—are still young. Their theories and research findings are often incomplete and subject to multiple interpretations.

Whatever their limitations and ambiguities, history shows that the currents of intellectual discourse in a society affect its social welfare system. Values are particularly important and have often had a far greater impact on social decision making than research findings or data. A working knowledge of the effectiveness of birth-control devices, for example, becomes useful only if one believes that practicing birth control is acceptable behavior. Further, values often influence the type of data collected and its interpretation. The struggle between values and data will undoubtedly continue to influence social welfare in the years to come. No matter how good the quality and extensive the scope of our data may become, the uses to which it is put, and the interpretations we reach, will always be influenced by our values.

SOCIETAL RESPONSES TO CATEGORIES OF THE POOR

Deciding Who Should Be Helped

Most societies have developed categories to sort people into groups to which help should or should not be offered. Often, even those considered worthy of help have been further subdivided into groups eligible for different kinds of help. There are two major reasons why categorizing the needy has been popular. First is the widely held intuitive belief that indiscriminant help is neither desirable nor practical. From this perspective, people should be self-reliant wherever possible in order to promote individual well-being and social prosperity.

Second is the recognition that resources are limited, and efficient distribution is needed. Categorization of the needy establishes a hierarchy of need, assuring the most effective use of resources by providing help for those whose needs are greatest. During the early stages of industrialization, for example, many people are displaced from their homes, work in unsafe or unhealthy factories, or find themselves unemployed—and thus in need—while the resources available for social welfare are limited. In such circumstances, limiting social welfare to the most needy is seen to be morally responsible and economically prudent.

Because we continue to categorize the poor today, it is useful to see how this process has developed historically. Over time, our knowledge of human behavior and how it is affected by environmental factors have modified the types of categories employed. Initially, under the old paradigm, only the most obvious misfortunes—illness and extreme age, for example—were considered to be grounds for unqualified help. Gradually, as the new paradigm has emerged, other sources of need—such as mental illness and illiteracy, single parenthood, family violence, or political refugee status—have become accepted as qualifications for receiving help. Slowly, there has been an increasing willingness to respond to the needs arising in predictable life-span transitions and crises. (See Medical Care in Sweden, Chapter 7.)

Early Categorizing Efforts and the Elizabethan Poor Law of 1601

The roots of categorizing are ancient. In Greek and Roman times, people who fell into need through no fault of their own were considered most worthy of assistance. This theme has endured through the ages. Those who suffer misfortune in spite of their best efforts to succeed have always been viewed more favorably than those who are seen as improvident or otherwise the cause of their own problems (Morris, 1986:88–98).

The *Elizabethan Poor Law of 1601* is often regarded as a major milestone in social welfare legislation. It was the result of 200 years of attempts by the state to control aid to the poor. The Poor Law provided for the right to assistance to those in need; ensured that relief would be provided at the lowest possible level of local government; established local overseers of the poor; encouraged private philanthropy in the form of free schools, hospitals, and almshouses, and other institutions to complement public efforts; and laid the foundation for the assistance and social control functions of social welfare by providing differential treatments for categories of dependency (Trattner, 1994:1–11; Reid, 1995). The needy were divided into three categories: the *helpless,* the *involuntarily unemployed,* and *vagrants* (Federico, 1983:95).

The *helpless* were those with a disabling condition over which they had no control. This has always been the easiest group to accept as deserving and includes the ill, those with severe mental or physical limitations, the disabled, the orphaned, and the frail elderly. The *involuntarily unemployed* were those who had suffered some kind of misfortune. These people were thought to bear some responsibility for their problems and thus were considered less worthy than the helpless. They included people who had been robbed, single mothers, families with many children, victims of fires, and those who had lost their jobs. *Vagrants* with no roots in the community were not considered to be the responsibility of the community and usually were not eligible for assistance. Instead, they were forced to return to their place of origin. What we see, then, is a progression from those considered to have no responsibility for their condition to those thought to be able to care for themselves if they wished to do so.

The type of assistance provided under the Elizabethan Poor Law varied by category of need. The more worthy one was considered, the less onerous was the social control to which one was subjected. Four types of services were provided: *outdoor relief* in one's own home, and *indoor relief* in three increasingly punitive types of institutions—almshouses, workhouses, and houses of correction (Leonard, 1965:137).

The poor considered most worthy were cared for in two ways. Those who were capable of living independently received outdoor relief consisting of financial aid, medical care, and other personal-care services while living in their own homes. The worthy poor who could not care for themselves were housed in **almshouses,** *institutional shelters in which spartan care to destitute individuals and families was provided* (Barker, 1991:10). In almshouses, people had a bed, food, and minimal physical care; little was provided beyond the basics. Most people preferred outdoor relief because it was less disruptive to their lives and less stigmatizing than being in an almshouse. By the twentieth century, almshouses had largely been replaced by home-based outdoor relief.

The involuntarily unemployed were sent to **workhouses,** *institutional residences in which government contracted with private individuals to feed and house* *the involuntarily unemployed in exchange for the work they could do.* Workhouses sheltered "infants, children, older and disabled people, and diseased as well as able-bodied adults" (Barker, 1991:252). Although considered worthy of aid, the involuntarily unemployed were expected to earn their assistance in the workhouse. They lived and worked in communal quarters that offered little privacy and few comforts, but in which food, clothing, and other necessities were provided. Because they were considered partially responsible for their condition, they were expected to work toward becoming independent. Additional incentive to do so was provided by the stigma associated with living in a workhouse.

The worst stigma and the most severe degree of social control was reserved for those who were committed to **houses of correction,** *residential institutions that housed criminals, vagrants, workhouse residents who violated the rules, and other persons deemed unworthy.* Living conditions in the houses of correction were primitive, and abuse was common. Houses of correction represented society's most controlling response to need, and were designed to punish those considered unworthy of humanitarian aid.

Crowding, lack of sanitation, substandard medical care, and poor nutrition resulted in high rates of sickness and mortality in almshouses, workhouses, and houses of correction.

The Elizabethan Poor Law also formalized a system of child welfare called *indenture.* **Indenture** involved *placement of orphans and children who had been removed from needy, therefore "unsuitable," families into the homes of "proper" people who agreed to provide care in return for the child's work.* In 1601, when the law was passed, child labor was widely practiced. Families that "could not maintain financial independence" were considered economically and morally dangerous, unable "by example, precept, or education to be expected to prepare the young for adult, independent living." Therefore, in the thinking of the times, it made sense to place their children with families that could provide what was considered a wholesome family environment (Axinn and Levin, 1992:13–15).

The Elizabethan Poor Law categorization of the needy and differentiation of services based on category was readily adopted in the American colonies because it was part of their English heritage and because it served colonists' needs for social control (Axinn and Levin, 1982:16–24). The colonies provided public assistance through public taxation. Treatment varied according to the "worthiness" of the dependent. Neighbors were treated better than were strangers. Medical care was frequently paid for by the town. Sometimes taxes were reduced or outdoor relief was provided; often the worthy poor were "auctioned off" to be cared for by the lowest bidder. To control the influx of those in need, residency requirements were established as a condition of eligibility for relief. Strangers who were deemed likely to become dependent were "warned away" or removed forcibly by law enforcement officials. For example, in Boston, poor Irish immigrants arriving by ship in 1719 were refused permission to disembark. (Consider the similar plight of Haitian and Cuban refugees in the 1990s.) Impoverished casualties of the frontier Indian wars also were turned away. The able-bodied unemployed were "bound out as indentured servants, whipped and run out of town, or put in jail." When such efforts at social control failed to stem rising need, the towns turned to the states for financial assistance (Trattner, 1994: 16–23).

The early colonists struggled to survive, American churches were not wealthy, and there was a scarcity of labor. Distinguishing between the truly helpless and those able to help themselves was functional for society. Further, providing help primarily at the community level made sense in a society without a strong national government.

The Use of Indoor and Outdoor Relief Today

The debate over the relative merits of outdoor and indoor relief emerged at a very early point (Axinn and Levin, 1992:48). Those who believed that outdoor relief was too expensive favored the use of indoor relief. The underlying assumption is that it is less expensive to serve supplicants in one location (such as an almshouse) than it is to provide services in their own homes.

Those favoring outdoor relief, however, pointed out that indoor relief isolated the needy from the community and created communal living conditions that could weaken families, promote illness, and foster violence and abuse. Outdoor relief was more consistent with citizens' rights of membership. It was less disruptive to established life patterns, even if it did not necessarily avoid such problems as unhealthy living conditions and abuse.

Although current thinking tends to view outdoor relief as more effective, more humane, and less costly (Dear and Wolch, 1987:61–68), many services continue to be provided in residential settings. Mental hospitals, treatment centers for delinquent or disabled youths, and prisons are still important elements in social welfare systems throughout the world. The appropriate balance between these two approaches remains an open question.

The policy of *deinstitutionalization* reflects contemporary ambivalence about the indoor and outdoor approaches. **Deinstitutionalization** is *the practice of releasing people from residential institutions and placing them in the community, where help can be provided in less restrictive ways through the use of community support systems.*

Deinstitutionalization is controversial when it is not linked effectively to community support systems. For example, it has been considered a significant cause of homelessness when "a steamroller policy of deinstitutionalization occurred without prior development of community-based service systems or proper preparation of communities that were expected to receive and support the flood of clients. . . . [As a result, clients] were left to fend for themselves in the community" (Dear and Wolch, 1987:65).

The *halfway house* is a community support system through which supervision and counseling are provided to help individuals readjust to independent living. **Halfway houses** are *small residential facilities that provide treatment and supervision while at the same time allowing clients to be at least partially integrated into community life.* Halfway houses have two principal uses. They shelter those who are able to function in the community but cannot, for whatever reason, live either with their own families or independently. Such persons include youths with relatively minor behavior problems, those with mild physical or mental limitations, abused or neglected people, and those struggling with substance abuse or other addictions that are not so severe as to be life-threatening. The halfway house provides help and support while enabling residents to participate in community life. Halfway houses are also used as an intermediary step between institutions, such as prisons or mental hospitals, and independent life in the community.

Plans to establish halfway houses frequently generate controversy. Persons who fear that residents of the facilities may be dangerous or that the presence of a halfway house may cause property values to fall may respond with a "nimby" (not-in-my-back-yard) attitude. (See The Human Face of Social Welfare 12: Not in My Back Yard.)

THE HUMAN FACE OF SOCIAL WELFARE 12

NOT IN MY BACK YARD

The homeless, elderly and mentally ill people who have gathered for years at the only soup kitchen in this seaside city may find soon that there is no such thing as a free lunch.

Five days a week for the last decade, the Long Beach Food and Friendship Inn has been serving meals at noon to the poor of this city of 34,000. But now that a local church has refused to renew its lease . . . the kitchen itself has joined the ranks of the homeless.

So today, the volunteers who run the kitchen took their tables, brown bags filled with sandwiches and ladles to dole out the minestrone to . . . a square in front of City Hall, where they continue feeding their clients in the open air.

The operators of the soup kitchen say their plight reflects the desire of officials and many residents to be rid of the 80 or so who come to the kitchen, a troubled group burdened by many problems and illnesses, from unemployment and alcoholism to drug addiction and schizophrenia. The kitchen's very presence, they say, may offend those who like to think that Long Beach, a racially mixed city of oceanfront cottages and condominiums, does not really have big city problems.

"The city wants us to go," Carey Friedman, chairwoman of the kitchen's board of directors, said as she stood in the square, watching volunteers hand out the cups of soup and ham-and-cheese sandwiches. "What they're basically telling us is, take a leap."

But Long Beach officials say they have not turned their backs on the soup kitchen, maintaining that in the past they were instrumental in finding it new quarters. Still, City Manager Edwin Eaton acknowledged that this time, finding the kitchen a home will be more difficult, because other churches and organizations in the city appear reluctant to help.

"I think that while everybody realizes the work they do is essential and needed, the prevailing attitude is 'We need to help people, fine, but not in my backyard,'" Mr. Eaton said. "We've reached out to any number of groups, but no one is interested."

Officials of the Food and Friendship Inn . . . had been negotiating to buy a Jewish War Veterans building in the west end of the city, . . . with a grant from the Federal Department of Housing and Urban Development.

The deal was scuttled . . . when city officials refused to support it. . . .

Mr. Eaton said that he indeed was involved in preliminary discussions with the soup kitchen's board about the site, but that the city had backed off from endorsing the deal when people who live near the building objected.

"I heard from a number of residents from around that block who advised me in no uncertain terms that they had heard what was taking

We can see how, nearly 400 years after the Poor Law created them, the concepts of indoor and outdoor relief remain with us as strategies for helping and social control. As with any social welfare strategy, effectiveness depends on the values on which the strategies are based, the ways in which they are implemented, and the resources that are made available.

Decisions about the most effective helping strategies inevitably return us to the issue of resources. How should we calculate the cost effectiveness of services? It may be cheaper to treat the mentally ill in the community rather than in mental hospitals. However, the stress of independent living may generate additional problems for the mentally ill and thus create community problems as well. The money saved by providing treatment in the community, therefore, must be balanced against the added costs of potential associated problems such as homelessness or violence. In addition, approaches to social welfare that

---

place and were adamantly opposed to it," Mr. Eaton said. "This is smack dab in the middle of a residential neighborhood. We made a judgment that the location of a soup kitchen would be inappropriate.". . .

The struggle to find a home for the kitchen has left its rotating staff of 80 volunteers demoralized and those who have come to depend on the food, anxious. Many of them said it was not just a hot meal they looked forward to, but the camaraderie at the tables that drew them day after day.

The difficulty faced by the Long Beach Food and Friendship Inn in its search for a home is typical of the conflict which often accompanies attempts to find locations for shelters for the homeless, halfway houses and other facilities for persons who are perceived as supplicants rather than citizens. We do not know if similar conflict accompanied the original siting of the Jewish War Veterans building in Long Beach. However, veterans are more likely to be treated as citizens than are the poor and homeless.

Although the soup kitchen paid the church about $10,000 per year to use its kitchen and dining room for 3 hours per day, the presence of the soup kitchen would cause wear and tear on the church facilities. It is possible, too, that the soup kitchen was perceived initially as a temporary, emergency measure for which need would disappear. When the social conditions that result in the need for private pro-

grams such as the soup kitchen were not addressed successfully, church members may have begun to experience "compassion fatigue." As a volunteer at a similar facility once put it to me [Bill Whitaker], "We didn't know this was going to be a life sentence." Such responses are becoming more and more common. They underscore the importance of working to influence public policies that can prevent—not just patch up—social problems.

This vignette also shows the close connection between the private and public sectors in the provision of social welfare. In this case more than 80 volunteers operated a private program for the poor in a private church. In all likelihood, some of the food they prepared for distribution was provided by The Emergency Food Assistance Program (TEFAP), a federal public program that purchases surplus food commodities and distributes them for use in programs serving the poor. In its attempt to purchase the Jewish War Veteran's building, the soup kitchen board hoped, also, to receive Community Development Block Grant funding from the federal Department of Housing and Urban Development. The attempt was blocked by the opposition of the Long Beach city government, another public organization.

Excerpted from Peter Marks, "Evicted Soup Kitchen Seeks a New Home," *The New York Times,* May 3, 1994, p. B5. Copyright © 1994 by the New York Times Company. Reprinted by permission.

address immediate needs without proper regard for long-term consequences may be less costly in the short run but more costly over the long haul. It is easy to see that a homeless person needs shelter and to provide it. But unless the forces that make that person homeless are addressed, the problem is likely to recur and worsen.

LET'S REVIEW

This chapter examines four important recurring themes that have shaped the historical development of social welfare: (1) developing a sense of responsibility for others, (2) the evolution of helping roles, (3) intellectual currents, and (4) societal responses to categories of the poor. Although our views about helping have ancient roots in the biological nature of human beings and the traditional religious injunction to be charitable, we have seen that the Industrial Revolution had a major impact on social welfare. The social changes brought by the Industrial Revolution affected people's needs, the ability of existing social structures to meet needs, and the application of scientific thinking to social welfare policies and processes.

Categorizing the poor to determine who should receive help has a long history. These categories reflect dominant social beliefs about the importance of personal responsibility and self-reliance through work. Many of our current programs and policies have their intellectual origins in the Elizabethan Poor Law of 1601, and feature eligibility requirements based on a continuing belief that those thought to be responsible for their own predicament should receive less assistance.

Other, and gradually less punitive, alternatives to categorizing the poor as a basis for allocating social welfare have emerged. Today, social values and available resources continue to influence our definition of needs. As the new paradigm for provision of social welfare has emerged, we can see in many societies a general movement toward outdoor relief coupled with less restrictive and less punitive definitions of who is needy. In part, this reflects the greater affluence of industrialized nations, an affluence that enables them to afford more services. It seems likely, however, that the widespread practice of categorizing the poor, which has endured for hundreds of years, will persist.

In Chapter 5 we consider social reform efforts that have influenced the development of social welfare in the United States. In many instances the events and circumstances to which reformers have responded also altered the dominant intellectual ideas of their eras; the interplay among events, ideas, and the struggle for a better society never ends.

STUDY QUESTIONS

1 Read about the 1994 proposal of the Clinton administration "to end welfare as we know it" and the 1995 Republican "Personal Responsibility Act." How did conflicting values, expressed by proponents and opponents of the welfare reform proposals, relate to the Poor Law concepts and the intellectual currents discussed in this chapter?

2 Do you think that highly industrial nations such as the United States can coexist peacefully with the much poorer and less industrially developed nations of the Third

World? In answering this question, try focusing on the kinds of needs that people have in each type of society, and the society's ability to meet them. To shed light on the differences between industrial and preindustrial societies, you might want to use Mexico as an example of a society in the midst of industrialization.

3 In what ways does the United States still categorize the poor in a manner similar to Elizabethan Poor Law practice? Try to focus on the thinking underlying these categories rather than the actual form each took. For example, we do not have work-houses, but we do have sheltered workshops for those with physical and mental limitations and "workfare" for welfare mothers.

4 Ask some social welfare professionals what contemporary ideas or theories they believe are having the greatest impact on social welfare. Ask them to explain their views. Then go to the library and look up the ideas in the *Encyclopedia of Social Work*.

5 Scan the chronological history of social welfare in the *Encyclopedia of Social Work*. You will find this a useful supplement to the material in this chapter and Chapter 5. What intellectual currents, events, or legislation would you like to know more about?

KEY TERMS AND CONCEPTS

family
Industrial Revolution
Elizabethan Poor Law of 1601
scientific method
scientific philanthropy
charity organization society
friendly visitors
Protestant Reformation
Protestant ethic
humanism
social contract
laissez faire economics

survival of the fittest
social Darwinism
socialism
Communist Manifesto
Marxism
democratic socialism
almshouses
workhouses
houses of correction
indenture
deinstitutionalization
halfway houses

SUGGESTED READINGS

Axinn, June, and Herman Levin. 1992. *Social Welfare: A History of the American Response to Need,* 3d ed. White Plains, NY: Longman. This is an excellent history of social welfare, focusing on the United States. It uses a chronological approach and includes excerpts from actual historical documents.

Forsberg, Mats. 1986. *The Evolution of Social Welfare Policy in Sweden.* Stockholm: The Swedish Institute. This small book provides interesting insight into the ideas and events that have influenced the development of social welfare in Sweden.

Fraser, Sara. 1986. *Tildy: Poorhouse Woman.* London: Futura Publications. A light novel that depicts life in an 1821 English poorhouse. A clear portrayal of the social control functions of the Poor Law system.

Morris, Robert. 1986. *Rethinking Social Welfare: Why Care for the Stranger?* White Plains, NY: Longman. An analysis of social welfare that combines a historical approach with an examination of philosophical underpinnings. Particularly strong on social welfare in ancient societies. Includes a stimulating discussion of contemporary social welfare issues and their significance.

Wilensky, Harold, and Charles Lebeaux. 1965. *Industrial Society and Social Welfare.* New York: The Free Press. A classic work. Parts One and Two are especially recommended for their thorough analysis of the impact of industrialization on social life and human need. Discusses, with insight and passion, the social welfare needs of societies struggling with the demands of industrialization.

REFERENCES

Axinn, June, and Herman Levin. 1992. *Social Welfare: A History of the American Response to Need,* 3d ed. White Plains, NY: Longman.

Barker, Robert L. 1991. *The Social Work Dictionary,* 2d ed. Washington, DC: National Association of Social Workers.

Berki, R. N. 1991. Socialism. In *Academic American Encyclopedia,* vol. 10. Danbury, CT: Grolier, pp. 19–24.

Bernard, Jessie. 1981. *The Female World.* New York: Free Press.

Brenner, Charles. 1957. *An Elementary Textbook of Psychoanalysis.* New York: Anchor Books.

Brieland, Donald. 1987. History and evolution of social work practice. In *The Encyclopedia of Social Work,* 18th ed., Silver Spring, MD: National Association of Social Workers, pp. 739–754.

Coll, Blanche. 1969. *Perspectives in Public Welfare.* Washington, DC: U.S. Government Printing Office.

Columbia University. 1987. *Columbia University Bulletin.* New York: Columbia University School of Social Work.

Dear, Michael, and Jennifer Wolch. 1987. *Landscapes of Despair: From Deinstitutionalization to Homelessness.* Princeton, NJ: Princeton University Press.

Federico, Ronald, with Janet Schwartz. 1983. *Sociology,* 3d ed. New York, Random House.

Freud, Sigmund. 1962. *Civilization and Its Discontents,* Trans. by James Strachey. New York: W. W. Norton.

Hellman, Judith. 1983. *Mexico in Crisis,* 2d ed. New York: Holmes and Meier.

Keith-Lucas, Alan. 1972. *Giving and Taking Help.* Chapel Hill: University of North Carolina Press.

Klein, Philip. 1968. *From Philanthropy to Social Welfare.* San Francisco: Jossey-Bass.

Laidler, Harry, and Florette Henri. 1992. Socialism. In *Collier's Encyclopedia,* vol. 21. New York: P. F. Collier, pp. 121–131.

Leonard, E. M. 1965. *The Early History of the English Poor Relief.* New York: Barnes & Noble.

Lieby, James. 1978. *A History of Social Welfare and Social Work in the United States.* New York: Columbia University Press.

Locke, John. 1690. Two treatises on government. London. In Talcott Parsons, Edward Shils, Kaspar Naegele, and Jesse Pitts, eds., *Theories of Society,* Glencoe, IL: Free Press, 1961, vol. I, pp. 101–103.

Macarov, David. 1978. *The Design of Social Welfare.* New York: Holt, Rinehart & Winston.

Madison, Bernice. 1968. *Social Welfare in the Soviet Union.* Stanford, CA: Stanford University Press.

Mencher, Samuel. 1967. *Poor Law to Poverty Program.* Pittsburgh: University of Pittsburgh Press.

Morris, Robert. 1986. *Rethinking Social Welfare: Why Care for the Stranger?* White Plains, NY: Longman.

New Encyclopedia Britannica. 1992. Chicago: Encyclopedia Britannica.

Redondi, Pietro. 1987. *Galileo: Heretic,* trans. by Raymond Rosenthal. Princeton, NJ: Princeton University Press.

Reid, P. Nelson. 1995. Social welfare history. In *The Encyclopedia of Social Work,* 19th ed. Washington, DC: National Association of Social Workers, pp. 2206–2225.

Reid, William, and Peter Stimpson. 1987. Sectarian agencies. In *The Encyclopedia of Social Work,* 18th ed. Silver Spring, MD: National Association of Social Workers, pp. 545–556.

Rosner, Jan. 1976. *Cross-National Studies of Social Service Systems: Polish Reports.* Ann Arbor, MI: Xerox University Microfilms.

Rousseau, Jean Jacques. 1762. A treatise on the social compact. Paris. In Talcott Parsons, Edward Shils, Kaspar Naegele, and Jesse Pitts, eds., *Theories of Society,* Glencoe, IL: The Free Press, 1961, vol. I, pp. 119–125.

Schenk, Quentin, with Emmy Lou Schenk. 1981. *Welfare, Society, and the Helping Professions.* New York: Macmillan.

Shapiro, Isaac. 1995. *Four Years and Still Falling: The Decline in Value of the Minimum Wage.* Washington, DC: Center on Budget and Policy Priorities.

Smith, Adam. 1776. Inquiry into the causes of the wealth of nations. London. In Talcott Parsons, Edward Shils, Kaspar Naegele, and Jesse Pitts, eds., *Theories of Society,* Glencoe, IL: The Free Press, 1961, vol. I, pp. 104–106.

Steinberg, S. H., ed. 1963. *A Dictionary of British History.* New York: St. Martins Press.

Streeten, Paul. 1992. Socialist economics. In *Collier's Encyclopedia,* vol. 21. New York: P. F. Collier, pp. 131–132.

Trattner, Walter. 1994. *From Poor Law to Welfare State: A History of Social Welfare in America.* New York: The Free Press.

Wilensky, Harold, and Charles Lebeaux. 1965. *Industrial Society and Social Welfare.* New York: The Free Press.

Woolf, Henry B. 1979. *Webster's New Collegiate Dictionary.* Springfield, MA: G. & C. Merriam.

Zimbalist, Sidney. 1977. *Historic Themes and Landmarks in Social Welfare Research.* New York: Harper & Row.

5

HOW HAVE SOCIAL MOBILIZATION AND SOCIAL REFORM MOVEMENTS AFFECTED SOCIAL WELFARE?

WHAT TO EXPECT FROM THIS CHAPTER

In Chapter 4 we examined some of the historical roots of contemporary views of social welfare and its role in society. These included the development of a sense of responsibility for helping others, the evolution of helping roles, and the influence of religious and secular intellectual currents including Protestantism, humanism, socialism, and social science. We saw that the concept of social welfare has gradually expanded from responsibility for family members to responsibility for members of society in general.

This chapter continues our historical analysis. However, instead of concentrating on the power of ideas to shape social welfare, it emphasizes the political role of social reformers and the mobilization of constituencies for social change. We see that shared experience of major events such as drastic changes in the economy, wars and natural disasters, and demographic shifts are important aspects of the social environment that help shape human behavior. Depending on the meaning given to such events by people acting on their own behalf or on behalf of others through social movements and advocacy organizations, such experiences may generate feelings of "we-ness" that increase the likelihood of supporting or opposing objectives of reform.

LEARNING OBJECTIVES

When you have finished studying this chapter, you should be able to:

1 Discuss ways in which beneficiary and conscience constituencies have contributed to the enhancement of social welfare in the United States.

2 List major milestones in the development of social welfare in the United States.

3 Discuss how events in the social environment such as wars and economic depressions have affected the evolution of social welfare.

4 Describe the role of the work ethic in welfare reform efforts in the second half of the twentieth century.

5 Discuss challenges to social welfare that have emerged in the late twentieth century.

SOCIAL MOBILIZATION AND SOCIAL REFORM

C. Wright Mills, in *The Sociological Imagination* (1959), made a distinction that is important to social work between *personal troubles* and *social issues*. **Personal troubles** are *private matters that occur when an individual feels that his or her cherished values are threatened.* Troubles are found within the character of individuals and within the range of their immediate relations with others. Social issues transcend personal circumstances and often involve crises in institutional arrangements. One person unemployed in a city of 100,000 is in personal trouble; one-third of the labor force without work constitutes an issue (Mills, 1959:8–9). In our discussion we use the terms *social problem* and *social issue* interchangeably.

In Chapter 3 we defined *social problems* as social conditions that are perceived "by significant numbers of the population, powerful groups, or charismatic individuals" to be threats to society "that could be resolved or remedied" (Maris, 1988:37). Social conditions are never inherently problematic: They become social problems when a sufficiently large number of persons *define* them as social problems (Mauss, 1975:3). By researching, writing, and speaking out, social reformers help define conditions as social problems that should be addressed. The challenge to reformers is to mobilize constituencies that believe that something should and can be done to ameliorate the conditions at issue.

For example, the social condition of young children working in the mines and mills of nineteenth-century North America did not become a social problem until social reformers in the settlement house movement, the labor movement, and others defined child labor as unacceptable. More recently, social reformers in the United States have successfully defined physical and sexual assault against children by family members and violence against women by their partners as social problems. Safe shelters for battered women have been created, and laws against spouse abuse and against child abuse and neglect have been enacted.

Definition of conditions as personal *troubles* or social *issues* is related to the perception of how well society is functioning.

If society believes itself to be operating effectively, and if most people feel they do well within the system, then those who find it hard to survive can be looked upon as individual failures. In such circumstances, the approach to the poor and to poverty issues is by way of remedial, residual programs aimed at uplifting the failures, at changing them to look like the rest of us . . . when society is considered to be operating ineffectively, the demand is for institutional change. (Axinn and Levin, 1992:5)

Expansion of social welfare has often involved struggle in which social reformers define a problem, develop a vision of its resolution, and attempt to mobilize the resources (people, time, and money) necessary to achieve their goals. The people forming the constituencies of reform movements can be seen as two distinct sorts, *beneficiary constituencies* and *conscience constituencies* (McCarthy and Zald, 1977:1221). **Beneficiary constituencies** are made up of *persons who stand to benefit directly if a social reform effort is successful.* They are motivated at least in part by their immediate self-interest. Workers striking to be recognized as a union, AFDC mothers organizing for welfare rights, and college students campaigning against cuts in federal support for their education are examples. **Conscience constituencies** are comprised of *supporters of a reform effort who do not themselves stand to benefit directly from its success.* Conscience constituents such as middle-class social workers or church members advocating on behalf of the poor or other oppressed groups of which they are not members are motivated more by altruism than by immediate self-interest.

Both beneficiary and conscience constituents have played important roles in mobilizing the resources necessary for the enhancement of social welfare in the United States. As we will see, throughout U.S. history, social reformers and—after the birth of social work in the late 1800s—social workers have helped shape social welfare policies and programs through advocacy and social mobilization.

Mobilization has also contributed to improvements in social welfare in Mexico, Sweden, and Poland. In Mexico, for example, land reform was a major goal of the Mexican Revolution. The successful revolutionaries created the *ejido* system of communally owned farmland, through which nearly half of all arable land in Mexico was distributed to peasant farmers. In Sweden, for decades most employers have signed a central agreement with labor concerning wages, working conditions, and other issues of collective bargaining. In 1995, when the U.S.-based firm Toys " Я " Us refused to sign the central agreement, workers went out on strike to protect their wages (Associated Press, 1995). (See "The Human Face of Social Welfare 13: Swedish Labor Policy.")

The outcomes of the struggles over preservation and enhancement of social welfare in each of our four countries in the future will depend to a significant extent on the mobilization of resources by constituent advocates.

THE HUMAN FACE OF SOCIAL WELFARE 13

SWEDISH LABOR POLICY

STOCKHOLM, Sweden—The U.S. retailer Toys "Я" Us, hit by widening strikes in Sweden, lashed out at unions Wednesday over a principle central to organized labor in Sweden.

The main issue in the week-old strike by 40 to 50 people is whether Toys "Я" Us will sign a centralized, nationwide agreement between federations of unions on one side and employers on the other.

The decades-old agreement system is central to the unions' broad influence in Swedish politics and business.

Unions "have forced our employees to strike solely because we will not unconditionally sign a collective agreement," the company said in a half-page ad in the daily *Dagens Nyheter.*

Union spokesperson Bill Erlandson conceded that workers did not have serious complaints about pay or conditions. They had been treated at least as well as other workers in Sweden, he said.

But he said the central agreement keeps all companies in line where individual unions may not be strong enough, and it creates a level playing field for all workers.

"About 90 to 95 percent of Swedish companies have signed this central agreement, concerning wages and working conditions, insurance, everything," said Erlandson of the Retail Clerks Union, which is leading the strike.

"The whole situation on the labor market is built on this central agreement," he said. "If we don't stop [Toys "Я" Us] now, this will continue with other foreign companies and even Swedish companies . . . This is a fight we cannot lose."

Without the central agreement, unions will be fractured and Sweden's deep-seated ideal of equalized wages across industry lines will be jeopardized, said economist Bengt Stymne of the Stockholm School of Economics.

"It could be dangerous for the Unions," Stymne said.

But he and other economists said the system has become "protectionist" and possibly outdated at a time when Sweden's troubled economy must be integrated.

So far other unions have supported the strike by refusing to deliver supplies or to pick up garbage at two Toys "Я" Us stores in southern and western Sweden.

The action is expected to spread next week to a store in Stockholm, and workers at a store in neighboring Denmark are negotiating with managers.

The strike comes as Sweden struggles to face up to tough times, in sharp contrast with its post-war boom upon which the labor policies were built.

Sweden faces a huge budget deficit, dangerously large national debt, 12 percent unemployment, a weak currency, and rising interest rates. Only exports still perform at levels that once supported the "Swedish Model" of cradle-to-grave welfare.

This article describes an example of a beneficiary constituency mobilizing to defend its interests. It also illustrates the interdependence of the global economy, as a firm from the United States does business in Sweden. Cultural expectations about how to conduct business appropriately may differ between Sweden and the United States. With more than 80 percent of Swedish employees belonging to labor unions (Swedish Institute, 1992), unions play a more central role in Sweden than in the United States. And, as we noted in the Introduction, Swedish welfare policy is designed to support work by both women and men. What may be the impact on people's lives in Sweden if the nationwide, centralized agreement between federations of unions and employers is lost? If you were a social worker in Sweden, what would be your position regarding the strike? Why? Why are Danish workers concerned about labor/management negotiations in Sweden?

SOCIAL REFORM AND SOCIAL WELFARE IN THE UNITED STATES

English Antecedents

As we noted in the previous chapter, social welfare in the American colonies was shaped by the values and principles of the Elizabethan Poor Law of 1601, which were brought to the New World by the English colonists. The Industrial Revolution marked a turning point in human history and in social welfare. Land ownership as a source of power was replaced by ownership of the means of production (factories, machines, technology, and the raw materials used in manufacturing). National governments gradually emerged and dominated local governing units. The rise of science challenged the dominance of religious ideas, and the power of the church was reduced as its landholdings became less valuable and as newly emerging national governments worked to establish their control over definitions of the "public interest." One consequence of all these developments was a gradually increasing role for government provision and control of social welfare. Beginning with the 1349 Statute of Laborers and continuing through the reigns of Henry VII, Edward IV, and Elizabeth I, the English government "established laws determining who could be given aid, where they could be given aid, how funds were to be raised, who should administer the aid, and what punishments should befall the poor and the providers of aid for failure to comply with the demands of law" (Reid, 1995:2207–2208).

The Industrial Revolution had other effects as well. Industrialization created a number of new social problems. Families were uprooted and became dependent on a wage economy. As jobs changed and moved, so did families. Smaller families could best adapt to a changed workplace that provided a set wage and encouraged geographic mobility. As families became smaller, however, their helping capacity was reduced, making it more difficult for them to care for children and the elderly. Also, as they moved into crowded cities, increasing numbers of people eventually found themselves unable to grow their own food to supplement their income and maintain self-reliance (Axinn and Levin, 1982:144).

The Colonial Period (1647–1776)[1]

In the Colonies prior to the American Revolution, the poor were generally tolerated and provided relief through a casually administered system that accepted community responsibility for the poor (Reid, 1995). In the 1720s the Great Awakening, a mass movement of religious revivals in North America, popularized philanthropy and involved working-class people in acts of charity. Enormously popular preachers such as George Whitefield took up collections for debtors, disaster victims, colonial colleges, and other causes. Advocates of the Enlightenment

---

[1]We will follow generally the practice of Axinn and Levin (1992) in dividing U.S. social welfare history into the colonial period (1647–1776), the pre-Civil War period (1777–1860), the Civil War and aftermath (1860–1900), the progressive reform era (1900–1930), and the Depression and the New Deal (1930–1940). We modify Axinn and Levin beginning with World War II, prosperity, the Great Society (1940–1980), and the Reagan reaction and social retreat (1980–1996).

argued that poverty is not natural, that all persons have the capacity to reason, and therefore the poor have a right to share in the nation's resources. The ideas of the Enlightenment generated social reform and humanitarianism.

> Groups "were formed for every imaginable . . . purpose: to assist widows and orphans, immigrants and Negroes, debtors and prisoners, aged females and young prostitutes; to supply the poor with food, fuel, medicine, [and] employment . . . ; to promote morality, temperance, thrift and industrious habits; to educate poor children in free schools, Sunday schools, and charity schools; to reform gamblers," drunkards, and juvenile delinquents (Mohl, 1969, quoted in Trattner, 1994:40).

By the time of the American Revolution, churches and a broad array of private organizations were providing aid to the needy. Mutual aid societies were formed by churches, nationality groups, fraternal societies, and other social organizations to aid the poor, provide for the sick, and bury the dead. Social welfare functioned as a partnership in which private charity complemented public aid. Social movement organizations, influenced by the emphasis of the Declaration of Independence on reason and human equality, focused attention on the need to improve the circumstances of common people. The antislavery movement mobilized the support necessary to abolish slavery in the northern states. Interest groups were formed that opposed imprisonment for debt and supported revision of the criminal codes and many other reforms (Trattner, 1994:32–41).

The Pre-Civil War Period (1777–1860)

Between the Revolution and the Civil War the working class in the United States was poorly organized compared with workers in England and Europe. Although there existed local associations of workers and scattered union protests, no national beneficiary constituency movement of poor persons emerged in the United States (Jansson, 1993:75–76). Other than the suffrage movement and parts of the abolition movement, reform efforts mobilized prior to the Civil War were based largely on conscience constituencies.

With the exception of federal aid to veterans and their survivors, public welfare remained largely a local and state responsibility. "[L]arge scale immigration, rapid industrialization, the advent of capitalism and the spread of wage labor, and widespread urbanization" resulted in increasing poverty and increasing local spending on relief (Trattner, 1994:49). Poverty came to be seen "as a social problem; as a potential source of crime, social unrest, and long-term dependence; and, therefore, as a proper target of reform." Attention turned to attempts to understand the causes of poverty in order to eliminate it (Reid, 1995:2209).

In spite of societal barriers such as substandard wages, and seasonal and technological unemployment, it was widely believed that any diligent person could become self-supporting. Although lip service was given to distinctions between worthy and unworthy poor, in reality all poor people—"no matter how hard they struggled . . . were still condemned as moral failures" (Trattner, 1994:55–56).

With an eye on social control of the poor, governmental commissions in New York and Massachusetts recommended reforms replacing outdoor relief with almshouses, where "through order, cleanliness, discipline, and routine, the poor could be transformed into useful and productive members of society" (Reid, 1995:2210).

Reliance on almshouses and workhouses expanded rapidly. The New York County Poorhouse Act of 1824 called for each county in the state to establish and operate one or more poorhouses to which all recipients of public assistance were to be sent. In that year Massachusetts had 83 county-operated almshouses; by 1860, there were 219. Conditions in the poorhouses were atrocious. Into these institutions, aptly described by Trattner as "social cemeteries,"

> were herded the old and the young, the sick and the well, the sane and the insane, the epileptic and the feebleminded, the blind and the alcoholic, the juvenile delinquent and the hardened criminal, male and female, all thrown together in a haphazard fashion. Nakedness and filth, hunger and vice, and other abuses such as beatings by cruel keepers were not uncommon (Trattner, 1994:61–62).

The reform movements of the early nineteenth century that resulted in the creation of almshouses also led to the founding of orphanages, reformatories, mental hospitals, and other institutions for special populations. Reformers worked to enact laws requiring the removal of children from county almshouses.

Concerned about the mentally ill, one social reformer, Dorothea Dix, traveled throughout the new nation and in several other countries investigating conditions in jails and prisons, reported her findings to state legislatures, and was instrumental in founding thirty-two mental hospitals and fifteen training schools for people with developmental disabilities. In 1854, she persuaded Congress to grant federal lands to the states to establish and endow hospitals for the deaf and the insane. The bill was vetoed by President Pierce, who argued that charity was constitutionally the province of the states and localities, not of the federal government (Wilson, 1975). Federal assistance would not be provided to state welfare programs until the economic and political crisis of the 1930s.

During the 1800s, major social movements were mobilized against slavery and for women's suffrage. "White women of all classes and all persons of the laboring classes (slave or free) were the driving forces for change." Sisters Sarah and Angelina Grimke were among those linking abolition and suffrage. Angelina, "the first 'respectable' American woman to speak in public," presented "the Massachusetts legislature with a petition signed by 20,000 women demanding an end to slavery." Other ardent abolitionists included Frederick Douglass, William Lloyd Garrison, Lucretia Mott, Elizabeth Cady Stanton, Lucy Stone, Sojourner Truth, and Harriett Tubman. Tubman, Douglass, Truth, and countless other unidentified opponents of slavery operated an *underground railway,* a system for spiriting fugitive slaves from the South to the North and Canada by hiding them in private homes. The *Seneca Falls* (New York) *Convention* on women's issues, organized by Cady Stanton, Susan B. Anthony, Douglass, and others, brought together 260 women and 40 men (but no people of color), who called for "equal educational rights; fairer laws for marriage, divorce, and property ownership; the end of a double moral standard; the right to write, speak, and teach on an equal basis with men; and equal participation in the trades, professions, and commerce" (Blockson, 1987; Day, 1989:192–195).

In 1853, the Reverend Charles Loring Brace, concerned about the plight of children on the streets and in the almshouses of New York, founded the Children's Aid Society, which over a 25-year period shipped more than 50,000 children from poor families by train to be adopted by families in the West, "where they might learn the benefits of hard work in an untouched environment" (Day, 1989:227–228). His book, *The Dangerous Classes of New York and Twenty Years' Work Among Them,* published in 1872, helped raise consciousness about the problems of the urban poor (Barker, 1991:261).

The Civil War and Aftermath (1860–1900)

Fierce fighting during the Civil War resulted in hundreds of thousands of casualties. In both the Union and the Confederacy, women volunteers formed organizations in support of the war effort. The *United States Sanitary Commission* was formed in 1861 in response to recommendations of the Women's Central Relief Association of New York for the creation of an organization to inform Northern women how best to be involved. Originally called the People's Commission on Sanitary Inquiry and Advice, the popular commission depended on voluntary donations of money and labor and channeled contributions for the relief and comfort of Union forces. Even though women's organizations funded and carried out its work, its nine officially appointed members were men (Axinn and Levin, 1992).

The *Freedmen's Bureau* was the first federally funded and operated welfare agency. Founded to assist former slaves, the agency distributed food and medical supplies to both blacks and whites, and established schools and orphanages for black children. Today, major institutions of higher education, including Howard, Atlanta, and Fisk universities, Hampton Institute, and Talladega College, trace their roots to the Freedmen's Bureau. Although its promise of land redistribution to former slaves ("40 acres and a mule") was not realized, from 1865 to 1869 the Freedmen's Bureau was an important federal counter to the southern states' *black codes,* which attempted to regulate the lives of black freedmen by limiting their property rights and their vocational and economic activities (Axinn and Levin, 1992).

During and after the Civil War, veterans' pensions were expanded and made more generous. A veterans' organization founded in 1866, the Grand Army of the Republic (GAR), constituted a beneficiary constituency "able to push for progressive liberalization of benefits and, when danger threatened, to secure those benefits against attack" (Axinn and Levin, 1992:87).

In 1800, there was no system of publicly funded education in the United States. Beginning in the 1820s, reformers—believing that an educated citizenry was essential to democratic participation and that education would instill morality enabling youth to avoid poverty, alcoholism, and crime—agitated for public education. By 1860, they succeeded in creating a national network of public primary and secondary schools serving both girls and boys, one of the major policy advances of the nineteenth century (Jansson, 1993:74–75).

During the Civil War, President Lincoln signed legislation that was a major step toward democratizing access to college education. The *Morrill Act of 1862* provided grants of federal lands to be sold by the states to fund education for the working classes. Agricultural and mechanical colleges were established that became the state "land grant" universities of today. Although tuition at these state universities has increased dramatically in recent years, they continue to make higher education accessible to persons who cannot afford to attend private colleges and universities.

Slavery was abolished by the Thirteenth Amendment to the Constitution in 1865. The Fourteenth Amendment, ratified in 1868, guaranteed that all native-born or naturalized U.S. citizens have rights that no state can abridge or deny. In 1870, ratification of the Fifteenth Amendment guaranteed the right of citizens, other than women, to vote regardless of race, color, or previous condition of servitude. The common interests of women and slaves, which had closely tied the suffrage and abolition movements, were ruptured; the suffrage movement itself split bitterly over the primacy of racial or gender rights (Day, 1989:194). Women were denied the right to vote for 50 years more. Finally, in 1920, the Nineteenth Amendment to the Constitution provided for women suffrage.

In the late 1800s, fortunes were made from oil, steel, aluminum, and meat packing. At the same time, farm sizes dropped and half of all farms became tenant operated. Federal land grants to the railroads made possible a transportation system linking the East and West—and sealed the fate of the Plains Indian nations by facilitating the slaughter of the vast herds of bison on which they depended. Farmers and workers, increasingly in conflict with corporate interests, organized granges and unions. By 1875, 30,000 local granges with some 2.5 million members were engaged in political activities to strengthen farmers vis à vis the railroads and other corporations. In 1883, the Knights of Labor had 50,000 members. Three years later there were 700,000 (Axinn and Levin, 1992).

Conflict existed, too, between organized labor and organized charity. Private charitable contributions in the United States had burgeoned until, as a percentage of wealth, they exceeded the effort of any European country. Metropolitan newspapers featured the activities of "Society," and charity work became an index of social status (Trattner, 1994:44–45). Supporters of the *charity organization societies*—frequently wealthy influential businessmen or their wives—believed their purpose was to suppress pauperism, not to aid the needy. Personal contact with middle-class role models, they believed, would help the individual "to rise above the need for relief. The ideal of charity was service on the part of the well-to-do, service whereby the poor could learn self-respect and resolution, which would build character." The focus on individuals as the cause of poverty diverted the attention of charity workers from its environmental causes. For example, immigrants and former slaves constituted a pool of surplus workers willing to accept jobs at almost any wage. When unions went on strike to try to prevent cuts in the inadequate wages of the day, charity workers opposed the strikes. Charity organizations were perceived quite correctly by workers as antiunion (Axinn and Levin, 1992:97).

Strengthening morality and character building were goals of the charity organization societies and of many middle-class reformers. Similar concerns resulted in rapidly spreading, locally based national membership organizations during the second half of the nineteenth and the early twentieth century. The Young Men's Christian Association (YMCA) was founded in London, England, in 1844 by drapery clerk George Williams and began in North America in Montreal in 1851. In 1855, the Young Men's Hebrew Association began in Baltimore, the YMCA was brought to Boston by retired sea captain Thomas C. Sullivan, and the Young Women's Christian Association (YWCA) was started in England. The first YWCA in the United States was organized in Boston by Grace Dodge in 1866. The Salvation Army, founded in London by the Reverend William Booth in 1878, was brought to the United States in 1880. The Volunteers of America was founded by Salvation Army dissidents in 1896. The Boys Clubs of America began in Boston in 1906, the Boy Scouts of America and Campfire Girls in 1910, and the Girl Scouts in 1912 (Day, 1989; Alexander, 1995).

The *settlement house movement* proved to be more sympathetic to organized labor than were the charity organization societies. **Settlement houses**—social "settlements"—were attempts to reduce the distance between socioeconomic classes by moving formally educated, middle- and upper-class volunteers into working-class neighborhoods. The ministers, educators, and college students "settled in" to exchange ideas and information with their new neighbors.

Settlement houses were generally located in cities, and they assisted immigrants with personal, family, health, housing, language, and employment problems by providing education programs, social services, counseling, and recreational services (Loavenbruck and Keys, 1987:556–557). Although settlement house residents often were motivated initially by charitable impulses, as they learned about the problems confronting the working-class poor, including sweatshops, child labor, unsanitary working conditions, long hours, starvation wages, and denial of the right to organize (Schlesinger, 1957:24), many became notable reformers. With the exception of organizing unions, settlement residents tended to act on behalf of rather than in concert with those for whom they advocated so passionately. Most settlement-based reformers were, then, prime examples of conscience constituents.

The original settlement house was Toynbee Hall, founded in London in 1884 by Vicar Samuel A. Barnett. The first U.S. settlement house, University Settlement in New York City, was founded in 1886 by Dr. Stanton Coit, an early resident of Toynbee Hall. Jane Addams, a young college graduate who, with Ellen Gates Starr, founded Hull House in Chicago in 1889, had also visited and been inspired by Toynbee Hall. The settlement movement grew rapidly in the United States in response to urban problems faced by working-class immigrants. After little more than a decade, residents in some 400 settlement houses in the United States were engaged in advocacy and reform, group work, and community development (Barker, 1991; Alexander, 1995).

Hull House, founded "as an instrument for social, educational, humanitarian, and civic reform" (Davis, 1967:12), and Henry Street, founded in New York by Lillian Wald in 1893, became incubators for many turn-of-the-century reform movements and innovations in social welfare. Most settlement residents were young, unmarried college graduates who remained for 1 to 3 years before moving on to another job or reform activity—making room for new settlement residents. The settlements "produced an extraordinary group of women whose vitality and enthusiasm reshaped American liberalism" (Schlesinger, 1957:24).

Among the most prominent reformers influenced by their Hull House residencies, Florence Kelley, socialist daughter of a protectionist congressman, changed Jane Addams from a philanthropist to a reformer, and worked for labor and political reform on behalf of children and immigrants. Her Hull House investigations of factories and sweatshops influenced her to organize the National Consumers League in 1899.

> The League's investigations turned up facts to stir the public conscience. Then the League's lawyers drafted bills, and the League's lobbyists sought to push them through legislatures. The League thus initiated the fight for minimum-wage laws and worked out a model statute, soon enacted in thirteen states and the District of Columbia. (Schlesinger, 1957:24)

The league established chapters in most major cities and carried out other successful campaigns against child labor and for shorter working hours and consumer protection (Schlesinger, 1957:24; Day, 1989; Barker, 1991:262; Alexander, 1995).

Hull House resident Mary O'Sullivan helped interest Addams in the problems of working women. She organized a union of women bindery workers, organized cooperative housing for working women, was one of Florence Kelley's investigators of tenement and sweatshop conditions, and in 1892 became the first woman organizer for the American Federation of Labor (Day, 1989:224).

Julia Lathrop personally investigated conditions in all 102 almshouses and poor farms in Illinois and was active in the mental hygiene and juvenile court movements. As the first head of the federal Children's Bureau, she initiated studies on "child labor, mothers' pensions, illegitimacy, juvenile delinquency, nutrition, and the mentally retarded." Grace Abbott became the head of the Immigrant's Protective League and succeeded Lathrop as head of the Children's Bureau. She and her sister Edith Abbott became professors of social work at the Chicago School of Civics and Philanthropy. Dr. Alice Hamilton studied industrial diseases and health problems of women in tenements and houses of prostitution (Day, 1989:224–225).

Still other Hull House women included Josephine Goldmark, who introduced the findings of social research into the courts as an instrument for social change and was a major figure in the campaign for shorter working days; Frances Perkins, Franklin Delano Roosevelt's Secretary of Labor and the first woman cabinet member; Mary Dewson, suffragist, preeminent authority on minimum wage legislation, Democratic Party activist who helped shape the Social Security Act of 1935; and Mary Anderson, Women's Trade Union League activist and head of the federal Women's Bureau (Wandersee, 1986).

Although the activities of Hull House reformers are the best known, staff of Henry Street Settlement, the Consumers' League, and other advocacy organizations also helped educate "an entire generation in social responsibility" (Schlesinger, 1957:25) as they worked collaboratively on key issues.

The Progressive Reform Era (1900–1930)

Progressivism was a "multi-faceted middle-class movement" that "emphasized parks and beautification, education, the 'Americanization' of new citizens, and professionalization, as well as social insurance and regulatory controls." Progressivism popularized the idea that charity is demeaning to both the giver and the receiver, and that collective responses to normal life risks through social insurance are superior to charity. Progressivism put "poverty, immigration, slums, child welfare, mental health, public health, and . . . gender and race (if not exactly class)" on the social policy and political agendas. Progressives enacted state legislation for workers' compensation, Mothers' Aid, and old age pensions, and created a context for federal intervention in social welfare (Reid, 1995:212–214).

The era of progressive reform was born out of social ferment. Organized labor grew stronger and mobilized. "Between 1880 and 1900, there were more than 30,000 strikes and lockouts involving 10 million American workers." Utopians such as Henry George and Edward Bellamy captured the public imagination with their writings (Reid, 1995:2212). Strikes and industrial violence, the growing populist movement, the march on Washington by Coxey's army of the unemployed, and industrial unions such as the United Mine Workers "were part of an agrarian/working-class coalition for reform" (Axinn and Levin, 1992:129).

Early in the twentieth century, the reform movement became more mainstream as conscience constituencies displaced beneficiary constituencies, reform activity emphasized opportunity for the underdog to become more like society's dominant social groups, and "[s]ocial protest became the property of intellectuals and professionals" (Axinn and Levin, 1992:129–130).

In 1904, social settlements in New York and Chicago organized the National Committee on Child Labor, which was instrumental in creating the 1909 White House Conference on Care of Dependent Children. The federal Children's Bureau was established in 1912, as recommended by the White House conferees. From its inception, however, the Children's Bureau existed in a hostile environment in which government programs were suspect, deemed "socialistic" by powerful organizations such as the American Medical Association. The reports of the Children's Bureau were important but refrained from attacking directly the poverty, malnutrition, and poor health of the nation's children (Jansson, 1993:123).

The greatest accomplishment of the Children's Bureau was the enactment of the 1921 *Sheppard-Towner Act,* through which nearly 3,000 child and maternal health centers were established, funded by federal grants to state health departments. Although infant and maternal mortality rates dropped significantly, the program was terminated in 1929 on grounds that it violated states' rights and represented socialized medicine. With the demise of the Sheppard-Towner Act, control over infant and maternal health was shifted from female-run public clinics to the hands of private, male physicians (Barker, 1991:264; Jansson, 1993:141).

Several books published near the turn of the century made important contributions to the mobilization efforts of reformers. *How the Other Half Lives,* a photo documentary of housing conditions in New York slums authored by Jacob Riis in 1890, for example, helped energize the movement for public housing. Robert Hunter's 1904 classic work *Poverty,* which reported that one out of every eight Americans was poor, provided grist for many reformers. Former mental patient Clifford Beers' 1908 exposé of life in a mental hospital, *A Mind That Found Itself,* graphically portrayed the inadequacies of mental institutions and helped Beers mobilize the mental health movement (Alexander, 1995). Upton Sinclair's. *The Jungle* exposed shocking conditions in the meat-packing industry and helped secure passage of the Food and Drug Act in 1906 (Axinn and Levin, 1992:131).

In 1905, the militant Niagara Movement was organized by W. E. B. Dubois—an Atlanta University sociologist who was the first African American to earn a Harvard Ph.D.—and Monroe Trotter to fight for "immediate recognition of the political, social, and economic rights of all black citizens," in opposition to the policy of gradualism espoused by Booker T. Washington (Hendrickson, 1986:250–251). The movement's leaders were among the black and white intellectuals vehemently opposed to racism who founded the National Association for the Advancement of Colored People (NAACP) in 1909–1910. Mary White Ovington, William English Walling, Henry Moskovitz, and five other settlement workers—whose previous reform activities had included organizing the Immigrant Protective League, the National Women's Trade Union League, a national investigation of women and children in industry, and the campaign for the federal Children's Bureau—were among the 35 founders. Believing that whites' ignorance of blacks was a major source of racism, the NAACP sought equality for blacks through persuasion and legal action (Davis, 1967:99–102; Morris, 1984:12–13; Barker, 1991).

A second major national organization focused on the needs of African Americans, the Urban League, was founded in 1910, with social worker George E. Haynes as its first director. Black people, he argued, would be integrated into American society by the removal of educational and employment barriers (Mayo, 1986).

The earliest form of social insurance in the United States, workers' compensation, was enacted by Congress in 1908. Between 1910 and 1920 all but six states implemented workers' compensation programs (Barker, 1991; Alexander, 1995).

At the beginning of the twentieth century, social reformers made effective use of social surveys to gather data, mobilize public opinion, and attempt to influence legislation. In 1912, members of Survey Associates, Inc., combined research and journalism toward that end. Their publications, *Survey Midmonthly* and *Survey Graphic,* edited by Paul Kellogg, were influential among both social workers and the general public. In 1913, I. M. Rubinow authored *Social Insurance,* advocating comprehensive protection against "sickness, old age, industrial accidents, invalidism, and unemployment." As executive secretary of the American Medical

Association's Social Insurance Commission in 1916, Rubinow was an important advocate of national health insurance (Alexander, 1995:2636). During that same year, Margaret Sanger opened the first birth control clinic in Brooklyn, defying the Comstock Law, which banned dissemination of information about contraception (Reed, 1995).

Small businessmen, writers, social workers, lawyers, clergy, and farmers joined the progressive struggle against "organized money." In 1912, Socialists elected more than 1,000 members to public offices, Socialist candidate Eugene V. Debs won 6 percent of the popular vote, and growing Socialist popularity catalyzed more moderate reform groups which defended capitalism. *Muckrakers* such as Upton Sinclair exposed unsanitary conditions in meat packing; fraud, graft, and monopolistic control in industry, railroading, and public utilities; and corruption in state and local governments, the courts, and the U.S. Senate. Their revelations "strengthened the movement for women's suffrage, the secret ballot, direct primaries, direct election of senators, the initiative, referendum, and recall, and municipal home rule." Social workers in charity organizations and settlements collaborated, seeking to strengthen family life through

> legislation to regulate tenement and factory construction; to prevent and compensate for industrial accidents and diseases; to prohibit child labor and provide for compulsory education; to improve sanitary and health conditions; to provide social insurance as security against unemployment, retirement, or death of the breadwinner; and to protect workers—especially women—in regard to minimum wages and working hours. (Axinn and Levin, 1992:130–134)

During the 1890s and the first two decades of the twentieth century, social worker reformers had viewed needy persons largely as products of impersonal social and economic forces. During the 1920s, however, a major shift occurred in the social work world view. Increasingly concerned with their professional status, many social workers turned to social and psychiatric casework, which perceived needy persons "as primarily a product of personal impulses." Concern shifted from social reform to preoccupation "with methods and techniques to help [the needy] become adjusted to their environment" (Trattner, 1994:254).

The focus of social work on personality and psychiatric casework did not, of course, eliminate "the social and economic causes of poverty—illness, injury, low wages, involuntary unemployment, old age, death of the family bread winner." These were issues that would reemerge as major social threats during the 1930s, issues with which the services provided by private sector social welfare agencies would be ill-prepared to cope (Trattner, 1994:270).

The Great Depression and the New Deal (1930–1940)

An **economic depression** is *"a socioeconomic condition in which business activity is lowered for a prolonged time, unemployment rates are high, and purchasing power is greatly diminished."* A **recession** is *"a milder or shorter version of economic depression"* (Barker, 1991:60, 196).

Recessions and depressions of varying degrees of severity had occurred periodically in the United States. The crash of the stock market in 1929, however, initiated the most severe depression in the nation's history. The Great Depression
began during the administration of Republican President Herbert Hoover. At first
Hoover was unwilling to intervene, probably believing that he faced an ordinary
depression that would run its course. For Hoover, "relief was a moral, not merely
an economic matter; private charity . . . was fine, but public aid, especially from
the national government, was a 'dole'" (Trattner, 1994:277).

By the end of 1930, however, it was clear that the current depression was not an
ordinary one. The national economy had collapsed, throwing millions of people out
of work through no fault of their own; states and cities were nearly bankrupt; and
private charity had dried up. Believing that relief would make government master
of the souls of those who received it, Hoover approved a federal appropriation to
feed stricken livestock but opposed an additional appropriation "to feed the starving
farmers and their families" (Trattner, 1994:278). In 1932, Hoover did sign a law creating the Reconstruction Finance Corporation, which could lend money to the states
for relief activities. Many of the heavily indebted states, however, were unwilling to
borrow such funds.

As manufacturing output dropped by 40 percent, average wages dropped 25 percent, unemployment neared 25 percent, and social unrest increased throughout the
nation in 1932, Franklin Delano Roosevelt (FDR) was elected President (Reid,
1995:2214). Declaring that the nation had "nothing to fear but fear itself," the Roosevelt administration fostered an alphabet soup of legislation that culminated in the
Social Security Act of 1935. Together, these programs constituted the **New Deal.**

The Civilian Conservation Corps (CCC) provided work and education for
young men ages 17–23. The National Youth Administration (NYA), under the
direction of social worker Aubrey Williams, funded part-time jobs that enabled
high school and college youth to stay in school. The Federal Emergency Relief
Agency (FERA) was the first major federally funded welfare program. Directed by
social worker Harry Hopkins, the FERA provided matching funds and grants to
the states for relief. During 4 months in 1933–1934, the Civil Works Administration (CWA) initiated 190,000 work projects employing 16 million persons in
locally proposed projects repairing and building roads and retaining walls, digging
ditches, cleaning local parks, recataloging books in public libraries, and much
more. Committed to providing work "for all able-bodied but destitute workers,"
FDR replaced FERA with the Works Progress Administration (WPA). The WPA
provided jobs to the unemployed—including artists, musicians, and scholars—
using their skills appropriately, and shifted federal support from home relief to
work relief. The National Recovery Act (NRA) established codes for wage and
price controls and the protection of workers' rights. The Agricultural Adjustment
Act (AAA) attempted to reform agriculture through farm production allotments
and stabilization of market prices (Barker, 1991; Jansson, 1993:160–161; Trattner,
1994; Alexander, 1995; Reid, 1995).

The **Social Security Act of 1935** was the jewel in the crown of the New Deal.
The legislation was drafted by FDR's Committee on Economic Security, in which

social workers Harry Hopkins, Frances Perkins, Ernest Witte, and Wilbur Cohen played key roles (Trattner, 1994). Its provisions included insurance-based protection of income for retirement, for disabled workers, and dependent survivors of a deceased breadwinner, and means-tested assistance for the elderly, blind, and disabled, and dependent children. Insurance for health care was a notable omission.

The United States had moved late and with considerable reluctance toward establishing its version of the welfare state. Enactment of the Social Security Act marked a dramatic shift in U.S. policy toward acceptance of federal responsibility for social welfare. This major change in public policy occurred in large part in reaction to social unrest and the mobilization of social movements with beneficiary and conscience constituencies. To understand the emergence of Social Security, we need to consider the political and economic environment that catalyzed that mobilization.

Social conditions and social policies are not abstractions; they have real impacts on the lives of real people. By 1932, the Depression was taking a heavy human toll. Wages were plummeting. Steel workers earned 63 percent less than they had in 1929. Pennsylvanians earned 5 cents per hour in sawmills, 6 cents in brick and tile works, 7.5 cents in general contracting. Women textile workers in Tennessee received less than 5 cents per hour for a 50-hour week. In more than a hundred sweatshops in Connecticut, young girls were working 55-hour weeks while earning as little as 1 to 2 cents per hour (Trattner, 1994:249).

Unemployed, "God-fearing members of the middle class" were standing in relief lines seeking handouts. Chicago had 50 percent unemployment. Between 1.5 and 2 million people abandoned their homes to roam "the country in an aimless search for the America of better days." The families of Pennsylvania miners subsisted on "wild weed roots and dandelions." In West Virginia people stole food to survive. Children starved in California. Suicides increased. Cardboard and tin "Hoovervilles"[2] sprang up beside luxury apartments; "people went hungry within sight of elevators bursting with grain" (Trattner, 1994:249–252).

And unrest grew stronger. In December 1931, Communist hunger marchers were greeted with machine guns in Washington, D.C. By the fall of 1932, the nation faced a serious threat. Disorder spread, and talk of revolution was heard among destitute, starving, disillusioned citizens. In Portland, Oregon, World War veterans organized a "Bonus Expeditionary Force" to assemble in Washington to demand early payments of bonuses scheduled to be paid in 1945. In all, 20,000 vets, many with their wives and children, camped on the marshy banks of the Anacostia River and lobbied for the bonus by their presence. After more than 2 months the unarmed bonus marchers were driven from the capitol by cavalry, tanks, infantry with fixed bayonets, and tear gas. Striking farmers declared a "holiday," refused to permit food shipments to several cities, and dumped milk into ditches in protest of low prices. Businessmen and even a U.S. Senator called for martial

---

[2]Shanty towns constructed by roving, homeless, unemployed persons seeking work were nicknamed Hoovervilles to mock the insensivity and inaction of the Hoover administration during the onset of the Great Depression. Similar housing for the homeless reappeared during the Reagan-Bush era.

law and fascist dictatorship to keep the unrest under control (Trattner, 1994:256–281).

The economic hard times spawned numerous social movements of potential beneficiaries agitating for various forms of social security. The first nationwide advocacy was carried out by the American Association for Old Age Security, organized in 1927 by Abraham Epstein. With a membership of less than 7,000 and an annual budget under $24,000, Epstein advocated through nationwide lecture tours, books, pamphlets, hundreds of newspaper and magazine articles, and legislative testimony. The National Old Age Pension Association, proposing monthly pensions of $30 for persons older than 65 who would retire and surrender their estates to the federal government, raised over $60,000—largely from 10-cent membership fees—before being exposed as fraudulent. In just 11 months, Upton Sinclair's EPIC movement organized more than 850 local clubs and sold 225,000 copies of his book, *I, the Governor of California and How I Ended Poverty,* which proposed a system of cooperatives raising food and producing goods for the impoverished. Dr. Francis E. Townsend claimed a membership of 2 million in 7,000 clubs across the nation supporting his proposal for monthly pensions of $200 for all Americans older than 60 who were willing to spend the money within a month of receiving it. Townsend Plan petitions signed by more than 10 million persons influenced significantly the passing of the Social Security Act as an alternative (Whitaker, 1970).

Organizations of the unemployed took their messages to the streets and added their impetus to the enactment of Social Security legislation. The National Council of the Unemployed, organized by the Communist Party in 1930, established local "unemployed councils" claiming half a million members in 800 cities and 8 states. In 1933, non-Communist "unemployed leagues" and "unemployed citizens' leagues," which had been organized by followers of A. J. Muste, federated into the National Unemployed League, which claimed a million members in 700 locals. In March 1935, groups of the unemployed that had been organized by the Socialist Party and the League for Industrial Democracy federated to form the Workers Alliance of America and claimed a membership of 600,000 with strongholds in Chicago, Baltimore, and New York (Whitaker, 1970).

While the Townsendites were often sick and feeble elderly middle-class voters, the organizations of the unemployed consisted of able-bodied workers. Unemployed workers blocked evictions, reconnected shut-off utilities, seized courthouses to prevent evictions, conducted rent strikes and hunger marches, held mass demonstrations at relief and municipal offices, and occupied state capitol grounds, governors' offices, and legislative chambers in at least five states. In Dearborn, Michigan, marchers organized by the Detroit Unemployed Council were fired upon by police while attempting to deliver petitions to the Ford plant. At least four were killed and several more wounded. Fifteen thousand persons attended the funeral, which featured red coffins and hearses draped in red (Whitaker, 1970).

The mobilizations of the unemployed, along with those of the Townsendites, the bloody strikes and organizing drives of the Congress of Industrial Organizations (CIO), and other movements of the day, contributed to the atmosphere which ensured passage of the Social Security Act of 1935 following the 1934 midterm elections, which brought many liberals into Congress (Whitaker, 1970; Reid, 1995).

While most social workers supported capitalism and the various reforms of the New Deal, as many as 15,000 rank-and-file social workers such as Mary Van Kleek and Harry Lurie sought a "fundamental reorganization of society" through "a planned socialist economy." They criticized the Roosevelt administration for its racism, political expediency, emphasis on work relief, and ties to big business. As an alternative to the proposed Social Security Act, they supported the Workers' Unemployment, Old Age and Social Insurance Bill, which proposed general-revenue-funded, flat, non-means-tested benefits at prevailing wage levels for workers and farmers who were involuntarily unemployed. They criticized the Social Security Act's contributory funding, limited coverage, low benefit levels, and lack of health insurance (Trattner, 1994:287).

The most glaring omission in the Social Security Act was its lack of health insurance. Although FDR's Committee on Economic Security had recommended inclusion of health insurance, congressional sponsors of the legislation deleted it, fearing that opposition to health insurance from the medical profession might defeat the entire Social Security Act. An agreement that Congress would act on health insurance shortly after passing Social Security was never implemented (Trattner, 1994). Subsequent attempts by presidents Truman and Clinton to enact health insurance failed, leaving the United States in 1996 the only modern, industrial nation without national health insurance.

The separation of social insurance and social assistance within the Social Security legislation segregated the very poor from mainstream programs and created a vulnerable class dependent on inadequately funded programs that have continued to be at the center of controversy (Reid, 1995:2216).

In spite of its shortcomings, however, the Social Security Act of 1935, as amended, remains the single most important piece of social welfare legislation in the history of the United States. Through it, giant steps were taken toward establishing a public safety net providing basic, albeit limited, economic security for American citizens.

The Great Depression ended as reindustrialization in connection with World War II stimulated the economy and resulted in a dramatic reduction in unemployment. By 1941 unemployment dropped to 10 percent; by 1944 it fell to 1.2 percent, the lowest rate for the century (Reid, 1995:2216).

World War II, Prosperity, and the Great Society (1940–1980)

War has had both short-term and enduring impacts on social welfare. Mobilization of able-bodied men into the armed forces during World War II created labor shortages in the United States. Consequently, women were encouraged to work outside the home to support the war effort. The 1942 Lanham Act provided federal matching grants to local communities for day care for children of working mothers. Private industry, too, provided on-site day care in order to attract women workers. Hundreds of thousands of women, celebrated as "Rosie the Riveter," demonstrated that they could excel in what had traditionally been "men's jobs." Ironically, after a few short wartime years with good pay, at the war's end the child care centers were closed and women were forced back into the home, giving up their jobs and income to returning male veterans.

Throughout U.S. history, public provision of income, medical care, and housing to veterans has been seen as an obligation of society. Needy veterans have been seen as worthy, and special efforts have been made to protect them from the stigma of being on welfare. The U.S. Veterans' Bureau was created in 1921 to coordinate and oversee medical care, pensions, vocational rehabilitation, and other benefits for veterans of World War I. The Servicemen's Readjustment Act of 1944, commonly referred to as the "G.I. Bill," helped World War II veterans adjust to civilian life by paying for education and job training, "VA loans" to purchase homes and businesses, employment services, and pensions. One outcome of the G.I. Bill was the initiation of many men into social work (Axinn and Levin, 1992:87; Alexander, 1995:2640).

In 1941, threatened with 50,000 to 100,000 African American workers marching on Washington under the sponsorship of the NAACP, the Congress on Racial Equality (CORE), and the Urban League, President Roosevelt banned discrimination in war industries and the armed services (Day, 1989:301).

Fearing that, without the economic stimulus of war, the Depression might recur, FDR proposed an Economic Bill of Rights establishing full employment as a federal responsibility. The policy was enacted as the Full Employment Act of 1946 but was never implemented (Alexander, 1995:2640; Reid, 1995:2216).

During the late 1940s there was no shift to the political left in the United States as occurred in Great Britain and Europe. The U.S. social welfare system was not under direct attack, but neither was substantial support mobilized for its expansion (Reid, 1995:2217). Nonetheless, the war and the draft had revealed the presence of significant health and mental health problems. Concerned that inadequate childhood nutrition had caused large numbers of men to fail their draft physicals, Selective Service head General Lewis Hersey, among others, became an advocate for a nationwide school lunch program. The National School Lunch Act of 1946 provided federal cash and commodities for school lunches, "as a measure of national security, to safeguard the health and well-being of the Nation's children" (Whitaker, 1993:36–37). The National Mental Health Act of 1946 recognized mental health as a national public health issue, created the National Institute of Mental Health, and laid the groundwork for community-based services. The Hill-Burton Act of 1946 (P.L. 79-725) increased federal involvement in health care through federal funding for a massive expansion of in-patient hospital facilities (Alexander, 1995:2640; Reid, 1995:2216).

After the war's end in 1945, the United Nations was founded and several affiliated agencies were established to deal with social welfare worldwide. These included the United Nations International Children's Emergency Fund (UNICEF), the United Nations Educational, Social, and Cultural Organization (UNESCO), and the United Nations High Commission for Refugees (UNHCR) (Barker, 1991:266).

In the national midterm elections of 1946, Republicans won control of both the U.S. House of Representatives and the Senate. The Republican antispending crusade, in combination with tax cuts, severely limited funding for social welfare expansion. Concurrently, President Truman, attempting to contain Soviet-inspired discontent and insurrection, developed the costly, but successful, Marshall Plan for the economic rebuilding of Europe.

Beginning in 1950 with the inception of the Korean War and the perceived threat of communism, the United States began a massive, ongoing increase in military expenditures, which consumed resources that might otherwise have been available for social welfare. The annual military budget quadrupled and, "after correcting for inflation, . . . remained at the same extraordinary level for the next forty-two years, leading to a military budget of roughly $300 billion in 1991." During the 1950s and as late as 1975, military and military-related budget expenses made up about three-quarters of federal expenditures (Jansson, 1993:203).

The 1950s saw a significant reduction in mobilization for social reform. Obsession with the fear of communist subversion resulted in **witch hunts** and **red baiting,** attempts to discredit the ideas and proposals of reformers and to destroy their careers by accusing them of being communists. One of the many victims was Marxist social worker Bertha Capen Reynolds, who, forced out of her job with the National Maritime Union and unable to find other social work employment, had to retire at the age of 62 (Freedberg and Goldstein, 1986:618).

Republican President Eisenhower, facing a Congress controlled once again by Democrats, sought support for his Cold War foreign policy in exchange for not attacking the surviving programs of the New Deal. Congress extended Social Security benefits to persons with disabilities, wives, widows, dependent children, and survivors. In response to Russia's *Sputnik,* the National Defense Education Act (P.L. 85-864) provided federal funds for math, science, and foreign language instruction (Barker, 1991; Jansson, 1993:205); Aid to Dependent Children was expanded to include care-taker relatives; the U.S. Department of Health, Education and Welfare was established in 1953; and the Housing Act of 1954 (P.L. 83-560) initiated massive urban renewal programs throughout the United States (Barker, 1991; Alexander, 1995).

In 1954, the Supreme Court ruled in *Brown v. Board of Education* that public school segregation was unconstitutional. Over the next 15 years the Court, under the leadership of Chief Justice Earl Warren, contributed to a fundamental shift in social policies affecting minorities and the poor (Dickinson, 1995).

When escalating violence threatened the lives of school children attempting to integrate the schools in Little Rock, Arkansas, President Eisenhower was forced to deploy federal troops to support desegregation. The Civil Rights Act of 1957 (P.L. 85-315), the first federal civil rights law since 1875, established the U.S. Commission on Civil Rights and strengthened federal enforcement powers (Jansson, 1993; Alexander, 1995).

The election of John F. Kennedy to the Presidency in 1960 marked the beginning of renewed interest in social reform. Sociologists such as William F. White, Lloyd Ohlin, and Kenneth Clarke were emphasizing the contributions of social structure and societally created social roles in shaping human behavior. A generation of college students was becoming aware of economic injustice through books such as *The Affluent Society* by economist John Kenneth Galbraith and *The Other America* by democratic socialist Michael Harrington (Alexander, 1995; Reid, 1995:2217). Most important, the civil rights movement played a crucial role in returning social reform to the public agenda.

Since 1910 the NAACP had worked persistently for legislation against lynching and debt slavery, for educational and employment opportunity, for access to unions and equal pay, and for desegregation. Since 1943 CORE had challenged segregation through Gandhian nonviolent direct action (Day, 1989:303). The 1955 lynching of Emmett Till and the exoneration of the whites accused of murdering him generated widespread outrage. The Montgomery, Alabama, bus boycott, initiated following the arrest of NAACP youth leader Rosa Parks for refusing to give up her seat to a white man, brought to prominence Dr. Martin Luther King, Jr., and resulted in the organization of the Southern Christian Leadership Conference (SCLC).

From 1961 to 1963, the civil rights movement brought sit-ins, freedom rides, and other forms of protest to the South and triggered increasing violence by segregationists. African American students created the Student Nonviolent Coordinating Committee (SNCC) to coordinate direct action and voter registration activity in the South. Pressured by the movement, President Kennedy became an advocate of civil rights. Although he was assassinated in 1963 (Day, 1989; Jansson, 1993), significant civil rights legislation was enacted during the ensuing Johnson administration.

The *Mississippi Summer Project,* organized by SNCC in 1964, brought hundreds of black and white students to the South to register black voters. In Birmingham, Alabama, television coverage of police dogs and high-pressure fire hoses being used against peaceful demonstrators further galvanized the nation (Day, 1989; Jansson, 1993). The civil rights mobilization resulted in enactment of the *Civil Rights Act of 1964* (P.L. 88-352) and the *Voting Rights Act of 1965* (P.L. 88-352). The Civil Rights Act prohibited discrimination based on "race, religion, or national origin in schools, employment, and service in places of public accommodation" and established the Equal Employment Opportunity Commission (EEOC) (Barker, 1991:37). The Voting Rights Act "prohibited the use of tests and other devices to disqualify black voters" and strengthened the federal role in protecting civil rights (Dickinson, 1995:1006).

Growing awareness of the issue of poverty generated by the civil rights movement, abhorrence to segregationist violence, and reaction to the Kennedy assassination helped create the context for the expansion of social welfare programs. Lyndon Baines Johnson was elected President in 1964 in a landslide victory over conservative Republican Barry Goldwater and initiated a **War on Poverty.** Under Johnson's **Great Society,** social welfare legislation was enacted that was exceeded only by that of FDR's New Deal.

There is controversy today about the effectiveness of the War on Poverty. Detractors contend that its programs were bureaucratic and failed to decrease dependency. Supporters point to its success in reducing poverty. Although expansion of military spending to finance the Vietnam War meant that the War on Poverty was never fully funded, nevertheless, as a result of Great Society programs, the percentage of people in poverty fell from 25 percent in the early 1960s to about 12 percent in 1969 (Dickinson, 1965:1007).

The centerpiece of Johnson's War on Poverty was the **Economic Opportunity Act of 1964** (P.L. 88-452). Coordinated by the Office of Economic Opportunity (OEO), its programs provided services through which it was hoped the poor would escape poverty; for a time, the OEO also attempted to shift the balance of political power in favor of the poor. Service programs for the poor under the Economic Opportunity Act included Job Corps residential training centers, employment for teens through the Neighborhood Youth Corps, neighborhood-based medical clinics, preschool education through Operation Head Start, and Upward Bound to encourage students from low-income families to finish high school and attend college. The act also supported legal aid societies and Volunteers in Service to America (VISTA), which advocated and sometimes helped organize the poor in addition to providing services.

Local *community action agencies* (CAPS) were established to coordinate service delivery. A requirement for "maximum feasible participation" of the poor in policy-making bodies, and early OEO efforts to bypass local political structures through direct funding to newly created community organizations, were vehemently opposed by local governments. After some early contributions to empowerment such as inspiring the Ohio Walk for Decent Welfare, around which George Wiley and social worker Tim Sampson organized the National Welfare Rights Organization (NWRO), the Community Action Program followed almost exclusively a services strategy and failed to mobilize poor people.

By offering modest salaries that were still significantly better than welfare benefits, the CAPs co-opted some of the best AFDC recipient-organizers of the welfare rights movement, helping to ensure that the NWRO would never become as strong as the Depression-era movements of the unemployed (Whitaker, 1970).

Three key social programs—Food Stamps, Medicare, and Medicaid—are the legacy of the Great Society. The *Food Stamp Act of 1964* (P.L. 88-525) provides food assistance to both working and nonworking poor people. Food stamps had been initiated in 1939 as a small program designed to dispose of surplus agricultural commodities. Under President Johnson the program was expanded dramatically, with recipients required to purchase coupons that could be exchanged for food valued at more than the purchase price of the coupons. ("A family of four with a monthly income of $140 could purchase $166 worth of coupons for $37.") In 1971–1973, under President Nixon, Food Stamps became a universal entitlement program for poor people. By 1995 Food Stamps were, following employment, the nation's first line of defense against hunger: One out of every ten persons in the United States received them (Barker, 1991:268; Whitaker, 1993; Alexander, 1995; Dickinson, 1995).

Medicare and Medicaid were enacted in 1965 as Titles 18 and 19 of the Social Security Act. **Medicare** is an entitlement program providing access to health care for the elderly through a combination of payroll taxes, premiums, and government subsidies. Hospital services are funded by mandatory Part A; doctors' services are funded by voluntary Part B. **Medicaid** is a federal/state matching grant program through which medical services are provided to recipients of Aid to Families with Dependent Children (AFDC) and other persons whose incomes do not exceed 133 percent of a state's AFDC minimum standard for health and decency (Dickinson, 1995:1007).

Costs of Medicare and Medicaid have increased dramatically. As Figure 5-1 illustrates, in fiscal year 1994 Medicare expenditures constituted 10.4 percent of the federal budget and Medicaid 5.3 percent. In comparison, Food Stamps constituted 1.6 percent, AFDC 1.1 percent, Social Security 20.6 percent, and military expenditures (not including military-related interest on the national debt) 18.3 percent of the FY 1994 federal budget (U.S. Congress, 1994). Increasing costs of Medicare and Medicaid fueled the unsuccessful campaign for health-care reform under President Clinton.

FIGURE 5-1   Federal budget, fiscal year 1994. (*Sources:* CBO, March 1995 and 1994 Green Book.)

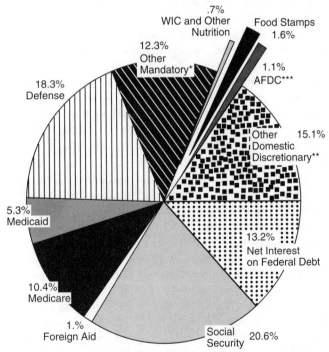

* Includes programs such as farm price supports, veteran's pensions, and Earned Income Tax Credit.

** Includes programs such as NASA, transportation and other infrastructure, and Head Start.

*** Includes AFDC cash benefits as well as AFDC child care programs and the Child Support Enforcement System.

Additional Great Society legislation focused on improved services for senior citizens, public housing, and education. The Older Americans Act of 1965 (P.L. 89-73) created the Administration on Aging, the first such federal governmental body to deal with the problems of aging, and a national network of Area Agencies on the Aging to provide nutrition and other services for elders. Housing and urban development legislation in 1961, 1964, and 1968 sought to improve public housing. The Elementary and Secondary School Act of 1965 (P.L. 89-10) provided services to "economically disadvantaged" pupils through the first major appropriation of federal funds to the U.S. education system (Alexander, 1995; Dickinson, 1995).

The civil rights movement was at its peak in 1963 when Dr. Martin Luther King, Jr., inspired 250,000 participants in the March on Washington and supporters throughout the nation with his "I Have a Dream" speech. As *de jure* legal barriers of segregation fell in the south and attention turned to *de facto* northern segregation, white liberal support for civil rights diminished. Rioting and civil unrest in northern and some southern cities further eroded support for the movement. Between 1965 and 1968, when King was assassinated, 8,133 persons were killed and 49,604 arrested in some 239 civil disturbances. President Johnson's National Advisory Committee on Civil Disorders (the Kerner Commission) identified white racism and limited opportunities for blacks as the major causes of the rioting (Day, 1989; Barker, 1991; Jansson, 1993).

President Johnson, whose escalation of the war against Vietnam had fragmented his coalition for reform, chose not to run for re-election in 1968. Republican President Richard M. Nixon, after narrowly defeating liberal Democrat Hubert Humphrey, began the process of dismantling the OEO and many programs of the Great Society, but also proposed a surprising array of social legislation. Significant reforms during the Nixon administration included the creation of the Occupational Health and Safety Administration (OSHA), the indexing of Social Security benefits, and enactment of the Earned Income Tax Credit (EITC), Supplemental Security Income (SSI), and revenue sharing programs (Jansson, 1993; Dickinson, 1995).

OSHA provides training programs on occupational health, conducts inspections, and requires employers to ensure that working conditions are safe (Barker, 1991). Indexing Social Security benefits to offset increases in the cost of living led to a decline in the poverty rate for elders from 29.5 percent to 15 percent between 1967 and 1979 (Jansson, 1993). The *Earned Income Tax Credit* encourages work by providing a tax credit equal to a percentage of the earnings of low-income workers. *Supplemental Security Income* (SSI) replaced state-subsidized Aid to the Aged, Aid to the Blind, and Aid to the Disabled with a federally financed and administered minimum benefit that reduced the stigma of welfare for those categories of the worthy poor. *General Revenue Sharing* provided "no strings attached" federal funds to state and local governments to use at their discretion. The 1973 Comprehensive Employment and Training Act (CETA) (P.L. 93-203), which consolidated many existing job-training programs, initiated *Special Revenue Sharing:* federal funds to states and local governments to spend with few regulations in general areas of need. These **revenue sharing** programs and, later under President Reagan, **block grants** for local health, education, and welfare needs, marked a major shift in federal/state responsibility for social welfare. Supporters touted increased efficiency and local control; opponents saw revenue sharing and block grants as a "covert way of reducing expenditures for social welfare needs" (Barker, 1991:24; Dickinson, 1995).

The *Family Assistance Program* (FAP) proposed by President Nixon, had it been enacted, would have dramatically changed public assistance and, perhaps, avoided the acrimonious, mean-spirited attacks on welfare in the late 1990s. Work, as we have seen, has always been highly valued in the United States. A major concern of welfare reformers has been how best to ensure that welfare recipients work hard enough, long enough, and effectively to move from "welfare dependence" to self-reliance.

"Nationwide retrogression in public welfare" was precipitated in 1960 when Newburgh, New York, initiated a set of punitive work requirements for welfare recipients (Alexander, 1995:2641). The Kennedy administration's Public Welfare Amendments of 1962 (P.L. 87-543) provided for social services through which AFDC recipients would be prepared for work and gave states the option of extending AFDC benefits to unemployed fathers with needy children. The 1962 amendments, together with the Manpower Development and Training Act of that year, marked a shift from an "old welfare" based on transfer payments to a "new welfare" based on opportunity and development (Reid, 1995:2218). The Johnson administration's 1967 Work Incentive Program (WIN) (P.L. 90-36) further encouraged work by permitting AFDC mothers to keep part of their earnings and by developing day-care and training programs (Barker, 1991).

Rather than reforming welfare, Nixon's 1969 Family Assistance Plan proposed replacing state-administered, state/federal-funded AFDC programs, whose benefits varied widely throughout the United States, with a federal guaranteed minimum income for all employed indigent families with children. FAP was approved twice by the House of Representatives but was defeated in the Senate. Opponents included conservatives who opposed federal support for social welfare, and liberals, including the National Welfare Rights Organization and the National Association of Social Workers, who argued that proposed benefit levels were too low and work requirements too strict (Barker, 1991; Alexander, 1995; Dickinson, 1995; Reid, 1995).

In 1977, Democratic President Jimmy Carter made his attempt to reform welfare. The Carter plan for Better Jobs and Income proposed replacing AFDC, Food Stamps, and SSI with a "national minimum income for families, individuals, and the elderly," with varying benefit levels based on work potential and participation. The proposal also called for creating 1.4 million public-service jobs for participants. The complicated Carter plan was never brought to a vote in Congress (Dickinson, 1995).

During the Carter administration, however, accessibility to Food Stamps was improved by eliminating the purchase requirement; poor families were helped to pay heating bills through the Low Income Home Energy Assistance Program (LIHEAP); the right of all Americans to employment was affirmed by the Full Employment and Balanced Growth Act (P.L. 95-523); and the Child Abuse Prevention and Treatment and Adoption Reform Act of 1978 (P.L. 95-266) and the Adoption Assistance and Child Welfare Act of 1980 (P.L. 96-272) were approved to address child abuse, improve adoption, and encourage the permanent adoptive placement of foster children (Barker, 1991; Alexander, 1995).

The civil rights movement inspired the development of a variety of social movement organizations advocating changes in social relationships. The rebirth of the women's movement was marked by Kennedy's appointment of a Commission on the Status of Women in 1961, the publication of Betty Friedan's *The Feminine Mystique* in 1963, and the founding of the National Organization for Women (NOW) in 1966. The gay rights movement was catalyzed by police violence at the Stonewall Inn in 1969. The American Association of Retired Persons (AARP), the largest U.S. senior citizens organization, was founded in 1958; and the Gray Panthers were founded by Maggie Kuhn in 1970 to advocate for the needs of the elderly and children (Alexander, 1995; Reid, 1995).

These new social movements fragmented the coalition for progressive reform by substituting concern about gender, ethnicity, religion, and sexual orientation for the traditional progressive emphasis on class and economic interests. The progressives' shift from economic and class concerns to those of status, along with a grass-roots tax revolt, manipulation of racial prejudice, and the rise of the political/religious right, helped lay the foundation for the "Reagan reaction" of the 1980s (Jansson, 1993:274–277; Reid, 1995:2221).

The 1950s and 1960s had been decades of rising standards of living for working- and middle-class people. An expanding U.S. economy seemed capable of benefiting all segments of the population, as Keynesian economists increased government spending to reduce unemployment or decreased spending to reduce inflation. The late 1970s, however, were characterized by *stagflation,* inflation without economic growth. Purchasing power was eroded by rising prices and taxes, as inflation pushed wage earners into higher income tax brackets. Economic discontent fueled the successful Proposition 13 initiative, which sharply reduced local taxes in California and inspired a nationwide tax revolt against government expenditures, in particular against costly "welfare" measures (Barker, 1991; Jansson, 1993; Trattner, 1994).

Republican strategists skillfully manipulated the racial prejudices of economically vulnerable voters. Aware from public opinion polls that many lower- and middle-class whites believed that their rising taxes were the consequence of social welfare programs which disproportionately benefited the "unworthy poor," especially women and racial minorities, Republicans portrayed Democrats as supporters of "welfare programs, urban riots, high taxes, busing, and affirmative action" and themselves as supporters of "the silent majority of law-abiding citizens" (Jansson, 1993).

In reaction to the gains of the civil rights movement and the social forces which were threatening the status quo, a strong conservative social movement mobilized support for a return to limited government, *laissez faire,* individual responsibility, traditional gender roles, school prayer, enforcement of morality, and the "right to life." By 1980, the new religious-political right coalition included some 90 constituent organizations and provided important support for Reagan (Day, 1989; Reid, 1995).

The Reagan Reaction and Social Retreat (1980–1996)

An early follower of Roosevelt and a Democrat until 1962, Ronald Reagan had become a popular conservative speaker attacking federal bureaucracy, federal regulations, welfare programs, high federal taxes, and the Warren Court's liberal interpretation of the Constitution. He espoused a frontier philosophy of self-sufficiency and believed that human needs should be met through work—augmented, if necessary, by private, voluntary charity but not by government programs. Believing that the United States was besieged throughout the world by communist expansion, Reagan advocated massive increases in military spending. Through **supply-side economics**—"a combination of reduced government spending on social programs, a heavy dose of military expenditures, the termination of government regulations, tax cuts (especially for the well-to-do), and a balanced budget"—benefits generated by investments of the wealthy, Reagan argued, would "trickle down" to the middle and working classes and to the poor. Promising a return to normal times following decades of unsettling reform, Reagan was elected President in 1980, obsessed with "lowering taxes, increasing America's defenses, and cutting social spending" (Jansson, 1993:274–277; Trattner, 1994:363).

With collaboration from Democratic legislators who feared the potential political power of the conservative movement, Republicans succeeded in lowering taxes for the rich, sharply increasing military expenditures, and decreasing public support for the unemployed and working poor.

The Omnibus Budget Reconciliation Act (OBRA) of 1981 (P.L. 97-35) cut federal funds for low- and moderate-income housing by 57 percent, AFDC by 17.4 percent, Food Stamps by 14.3 percent, and an array of social services for poor people by 23.5 percent. The act toughened eligibility standards for AFDC, Food Stamps, and unemployment insurance; eliminated AFDC work incentives; and folded 57 programs into seven block grants funded at amounts substantially lower than those allocated previously to the individual programs. The OBRA focused its cuts on means-tested programs and avoided cuts to the more costly entitlement programs, which had more powerful constituencies. When Reagan proposed cuts in SSI and Social Security, Save Our Security (SOS), a new coalition of old-age groups, unions, and other liberal organizations vigorously protested and forced the administration to back down (Jansson, 1993:284–286; Trattner, 1994:366; Dickinson, 1995:1009).

From 1980 to 1983, total funding for social welfare programs was reduced by 7 percent. Some programs, however, took much heavier hits. School breakfasts and lunches, the summer feeding program for children, and the Special Food Program for Women, Infants, and Children (WIC) were cut by 29 percent, AFDC and Food Stamps by 13 percent, compensatory education by 17 percent, and unemployment and training programs by 60 percent (Day, 1989:389).

The Economic Recovery Tax Act of 1981 addressed Reagan's second area of concern, with a 20 percent reduction in personal income taxes over 3 years and major reductions in corporate income taxes. After a battle within the administration between "supply siders" and persons concerned about the rapidly escalating federal deficit, the Tax Equity and Fiscal Responsibility Act of 1982 (P.L. 97-248) took a new tack. Arguing that "everyone has to suffer" because of the fiscal crisis facing the country, the act took back part of the corporate tax cuts and slashed Medicaid and Medicare services, AFDC, child support enforcement, SSI, and Unemployment Compensation (Jansson, 1993:285–286; Alexander, 1995:2645).

Reagan sought unprecedented peacetime increases in military spending, proposing to increase the military budget by $1.46 trillion[3] over 5 years. More than $1 trillion was proposed as down payment for the Strategic Defense Initiative, better known as "Star Wars," a space-based, laser-guided antimissile system that many scientists believed was unattainable. Although the Democrat-controlled Congress did not appropriate all the military funds Reagan requested, by 1986 annual military expenditures totaled $268 billion, more than double the 1980 level (Day, 1989:381; Jansson, 1993; Trattner, 1994:273–274).

Having come into office promising to balance the budget, the Reagan/Bush administration ran the highest deficits in the nation's history, more than doubled the national debt to $2.6 trillion (Trattner, 1994:369, 379), and created the stimulus for the balanced budget movement that would prove a grave threat to social welfare programs by the mid-1990s.

Other significant social legislation, sometimes restricting and sometimes expanding social welfare, was enacted during the Reagan presidency. Pell grants, loans, and work-study support for college education became less available and more costly. The Comprehensive Employment and Training Act (CETA) was terminated, destroying 400,000 government-subsidized jobs, and replaced by the Job Training Partnership Act (JTPA), which subsidized private-sector job training organizations. Amendments to the Social Security Act (P.L. 98-81) placed Social Security on a financially stable basis by expanding mandatory participation, reducing benefits, and delaying the age of retirement. The Tax Reform Act of 1986 (P.L. 99-514) reduced income taxes and increased the benefits of the Earned Income Tax Credit. The Education of the Handicapped Act (P.L. 99-457) provided federal assistance for early intervention services for infants and toddlers with disabilities. The Stewart B. McKinney Homeless Assistance Act (P.L. 100-77) established the Interagency Council on Homelessness to coordinate and fund public programs for homeless people. The Hunger Prevention Act (P.L. 100-435) expanded and strengthened Food Stamps (Day, 1989; Alexander, 1995).

By the mid-1980s, "workfare"—state and local welfare programs requiring recipients to work for all or part of their benefits—seemed to be an idea whose time had come. By 1987, workfare programs existed in some forty states but, according to a General Accounting Office study of sixty-one programs, had little effect in moving recipients off welfare. Reagan's contribution to welfare reform was the Family Support Act of 1988 (P.L. 100-485). The act improved child sup-

---

[3]When we read about expenditures of millions, billions, and trillions of dollars, most of us have a difficult time imagining just how much money is being talked about. If you had $1 million and spent it at the rate of $1,000 per day, you would be broke in about 2 years and 9 months. If you spent $1 billion at the same rate, you would be broke in about 2,740 years. It has been estimated that $1 trillion would be equal to a tightly packed stack of $1,000 bills 67 miles high, two to three times the cruising altitude of commercial airliners.

port enforcement and created the Job Opportunities and Basic Skills (JOBS) program to improve employability of AFDC recipients through education and training, reimbursement for work-related expenses, and child care and health care for up to a year after leaving AFDC for employment. Single AFDC parents with children older than 3, and at state option older than 1, were required to work (Barker, 1991:122; Trattner, 1994:375–376; Alexander, 1995:2645).

During the first 3 years of the Reagan administration, the rate of poverty increased from 11.7 to 15.3 percent, "the highest rate and the greatest number (some 35.3 million) since the mid-1960s." In 1985, the Physicians Task Force on Hunger in America, headed by social worker Larry Brown, reported that hunger was widespread and serious, affecting some 20 million persons, largely because of the failure of Reagan's supply-side economics. In 1986, the National Coalition for the Homeless reported a "new wave of destitute citizens [living] in the nation's streets . . . a great many of whom were children and infants." In 1988, a cover story on "Begging in America" ran in *Time* magazine. The principle of *progressive taxation,* the idea that those with higher incomes should pay a higher percentage in taxes than those with lower incomes, was turned on its head by Reagan. Between 1981 and 1985, taxes paid by the poorest one-fifth of the population increased an average of $137, while the taxes of the wealthiest one-fifth decreased by $2,531 per taxpayer (Jansson, 1993:285; Trattner, 1994:369–376). The policies of "Reaganomics" resulted in "falling wages, cuts in social benefits and services, and higher taxes," which took their toll in the lives of the poor (Dickinson, 1995:1010).

George Bush, who had served as Reagan's Vice President, followed Reagan's lead in playing to racial prejudice during his Presidential campaign against Michael Dukakis. Promising to foster "a kinder, gentler America," Bush continued the Reagan policies of support for massive military expenditures and opposition to tax increases. Even after the Soviet empire dissolved, and social reformers saw a once-in-a-lifetime opportunity for a "peace dividend" through which the high military expenditures of the Cold War could be shifted to other purposes, Bush adamantly opposed cuts in the military budget. Under pressure to reduce the federal deficit, Congress agreed to reduce domestic and military spending proportionately over several years, with the stipulation that the military budget could not be "raided" to increase social expenditures (Jansson, 1993:294–296).

Although homelessness, poverty, and economic inequality grew during the Bush administration, people with disabilities were protected against discrimination in employment, housing, and public accommodations by enactment of the Americans with Disabilities Act of 1990 (P.L. 101-336); and discrimination based on race, gender, disability, or religion was restricted by the Civil Rights Act of 1991 (P.L. 102-166) (Alexander, 1995; Dickinson, 1995; Reid, 1995).

In the three-way race for the Presidency in 1992, Democrat Bill Clinton defeated Bush and Independent millionaire Ross Perot. Clinton emphasized domestic issues, proposing to strengthen the economy, reduce taxes on the middle class, provide universal health insurance, and "end welfare as we know it." Clinton signed the Family and Medical Leave Act (P.L. 103-3), which had been vetoed by Bush, providing unpaid leave for childbirth, adoption, and family health-care needs; lifted the "gag rule," which prevented federally subsidized family planning clinics from discussing abortion; initiated a campaign for free immunization of every child; and attempted to end discrimination against gay men and lesbians in the military (Trattner, 1994:387–395; Alexander, 1995:2647; Reid, 1995:2223–2224).

The Clinton health-care reform legislation proposed reducing costs and increasing accessibility by enrolling all citizens in "regional health alliances," which would contract with health-care providers for "managed care" of basic health coverage. Competing legislation backed by the National Association of Social Workers proposed a "single-payer" model similar to the Canadian health-care system. Conservative critics launched a media campaign contending that the Clinton plan would decrease the benefits and quality of services available to those currently insured. Congress adjourned for the 1994 election campaign without enacting health-care legislation (Trattner, 1994; Dickinson, 1995).

Clinton proposed welfare reform which would "make work pay"; improve child support enforcement; provide education, training, and services "to help people get off and stay off welfare"; and limit benefits to 2 years (Reed and Ellwood, 1993). The Clinton proposal was scheduled for consideration after health care. The midterm elections of 1994 brought Republican majorities to the House of Representatives and the Senate for the first time in 40 years, and shifted the debate over welfare reform and the role of government in social welfare activity dramatically to the political right.

The Republicans campaigned in 1994 on a platform packaged as a **Contract with America.** Appealing simplistically to mainstream values and fears, the contract promised to debate and vote during the first 100 days of the 104th Congress on the Fiscal Responsibility Act (balanced budget and line-item veto), the Taking Back Our Streets Act (getting tough on crime), the Personal Responsibility Act (welfare reform), the Family Reinforcement Act, the American Dream Restoration Act (middle-class tax relief), the National Security Restoration Act (increased military funding), the Senior Citizens Fairness Act (reduced taxes on Social Security benefits), the Job Creation and Wage Enhancement Act (capital gains tax cuts and business incentives), the Common Sense Legal Reform Act (limiting corporations' product liability), and the Citizen Legislature Act (term limits) (Facts on File, 1994). Under the leadership of the right-wing Speaker of the House, Newt Gingrich, legislation related to each of the proposals except congressional term limits was passed by the House of Representatives.

The House Republican proposals for welfare reform enacted in the Personal Responsibility Act included: changing AFDC from an entitlement program to fixed-funding block grants under which states would set eligibility criteria and benefit levels; denying AFDC benefits to unmarried women under 18; establishing "family caps" denying AFDC benefits to additional children born to a family receiving AFDC; requiring adults to work after 2 years of education or training; and setting a 5-year lifetime limit on AFDC assistance. The Personal Responsibility Act as passed by the House maintained Food Stamps as an entitlement but reduced benefits by 14 percent over 5 years; terminated Food Stamps after 90 days to able-bodied unemployed adults willing to work but unable to find jobs; eliminated federal nutrition standards; ended the federal guarantee of a free lunch for every poor school child; converted the WIC, school lunch, and school breakfast programs into block grants; ended the eligibility of legal immigrants for federal safety-net programs; and eliminated 360,000 disabled children from SSI (Pear, 1995). Conflict over how to allocate block grant funds to states with differing needs delayed action in the Senate. In early 1996, the House/Senate conference report was vetoed by President Clinton and the Republican proposals for welfare reform failed to become law.

Although the future of social welfare's response to human needs in the United States is uncertain, during the course of the twentieth century social welfare has developed into a system of support that goes far beyond day-to-day survival needs. Although survival needs continue to be crucial for the millions who still live in poverty, the biological, social, and psychological aspects of human existence are being addressed in new and expanded ways. As we will see in Chapters 6 and 7, however, the programs comprising the U.S. social welfare system are often quite fragmented and fail to deal holistically with human needs. Nevertheless, social welfare has over the centuries proven to be an adaptable and effective element in enabling people to improve their lives.

LET'S REVIEW

This chapter focuses on the role of mobilization by social reformers in responding to and influencing historical events that have shaped the development of social welfare in the United States. The chapter traces the increasingly crucial role played by public social welfare in responding to human need.

Together, Chapters 4 and 5 have provided a foundation for understanding the current social welfare system in the United States. Chapters 6 and 7 will describe the structure and day-to-day operation of the current social welfare system in the United States, and will include glimpses of social welfare in our other three societies. The current social welfare system of the United States is comprised of many programs, each of which tends to focus on specific needs. An overall framework to coordinate service delivery is lacking, leading to gaps in coverage and administrative inefficiencies.

STUDY QUESTIONS

1 How has mobilization by social reformers affected the development of social welfare in the United States?

2 Some people believe that immediate self-interest is the only viable motivation for participation in attempts to change social policies. Others believe that altruistic concern about the welfare of others is a viable motivation for participation. As you reflect upon the efforts of social workers and other reformers that have been referred to in this chapter, what do you think? What potential social reform roles are there for you as a social worker or citizen?

3 How is it that social conditions that are accepted as normative during one historical era come to be seen as social issues requiring reform in another?

4 Select a piece of social welfare legislation in which you are interested. In your university library, use the index to a major newspaper such as *The New York Times* or the *Washington Post* to locate contemporary news articles describing the social issue and enactment of the legislation. Try to identify social reformers and organizations who advocated for or against the legislation. Were they beneficiary or conscience constituents?

5 Read a biography or autobiography about the life and work of a reformer who worked on an issue about which you care. How were the reformer's efforts affected by the economic and other events in the social environment of the time? How did gender, race, and socioeconomic class affect the reformer's work? A good place to begin your search is in the biographical section of the *Encyclopedia of Social Work,* 19th ed. (Edwards, 1995).

KEY TERMS AND CONCEPTS

personal troubles	witch hunts and redbaiting
beneficiary constituencies	War on Poverty
conscience constituencies	Great Society
Freedmen's Bureau	Economic Opportunity Act of 1964
settlement houses	Medicare
progressivism	Medicaid
economic depression	revenue sharing
recession	block grants
New Deal	supply-side economics
Social Security Act of 1935	Contract with America

SUGGESTED READINGS

Davis, Allen F. 1967. *Spearheads for Reform: The Social Settlements and the Progressive Movement 1890–1914.* New York: Oxford University Press. An inspiring description of the contributions of social reformers to social welfare during a time of social ferment in the United States.

Franke, Richard W., and Barbara H. Chasin. 1994. *Kerala Radical Reform as Development in an Indian State,* 2d ed. Oakland, CA: Institute for Food and Development Policy. Kerala now has some of the Third World's highest levels of health, education, and social justice. Without idealizing Kerala's achievements, the authors describe the role of movements for social justice in its successful struggle to redistribute wealth and power.

Jansson, Bruce S. 1993. *The Reluctant Welfare State: A History of American Social Welfare Policies,* 2d ed. Pacific Grove, CA: Brooks/Cole. An excellent history of the development of social welfare in the United States.

Olsson, Sven E. 1990. *Social Policy and the Welfare State in Sweden.* Lund, Sweden: Arkiv. The author describes the development of social welfare policy in Sweden during the late nineteenth and twentieth centuries. The roles of radical intellectuals and popular social movements in the development of the modern Swedish welfare state are discussed, and issues of decentralization and privatization are explored.

Wilson, Dorothy Clarke. 1975. *Stranger and Traveler: The Story of Dorothea Dix, American Reformer.* Boston: Little, Brown. Biography of the first major woman social reformer in the United States.

REFERENCES

Alexander, Chauncey A. 1996. Distinctive dates in social welfare history. In *Encyclopedia of Social Work,* 19th ed. Washington, DC: National Association of Social Workers, pp. 2631–2647.

Associated Press. 1996. Strike against Toys "Я" Us widens as firm resists Swedish labor policy. *Bangor* (Maine) *Daily News,* May 18, p. A7.

Axinn, June, and Herman Levin. 1982. *Social Welfare: A History of the American Response to Need,* 2d ed. White Plains, NY: Longman.

———. 1992. *Social Welfare: A History of the American Response to Need,* 3d ed. White Plains, NY: Longman.

Barker, Robert L. 1991. *The Social Work Dictionary,* 2d ed. Washington, DC: National Association of Social Workers.

Blockson, Charles L. 1987. *The Underground Railway: First-Person Narratives of Escapes to Freedom in the North.* New York: Prentice Hall.

Davis, Allen F. 1967. *Spearheads for Reform: The Social Settlements and the Progressive Movement 1890–1914.* New York: Oxford University Press.

Day, Phyllis J. 1989. *A New History of Social Welfare.* Englewood Cliffs, NJ: Prentice Hall.

Dickinson, Nancy S. 1995. Federal social legislation from 1961 to 1994. In *Encyclopedia of Social Work,* 19th ed. Washington, DC: National Association of Social Workers, pp. 1005–1013.

Edwards, Richard L., ed. 1995. *Encyclopedia of Social Work,* 19th ed. Washington, DC: National Association of Social Workers.

Facts on File. 1994. Text of the Republican Party candidates' "Contract with America." November 10, p. 827.

Freedberg, Sharon M. and Joan L. Goldstein. 1986. Reynolds, Bertha Capen. In Walter I. Trattner, ed., *Biographical Dictionary of Social Welfare in America.* New York: Greenwood Press, pp. 616–619.

Hendrickson, Kenneth E. 1986. DuBois, William Edward Burghardt. In Walter I. Trattner, ed., *Biographical Dictionary of Social Welfare in America.* New York: Greenwood Press, pp. 250–252.

Jansson, Bruce S. 1993. *The Reluctant Welfare State: A History of American Social Welfare Policies,* 2d ed. Pacific Grove, CA: Brooks/Cole.

Loavenbruck, Grant, and Paul Keys. 1987. Settlements and neighborhood centers. In *Encyclopedia of Social Work,* 18th ed. Silver Spring, MD: National Association of Social Workers, pp. 556–561.

Maris, Ronald W. 1988. *Social Problems.* Chicago: Dorsey Press.

Mauss, Armand L. 1975. *Social Problems as Social Movements.* Philadelphia: J.B. Lippincott.

Mayo, Marjorie Henton. 1986. Haynes, George Edmund. In Walter I. Trattner, ed., *Biographical Dictionary of Social Welfare in America,* New York: Greenwood Press, pp. 362–364.

McCarthy, John D., and Mayer N. Zald. 1977. Resource mobilization and social movements: A partial theory. *American Journal of Sociology,* 82(6):1212–1241.

Mills, C. Wright. 1969. *The Sociological Imagination.* New York: Grove Press.

Mohl, Raymond A. 1969. Poverty in early America, a reappraisal: The case of eighteenth century New York City. *New York History,* 50(1):5–27.

Morris Aldon D. 1984. *The Origins of the Civil Rights Movement: Black Communities Organizing for Change.* New York: The Free Press.

Pear, Robert. 1995. House backs bill undoing decades of welfare policy. *The New York Times,* March 25, p. 1.

Reed, Bruce, and David Ellwood. 1993. Charge to the working group on welfare reform, family support and independence. Washington. DC: Welfare Reform Working Group, September 23.

Reed, James. 1996. Sanger, Margaret. In Walter I. Trattner, ed., *Biographical Dictionary of Social Welfare in America.* New York: Greenwood Press, pp. 656–660.

Reid, P. Nelson. 1996. Social welfare history. In *Encyclopedia of Social Work,* 19th ed. Washington, DC: National Association of Social Workers, pp. 2206–2225.

Schlesinger, Arthur M., Jr. 1967. *The Age of Roosevelt: The Crisis of the Old Order, 1919–1933.* Boston: Houghton Mifflin.

Swedish Institute. 1992. *Labor Relations in Sweden.* Stockholm: The Swedish Institute, Fact Sheets on Sweden (FS3). Pamphlet.

Trattner, Walter I. 1994. *From Poor Law to Welfare State: A History of Social Welfare in America.* New York: The Free Press.

U.S. Congress, House of Representatives. 1994. *Green Book.* Washington, DC: U.S. Government Printing Office.

Wandersee, Winifred D. 1986. Dewson, Mary (Molly) Williams. In Walter I. Trattner, ed., *Biographical Dictionary of Social Welfare in America,* New York: Greenwood Press, pp. 231–233.

Whitaker, William H. 1970. *The determinants of social movement success: A study of the National Welfare Rights Organization.* Ph.D. dissertation, Brandeis University, Florence Heller Graduate School for Advanced Studies in Social Welfare, Waltham, MA.

———. 1993. *Maine Community Childhood Hunger Identification Project Report.* Orono: University of Maine School of Social Work.

Wilson, Dorothy Clarke. 1975. *Stranger and Traveler: The Story of Dorothea Dix, American Reformer.* Boston: Little, Brown.

A SOCIETY IN PICTURES—
MEXICO

PASEO DE LA REFORMA, MEXICO CITY

Mexico City is the second largest city in the world. In overall appearance, it resembles many other large, modern cities. It has beautiful boulevards and narrow side streets, modern high-rise buildings and elegant older structures, and a wide range of restaurants and shops. (See "On the Street in Mexico City," Introduction.) (Russell Dian/Monkmeyer)

WORKER DISPLACED BY NAFTA

The promise of the North American Free Trade Agreement (NAFTA) has gone unfulfilled for many in Mexico. Flavio Ortega, 35, is a former computer technician who now makes his living shining shoes in front of a Howard Johnson's in Monterrey (DePalma, 1995:A1). (Phillip Diederich/*The New York Times*)

A SHANTY TOWN IN JUAREZ

Shanty towns are found throughout Mexico, particularly surrounding the major cities, where they often provide housing for large numbers of people. Some 38 percent of the residents of Mexico City live in such towns, of which the largest, Nezahualcoyotl—commonly called Neza—houses some 2.7 million people. (See "The Human Face of Social Welfare 4: Self-Help and Dignity," Chapter 1.) (Abbas Magnum)

STREET VENDOR IN TAXCO, MEXICO

Street vendors are a common sight in many Mexican cities. Once a predominantly agricultural society, Mexico has in recent years experienced a great increase in its urban population as rural families—increasingly forced off the land as a result of NAFTA—move to the cities in search of better living conditions. One of the ways in which many of these families support themselves is by selling goods on the street. (F. B. Grunzweig/Photo Researchers)

A CLASSROOM SCENE IN A SCHOOL OUTSIDE MEXICO CITY

In a developing country such as Mexico, money for capital-intensive public facilities is limited. These children from a poor suburb attend school in a building where their desks are constructed from concrete building blocks. All Mexican children are given, free of charge, new textbooks and workbooks, which they are permitted to keep. (Abbas/Magnum)

A SOCIETY IN PICTURES—POLAND

A VIEW OF WARSAW TODAY

The business district of Warsaw looks like the downtown of any contemporary city in Western Europe. There are many high-rise office buildings, hotels, and apartment buildings. The view here is of the city center looking north from the Palace of Culture over office and apartment buildings. (Porterfield-Chickering/Photo Researchers)

OLD TOWN, WARSAW

The Old Town, like much of Warsaw, was destroyed during World War II following an uprising against the Nazis. As an expression of their commitment to cultural survival, Poles reconstructed the Old Town to look exactly as it had before the war. They did such a good job that today it is hard to believe the buildings are not hundreds of years old. (See "On the Street in Warsaw," Introduction.) (Tony Stone/Tony Stone Images)

SMALL VILLAGE IN POLAND NEAR THE RUSSIAN BORDER

While nearly 60 percent of the Polish people live in cities, the remainder live in rural settings, where traditional extended families are still common. As a consequence of the Holocaust, deportation of ethnic Germans, and redrawing of national borders following World War II, Poland is now a homogeneous society in which 98 percent of the population, like this grandmother and her two grandsons, is of pure Polish extraction. (Jill Hartley/Photo Researchers)

WORSHIPPERS IN LOWICZ, POLAND

The Roman Catholic Church continues to be very popular and powerful in Poland. Following the defeat of the Communists, it won back much of its confiscated property, won adoption of one of Europe's most restrictive antiabortion laws, and prevented the constitutional protection of the rights of gay men and lesbians. A 1995 survey of public opinion reported that 72 percent of Poles trust the church, but 69 percent believe that the church is too involved in politics, and more than half of all Polish Catholics believe abortion laws should be liberalized (Perlez, 1995a). (Witold Krassowski/*The New York Times*)

POLISH POLICE INTERVENE TO STOP DOMESTIC VIOLENCE

During a domestic violence call in Warsaw, a police officer arrests a man for beating a woman. Polish police today are young, often inexperienced replacements for the former Communist militia. With police hampered by lack of experience and resources, street crime has been increasing (Perlez, 1995b). (Witold Krassowski/Matrix International)

A SOCIETY IN PICTURES—SWEDEN

A SWEDISH CHILD WELFARE CLINIC

The first child welfare clinics appeared in Sweden in the early 1940s. Emphasizing preventive medicine, the 1,260 clinics located throughout the country provide checkups for 99 percent of all 1-year-olds and two-thirds of all other preschool children. Infants are brought to the clinics an average of ten times per year, 1-year-olds three times, and older children two times per year. In addition, clinic nurses make house calls, mainly to families with infants. (See "Health Care in Sweden," Chapter 7.) (Courtesy of Swedish Information Service)

NURSERY SCHOOL IN GIDEONSBERG, SWEDEN

Nursery schools in Sweden are primarily run and financed by county government. Kindergartens hold two classes a day, one in the morning and one in the afternoon, each for 3 hours. In addition, many day nurseries provide day care for children whose parents are employed outside the home. Day nurseries are open from 6:30 a.m. until 6:30 p.m. and provide instructional programs similar to those offered in kindergarten. (Rolf Carlson/Pressens Bild)

INTERIOR OF A SWEDISH NURSERY SCHOOL

In Sweden, it is considered desirable for children to attend either a kindergarten or a nursery school beginning at the age of 4 or 5 at the latest. Both kindergartens and day nurseries provide free health care and, as here, meals when appropriate. (Eva Wernlid/Tiofoto AB)

PHYSICALLY LIMITED STUDENTS IN A SWEDISH SCHOOL

One of the goals of Swedish social welfare policy is to enable people who encounter major difficulties in their daily lives because of physical, mental, or other problems to participate in social activities and live like other people. This philosophy extends to education, where the physically limited are integrated into regular classrooms and attend school with other children. (Courtesy of Swedish Information Service)

TAXIS FOR THE PHYSICALLY LIMITED IN SWEDEN

Among the steps taken in Sweden to provide access to public places for those with physical limitations are audible signals on traffic lights and access ramps in buildings. In addition, the municipal transport system enables the physically limited, as well as the elderly, to ride taxis or specially equipped vehicles while paying about the same fares as on the regular public transportation network, which is itself designed to be accessible to those with limitations. (See "On the Street in Sweden," Chapter 2.) (Bent-Göran Carlsson/Tiofoto AB)

A SOCIETY IN PICTURES— THE UNITED STATES

CINCINNATI, OHIO

Like many other large American cities, downtown Cincinnati has experienced an economic rebirth. Sleek new high-rise office buildings and hotels have replaced decayed buildings, and many of the older buildings that remain have been restored or refurbished. Such urban renewal projects may increase homelessness by destroying affordable housing. Community land trusts are one solution. (See "On the Street in Yonkers, New York—the REAPS Community Land Trust," Chapter 7.) (Tom McHugh/Photo Researchers)

AN IRON CURTAIN ON THE U.S.–MEXICAN BORDER

In an effort to turn away increasing numbers of illegal immigrants who try to enter the United States to obtain jobs to feed their families, the U.S. Immigration and Naturalization Service has erected walls of steel at popular crossing points on the U.S.–Mexican border. Such barricades hinder but seldom stem the flow of immigrants. (See "The Human Face of Social Welfare 21: They've Gone to the Other Side," Chapter 10.) (Lenny Ignelzi/AP/Wide World)

A SWEATSHOP IN CHINATOWN

Throughout American history, immigrants have provided a continuing source of vitality, new cultural ideas and, in many instances, low-cost labor. In the garment factories of Chinatown, where the average worker's annual income is less than $6,000, women hunch over sewing machines in the glare of overhead lamps. (See "The Human Face of Social Welfare 10: The Government and the Workplace— Sweatshops," Chapter 4.) (Eugene Gordon)

HOMELESSNESS IN GREENWICH VILLAGE, NEW YORK CITY

Every large American city has a population of homeless people living on the street. Popular living areas include grates over exhaust vents, where the escaping air provides life-giving warmth. Others find corners or doorways in which to set down cardboard "beds" on which they sleep and live. (See "On the Street in the United States—Homelessness," Chapter 1) (Bob Combs/Rapho/Photo Researchers)

WORKFARE ON THE LOWER EAST SIDE, NEW YORK CITY

In New York City all able-bodied, childless applicants for Home Relief are required to work in exchange for their benefits. Critics of workfare say that recipients take jobs away from city workers, without learning skills. Meeting workfare requirements prevents some participants from attending school, which might enable them to leave the welfare roles (Martin, 1995:A1). (Librado Romero/*The New York Times*)

NOTES

DePalma, Anthony. 1995. For Mexico, NAFTA's promise of jobs is still just a promise. *The New York Times,* October 10, p. A1.
Martin, Douglas, 1995. New York workfare expansion fuels debate. *The New York Times,* September 1, p. A1.
Perlez, Jane, 1995a. Shrinking gap between Church and Polish state. *The New York Times,* July 17, p. A13.
———. 1995b. Poles dismayed at unchecked crime: Citizens bypassing the police in a weak justice system. *The New York Times,* June 19, p. A7.

6

WHAT IS THE STRUCTURE OF SOCIAL WELFARE TODAY?

WHAT TO EXPECT FROM THIS CHAPTER

In Chapter 5 we discussed how social reform movements have influenced the historical development of social welfare in the United States. This chapter focuses on the present: How are social welfare services organized in today's world? This chapter and the one that follows are closely related. This chapter examines the various ways in which social welfare services may be structured. Chapter 7 describes specific social welfare programs in the four countries we are comparing: the United States, Sweden, Poland, and Mexico.

We have seen in earlier chapters that people have biological, psychological, and social needs. Often times social welfare programs are organized to respond to such needs at predictable points in the human life cycle. One way to think about social welfare programs is in terms of the age group that is being targeted. Programs may focus on the needs of children or the elderly, for example. Other programs may focus on needs such as adequate nutrition, housing, and health care, which are present throughout the life span.

Knowing that we wish to devise a program to meet a specific human need does not tell us much about how to structure the program to ensure its effectiveness. How the program will be financed, who will be eligible, and how the program will be administered are among the questions that must be answered.

The design of specific programs is often determined by the overall structure of the social welfare system. It is this structure, or design, that we will be studying in this chapter. Once grasped, it will be easier to understand specific programs such as Medicare, Social Security, and Unemployment Insurance, which are the subject of the next chapter.

LEARNING OBJECTIVES

When you have finished studying this chapter, you should be able to:

1 Explain the relationship between informal helping networks, social agencies, and social welfare programs.

2 Discuss competing rationales for distributing social welfare resources in cash and in kind.

3 Discuss advantages and disadvantages of public and private social welfare programs.

4 Distinguish between residual and institutional perspectives on social welfare.

5 Identify and define five "pillars" of social security.

INFORMAL HELPING NETWORKS, FORMAL AGENCIES, AND PROGRAMS

Let us begin by returning to familiar territory: formal and informal social welfare. Responsibility for the social welfare of others can be carried out in very direct personal activity, or less directly through organizations. As we indicated in Chapter 1, **informal (or natural) helping networks** consist of activities of *family, friends, neighbors, local churches, synagogues, and mosques, service organizations, and others who provide either spontaneous charity or mutual support in times of need.*

Each of us participates in informal helping networks. For example, out of concern about hunger, we might take part in a hunger walkathon, give money to a food pantry, or contribute nonperishable food to the annual letter carriers' food drive. Informal social welfare activities are most likely to occur at the local community level, although sometimes they benefit persons distant from the locality. "Trick-or-treat" for UNICEF is an example.

We also support more formal social welfare programs, which are organized, structured responses to need. Informal and formal helping activities range along a continuum from least to most formal, from spontaneous to planned. Formal social welfare programs are more structured, ongoing responses to need than are informal activities. Out of concern about hunger, formal responses might include volunteering monthly in a soup kitchen, or meeting regularly with a group of friends to write letters urging elected officials to support antihunger legislation. This formally organized letter writing might result in strengthening and expanding formal public antihunger programs such as Food Stamps or the Earned Income Tax Credit. Formal social welfare programs may be organized in the local community, or at the state, national, or even international level.

There is considerable controversy over whether it is better to provide help informally or on a formal basis (Gilbert, 1986:254). Some people today, for example, decry the diminished role of families in meeting the needs of their members, seeing in this change a deterioration in our sense of moral responsibility. Replacing natural care givers such as the family and the local community with large, formal, potentially rigid and impersonal public and private agencies is seen as being detrimental to the quality of help provided and as undermining important interpersonal relationships.

Others disagree, believing that the institutionalization of social welfare is indicative of a stronger commitment by individuals and society to helping others. Organized responses to need, they contend, are necessary because informal responses are insufficient to address the scope of needs that persists.

Both formal and informal means of providing social welfare resources can be effective. Wealthy, industrialized nations tend to emphasize formal helping because of the scale of their social and economic systems. In less affluent countries, more needs are dealt with informally.

In Mexico, for example, informal helping networks play a major role in dealing with many social problems. The approach to social welfare in a Mexican city such as Nezahualcóyotl—you may wish to refer to Chapter 1, "The Human Face of Social Welfare 4," for details—is basically informal. The problem of homelessness is solved by the homeless themselves, who exploit Mexico's political and economic disorganization to establish a toehold for themselves at the fringes of urban areas. They then work together to gain access to the social welfare system, eventually building stable communities in which they have an economic stake and that are served by formal service delivery structures.

Homelessness is handled quite differently in the United States. (See Chapter 1, "On the Street in the United States: Homelessness".) The pervasiveness of property ownership has eliminated fringe areas in which U.S. homeless can establish squatters' rights, and the U.S. political system usually is sufficiently powerful to prevent the takeover of property by homeless squatters. Instead, the available housing options—public shelters, welfare hotels, low-cost housing, rent subsidies, and so on—are choices within the formal social welfare system.

Another difference between the United States and Mexico is the composition of the homeless themselves. In the United States, the homeless poor are mixed with others who have been discharged from treatment centers but are still mentally ill or are substance abusers. With such a mixed group, it is difficult, although not impossible, to develop the kind of self-help networks that are common in poor Mexican communities.

We can see, then, that formal social welfare programs provide the structure and continuity necessary for long-term solutions to needs. The residents of Neza know that, which is why they struggle to gain access to the formal system, relying in the interim on informal helping networks to meet their basic survival needs. The Mexican response to the problem of homelessness illustrates the way in which the formal and informal helping systems can complement one another, a goal the United States still struggles with when trying to meet the needs of its homeless.

Social welfare should not become so formalized that people have difficulty utilizing their own informal helping networks. Nor should programs become so formalized that those seeking help become nameless, faceless "cases" instead of being treated as citizens and human beings.

The formal social welfare system works by making resources available to people in the form of programs administered by agencies. **Formal social welfare programs** are *organized, structured responses to need, carried out under public or private auspices, which distribute income or social services to targeted recipients.* The U.S. Social Security retirement program, for example, distributes retirement income to eligible people who are ages 62 or older. **Social welfare agencies** are *formal organizations whose manifest function is to administer social welfare programs so that they effectively and efficiently meet people's needs.* It is important to keep in mind that social welfare agencies and programs also have latent functions such as exercising control over the behavior of participants.

We are so accustomed to hearing about programs and agencies that we sometimes take their existence for granted. However, resources exist only if programs are created to make them available. Furthermore, the way programs are designed very much affects the resources provided. For example, unemployment insurance in the United States generally lasts for 26 weeks. No further benefits are paid after that time, whether or not the recipient has found a new job. Or consider education. Free public education is provided through high school, but not beyond. Because there is no free education beyond high school, many people in the United States are denied access to higher education.

This book is concerned primarily with formal social welfare services provided in a purposeful way by society for its members. Nevertheless, informal helping networks also make important contributions to the social welfare institution. Informal helping networks and formal social agencies are mutually interdependent. Sometimes that interdependence is planned. Sometimes it is not.

Let us look at Poland to illustrate how these relationships can develop. By law, the Polish family is responsible for meeting the needs of its members, both young and old (Brzozowski et al., n.d.:18). Given this mandate, the family becomes an important source of informal social welfare services. It is also people's primary link with the formal social welfare structure, because services to individuals are generally provided through their families. The Polish family, then, represents an important link between informal and formal helping structures.

However, Poland suffers from a severe housing shortage. It often takes 10 years or more of waiting before apartments become available for families that need them (Les, 1985:2–3). As a result, three or even four generations may live together in rather small apartments. In this sense, the Polish family functions as an informal social welfare system, providing housing for its members when the formal structure is unable to do so. However, data show that such crowded living conditions create problems for family members (Les, 1985:4). The inability of the formal social welfare system to provide adequate housing strains the informal resources of the family, thereby generating additional needs for counseling and other kinds of help.

Unlike in Poland, families in the United States are not legally responsible for caring for their adult members. Nevertheless, the current shortage of affordable housing has created a relationship between the informal and formal social welfare networks that is similar to the one in Poland. When people in the United States cannot find affordable housing, their first recourse is often to stay with friends or family while looking for a place to live. This was what happened to Toy Santiago's family—discussed in the Introduction—after there was a fire in their building. This is usually a temporary solution, and eventually either housing is found or the family becomes homeless. If homelessness occurs, other problems may follow: marital instability, difficulty getting the children to school, exposure to violence, and so on. (You will recall the problems encountered by the Brand family, when the Brands lived in a shelter for the homeless. See Chapter 1.)

We can see in the above examples how the informal helping network can be a valuable supplement to the formal system. However, informal resources are usually limited, and they can be easily overwhelmed by serious needs. Ideally, the informal system would provide as much help as it could and then the formal system would take over. In Sweden, the government is experimenting with an innovative housing policy designed to deal with the problems that arise when several generations live together. The proposed solution involves building apartments that contain separate miniapartments for elderly family members or teenagers. This allows the family members involved to have some independence while still participating in family life. It improves the family's chances of meeting more needs of its members and avoiding the need for formal social welfare services.

As we have already seen, the informal and formal systems do not always work well together. Both systems may become overburdened resulting in new problems. Nevertheless, it is important to remember that the two systems are linked, sometimes by design (the role of the family in Poland) and sometimes by necessity (the homeless in the United States). How well they work together is a function of the overall design and basic structure of the social welfare system.

PUBLIC AND PRIVATE SOCIAL WELFARE PROGRAMS

Another important characteristic of social welfare programs is the source of their funding. In theory, there is a clear distinction between publicly and privately funded social welfare programs. *Public social welfare programs* are funded by taxes. *Private, or voluntary, social welfare programs* are funded by voluntary charitable contributions of individuals and private organizations, by fees people pay for the services they receive, or by funds spent by corporations to provide social welfare services to their employees. In reality, the public–private distinction is not as clear. Government subsidies to "private" social agencies in the form of fees for the purchase of services, and as income tax write-offs of the costs of social welfare benefits provided to their employees by corporations has blurred the public–private distinction in many countries today. In the United States, for example, *Nonprofit Times* estimates that the top 100 domestic nonprofit organizations received government funds totaling $3.58 billion in 1990 (Beckman and Hoehn, 1992:27). In 1992, private social welfare organizations participating in United Way federated fund-raising campaigns received 45.4 percent of their income from government funding, 20.9 percent from fees and dues, 11.6 percent from United Way contributions, 10.5 percent from non-United Way fund raising, and 11.6 percent from other sources (Brilliant, 1995:2476).

Matters are further complicated by the existence of two major types of private social welfare organizations: traditional, *not-for-profit* voluntary agencies and an increasing number of for-profit, *proprietary* social welfare businesses. **Not-for-profit agencies** are *social welfare organizations established for social purposes other than making money for investors* (Barker, 1991:157). Examples include organizations such as Catholic Charities USA, the Child Welfare League of America, Big Brothers/Big Sisters, and settlement houses. **Proprietary social agencies** are *businesses that attempt to make a profit for their investors by selling personal social services.* For-profit nursing homes and halfway houses, and social workers in private practice, are examples of proprietary social welfare organizations. In Texas, even prisons are privately owned and operated for profit. Both not-for-profit and proprietary agencies may receive government funding as part of their income. Indeed, a 1986 study indicated that approximately one-third of the budget of an average private agency comes from public money (Sosin, 1986:44).

In countries with free-market economic systems, such as the United States, the public sector is intended to be "a counterforce to balance against the excesses and hazards of capitalism without inhibiting the free market's productive energies" (Gilbert, 1983:164). In other words, a manifest function of social welfare is to protect—without altering the fundamental nature of the capitalist economic system—those who are jeopardized by free market competition.

In other countries the objectives of the economic and social welfare systems may be more closely linked. Wojciechowski (1975:191), for example, notes that Poland under socialism was "a country strongly committed to the concept of governmental intervention through planning." In a socialist society, one of the purposes of the economic system is to achieve certain social welfare goals. Similarly, Sweden uses centralized planning as a way of managing market forces to achieve agreed-upon social goals. In both countries, the public sector is by far the largest component of the social welfare system. Private services are either very limited, as in Sweden, or closely tied to the government, as in Poland. (See "Approaches to Taxation in Sweden and the United States.")

In the United States, on the other hand, private agencies are a very important part of the social welfare system. Many people in the United States believe that

APPROACHES TO TAXATION IN SWEDEN AND THE UNITED STATES

There are interesting similarities and differences in the way Sweden and the United States make use of taxation for social welfare purposes. Both have a progressive income tax, but tax rates in Sweden are much higher than in the United States because of Sweden's much more extensive network of social welfare services. Social welfare services in Sweden are in part funded by an income tax levied by local governments. In contrast, municipalities in the United States rely heavily on property taxes.

Both Sweden and the United States offer tax exemptions for interest on home mortgages, but these are more generous in the United States. Other types of tax exemptions in the United States, such as for child-

care expenses incurred by working parents and for charitable contributions, are not widely used in Sweden. This is because Swedish child care is provided as a social welfare benefit, and because private charitable organizations are uncommon in a country with so extensive a public social welfare system. Finally, many social welfare income benefits are taxed in Sweden. Pensions and benefits paid to workers when they are ill, for example, are considered taxable income. In contrast, social welfare benefits sometimes are not taxed in the United States. U.S. Social Security retirement pensions paid to individuals whose total income exceeds a specified amount are one notable exception.

Source: Interviews and personal observations of Ron Federico, 1987.

government activity should be limited to those areas where it is absolutely necessary: levying taxes and providing for the national defense, for example. There is a strong tradition of neighbors helping neighbors—originally through informal helping networks and later through formally organized voluntary efforts. Motivated by the Judeo-Christian tradition of helping those in need, religious organizations have played an especially important role. In 1983, U.S. religious groups contributed an estimated $7.5 billion to social welfare concerns, exceeding the contributions of both corporations and foundations (Ortiz, 1995). Catholic, Protestant, Jewish and other sectarian agencies provide a wide range of personal social services.

Catholic Charities USA is the largest private social service network in the United States. The organization works to reduce poverty, support families, and empower communities through a network of 1,400 local agencies with more than 234,000 staff members and volunteers. Table 6-1 reports the numbers of people receiving various social services and emergency services through Catholic Charities in 1994. More than 11.1 million different persons were served. In addition to providing services, 134 Catholic dioceses worked at the national, state, and local levels on social policy and legislation related to income security and welfare reform, international justice and refugees, health care and insurance, hunger and nutrition, housing, and family life. Federal, state, county, and city governments provided 62 percent of Catholic Charities USA's $1.9 billion budget (Flynn, 1995).

Public and private agencies in the United States can be differentiated in terms of *accountability, responsibility, resources,* and *flexibility.* Later we will see how, in spite of their differences, public and private social welfare agencies work closely together.

TABLE 6-1   ROMAN CATHOLIC SOCIAL AND EMERGENCY SERVICES IN THE UNITED STATES, 1994

Social services	People served
Social support	913,256
Counseling	878,274
Education and family support	613,307
Socialization and neighborhood	503,728
Refugee settlement and immigration	246,476
Foster home, group home, and residential care	110,695
Pregnancy	109,947
Health care	87,315
Permanent housing	74,196
Adoption	42,174
Other	323,942
Total social service clients (unduplicated)	**3,903,270**
Emergency services	
Soup kitchens	1,236,731
Food pantries	2,615,759
Other food services	1,092,689
Temporary shelter	295,893
Other emergency services	1,984,663
Total emergency service clients (unduplicated)	**7,225,735**
Total social and emergency service clients (unduplicated)	**11,129,005**

Source: Patrice Flynn, *Catholic Charities USA 1994 Annual Report: Responding to Changing Times.* Washington, DC: The Urban Institute, 1995.

Accountability.   By law, public agencies are accountable to the public, whereas private agencies are accountable only to their governing body, usually a board of directors. As a result, the public has the legal right to obtain information about the operation of public agencies. Access to similar data about private agencies is likely to be limited to those who are part of the organization that runs the agency.

Responsibility.   Public agencies form the backbone of the social welfare system because they have been created to meet the basic needs of all citizens. Private agencies can be much more specialized, providing certain kinds of services to targeted user groups.

Resources.   Public programs have access to government funds, whereas private agencies depend on contributions, fees, and contracts. Therefore, most public agencies have a much larger resource base than do private ones. This usually enables them to assist many more people and to provide a wider range of services than private agencies can. Given their limited resources, private social agencies tend to distribute in-kind rather than cash benefits (Sosin, 1986). The Salvation Army, for example, provides meals and overnight shelter. Some private agencies, such as South Side Settlement, do provide limited cash grants and loans.

Flexibility.   Public agencies are open to input from citizens through the political process. However, this is usually time consuming and cumbersome, so these agencies may find it difficult to respond quickly to new situations or problems.

Private agencies receive input from their members, and decisions are made by their governing body. As a result, they may be able to respond fairly quickly to new ideas, needs, or situations.

Sometimes, private social agencies develop program innovations that demonstrate the need for and feasibility of new programs. Later the programs are sponsored more widely by public agencies that have greater resources. Settlement houses, for example, developed nursery school programs that were the forerunners of the federal Head Start Program.

Although voluntarism was lauded by President Bush and others using the rhetoric of "a thousand points of light," the private sector has been unable to keep up with increasing need as public funding for social welfare programs has been decreased.

Some of the differences between public and private agencies are illustrated by the New York City foster-care example ("The Human Face of Social Welfare 14"), which describes collaboration between public and private providers of social services.

The Role of the Market

Gilbert (1983:6) describes the current phase of welfare capitalism as one in which it is believed that profit-making strategies can and should be used by the welfare state. This has encouraged the commercialization of health and welfare through what is commonly called **privatization:** *the reliance on for-profit corporations, partnerships, private practice, and proprietary social services within the private sector to meet social needs* (Barker, 1991:181–182). Privatization involves transferring to the private, for-profit-sector personal social services that previously were provided by the public sector.

Privatization is seen by its advocates as a way to make service delivery more efficient and effective by reducing the size and power of large governmental social welfare bureaucracies. Reducing the cost of public services is attractive to those who believe that taxes are too high. In market-oriented societies such as the United States, the profit incentive is believed to increase efficiency and reduce the cost of services, a desirable goal in the eyes of many. Competition among social agencies is valuable, some contend, if it gives users a choice and encourages competing agencies to provide more efficient and appealing services.

Critics of privatization point to a number of drawbacks (Abramovitz, 1986). First, they raise the fundamental ethical question of whether public money spent on social welfare should go to pay profits or, to state the issue more dramatically, whether proprietary agencies should be permitted to make money from people's misery. There is a basic distinction between not-for-profit private agencies that use all of their resources to provide services, and for-profit agencies that seek to maximize income and reduce expenditures so that they make money for their owners. A related ethical issue is whether the profit motive leads proprietary agencies to reduce the quality of services and to exclude the most needy, who are usually the most expensive to help.

THE HUMAN FACE OF SOCIAL WELFARE 14

PUBLIC RESOURCES, PRIVATE SERVICES

Though New York City is legally responsible for children in foster care, the city actually provides little of the services the youngsters receive. Only about 1,700 youngsters are housed in city-operated foster homes. The remaining children are distributed—literally allocated in a process that often resembles a human bazaar—among the 57 [private] agencies that care for the children, under contracts [between the city and the private agencies] worth $300 million a year. . . .

The public and private agencies that run New York City's . . . foster care system are deeply split over who should control the system. . . .

Even government officials who are nominally in charge are saying that a major part of the problem is that the system is complex, unwieldy and not really under anyone's control. . . .

A 15-year-old Protestant girl who had given birth a year earlier was sent to the Mission of the Immaculate Virgin, a foster care center . . . run by the [Catholic] archdiocese. She told administrators there that she was sexually active, but they refused to provide her with birth control services. When she obtained birth control pills on her own, administrators took them away. A few months later, she became pregnant again.

A Protestant teenager was at the top of a list for placement in a group home run by a Jewish agency, but the spot was taken by a Jewish youngster lower on the list. The teenager had to go instead to a group home run by the city that did not have the supervision or the care for which the Jewish agency was known. The teenager dropped out of the program and ended up in prison on a weapons charge. . . .

"I just can't say, 'Do it,' and it gets done," [a city official] said. "There is a diffusion of responsibility and control that makes it difficult to manage. When you want to change something to make the system more efficient or more effective there are an awful lot of steps."

The preceding excerpt illustrates some of the differences between private and public agencies. Major responsibility for foster care in New York City rests with the public sector, which, in part because of the much greater scope of its responsibilities, is far larger and has far greater resources than the private agencies involved. Unfortunately, as the example also suggests, accountability is sometimes difficult to maintain in such a large system.

The case also illustrates the ability of private agencies to establish their own policies about service delivery. While public agencies must serve all who qualify, private agencies often provide services only to special groups.

Excerpted from Ari Goldman and Michael Oreskes, "New York Foster Care: A Public-Private Battleground," *The New York Times,* April 9, 1987, p. B1. Copyright © 1987 by The New York Times Company. Reprinted by permission.

Abramovitz (1986:261) presents data and arguments to suggest that the level of care and its availability to those who are especially disadvantaged suffer in profit-making agencies. If proprietary services are more expensive than those provided through the public or not-for-profit sectors, their costs may exclude those who are most needy but least able to pay. Allowing proprietary agencies to "skim" the easiest-, least-expensive-to-serve persons leaves the public and not-for-profit agencies to deal with the most difficult and costly needs. People seeking services may lack the information needed to compare and evaluate the quality of services available from competing sources, or they may lack access to the transportation or money necessary to use the services they prefer. Critics worry, too, that shifting responsibility away from the public sector will undermine societal commitment to social welfare. Then, if the proprietary sector proves unable or unwilling to provide adequate services, scaled-back public and not-for-profit agencies may be unable to meet the demands placed upon them. Finally, critics argue, because a devalued and poorly funded public sector might be expected to deliver shoddy services, those forced to use that system could end up being considered second-class citizens.

Privatization is not new. What is new is the belief that private services can be profit making, and the extent to which public funds are used to support private services. Abramovitz (1986:261) notes that by 1977 nearly 80 percent of U.S. nursing homes were operated for profit, and public funds accounted for about two-thirds of their revenues (primarily through the Medicare and Medicaid programs). For-profit hospital chains are especially lucrative. Columbia/HCA Healthcare, for example, is the fastest growing for-profit hospital chain in the United States. Columbia/HCA employs 157,000 persons in 320 hospitals and more than 125 outpatient centers in 36 U.S. states, Switzerland, and Great Britain. In 1994, it reported $630 million in net income on gross profits of $4.9 billion (Spain and Talbot, 1996:246–247; Columbia/HCA Healthcare, 1995).

"Contracting" between public and private agencies is becoming increasingly common. **Contracting** is *the practice of hiring private agencies to carry out specified public social welfare activities—such as delivering social services—in return for payment from public funds.* Public agencies contract with private agencies either because the private agency is better able to provide the service, or because it is less expensive to use an existing private service than for the public agency itself to develop a similar program. The New York City foster-care situation (described in "The Human Face of Social Welfare 14") is an example. The need for additional foster care was met faster and at less expense by contracting with several existing private foster-care agencies than it would have been by creating a new public program. When private agencies are able to provide services that are superior in quality to those likely to be available from the public system, contracting seems to make sense. This arrangement enables the public agencies to specify the type and quality of services to be provided while at the same time taking advantage of the flexibility and specialization characteristic of private agencies.

In evaluating the proper relationship between public and private for-profit agencies, one question to be addressed is whether the operating assumptions of capitalism fit social welfare. When businesses compete, three assumptions are made: (1) consumers will be able to make informed choices; (2) they will be able to make choices freely; and (3) competition is "free," meaning that anyone can choose to compete and the market will select the most efficient and desirable services.

It is questionable whether these conditions prevail in the social welfare market. People needing help may lack the education or the psychological ability to make informed choices. Their freedom of choice may be limited by a lack of resources, the nature of their need, lack of geographic mobility, lack of information, or inability to meet eligibility standards.

Whether competition is really "free" is also questionable. For example, the shortage of nursing-home beds and the fact that government payments are tied only loosely to the quality of nursing-home care makes it questionable whether the market can select the most efficient and effective providers of residential care for the elderly.

Preoccupation with profit can overshadow all other considerations. In the United States, runaway health costs are a classic example of failure to put a cap on profit. As a consequence, those in need of medical care pay higher costs and often receive fewer benefits than in other industrialized nations. Meanwhile, insurance firms and physicians continue to reap windfall profits, the nation endlessly debates the pros and cons of universally available health insurance, and millions of uninsured and underinsured persons continue to suffer.

In spite of such problems, collaboration between public and private agencies is growing. Not only is it increasingly popular in the United States, it is also being studied in Sweden, where the private social welfare sector is minimally developed at the present time, and in Poland, where efforts are being made to reduce the government's control over the formation of self-help organizations. Mexico has for some time had a system that encourages the use of private funds to build agencies, with operating funds then coming from the public sector.

To summarize, public and private agencies are fundamentally different in their structure and functioning. Each developed in response to different needs: the public sector to meet the basic needs of all citizens; the private not-for-profit sector in response to the particular needs of special groups. The recent past has seen an upsurge in contracting between public and both private not-for-profit and proprietary agencies, and in the use of public benefits to pay for services delivered privately. While privatization and the growth of proprietary agencies raise a number of ethical and practical issues, there is little indication that relationships between public and private agencies in the United States will weaken in the near future. A public–private partnership is likely to continue to be the path followed for addressing the need for personal social services in the United States.

Table 6-2 lists some of the public and private agencies providing social welfare services in Westchester County, New York (the former home of Ron Frederico). Although it is incomplete, the list will give you some sense of the complexity and scope of the social welfare system, and of the many types of agencies involved. As you review Table 6-2, it is important to keep in mind that New York is a relatively wealthy state, whose social welfare system is more extensive than those of many other states. Also, Westchester County, which borders New York City on the north, is not typical of counties across the United States. Even though it has pockets of severe poverty, it is a generally wealthy county with household incomes well above the national average.

RESIDUAL AND INSTITUTIONAL APPROACHES TO SOCIAL WELFARE

Some years ago, Wilensky and Lebeaux (1966:138–140) explained that there were two ways in which to view social welfare: as "residual" or as "institutional." In the

TABLE 6-2   PUBLIC AND PRIVATE SOCIAL WELFARE AGENCIES IN WESTCHESTER COUNTY, NEW YORK

Service area	Public	Private
Child welfare	Municipal Youth Boards (prevention of juvenile delinquency); Westchester County Department of Health (preventive health services, maternal health care); Westchester County Department of Social Services (adoption, foster care)	Children's Village (special education and clinical treatment for emotionally disturbed youngsters); Blythdale Children's Hospital (care for emotionally and physically limited children); Exchange Club/Child Abuse Prevention Center of Westchester (counseling for families with child abuse problems); Parents Place, Inc. (services to improve parenting skills); Grace Church Community Center (day-care center, day camp)
Counseling	Westchester County Department of Community Mental Health and municipal Departments of Community Mental Health Services (a wide range of personal and family counseling and psychological therapy services); Legal Services Corporation (legal counseling)	Jewish Board of Family and Child Services; Family Service Association (both agencies provide personal and family counseling); Women in Self-Help; Legal Aid Society (legal counseling)
Community development	Municipal Councils of Community Services (facilitates cooperation between the many social welfare agencies in the community); New York State Ombudsman Program (works on improving communication between citizens and the government); Town of Greenburgh Department of Community Development and Conservation; New York State Division of Housing and Community Renewal (improvements in housing)	Council for the Arts (promotes cultural development in communities); Housing Action Council for Community Development and Preservation (improved housing); Latin American Community Enterprises (helps form tenants organizations and develop neighborhood conservation programs in areas with many Hispanic residents)
Criminal justice	New York State Division for Youth (counseling for youth involved with the courts); Westchester County Office of Criminal Justice Planning; Westchester County Department of Probation; municipal Bureau of Youth Services (efforts to prevent juvenile delinquency)	Juvenile Law Education Project (concerned with improving the quality of legal services available to juveniles); Lawyer Referral Service; Victims Assistance Service of Westchester (assistance for victims of crimes)
Education	Greenburgh 11 Union Free School District (municipal special education program for emotionally disturbed youngsters); New Rochelle Youth Employment Service (municipal employment counseling program in the public school system); local community school boards (responsible for primary and secondary schools)	Educational Opportunity Center of Westchester (free remedial education for low income people); Ferncliff Manor (education and training for the severely retarded); Literacy Volunteers of Mt. Vernon (tutoring and teaching English as a second language); New York School for the Deaf

(Table continues on next page.)

TABLE 6-2   PUBLIC AND PRIVATE SOCIAL WELFARE AGENCIES IN WESTCHESTER COUNTY, NEW YORK,
(*Cont'd.*)

Service area	Public	Private
Employment and unemployment	New York State Commission for the Blind and Visually Handicapped (vocational rehabilitation services); New York State Department of Labor (employment offices); New York State Education Department and Office of Vocational Rehabilitation	Westchester Hispanic Coalition (employment training and placement primarily for hispanics); Senior Personnel Placement Bureau (employment service for elderly people who want to work); Urban League of Westchester (job placement assistance primarily for African Americans)
Family counseling	Westchester County Department of Health (parenting counseling); Westchester County Department of Social Services (financial and other resource management counseling); Mt. Vernon Diversion and Counseling Program (municipal personal and family counseling service)	Family Service of Westchester; Catholic Charities Family and Children's Services; Center for Family Learning; Guidance Center of New Rochelle (services to strengthen all aspects of family life); Northern Westchester Shelter (for victims of domestic violence)
Health	Westchester County Medical Center (in and out-patient services); Westchester County Department of Health (health information, screening, inoculations); Veterans Administration Hospital (medical service for veterans)	Nursing homes; hospitals; American Cancer Society; Red Cross; Burke Rehabilitation Center (rehabilitation services for those with physical limitations)
Income maintenance and basic needs	Department of Social Services (public grant and in-kind programs); Social Security Administration (local offices for public social insurance programs); New York State Division of Housing and Community Renewal (housing assistance)	Salvation Army (food and housing assistance); Freedom Gardens for the Handicapped (low-cost housing); Cortlandt Emergency Food Bank; Meals-on-Wheels (home delivery of meals for the home-bound elderly)
Mental health and developmental disabilities	Westchester County Department of Community Mental Health (diagnostic and counseling services); New York State Office of Mental Retardation and Developmental Disability (group homes; in-patient services; information and referral)	Four Winds Hospital (psychiatric hospital); Community Based Services (rehabilitation for the developmentally disabled); Young Adult Institute (group homes for the mentally retarded); Harlem Valley Psychiatric Center (outpatient treatment); North East Westchester Special Recreation, Inc. (therapeutic recreation for the developmentally disabled)
Recreation	Municipal departments of recreation; Westchester County Department of Parks, Recreation, and Conservation (county recreation facilities); municipal Offices for the Aging (day care, meals, information, transportation, recreation)	Neighborhood House (recreation for the elderly and the disadvantaged); Boys Clubs; Don Bosco Community Center; YM/YWCA (recreation and continuing education programs); Westchester/Putnam Special Olympics (athletic program for the disabled)

TABLE 6-2   PUBLIC AND PRIVATE SOCIAL WELFARE AGENCIES IN WESTCHESTER COUNTY, NEW YORK, (*Cont'd.*)

Service area	Public	Private
Retirement	Department of Social Services (public grant and in-kind programs); municipal and county Offices for the Aging (information, day care, recreation, meal programs, advocacy); Social Security Administration (public insurance programs)	American Association of Retired People (advocacy, information); Visiting Nurse Service (home health care); Volunteer Service Bureau (telephone reassurance, volunteer opportunities); nursing homes
Substance abuse	Municipal Youth Advocate Programs (prevention and early identification of youth at-risk); municipal Drug Abuse Prevention Councils (information); Veterans Administration Hospital (in and out-patient treatment for veterans who are substance abusers); Westchester County Department of Community Mental Health (substance abuse counseling)	Daytop Village (drug rehabilitation); Alcoholics Anonymous (rehabilitation of alcoholics); Halfway House of Westchester (group home for recovering alcoholics); National Council on Alcoholism (information, training); Renaissance Project (drug counseling and information)
Workplace	New York State Department of Labor, Unemployment Insurance Division (operates state unemployment insurance program) and Job Service Division (employment service to provide training and help in finding jobs)	Union benefit programs; health, pension, and other benefits provided by employers; employer-run day-care centers

Source: Westchester Services Directory, White Plains, NY: Westchester Community Service Council, 1984

residual view, social welfare is a limited response to breakdowns in the normal functioning of the market, the family, or the individual. Social welfare from the residual perspective should operate as a safety net in which programs under unusual circumstances temporarily substitute for failures in the functioning of individuals or institutions (Barker, 1991:201). In the **institutional view,** social welfare is a "mainline" social institution—on equal footing with the family, religion, the economy, and government—"in which programs are permanent and provide for the overall security and emotional support of people" (Barker, 1991:116). From the institutional perspective, social welfare should play a normative, ongoing role in modern industrial societies.

In other words, from the residual perspective, social welfare is designed to help people after their needs become problematic; from the institutional perspective, social welfare functions to prevent needs from becoming problems.

When social welfare is perceived as a mainline institution, its benefits are more likely to be made universally available. *Universal benefits* are social resources distributed to a nation's citizens as rights of membership independent of employment status or income.

The difference between the residual and institutional approaches can be seen in the way different societies deal with pregnancy leave and the need for emergency child care. In Sweden, all parents have had for many years the right to paid absence from work to care for very young or ill children. In the United States, until enactment of the Family and Medical Leave Act of 1993, working parents who were absent from work because of pregnancy or family illness risked losing their jobs. Sweden's policy was more institutional, that of the United States more residual. Following enactment of the Family Leave Act, U.S. parents employed in public agencies, public and private elementary and secondary schools, and private organizations with fifty or more employees became eligible to take up to 12 weeks of job-protected unpaid leave when a new child joined their family or a family member experienced a serious health problem (NASW, 1995). Although not all employees are covered, U.S. policy has become more institutional than it was previously.

The difference between the residual and institutional approaches is reflected in the way social services are structured. Kahn and Kamerman (1977:7–8), distinguish between two distinct types of personal social services: "case services" and "public social utilities." *Personal social services,* as you probably recall from Chapter 1, are nonfinancial social welfare programs that enhance people's personal development and functioning. *Case services* are personal social services such as counseling and medical care, which are intended to help persons with personal maladjustments, problems, illness, or other difficulties. Case services are provided selectively. Not only must clients have the specific need the service is designed to meet, they must usually also meet additional criteria—such as paying a fee or being able to demonstrate that they are poor—before qualifying. Case services, then, are remedial responses to the breakdown of individuals often perceived to be deviant, helpless, or in need of emergency support—the hallmark of the residual perspective.

Public social utilities, however, are personal social services seen as part of the normal system of response to needs that most people experience at various times during their lives. Public social utilities reflect an institutional perspective in which personal social services are seen as part of the societal infrastructure comparable to libraries, museums, and public systems of transportation, education, mail delivery, and water and sewerage. Public social utilities are usually available to everyone, at least to everyone for whom they are intended. For example, free public education is automatically available to all children between the ages of 5 or 6 and 16 or 17 in the United States. People who use public social utilities, "and thus rely on others in society," are defined as normal persons with strengths that can be built on rather than as deviant or helpless (Barker, 1991:221).

Consider the difference between two approaches to drug abuse: *drug counseling* and free public *drug education.* Drug counseling is provided selectively as a case service via clinics and counseling centers to those with drug problems. Drug counseling reflects a remedial, residual approach to the issue of drug abuse. Drug education included in the public school curriculum, however, functions as a public social utility, providing preventive social services to all students. Drug education in the school curriculum reflects an institutional approach to the issue of drug abuse.

The public social utilities approach to social welfare is more popular in nations such as Sweden and Poland than in the United States. At least in part, this reflects differences in the acceptance of centralized economic and social planning. Countries that make greater use of centralized planning tend to approach social welfare from an institutional perspective. Those, like the United States, which make less use of centralized planning, often take a more residual approach to social welfare.

CASH AND IN-KIND BENEFITS

Social welfare resources may be provided as cash benefits or as in-kind goods or services. **Cash benefits** are *social welfare resources provided in the form of money.* Cash benefits foster maximum freedom of choice for those who receive them. The U.S. program Aid to Families with Dependent Children (AFDC), for example, is a cash benefit provided to eligible parents to help them purchase shelter, clothing, and other basic necessities for their families. Because the AFDC benefits are in cash, the parent can decide how best to spend the money to meet family needs.

Although cash benefits most often are distributed directly as checks to recipients, they may also be distributed indirectly as tax expenditures. Deduction of interest on home mortgage payments and deduction of charitable contributions from the income on which taxes are paid—to name only two of many tax "loopholes" that benefit middle- and upper-income families—reduce income tax liabilities of the nonpoor and tend to redistribute income from persons with low incomes to those with greater incomes. This occurs for two reasons.

First, when taxes are reduced, the amount of revenue that is available to spend for social welfare programs decreases. If government spending is constrained by a balanced budget policy, reductions are likely in allocations for programs which benefit unpopular, unorganized populations such as poor persons. The 1995 Republican Contract with America is illustrative. The contract proposed 5-year tax cuts of $180 billion, over half of which would go to the 12 percent of U.S. families with annual incomes exceeding $100,000. During the same 5 years, funding for programs benefiting poor families would be reduced by more than $100 billion (Lav, et al., 1995; Shapiro, et al., 1995).

Second, tax exemptions are usable only by people who pay taxes. The more taxes they pay, the more valuable the exemptions are. Because the poor often do not earn enough income to be liable for income tax, tax incentives are of greatest value to those who are not poor. One provision of the Contract with America was for a $500, nonrefundable Child Tax Credit. Children in the poorest one-fifth of the population would receive no benefits. Children in the poorest two-fifths of U.S. families would receive only 3.5 percent of the benefits, while children in the richest two-fifths would receive 64 percent of the benefits, nine times as much as the poorer children (Center on Budget and Policy Priorities, 1995:4).

In-kind goods and services are *social welfare resources provided in a form other than money.* In Mexico, tortillas are sometimes provided by the government directly to low-income families. Distribution of surplus commodity food in "cheese lines" through The Emergency Food Assistance Program (TEFAP), provision of health care through Medicaid, and clothing contributed to the poor by the Salvation Army are examples of in-kind goods and services in the United States. Provision of social welfare resources as in-kind benefits limits the freedom of participants to determine which of their needs are of highest priority. Eligibility for Medicaid, for example, cannot be exchanged for shelter by homeless families.

A common rationale for providing resources in-kind is the assumption of dominant groups that poor people either cannot or will not make "appropriate" choices if left to their own devices. When members of the Family Council of South Side Settlement, where I [Bill Whitaker] worked for 10 years, decided to give out cash instead of food baskets during the Christmas holidays, many long-time contributors refused to support the effort. Their argument: Parents might spend the money on alcohol or cigarettes instead of on food for their families. In reality, most of the families in the Settlement community did an excellent job of deciding how best to use their limited resources to meet family needs. They had to in order to survive.

In-kind goods and services are often used in the attempt to minimize the costs of helping others by distributing surplus or unwanted items such as surplus commodities or used clothing. The highly visible manner in which in-kind goods are sometimes distributed—through "cheese lines" and soup kitchens, for example—is considered humiliating and degrading by many people. Although private in-kind programs may provide a way of responding to short-term, emergency needs, they are unlikely to have much of an impact on prevention or long-term solutions of the needs to which they try to respond.

Food Stamp coupons and the food vouchers distributed by the U.S. Special Supplemental Food Program for Women, Infants, and Children (WIC) have characteristics of both cash and in-kind programs. Although Food Stamps can be spent only for the purchase of food, Food Stamp recipients may choose which foods they wish to buy. WIC vouchers, in contrast, must be redeemed for fixed amounts of specified foods containing specific nutrients.

ORGANIZATIONAL COMPLEXITY

In the United States, formal social welfare services are made available to those in need through an often-complex partnership of federal, state, and local social welfare agencies. Benefits are commonly delivered through local or state agencies, with major funding provided through federal tax dollars. Because the person paying the piper generally calls the tune, states and localities usually are required to carry out programs in ways consistent with federal guidelines.

Let's think about how organizational complexity affects a person seeking assistance—say, a person experiencing hunger. First of all, the potential applicant must be able to find out about the existence of programs addressing hunger and learn where they are located. Because social benefits are delivered by a large number of public and private social welfare agencies, some communities publish directories of social services to help people find the programs they need. Others establish information and referral services for the same purpose. The Yellow Pages of most phone books contain listings of social and human services. Social workers in their role as brokers may help link the person in need with appropriate resources.

In an emergency situation the hungry person may turn first to a private soup kitchen or food pantry, which will be able to provide limited, short-term help. In order to meet ongoing needs, however, participation in the federal Food Stamp Program may be necessary. Because the public agency that administers the program is likely to have other responsibilities as well, the applicant will need to identify the appropriate social welfare worker. This task may be complicated by the complexity of the agency. Organization of the New Hanover County, North Carolina, Department of Social Services is typical (see Figure 6-1). Once contact has been made with the appropriate intake worker, help received will depend on the rules and regulations of the agency and on the worker's interpretation of those rules, and his or her competence in filling out forms correctly, meeting deadlines, and straightening out any problems that may arise.

But the situation is more complicated still. The local agency is likely to be part of a much larger network. For example, the New Hanover County Department of

FIGURE 6-1 Organization of the New Hanover Department of Social Services. (Courtesy New Hanover County Department of Social Services, Wilmington, NC, F. Wayne Morris, Director.)

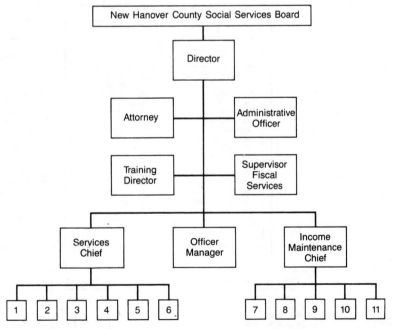

1. Case Management
2. Protective Services for Children
3. Permanency Planning for Children
4. Children's Services
5. Placement and Rehabilitative Services for Adults
6. Maintenance and Support Services for Adults
7. Eligibility Intake Unit
8. Child Support Enforcement
9. Aid to Families with Dependent Children
10. Food Stamps
11. Medicaid

Social Services is part of the larger, statewide North Carolina Department of Social Services. Further, many of the programs administered by the state agency originate with and are at least partially funded by the U.S. Department of Health and Human Services (USDHHS). As Figure 6-2 suggests, USDHHS is itself a very complex agency.

FIGURE 6-2   Organization of the United States Department of Health and Human Services. (*Source:* Office of the Federal Register. National Archives and Records Administration. 1986. *1986/87 United States Government Manual.* Washington, DC: U.S. Government Printing Office, p. 856.)

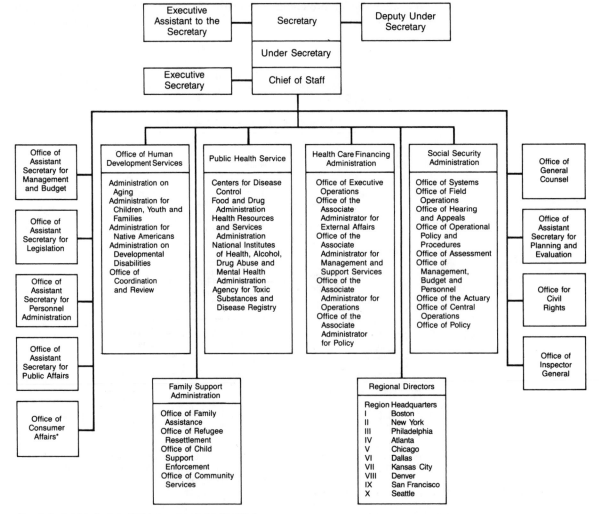

United States Department of Health and Human Services

*Located administratively in HHS but reports to the President.

The request for Food Stamps ultimately depends on activities of the Office of Family Assistance in the Family Support Administration of USDHHS and the U.S. Department of Agriculture (USDA). State and local departments of social service implement policies established there. Just as the competence of the local Food Stamp intake worker affects the resources that are received, so do the activities of the administrative staff of the local and state agencies. The success of their efforts as advocates helps determine the programs and resources that will be available.

USDHHS is the federal agency most concerned with social welfare programs. Many other federal agencies, however, are also involved. The USDA is responsible for a number of nutrition and supplemental food programs. The U.S. Department of Commerce's social welfare responsibilities include operation of the Census Bureau and assistance to minority businesses. The U.S. Department of the Interior administers certain training and employment programs for youth, the recreational services of the National Park Service, and the Bureau of Indian Affairs. The U.S. Department of Justice is responsible for civil rights and criminal justice programs, the Department of Education for educational policy and enrichment, and the Department of Labor for extensive employment-related assistance.

To summarize, we have seen that social welfare resources are organized and delivered through programs that are themselves administered by agencies. It is sometimes difficult to identify programs and locate agencies. Even when one has established contact with an agency, the agency's organization and functioning can influence the effectiveness and sensitivity with which its programs operate. Since individual agencies are frequently part of larger networks, their actions and policies are shaped at least in part by decision making at these higher levels.

A final point about the relationship among resources, programs, and agencies is that often multiple programs and agencies address the same problem. Consider, for example, Figure 6-3, which depicts the way in which the Red Cross and the government work together in the event of a disaster.

You can see from Figure 6-3 that relief efforts in the case of a community disaster involve many agencies, of which the Red Cross is only one. Others include the government agencies responsible for such services as child welfare, income maintenance, and the police. Many private agencies not included in Figure 6-3 would undoubtedly also respond (churches, synagogues, and mosques, for example). Since each agency has its own programs and its own policies, there is ample room for duplication of services and confusion among those receiving help.

Let us review for a moment the terms we have discussed so far in connection with social security programs. We have distinguished between informal and formal social welfare resources, public and private program funding, residual and institutional perspectives on social welfare, and cash and in-kind benefits. We have defined the personal social services that are an important component of social security and have distinguished between case services and public social utilities. Before we move on to consider the five "pillars" on which social security is based throughout the world, let us review the definitions of two final terms: "social insurance" and "social assistance."

WHEN DISASTER STRIKES

Government Provides*

Emergency Community Services
- Police services
- Safeguards to public health and sanitation
- Special police and fire protection for disaster area
- Identification and care of dead, including temporary morgues
- Designation of hazardous buildings and areas
- Emergency communication and transportation services

Usual Community Welfare Services
- Financial and medical assistance to eligible persons
- Social services for families, including casework and rehabilitation services; foster family, institutional, or day care for children; services and care for aged persons, mentally retarded children, and others with special problems

Assistance in Community Restoration**
- Repair or replacement of sewage and water systems, streets, and highways
- Removal of debris
- Restoration of public transportation and communication facilities
- Repair or replacement of public buildings (schools, hospitals, etc.)
- Inspection of private property for health and safety
- Salvage of unclaimed property

Aid for Recovery to Families**
- Disaster loan programs, such as those provided by Small Business Administration, Farmers Home Administration, etc.
- Food stamps and donated foods from Department of Agriculture
- Disaster unemployment insurance provided by Department of Labor through state unemployment offices
- Temporary housing
- Specialized counseling and advice to families, such as that provided by Public Health, Department of Agriculture, and other agencies or departments
- State grants for serious and unmet needs
- Emergency welfare services to families with children, in some states

Red Cross Provides*

Emergency Mass Care Assistance
- Food for disaster victims and emergency workers
- Temporary shelter
- Medical and nursing aid
- Clothing
- Blood and blood products

Emergency Assistance on Individual Family Basis
- Welfare inquiry and information services
- Emergency assistance for food, clothing, rent, bedding, selected furnishings, transportation, medical needs, temporary home repairs, and occupational supplies and other essentials
- Referral to government disaster programs

Aid for Additional Assistance to Families for whom Government Programs Not Available
- Casework services
- Food, clothing, and other maintenance until normal sources of support are restored
- Building and repair of owner-occupied homes
- Household furnishings
- Medical and nursing care
- Personal occupational supplies and equipment

*The chart shows how distinct and yet how closely related are the responsibilities of Red Cross and of government in natural disasters.

**Some of these programs are activated only after a Presidential Declaration of a major disaster. Federal disaster assistance is coordinated by the Federal Emergency Management Agency (FEMA).

Red Cross and government are both needed to perform disaster functions.

Social insurance programs are programs "which depend on previous employment history and, in general, are independent of a claimant's personal or family income." *Social assistance programs* are government-financed, "means-tested public transfers provided to people in need who meet certain eligibility conditions for regular or occasional income support" (Cornia and Sipos, 1991: xv–xviii).

FIVE "PILLARS" OF SOCIAL SECURITY

In the United States, the term "social security" commonly refers to the social insurance system of retirement pensions established through the Social Security Act of 1935. Most other nations, however, define *social security* more broadly, as a nation's set of social insurance and social assistance programs aimed at providing essential security to its population. In international social welfare circles, social security is commonly discussed in terms of five major "pillars" that support the protective shelter of social security. The five are: old age, disability, and death benefits; health care, sickness, and maternity benefits; work-injury benefits; unemployment support; and family allowances. In our discussion we will follow international practice. Unless otherwise noted, the following information about the five pillars of social security is drawn from *Social Security Programs throughout the World—1991* (U.S. Department of Health and Human Services, 1992).

Old Age, Disability, and Survivor Programs

Social security programs addressing the long-term needs of old age, disability, and survivors are found in 138 countries throughout the world. Benefits are usually in the form of pensions payable for life, financed by a combination of worker contributions, employer payroll taxes, and government contributions. Historically, most systems begin by providing coverage first to government workers and members of the armed services, next to workers in industry and commerce, and later to other wage earners and salaried employees. Economically weak groups such as domestic servants, agricultural workers, and the self-employed often are excluded—at least initially—from coverage.

To receive an *old age pension,* a person must usually have reached a specified age and have worked in covered employment for at least a minimum period of time. In many countries women may draw a full pension sooner than men in spite of their longer life expectancies. In some countries workers employed in especially hazardous occupations such as underground mining may retire early with full benefits. Most old age pensions are supplemented if the retiree is supporting a spouse or minor children. *Pensions for partial or full disability* function much like old age pensions and may also provide rehabilitation and training services. *Survivor pensions* generally pay a percentage of the benefit that was being paid to the insured wage earner at death. Survivor pensions paid to elderly or disabled

FIGURE 6-3   The operation of multiple systems when disaster strikes. (*Source: Your Community Could Have a Disaster.* 1979. American Red Cross pamphlet.)

widows usually continue until the widow's death, while survivor pensions paid to younger mothers typically end after their youngest child has reached a certain age. In general, widows' pensions cease upon remarriage.

Health Care, Sickness, and Maternity Programs

The second pillar of social security consists of programs which respond to needs associated with temporary incapacity resulting from short-term illness and pregnancy. Such programs provide either cash benefits to replace lost wages, or in-kind medical, hospital, and pharmaceutical benefits. Eighty-six nations have some kind of sickness or pregnancy social security program.

The proportion of a country's population eligible for sickness and pregnancy benefits varies according to its level of economic development. Developing countries often initiate programs in the capital city and other urban centers and later expand coverage to smaller towns and rural areas.

In order to qualify for cash sickness benefits, one must usually have worked for a minimum length of time, be gainfully employed when becoming ill or pregnant, be unable to work, and not be receiving sick-leave pay from an employer. Most cash sickness benefits require a waiting period of several days to exclude short-term claims for periods during which income loss is small. Some maternity programs provide for the purchase of a layette or make a lump-sum "maternity grant" following the birth of a child.

Medical benefits typically include general practitioner care, hospitalization, and essential drugs. Sometimes services of medical specialists, surgery, maternity care, dental care, physical appliances, transportation, and nursing-home care also are included. Health-care costs usually are paid for either through national health programs that offer direct services to those needing them, by the government directly to the provider, or by government reimbursement of costs paid by the patient. In some countries, such as the United States, privately purchased health insurance plays an important role.

Pensioners often receive publicly funded health-care benefits either free as part of their retirement benefits or after paying a premium. Dependent spouses and young children of insured workers usually are eligible for health-care benefits, but sometimes receive lesser levels of coverage. In countries with national health services, health-care and maternity benefits often are available to virtually all residents, although special restrictions may apply to noncitizens. National health-care programs and private health insurance programs generally require cost sharing by the patient to discourage overutilization.

Work-Injury Programs

Benefits which accrue as a consequence of incapacity or death from injury on the job or occupational illness make up the third pillar of social security. Such programs provide short- and long-term benefits depending on the duration of the compensated incapacity and the age of dependent survivors. Workers' compensation programs are the oldest form of social security. Dating from the early nineteenth century, today workers' compensation is widespread, with programs operating in 139 countries.

Most work-injury programs are organized as publicly funded social insurance, but about 20 countries, including the United States, operate with legally mandated private arrangements. Workers' compensation programs ordinarily insure wage and salary workers, and exclude the self-employed. They are usually employer funded, recognizing the employer's responsibility for providing a safe and healthy workplace. Work-injury social security programs replace varying percentages of the worker's average income for varying lengths of time depending on whether the disability is temporary, permanent and partial, or permanent and total. In addition to cash payments, workers' compensation also provides hospital care and rehabilitation services. Workers' compensation may also provide funeral benefits and cash payments to survivors of deceased workers.

Unemployment Benefit Programs

The fourth pillar of social security consists of programs that partially replace income lost through unemployment and help the unemployed find new jobs. Since unemployment benefits usually are available only in wealthier, industrialized countries, they exist today in only forty-four nations. Most unemployment compensation programs are publicly funded, but some are operated by trade unions for their members.

To qualify for unemployment benefits, a worker must be involuntarily unemployed following a minimum period of covered employment, must be capable of and available for work, and must register at an unemployment office. The worker must not have left a job voluntarily without good cause, must not have been fired for misconduct, must not be unemployed as the result of a strike, and must not refuse reasonable offers of suitable work.

Benefits are paid weekly for up to a maximum number of weeks, which theoretically is sufficient to find a new job. In addition to providing replacement income, several programs in Western Europe utilize elaborate measures to prevent or counteract unemployment by promoting occupational and geographic labor mobility and by subsidizing worker retraining and relocation from declining or restructuring industries.

Family Allowances

Programs that provide supplemental income to families to help meet the costs of raising young children make up the fifth, and final, pillar of social security. **Family allowances,** sometimes known as *children allowances,* are *benefits "in which every eligible family, regardless of financial need, is allocated a specified sum of money"* (Barker, 1991:80). Benefits usually are provided as general grants, but sometimes also include grants for school, for the birth of a child, and for dependent adults. Family allowances originated in nineteenth-century Europe as employer subsidies to workers with large numbers of children, and are available today in sixty-three countries—including every industrialized nation except the United States.

Eligibility is determined by family size and sometimes income. Payments typically begin with the birth of the first child, and continue until the child reaches the legal age for leaving school or beginning work. Usually, benefits continue for children who remain in school, apprenticeship, or vocational training. In Germany, for example, family allowances may be continued until the age of 27 under such circumstances. The cost of universal family allowance programs is paid from general revenue; employment-related family allowances are funded through employer payroll taxes.

Means-Tested Programs of Social Assistance

Income-tested programs also contribute to social security. Such programs constitute the primary form of social security in only a few countries, but supplement income-maintenance programs in many others. Generally, means-tested programs help fill the income gap for persons who are not in covered employment or whose employment-related benefits and other resources are inadequate to meet family survival needs. In the next chapter, we describe several major means-tested programs in addition to programs that constitute the five primary pillars of social security.

LET'S REVIEW

This chapter provides some sense of the larger design of the social welfare system. Social welfare is not just a collection of programs; rather, it is a system that seeks to address certain needs by distributing and redistributing resources in a way that helps to meet the human needs of the total population. It does so through structural arrangements that reflect concerns with cost, effectiveness, and maintaining people's sense of personal responsibility. In general, the structure of the system reflects the linkage between these concerns and other societal values.

The structure and organization of social welfare programs are affected by many factors: the basic human needs spelled out in Chapter 2, the value conflicts discussed in Chapter 3, the philosophical and historical developments described in Chapter 4, and the social mobilization efforts of reformers delineated in Chapter 5. The clash of ideas and social forces in the arena of politics within the context of the socioeconomic environment of a given nation helps determine the shape and structure of social welfare in that country. Having mastered the Introduction and the first six chapters of this text, you are now ready to look critically at the social security programs of our four countries.

This chapter should have helped you to understand better the overall design of social welfare systems. In Chapter 7 we will examine the specific programs that make up the systems through which resources are distributed to people in the United States, Sweden, Poland, and Mexico. As you learn about these programs, you will want to keep in mind their roles in each nation's social welfare institution.

STUDY QUESTIONS

1 Consider your own family. List the ways in which family members contribute informally to your social well-being. In what ways does your family help you meet your needs for income? What informal personal social services does it provide? How does your family help you meet your needs for personal empowerment? If this last question seems difficult to answer, consider your family's attitudes toward women's career choices, what you have been taught about your racial or ethnic group, and similar matters relating to your ability to advocate effectively on your own behalf.

2 Make a list of the social programs from which you are receiving resources for meeting your needs. Classify the programs as formal and informal, public and private. Then summarize in a brief report the extent of your current involvement with the elements of the social welfare system discussed in this chapter.

3 What are your feelings about social insurance, social assistance, in-kind programs, and tax benefits? Do you think that some of these types of programs are better than others? If you had your way, would you eliminate some and increase the use of others? Which ones and why? If you believe they all have a place in the design of social welfare, do you think they are currently being used effectively? If not, what changes would you make?

4 Do you think that social welfare should be exclusively for the poor? Explain the reasons for your thinking. Then compare your analysis with that of a friend who is not taking this course. What differences are there in your perspectives?

KEY TERMS AND CONCEPTS

informal (or natural) helping networks
formal social welfare programs
social welfare agencies
not-for-profit agencies
proprietary social agencies

privatization
contracting
cash benefits
in-kind goods and services
family allowances

SUGGESTED READINGS

Cornia, Giovanni Andrea, and Sándor Sipos. 1991. *Children and the Transition to the Market Economy: Safety Nets and Social Policies in Central and Eastern Europe.* Brookfield, VT: Gower. A sobering examination of the effects on children of the transition to capitalism in Poland, Hungary, Czechoslovakia, and Bulgaria. A call for greater emphasis on safety nets and social policies that will benefit children and families most at risk.

Fernandez, John. 1986. *Child Care and Corporate Productivity.* Lexington, MA: Lexington Books. This book uses the issue of child care for working parents to illustrate the relationship between public policy and adequate social welfare services. It focuses on how workers and the corporations that employ them attempt to find solutions to the need for adequate child day care in the absence of adequate public services.

Kahn, Alfred, and Sheila Kamerman. 1975. *Not for the Poor Alone.* Philadelphia: Temple University Press. The authors use examples from several European countries to illustrate how the public sector can meet different kinds of human needs. They focus on nonfinancial services, which, they argue, should be made available to the entire population, not just the poor.

Sosin, Michael. 1986. *Private Benefits: Material Assistance in the Private Sector.* Orlando, FL: Academic Press. A study of private agencies and their use of income maintenance, grant, and in-kind services. Clearly illustrates the interdependence of private and public agencies, as well as the different functions and characteristics of each.

REFERENCES

Abramovitz, Mimi. 1986. The privatization of the welfare state: A review. *Social Work,* 31(4):257–264.

Barker, Robert L. 1991. *The Social Work Dictionary,* 2d ed. Washington, DC: National Association of Social Workers.

Beckman, David, and Richard Hoehn. 1992. *Transforming the Politics of Hunger.* Washington, DC: Bread for the World Institute on Hunger and Development.

Brilliant, Eleanor L. 1995. Voluntarism. In *Encyclopedia of Social Work,* 19th ed. Washington, DC: National Association of Social Workers, pp. 2469–2482.

Brzozowski, Ryszard, et al. n.d. *Social Welfare and the Lines of Its Development in the Polish People's Republic.* Warsaw: Polish Medical Publishers.

Center for Budget and Policy Priorities. 1995. The child tax credit: Who would be helped? Washington, DC: CBPP, March 28.

Columbia/HCA Healthcare Corporation: Complete Company Records, April 1995. *Compact Disclosure.* CD-ROM. Disclosure Incorporated, August 1995.

Cornia, Giovanni Andrea, and Sándor Sipos. 1991. *Children and the Transition to the Market Economy: Safety Nets and Social Policies in Central and Eastern Europe.* Brookfield, VT: Gower.

Flynn, Patrice. 1995. *Catholic Charities USA 1994 Annual Report: Responding to Changing Times.* Washington, DC: The Urban Institute.

Gilbert, Neil. 1983. *Capitalism and the Welfare State.* New Haven, CT: Yale University Press.

Goldman, Ari, and Michael Oreskes. 1987. New York foster care: A public-private battleground. *The New York Times,* April 9, p. B1.

Kahn, Alfred, and Sheila Kamerman. 1975. *Not for the Poor Alone.* Philadelphia: Temple University Press.

Lav, Iris, Cindy Mann, and Pauline Abernathy. 1995. Tax proposals grow in cost and inequity over time. Washington, DC: Center on Budget and Policy Priorities, April 10.

Les, Ewa. 1985. Some social threats in Poland in relation to procedures and models of social policy. Paper presented at the 13th Regional Symposium on Social Welfare of the International Committee on Social Welfare, Turku, Finland, June.

NASW. 1995, March 3. *Issue Brief: The Family and Medical Leave Act of 1993.* Washington, DC: National Association of Social Workers.

Ortiz, Larry P. 1995. Sectarian agencies. In *Encyclopedia of Social Work,* 19th ed. Washington, DC: National Association of Social Workers, pp. 2109–2116.

Shapiro, Isaac, Richard Kogan, and Pauline Abernathy. 1995. Assessing the first 100 days: The combined distributional effects of the House spending and tax proposals. Washington, DC: Center on Budget and Policy Priorities, April 7.

Sosin, Michael. 1986. *Private Benefits: Material Assistance in the Private Sector.* Orlando, FL: Academic Press.

Spain, Patrick J., and James R. Talbot. 1996. *Hoover's Handbook of American Companies: 1996.* Austin, TX: The Reference Press, pp. 246–247.

U.S. Department of Health and Human Services, Social Security Administration, Office of International Policy. 1992. *Social Security Programs throughout the World—1991.* SSA Publication No. 61–006. Washington, DC: U.S. Government Printing Office.

Wilensky, Harold, and Charles Lebeaux. 1966. *Industrial Society and Social Welfare.* New York: The Free Press.

Wojciechowski, Sophie. 1975. Poland's new priority: Human welfare. In Daniel Thursz and Joseph Vigilante, eds., *Meeting Human Needs,* Beverly Hills, CA: Sage, Vol. I, pp. 169–195.

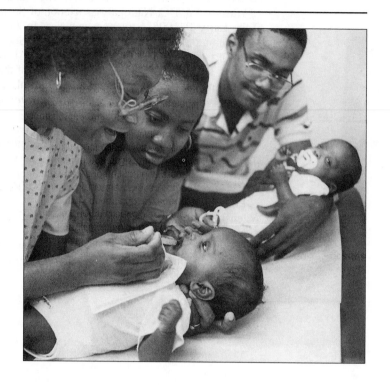

7

WHAT DOES SOCIAL WELFARE LOOK LIKE IN DAILY LIFE?

WHAT TO EXPECT FROM THIS CHAPTER

This chapter describes the major public programs which make up each of the five pillars of social security in the United States, Sweden, Poland, and Mexico. You will learn how these programs are structured, what services they provide, and how people gain access to them. Knowing what services and programs are provided by which agencies is basic to participation in the social welfare system of one's country, either as a worker or as a user.

The chapter concludes our discussion of the evolution and organization of the programs that, together, constitute the social welfare institution in each of our four countries. Starting with Chapter 1, we learned about the concept of social welfare and the way it has been implemented in the United States, Mexico, Poland, and Sweden. In Chapter 2 we saw how social welfare is a response to predictable life-cycle needs, and in Chapter 3 we discussed some of the conflicting values that make social welfare controversial. Chapters 4 and 5 traced the historical development of social welfare in response to intellectual currents, social reformers, and economic, political, demographic, and environmental conditions. Chapter 6 examined the overall design of social welfare systems.

This chapter goes a step further by looking at the actual programs through which services are delivered. At the conclusion of this chapter you will have moved from a general understanding of what social welfare is to specific knowledge about the actual programs and resources that are available to people in our four countries. As you read about each country's programs, try to keep in mind the different ways in which policymakers in each country have responded to the needs of their citizens and other residents.

In the remainder of this book, we will use what you have learned to relate social welfare to the rest of society. We will explore its relationships with the other social institutions—the family, education, religion, government, and the economy; we will discuss the major social welfare professions; and we will conclude by trying to foresee what the future may hold for social welfare. But that is getting ahead of ourselves. Let's turn now to the specific social welfare programs that affect our daily lives.

LEARNING OBJECTIVES

When you have finished studying this chapter, you should be able to:

1 List six elements of a framework that is useful for analyzing any social welfare program.

2 Use the framework to describe a public social welfare program of your choice in the United States, Sweden, Poland, and Mexico.

3 Identify similarities and differences among the five pillars of social security in the four countries we are studying.

4 Describe in detail the social welfare programs included in the five pillars of social security in your own country.

UNDERSTANDING SPECIFIC SOCIAL WELFARE PROGRAMS

In this chapter we will describe a large number of social welfare programs, each addressing one or more particular needs. No one can master the details of all of them. It is possible, however, to devise a general approach for understanding whatever programs may be of greatest interest. You will find this approach useful for thinking about any program that you, or someone you know, may need to access. Such a framework will be particularly useful if you become a social welfare professional; familiarity with the programs that provide services in your field of practice will be an important part of your work.

A two-stage framework is used in this book. First, as you already know, we organize our discussion according to the five pillars of social security. Second, we answer a series of questions about the programs within each pillar: What is the program's purpose? What are the program's eligibility requirements? What benefits does the program provide? How are benefits provided? How is the program administered? What, if any, are the program's shortcomings? Before turning to the five pillars of social security in each country, let's say a little bit more about these six questions. Used as a checklist, the questions will help you identify and understand the programs most likely to be useful to you for any given purpose.

What is the program's purpose? What type of need is the program designed to meet? Does it, for example, help people obtain better health care, provide them with more money, better housing, more education, or assistance in finding a job?

What are the program's eligibility requirements? **Eligibility requirements** are *the conditions that must be met before people qualify to receive benefits from a social welfare program.* Who qualifies to receive the program? Is there an age requirement, an income limit, a requirement that one's degree of disability be certified, an employment history requirement, or any other specific requirement that must be met in order to be eligible?

What benefits does the program provide? Social welfare benefits are the actual resources a particular social welfare program provides to users. In the case of a health-care program covering the cost of treatment associated with certain illnesses, you would want to ask exactly what illnesses are covered. Similarly, when dealing with a financial aid program, you would need to know how much aid is provided and for how long. Only by asking the appropriate questions can you determine exactly what help people should expect to receive. Keep in mind, too, that benefits from a single program are often insufficient to meet one's total needs. As a result, people often have to make use of several programs.

How are benefits provided? How do benefits reach people? Is a check sent through the mail? Does it come automatically every month, or is it necessary to reapply each time? Are the benefits payable to other parties, such as hospitals and physicians, or are they paid to the client, who is then responsible for paying these other parties? Do you have to wait in line to receive a meal, or is it delivered to your home? It is important to ask such questions in order to be certain the benefits are provided in such a way that the person in need can actually use them.

How is the program administered? Knowing this tells you where to go to apply for benefits and provides an indication of the procedures that may be involved. If it is a federal program, for example, there are likely to be well-defined appeals procedures in the event that benefits are denied. Such procedures may not exist if the program is administered privately or by a state. Remember, too, that the structure and organization of the agency itself can affect the effectiveness of the program and the efficiency with which benefits are provided.

What are the program's shortcomings? Is the program available, accessible, adequate, and efficient? Does the program serve all persons who need it? Is the program accessible to those who need its services? Are applicants treated with dignity and respect? The way in which benefits are made available can sometimes be troublesome. For example, benefit checks mailed to poor people living in crime-ridden neighborhoods are sometimes stolen. Having the check deposited directly in the recipient's bank account makes sense in such cases, provided, of course, the person has enough money to maintain an account and there is a bank near where the person lives. Some homeless people are reluctant to go to shelters because they fear they will be robbed or assaulted. Elderly people may not have the strength to go and wait in line where free food is being distributed. Ensuring that resources actually get to the people who need them is a major concern for users of services and social welfare professionals. In order for this to occur, not only must the resources be available, people must know about and be able to access them without fear or loss of dignity.

Now let's apply this framework to some specific social welfare programs in each of our four countries.

FIVE PILLARS OF SOCIAL SECURITY: THE UNITED STATES

As the United States and other countries throughout the world were transformed from agrarian to industrial societies, families, private charities, and local governments proved inadequate to meet all the social welfare needs of their citizens. Social security programs shaped by the varied historical, cultural, demographic, political, and economic contexts of each country emerged in response to unmet need. The geographic size, ethnic diversity, and frontier tradition of self-reliance of the United States resulted in a U.S. social welfare institution characterized by pragmatism and incremental development, considerable decentralization, and a public–private partnership in providing and paying for social welfare benefits.[1]

In fiscal year 1990, U.S. governmental social welfare expenditures totaled $1,045.4 billion (19.1 percent of gross domestic product). The federal government provided about 59 percent, and state and local governments about 41 percent of the funds. Private expenditures for health and medical care, social welfare services, education, and employee benefits such as pensions, group life insurance, and sickness benefits totaled an additional $680.7 billion (USDHHS, 1993:3–5).

Old Age, Disability, and Death Benefits

The largest income-maintenance program in the United States, **Old Age, Survivors, and Disability Insurance (OASDI),** *"provides monthly cash benefits to replace, in part, the income that is lost to a worker and his or her family when the worker retires in old age, becomes severely disabled, or dies"* (USDHHS, 1993:7). Popularly referred to as Social Security, OASDI is financed through 12.4 percent payroll taxes divided equally between workers and employers. In 1996, OASDI payroll taxes were paid on the first $62,700 of a worker's income. With about 95 percent

---

[1]An excellent description of the historical development and current status of most public programs that make up the five pillars of social security in the United States may be found in *Social Security Programs in the United States,* a 1993 publication of the U.S. Department of Health and Human Services (USDHHS), SSA Publication No. 13–11758. A brief summary may be found in *Social Security Programs throughout the World 1993,* a 1994 publication of the USDHHS, SSA Publication No. 13–11805. Unless noted otherwise, our discussion of U.S. programs is based on these sources.

of U.S. jobs covered, OASDI provides at least half the income of three out of five retirees, ensures continuing income for 95 percent of U.S. children and surviving parents if the family breadwinner dies, and protects about 80 percent of U.S. workers and their families in the event of a breadwinner's long-term severe disability. Each covered worker must apply for a Social Security number, which is used to track lifetime contributions, on which benefits are based. Contributions are held in trust funds, which may be used only to pay program benefits and operating costs.

Old age pensions are provided for life to insured workers with 40 or more quarters of coverage. Full pensions, paying a maximum of $1,128 per month in 1993, may be taken up at age 65 (phasing to 67 by 2027). A spouse, divorced spouse if the marriage lasted at least 10 years, or dependent child is eligible for an additional 50 percent benefit. Maximum family pension is 150–188 percent of the worker's benefit. *Disability pensions* are provided for life to workers who are unable "to engage in substantial gainful activity due to impairment expected to last for at least one year or result in death." Disability benefits are the same as old age benefits except that the maximum family pension is 100–150 percent of the worker's pension. Surviving spouses, or divorced spouses if the marriage lasted 10 years, are eligible for *survivor pensions* of 100 percent of the worker's pension. Dependent orphans are each eligible for 75 percent; one dependent parent is eligible for 82.5 percent; two dependent parents are eligible for 150 percent (USDHHS, 1994:344).

OASDI is administered by the Social Security Administration of the U.S. Department of Health and Human Services through regional program centers, district offices, and branch offices. Proof of age must be provided when applying for retirement benefits. Once declared eligible, retirees receive monthly benefit checks for the remainder of their lives. Payroll taxes are collected by the Internal Revenue Service, and checks are issued by the Department of the Treasury.

Because the payroll taxes of currently employed workers are used to fund the OASDI benefits of those who have retired, and because the ratio of employed to retired workers is shrinking, concern has been expressed about the future viability of the program. In 1995, the annual Social Security report to Congress projected that, as the program is currently structured, trust funds will continue to grow until the year 2020 and then decline until depleted in 2030 (Pear, 1995).

Health Care, Sickness, and Maternity Programs

In 1991, U.S. health and medical care expenses totaled $751.8 billion (13.2 percent of gross domestic product). The private sector originated about 56 percent of these expenses; local, state, and federal governments, about 44 percent. More than two-thirds of public expenditures were for Medicare and Medicaid. The remaining third consisted largely of military-related medical care, Workers' Compensation medical costs, public health, medical research, and construction of medical facilities. Health-care programs in the United States are the most costly yet least effective among industrialized nations when measured in terms of infant mortality rate and percentage of the population uninsured or only partially insured.

Medicare is *a social insurance program that provides health care for the aged and disabled.* Persons age 65 or older who are eligible for Social Security and persons who have received Social Security disability benefits for at least 2 years are eligible for Medicare. Medicare services are provided through two separate but coordinated plans. Medicare Part A consists of compulsory hospital insurance covering inpatient hospital care, inpatient skilled nursing-home care following hospitalization, home health care, and hospice care. Medicare Part A is funded by 1.45 percent payroll taxes paid by both workers and employers into the hospital insurance trust fund.

Medicare Part B is optional supplementary medical insurance covering services of physicians and surgeons, certified registered nurse anesthetists, clinical psychologists, clinical social workers, physician assistants, nurse practitioners, and clinical nurse specialists. Part B also covers emergency room or outpatient clinic services, laboratory tests and X-rays, partially hospitalized mental health care, physical and occupational therapy, rural health clinic services, limited organ transplants, durable medical equipment such as wheelchairs and hospital beds for home use, and drugs and vaccines. In 1995, participants in Medicare Part B share the costs of their health care through an annual deductible of $100, monthly premiums of $46.10, 20 percent co-payments for services received, and payment for health services not covered or not fully covered by Medicare.[2]

Medicare eligibility is determined by the Social Security Administration, payroll taxes are collected by the Internal Revenue Service, and the program is administered by the Health Care Financing Administration—three federal agencies. As is the case with OASDI, Medicare is experiencing funding problems. Rapidly escalating health-care costs are threatening the solvency of the program. The Part A trust fund is currently projected to be depleted in 2002; in 1994, the Part B trust fund paid out $4 billion more than it took in (Pear, 1995).

Medicaid[3] is *the largest U.S. program providing health care to the poor. Beneficiaries must have low incomes and minimal assets.* Medicaid is primarily for persons eligible for Aid to Families with Dependent Children or Supplemental Security Income. Children under age 6 and pregnant women in families with income less than 133 percent of the federal poverty line, certain low-income Medicare beneficiaries, and (temporarily) former AFDC and SSI recipients who lose eligibility because of earned or Social Security income also qualify. In addition, states may choose to provide Medicaid to "categorically needy" groups such as infants under 1 year old and pregnant women in households with incomes up to 185 percent of the federal poverty line, and persons who are "medically needy" as a consequence of excessive medical expenses.

Medicaid costs are shared between federal and state governments according to a formula that compares each state's per-capita income with national per-capita

---

[2]Legislation before Congress in September 1995, if enacted, is likely to more than double Medicare Part B cost to participants.

[3]If legislation currently (September 1995) before Congress is enacted, Medicaid will be converted from an entitlement program to a state-administered block grant with reduced funding. States will have to cut costs by tightening eligibility requirements, reducing medical services, or both.

income. Because Medicaid is an entitlement program, costs are not capped. The federal government matches between 50 and 83 percent of state Medicaid expenditures according to the established formula.

State Medicaid programs operate, within broad federal guidelines, with considerable flexibility vis á vis the services and duration of services they will provide. Each state must provide to eligible beneficiaries inpatient and outpatient hospital services, physician services, nursing-home services for persons 21 years old or older, home health care, family planning services and supplies, rural health clinics, pediatric and family nurse practitioner services, nurse midwife services, and early and periodic screening, diagnosis, and treatment (EPSDT) services for children under 21. States also may choose to provide clinic services, nursing-home services for the elderly and disabled, intermediate-care facilities for the mentally retarded, optometrist services and eyeglasses, prescribed drugs, prosthetic devices, and dental services.

Medicaid benefits are obtained by applying at the local welfare department, filling out an application, having an interview, and providing proof of income, assets, and age. When approved for the program, users receive a Medicaid card that must be shown whenever services are provided. Continued eligibility to receive benefits must be reestablished periodically.

Medicaid, like Medicare, is administered by the Health Care Financing Administration. Payment is made directly to the individual or organization providing the health care. Participating physicians and health-care facilities must agree to accept the benefit levels established by the program. Many services must be approved in advance by state health officials in order to be eligible for payment. There is an appeals procedure for Medicaid applicants who believe they have been improperly found to be ineligible for coverage or users who are dissatisfied with the handling of their benefits.

Because Medicaid is means tested, public support is weaker than for Medicare. Because the program lacks a well-organized, powerful constituency, it is vulnerable to budget cuts. Medicaid expenditures have been growing rapidly—largely because of health-care costs increasing faster than the cost-of-living index, economic recession resulting in increased numbers of eligible persons, growing numbers of very old and disabled persons requiring acute long-term care, and technological advances that extend life at very high economic costs. The federal share of Medicaid costs increased by 67 percent between 1990 and 1992.

Federally funded military-related medical programs include *health and medical care for active-duty personnel,* a nationwide system of *veterans' hospitals,* the *Civilian Health and Medical Program of the Department of Veterans Affairs* (CHAMPVA) for dependents and survivors of veterans with service-related disabilities or deaths, and the *Civilian Health and Medical Program of the Uniformed Services* (CHAMPUS) for military dependents and retirees.

The **Special Supplemental Food Program for Women, Infants, and Children (WIC)** is one of the most popular and successful U.S. preventative health programs. WIC *provides a monthly package of nutritious foods tailored to the dietary needs of infants, children younger than 5, and pregnant, postpartum, and breast-*

feeding women. The foods provide protein, iron, calcium, zinc, and vitamins A, B$_6$, and C—nutrients likely to be missing from the diets of low-income women and children. WIC participants also receive nutrition education and referrals to other health and social services (Whitaker, 1993).

WIC program participants must be nutritionally at risk and have household incomes less than 185 percent of the federal poverty line. WIC foods are purchased with vouchers that may be exchanged for specific foods in participating grocery stores and farmers' markets. In fiscal year 1992, the vouchers were worth about $30 per person per month. WIC is federally funded and is administered by the Food and Nutrition Service of the U.S. Department of Agriculture in cooperation with state departments of human services. Applicants are screened and benefits approved by a network of about 8,900 state-approved local clinics. In 1992, 5.4 million women, infants, and children received WIC benefits. More than 40 percent of U.S.-born infants participate in WIC (USDHHS, 1993).

Although WIC is perhaps the most cost-effective U.S. social welfare program—studies report, for example, that each dollar spent in WIC's prenatal component saves between $1.77 and $3.13 in Medicaid expenses alone during the first 6 months of a child's life—WIC is not an entitlement program. Funds must be appropriated by Congress annually. Coverage has been increasing steadily, but in 1992 funding limitations still denied WIC services to nearly half of those eligible (Whitaker, 1993).

Work-Injury Programs

Workers' Compensation, the earliest widely developed form of social insurance in the United States, *provides cash benefits and medical care to workers injured on the job, and to surviving dependents of workers who die in work-related accidents.* In 1991, about 88 percent of U.S. workers were protected by state and federal workers' compensation laws. Compensation is paid if the injury or death arises "out of and in the due course of employment" and is not a result of the worker's intoxication, willful misconduct, or gross negligence. Compensation usually is based on the degree and permanence of the injury and varies widely from state to state in amount and duration of payments (USDHHS, 1993:29).

Based on the assumption that the employer is responsible for providing safe working conditions, and that therefore the cost of workplace accidents should be a business expense, workers' compensation programs are financed primarily by employers. In addition to money payments, the programs provide for health care and rehabilitative services as needed. Administration is usually by boards or commissions created through state legislation. The *Black Lung Benefit Program* is a special federal workers' compensation program for coal miners who are totally disabled by black lung disease. Domestic servants, farm workers, and casual laborers often are excluded from workers' compensation coverage.

Temporary disability insurance programs that provide time-limited payments to offset loss of wages from temporary non-job-related disability and maternity currently are offered in Rhode Island, California, New Jersey, New York, Puerto Rico, and Hawaii. These programs cover about 22 percent of U.S. workers employed in private industry, are funded by worker and/or employer contributions, and vary considerably in benefits. Typically, disability is defined as "inability to perform regular or customary work because of a physical or mental condition" (USDHHS, 1993:37). Private insurance programs offering temporary disability benefits are more widespread than public programs.

Unemployment Benefit Programs

Unemployment insurance *partially replaces the wages of most regularly employed U.S. workers who become involuntarily unemployed and are able and willing to work.* Workers who quit their jobs without good cause, are fired for misconduct, go on strike, or refuse to apply for or accept suitable work are disqualified from receiving benefits.

After a 1-week waiting period, unemployed workers in most states receive cash benefits of about 50 percent of their earnings during a previous base period, with maximum weekly payments varying from $133 to $335 in 1992. Weekly benefits are reduced by earnings that exceed a specified amount. A worker ordinarily is eligible for unemployment benefits for a maximum of 26 weeks during the year following establishment of eligibility. Under limited circumstances in states experiencing periods of sharply increased unemployment, benefits may be extended for an additional 13 weeks. Between 1991 and 1993, federal emergency unemployment compensation legislation extended benefits for an additional period, with the result that, for a time, an unemployed U.S. worker could receive a total of 52 to 59 weeks of benefits.

Unemployment insurance is a federal–state system funded by employer-paid payroll taxes. Basic coverage is paid from state funds, extended coverage is paid equally from state and federal funds, and emergency extended benefits from federal funds. States, subject to federal standards, decide levels and duration of payments, contribution rates, and eligibility requirements. States also administer the program. Significant shortcomings of unemployment insurance include program complexity and the limited duration of benefits. Many unemployed workers exhaust their benefits before they are able to find new jobs.

Family Allowances and Other Social Benefits

Family allowances are cash grants paid to every qualifying family—regardless of income—for the benefit of the family's children. The United States is unique among industrialized nations in having no family allowance program.

Although the United States lacks a family allowance program, it has several means-tested programs that provide income or income substitutes to families and, less commonly, to individuals. These include both cash and voucher programs—*Supplemental Security Income, Aid to Families with Dependent Children, Food Stamps, the Earned Income Tax Credit, the child tax credit, general assistance,* and *Low-Income Home Energy Assistance*—and in-kind programs—*school breakfasts and lunches, and public housing.*

Supplemental Security Income (SSI) is *a federally funded (frequently state-supplemented) assistance program guaranteeing a minimum monthly income to low-income persons who are blind, disabled, or older than 65.* In 1992, a total of 5,647,000 persons received SSI benefits. Of these, 4,055,000 were disabled, 1,505,000 elderly, and 86,000 blind. In 1994, SSI paid monthly means-tested cash payments up to a maximum of $446 for eligible individuals and $669 for couples. Payments were reduced by a recipient's other income and ceased when individual countable income reached $5,352 per year. Persons whose assets—other than a house, and personal goods and household effects with a maximum value of $2,000—exceed $2,000 for an individual or $3,000 for a couple are ineligible for SSI. Federal payments—which states may elect to supplement—are increased automatically to reflect rises in the cost of living.

Federal costs of SSI are financed from general tax revenues; the program is federally administered. Determination of eligibility is made in Social Security Administration district offices, and monthly checks are issued through the Treasury Department.

Aid to Families with Dependent Children[4] (AFDC) was, in 1996, *a federal–state funded assistance program for children "in families where need is brought about by incapacity, death, continued absence, or unemployment of a parent."* AFDC provided part of the difference between a family's income and its state's **standard of need,** *the amount of money—taking into account costs of food, clothing, shelter, utilities, and other necessities—that a state determines is necessary to provide a minimum standard of living in that state for a family of a given size.* As one might expect, standards of need varied from state to state. In 1993, for example, the monthly standard of need for a family of three was $577 in New York, $421 in Colorado, and $368 in Mississippi. Families with income not exceeding 185 percent of a state's standard of need, after some disregards intended to encourage self-support, were eligible for AFDC. AFDC recipients could not own assets—other than a home, equity in a car or burial plot up to $1,500 each, or, at state option, basic clothing and furniture—valued at more than $1,000. AFDC recipients had to agree to allow the child-support enforcement agency to enforce child-support payment obligations by absent parents. Application for AFDC was made at local public welfare offices. Persons who qualified for AFDC usually qualified also for Medicaid and Food Stamps.

As part of its AFDC program, each state was required to operate a *Job Opportunities and Basic Skills Training* (JOBS) program to help prepare adult AFDC recipients for employment. Mandatory JOBS services included high

---

[4]In 1995, Congress enacted the Personal Responsibility Act, part of the Republican Contract with America. The act was intended to end 60 years of AFDC as a federal entitlement that ensured at least a modicum of income security to low-income families with children. The act proposed transferring responsibility for AFDC to the states in the form of block grants, reducing federal funding levels, and requiring states to contribute 80 percent of their present AFDC appropriations for a period of 5 years. In response to widespread opposition by social workers and other advocates, the act was vetoed by President Clinton. At this writing in April 1996, the fate of AFDC and welfare reform remains to be determined. See addendum on pages 347 to 350.

school equivalency education, basic and remedial education, jobs skills training, job readiness, and job development and placement. In consultation with the AFDC recipient, an employability plan was developed and the state decided what services, such as child care, transportation, or books and fees, it would provide in support of the plan.

AFDC was administered collaboratively by the federal Department of Health and Human Services Administration for Families and Children and state departments of human services. The federal agency reviewed and approved state plans and grants, provided technical assistance, evaluated state operations, set standards, and collected and analyzed statistics. The states established eligibility and mailed monthly checks. Fifty to 83 percent of a state's AFDC contributions were matched by federal funds according to a formula that provided higher federal support to states with lower per-capita incomes (USDHHS, 1993:70).

Substandard grant levels and a number of widely believed but inaccurate myths about AFDC recipients were two of the program's major shortcomings. State AFDC grants were not required to bring family income up to state standard. In fiscal year 1992, "average monthly payments per family ranged from a low of $121.58 in Mississippi [one-third of its need standard] to a high of $742.22 in Alaska." That year 4.9 million families including 9.5 million children received $22.1 billion in AFDC payments (U.S. Department of Commerce, 1994:383). Growing program costs and public perceptions that AFDC recipients were unwilling to work, lived "high on the hog," bore additional children in order to increase their monthly checks, and stayed on AFDC indefinitely, resulted in increasing attacks on the program and scapegoating of beneficiaries under the rubric of welfare reform.

The *Food Stamp Program* is the largest, most far-reaching, and most important food assistance program for low-income families in the United States. After employment, Food Stamps are the nation's first line of defense against hunger (Whitaker, 1993:32). **Food Stamps** are *coupons redeemable in most retail grocery stores "for food for human consumption and garden seeds and plants"* (USDHHS, 1993:70). Food Stamps may not be redeemed for nonfood items such as household supplies, alcohol, or cigarettes. Food Stamp benefits are based on the cost of the *Thrifty Food Plan,* the least generous of several food market baskets priced periodically by the U.S. Department of Agriculture. Coupons are issued monthly in amounts determined by household size and income. In October 1993, an eligible household of four with no income received Food Stamps worth $375 per month. Households with income receive stamps equal to the difference between 30 percent of their income after deductions and the maximum benefit.

To be eligible for Food Stamps, a household must have gross income less than 130 percent of the federal poverty level; net income after certain deductions for earnings, work-related dependent-care expenses, out-of-pocket medical expenses, and excess shelter costs of less than the poverty level; and less than $2,000 ($3,000 if one member is 60 or older) in disposable assets.

Food Stamp costs are paid for entirely by federal general tax revenues, but administrative costs are shared by the states. The program is administered nationally by the Food and Nutrition Service of the U.S. Department of Agriculture, and is operated through local welfare offices, grocery stores, and banks. Application for Food Stamps is made at local welfare offices except that recipients of SSI may apply at Social Security district offices. In 1994, 27 million persons per month (approximately one out of ten U.S. citizens) received Food Stamps providing an average of about 76 cents per person per meal (FRAC, 1995:34). In fiscal year 1992, annual benefits totaled $20.9 billion.

There are three major shortcomings of Food Stamps. First, benefits are inadequate. Although in theory the Thrifty Food Plan will provide a nutritionally adequate diet, the plan is inadequate for extended use. Although Food Stamps are not intended to provide for the total food needs of a household, excessive shelter costs often limit the ability of families to supplement Food Stamps with cash. In a study of childhood hunger in Maine, for example, 35 percent of households receiving Food Stamps spent more than half of their total incomes on shelter. Four out of five Food Stamp households reported running out of Food Stamps before the end of each month. Second, many eligible households do not receive Food Stamps. In the Maine childhood hunger study, 17 percent of households apparently eligible for Food Stamps received no benefits. Of households that had applied for but were not receiving Food Stamps, 13 percent indicated discomfort in using the coupons, and 11 percent said that attitudes they encountered in the welfare office discouraged them from completing their applications. Third, strict assets limitations often disqualify low-income applicants. In rural areas, where reliable transportation is a high-priority need, possession of a vehicle worth more than $2,000 (even if it is essential for travel to work or to seek work) disqualifies many persons who would otherwise be eligible for Food Stamp benefits (Whitaker, 1993).

AFDC and Food Stamps, together with access to health care, have made a major difference in the lives of poor people throughout the United States. "The Human Face of Social Welfare 15: Up from Hunger," documents that progress in Beaufort County, South Carolina, between 1969 and 1995. Policy changes being considered by Congress in 1996 threaten these gains in human well-being.

The **Earned Income Tax Credit (EITC)** is *a means-tested, refundable federal tax credit that supplements the wages primarily of low-income working families with children.* Modified benefits are available to working families without qualifying children. Unlike the child tax credit (discussed below), the EITC benefits low-income, working families with or without children, regardless of whether the family earns enough income to owe income tax. The EITC pays eligible workers a percentage of their earnings up to a threshold. Beyond the threshold the credit is reduced by a phase-out percentage, with the result that the credit reaches zero at a "breakeven" point. In 1994, a family with one child received a credit of 26.3 percent on creditable earnings up to $7,750. This yielded a maximum credit of $2,038, which was received by families with earnings between $7,750 and a threshold of $11,000. Beyond the threshold the credit was phased out until it disappeared at breakeven income of $23,753. Families with two or more children are eligible for a larger credit.

Since the EITC is a "refundable" credit, families receive it as a reduction in income tax liability or, if the credit is larger than their tax liability, as a cash payment.

EITC benefits are not counted as income or assets when determining eligibility for AFDC, Food Stamps, Medicaid, SSI, Low-Income Home Energy Assistance, or low-income housing. The EITC is administered by the Internal Revenue Service. Application is made by filling out a simple, one-page form when filing one's federal income tax return. In 1994, 14.6 million U.S. families with children and 4.8 million families without children received EITC benefits totaling $21 billion (USDHHS, 1993:77–79). Proposals before Congress in November 1995, if enacted, will reduce EITC benefits for low-income workers by $43 billion between 1996 and 2002 (Center on Budget and Policy Priorities, 1995).

In November 1995, Congress passed *child tax credit* legislation intended to reduce family income tax payments by $500 per year for each child under 19. Like the EITC, the child tax credit would be easily administered through the Internal Revenue Service. Although at first glance the child tax credit resembles a family allowance program, there are significant differences between them. The child tax credit is not "refundable." Because families must owe income tax in order to receive any benefit, only relatively affluent families would receive maximum benefits.[5] "Approximately 23.7 million children living in families with low or moderate incomes—constituting one-third of all U.S. children—would receive no aid from the child credit. Another 7 million children in moderate-income families would receive a partial credit of less than $500." While the richest 13 percent of U.S. taxpayers—those with incomes of $75,000 or more—would gain $24 billion from the child tax credit between 1996 and 2000, the poorest half of taxpayers would lose $12.4 billion from the effects of the child tax credit combined with the proposed cuts in the EITC (Center on Budget and Policy Priorities, 1995).

General assistance (GA), sometimes referred to as "general relief" or "town assistance," is *means-tested financial and other aid provided from state and/or local funds, most often to persons who are ineligible for federally subsidized assistance programs such as SSI or AFDC.* Benefits vary from state to state but are usually small, highly restricted, and of short duration. A typical recipient of GA is a single adult, living alone, aged 30–40. Employable single adults and childless couples frequently are denied GA. Rarely, general assistance provides additional resources to AFDC or SSI beneficiaries with unmet needs (USDHHS, 1993; Whitaker, 1993; Rein, 1995).

GA is administered by states, local government, or local government under state supervision. Application ordinarily is made in local welfare departments. In 1990, GA cash benefits ranged "from $27 in Charleston County, South Carolina (5 percent of the poverty line) to $385 in Maine (77 percent of the poverty line)." A 1982–1990 study by the Department of Health and Human Services reported some form of GA program in forty-five states. During 1991 and 1992 many states cut back or eliminated their GA programs. In fiscal year 1991, thirty-five states and the District of Columbia reported distributing general assistance totaling $2.9

---

[5]A family with two children with income too low to owe federal income tax would receive nothing, with income high enough to owe $600 in tax would receive $600, and with a tax liability of $1,000 or more would receive $1,000.

UP FROM HUNGER

Bluffton, S.C.—Viola DuPont says "the worms" already had killed two of her daughters and had afflicted a third, Corretta, when Sen. Ernest F. Hollings knocked on the door of their shack.

The 1969 visit was part of a Hunger Tour of South Carolina that exposed the desperate condition of the poor here. Corretta's plight, as well as her parasites, were taken to Washington as evidence in Senate hearings. In response, a federally funded health clinic was opened in 1970. Septic tanks and running water were installed.

Corretta survived, and today her own three children are kept healthy by a raft of anti-poverty programs: Medicaid, food stamps, school lunches, Head Start, and the Women, Infants and Children nutrition program.

"We came through rough times, we sure did," Ms. DuPont says. "It's a whole lot better now."

In 1969, Beaufort County was one of the poorest spots in the nation, and the hearings contributed to an escalation of the government's war on poverty. . . .

How successful has the federal government's antipoverty effort been over the past quarter century? To answer that, it may be helpful to retrace Sen. Hollings's path through the collection of coastal hamlets known as the Lowcountry.

Hollings's tour makes clear that the health, nutrition, and overall living standard of the poor here in the Lowcountry have improved. But it is difficult to determine how much of the improvement comes from specific federal programs and how much from a growing economy. In Beaufort, the steady expansion of Hilton Head resorts, for instance, has brought jobs—albeit low-paying ones—to the poorer parts of the county.

Some say the antipoverty programs in Beaufort also have had a role in exacerbating other problems: dissolved families, teenage pregnancy, dependency on welfare. . . .

Still, here in the Lowcountry, the lives of the poor are less harsh than they were a generation ago. At least some of this has to do with government help.

Back in 1970, for example, there were only two doctors in Beaufort known to serve the poor; now, there are some 72 doctors who rely in part

on the Medicaid health program for the poor. With government-supported clinics for the indigent and expanded nutrition programs for mothers, infant mortality in Beaufort has dipped to fewer than 10 deaths per 1,000 births, from 62 in 1965. Of the dozens of people interviewed for this article, not one knew of a person here who regularly goes hungry.

Modest homes, many bought with federal mortgage subsidies, have replaced leaky "shrimp shacks." Running water and septic tanks laid with federal funds have replaced disease-causing outhouses. A recent study by the Annie E. Casey Foundation found that the number of children living in poverty here declined to 20.1% from 35.1% in the two decades following 1969. . . .

The first stops on today's tour are the sea islands of St. Helena and Warsaw—now, as then, some of the poorest places in America. In his 1970 book, *The Case Against Hunger,* Sen. Hollings says he visited a Beaufort County shack, "typical of thousands of hovels," housing 15 African Americans with no heat, electricity, or water. They were dressed in rags and suffered nutritional-deficiency diseases such as pellagra, scurvy and rickets. Now, the improvement in St. Helena is all around: new, paved roads, water to all homes and government-financed dwellings.

"You won't see the poverty in the raw because it's not there," says William Grant, a community activist who guided the first hunger tour. . . .

Mathilda Middleton lived in St. Helena during the Hollings tour and today shares the same house with her granddaughter and two grandchildren. Mrs. Middleton, who stopped working 10 years ago at age 77, recalls that in the 1960s the only food on the table was often what they could grow in their own yard. They carried water from a shallow well, there was no electricity and the only heat came from burning wood . . .

Today the home is no palace, a sloping structure with worn out furniture, a rusted metal roof and ripped screens. But the war on poverty has won some small skirmishes here. Mrs. Middleton's granddaughter, Delores Simmons, gets [monthly] vouchers for milk, eggs, cereal, juice and peanut butter from the federal WIC program for her two-year-old daughter. Her eight-year-old boy went through the Head Start preschool program and now receives free lunches at school—both federal programs that weren't available to Ms. Simmons, a ninth-grade dropout.

Another victory: Ms. Simmons receives just over $200 a month in food stamps, so she can afford to feed the children chicken or fish most nights—another improvement on her childhood. An AFDC payment of another $200 gives her clothing money. Perhaps most important is the Beaufort-Jasper Comprehensive Health Clinic, formed in the wake of the hunger tour and funded today 94% by Medicaid and U.S. Public Health Service funds. Ms. Simmons takes her children there about twice a month, and can get medicine on the spot.

Mrs. Middleton's septic tank and running water were installed about a decade ago, again courtesy of Comprehensive Health. The area's septic tanks were paid for by the now-defunct U.S. Office of Economic Opportunity, which also funded wells for clean drinking water. Comp Health has installed 1,000 septic tanks, and the program is now paid for by the United Way. It costs residents $600 for a tank that otherwise would be $2,000 or more.

The antipoverty programs have clearly softened Ms. Simmons life—perhaps too much, some might argue. Asked why she doesn't work, Ms. Simmons replies: "There ain't no reason." . . .

Next stop on the tour is Bluffton, a town just across the bridge from the Hilton Head resorts. Here, as elsewhere in Beaufort, the introduction of $20,000 mobile homes, which can be had for 5% down and $200 monthly payments, has proven a big improvement over the shacks. . . .

An hour's drive across the county brings the tour to Jesse Coakley's home in the town of Dale. Here at the Coakley place, those on the 1969 Hunger Tour found children with worms and other illnesses. With no outhouse, an adjacent field was used as toilet.

These days the house has a septic tank and running water from a deep well, installed in the 1980s by Comp Health. The home, though dilapidated, has a heater, refrigerator and television. And Mr. Coakley and his 18-year-old grandson, who lives with him, eat three square meals a day. . . .

If there is one emblem of the success of the antipoverty programs here, it can be found in Sheldon, the last stop of the hunger tour and home to one of the clinics of Beaufort-Jasper

Comprehensive Health Service. Its 14 doctors receive 94,000 visits a year from 18,000 poor or near-poor patients. Of its $6.8 million budget, $3 million comes from the U.S. Public Health Service and almost all the rest from Medicaid. It is the most visible symbol of a vastly improved healthcare system for the poor.

The results are impressive: not a single case of worms in 15 years, and not a single case of malnutrition that didn't come from neglect. The clinic's infant mortality rate is less than half the national and state averages. "We have wiped out pediatric hunger in this county and we don't see malnutrition," says Francis E. Rushton, a private Beaufort pediatrician who credits the WIC and school-lunch programs. . . .

Revisiting communities in Beaufort County, South Carolina, in which hunger, malnutrition, and disease were rampant 25 years earlier, demonstrates many positive impacts of the War on Poverty initiated by President Johnson. The visit also reveals persons who have chosen not to work at low-wage jobs which would provide fewer benefits than those sometimes available through a combination of federal programs. The Beaumont experience illustrates the linkage between the economy and social welfare and the importance of economic development and decent wages in fostering increased self-reliance.

In 1995, with proposals being considered by Congress to end entitlements, to reduce spending for antipoverty efforts, and to overhaul or hand over to the states many of the programs—Food Stamps, child nutrition, WIC, AFDC, the Earned Income Tax Credit, Medicaid, Supplemental Security Income, and others—which have made such a difference to poor people in Beaufort County and throughout the United States, the challenge is to address the problems of dependency and family dissolution without reintroducing hunger and illness to places such as the Lowcountry. The policy choices which are being made will have enormous impact on children and their families.

billion to 1.35 million persons. In fiscal year 1992, thirty-four states reported a total of only 1.1 million GA recipients (USDHHS, 1993; Rein, 1995).

GA tends to be treated as assistance of last resort. Participants are often highly stigmatized. In some New England states, for example, GA is still administered by the "overseer of the poor," an elected position tracing its roots to the Elizabethan Poor Laws.

The **Low-Income Home Energy Assistance Program (LIHEAP)** *provides federally funded block grants to states and other jurisdictions to help households with incomes less than 150 percent of the federal poverty line meet the costs of home heating and/or cooling.* Benefits are provided as cash, fuel, prepaid utility bills, home weatherization, or as vouchers that may be exchanged for energy supplies. LIHEAP is administered by the U.S. Department of Health and Human Services. Application is through designated local agencies such as Community Action Program (CAP) offices. In fiscal year 1993, Congress appropriated $1.346 billion for LIHEAP, down from $1.5 billion in 1992. In 1995, as is the case with many means-tested assistance programs, majority Republicans in Congress have targeted LIHEAP for further cuts or program elimination.

Three nutrition programs for school-aged children—the *National School Lunch Program,* the *National School Breakfast Program,* and the *Summer Food Service Program*—play major roles in preventing and reducing hunger among children in the United States. The programs are intended to help the states provide "an adequate supply of nutritious food for all children at a moderate cost" and to support farmers by encouraging "the domestic consumption of nutritious agricultural commodities" (USDHHS, 1993).

The *National School Lunch Act of 1946* was created as a "measure of national security, to safeguard the health and well-being of the Nation's children." Among its chief advocates was General Lewis Hersey, who headed the Selective Service and was gravely concerned that many young men failed their World War II draft physicals as a consequence of poor childhood nutrition. The *National School Breakfast Program* was permanently authorized in 1975 with a statement of Congressional intent that the program "be made available in all schools where it is needed to provide adequate nutrition for children in attendance." The *Summer Food Service Program* provides nutritious meals to children when school is not in session (Whitaker, 1993).

Children living in households with incomes less than 130 percent of the federal poverty line receive free school breakfasts and lunches. Those from households with incomes between 130 and 185 percent of the poverty guidelines receive reduced price meals costing (in FY 1992) no more than 30 cents for breakfast and 40 cents for lunch. Summer meals are offered free to all children at sites where at least half the participants are from households with incomes less than 185 percent of the poverty line.

The school nutrition programs are funded with federal general tax revenues and administered by the Food and Nutrition Service of the U.S. Department of Agriculture through state educational agencies. States contribute state administrative costs. In fiscal year 1992, 852 million school breakfasts and 4.1 billion school lunches were served at a cost totaling approximately $5.2 billion. Although most elementary, middle, and high schools provide school lunches, far fewer schools provide breakfasts. Many children eligible for free or reduced-price breakfasts have no access to the program. Other children decide not to eat school breakfasts or lunches because of the possible stigma of being labeled poor. Even fewer children are able to participate in the summer food program. In the state of Maine, for example, only about 3 percent of the children eating free or reduced-price school lunches also have access to summer meals (Whitaker, 1993).

The Housing Act of 1949 established the policy of ensuring "a decent home and suitable living environment for every American family." Unfortunately, the United States has fallen far short of realizing that goal. Mulroy (1995:1377) graphically illustrates the gap between policy and reality:

• During the 1980s, the federal budget for affordable housing was cut 75 percent, whereas the number of applicants soared.
• [During the 1990s] waiting lists for public housing grew dramatically, forcing more than two-thirds of U.S. cities to close their lists to new applicants.
• [In 1991] 91 percent of all current renter families could not afford to purchase a home.
• Anywhere from 300,000 to 500,000 people are homeless on any one night in the United States, and the homeless population is estimated to be more than 1 million.

Federal programs that meet some of the need for "decent, safe, sanitary, and affordable housing for all Americans" (USDHHS, 1993:75) include public housing, rental assistance, and programs for the homeless.

Public housing consists of *residences "that are built, maintained, and administered by . . . government to provide low-rent or no-rent homes for needy people"* (Barker, 1991:190). Through the Housing Act of 1937, federal funds are provided to local or Native American public housing authorities for the construction, operation, and maintenance of housing projects for low-income families with children, the elderly, disabled, or handicapped. Families whose income is less than 50 percent, or in some cases up to 80 percent, of an area's median income are eligible when spaces are available. Successful applicants pay rent equal to 30 percent of their adjusted monthly household income. Most federal public housing funds are administered by the U.S. Department of Housing and Urban Development (HUD). In fiscal year 1992, there were 1.4 million public housing units operated at a federal cost of $2.8 billion.

HUD *Section 8 rental programs* provide vouchers or certificates giving assisted families "the opportunity to lease rental housing that is suitable to the family's needs and desires" (USDHHS, 1993:76). Families receiving rental certificates generally pay 30 percent of their adjusted income toward rent below a set maximum. With rental vouchers, families receive the difference between an area standard rent and 30 percent of their adjusted income. If their housing costs exceed the area standard, they must pay the difference; if they are able to find housing costing less than the area standard, they may keep the difference. In

1992, about 2.8 million housing units were provided through Section 8 at a federal cost of $12.3 billion.

HUD administers a variety of *programs for the homeless,* including grants for emergency shelters, transitional housing in which homeless families may remain for up to 2 years while seeking permanent shelter, and permanent housing for persons with disabilities. Usually, programs for the homeless include funds for supportive services in addition to shelter. In fiscal year 1992, HUD administered $450 million in grants for the homeless.

The largest federal housing subsidy is the *income tax deduction of interest on home mortgage loans.* Such tax breaks benefit middle- and upper-class homeowners rather than the poor. In 1981, for example, the federal government spent less than $7 billion on all subsidies for low-income housing, but forgave $30 billion in taxes for homeowners (Abramowitz, 1983).

Honorably discharged veterans of active-duty military service in the United States are eligible for many income maintenance and personal social service benefits that are not generally available to nonveterans. Such programs, administered through the U.S. Department of Veterans Affairs, include: *"G.I. Bill" education grants, Veterans Administration housing loans* for the purchase or improvement of homes, medical care through *V.A. hospitals, life insurance,* and *burial benefits.* Disabled veterans, those retired after 20 years or more of military service, their dependents, and dependents of veterans with service-related deaths are eligible for many special benefits, including shopping in government-subsidized commissaries. Veterans may retire with half pay and other privileges after 20 years of service (U.S. Department of Veterans Affairs, 1995).

This concludes our review of the major public programs that constitute the five pillars of social security in the United States. There are, of course, many more federal social welfare programs. In fact, the *1993 Catalog of Federal Domestic Assistance,* "a government-wide compendium of Federal programs, projects, services, and activities that provide assistance or benefits to the American public," describes 1,308 programs administered by fifty-one federal agencies (U.S. Office of Management and Budget, 1993)!

The *voluntary sector* in the United States complements the public social welfare activity we have described, and is much more extensive than in Sweden, Poland, or Mexico. In the words of the 1975 Commission on Private Philanthropy and Public Needs: "Few aspects of American Society are more characteristically, more famously American than the nation's array of voluntary organizations, and the support in both time and money that is given them by its citizens." By the 1990s there were more than a million voluntary "formal organizations and countless other informal groups and associations" in the United States (Brilliant, 1995:2469). (See "Big Brothers/Big Sisters of Yonkers, New York.")

In 1993, the Internal Revenue Service listed more than 575,000 *501(c)3* charitable nonprofit organizations and more than 142,000 *501(c)4* social welfare organizations in its master file of tax-exempt organizations. Functioning as *nonprofit, public-benefit organizations,* **501(c)3 and 501(c)4 organizations** *are exempt from paying federal and many local and state taxes. In addition, contributions to*

BIG BROTHERS/BIG SISTERS OF YONKERS, NEW YORK

The Yonkers, New York, Big Brothers/Big Sisters social agency is one example of the thousands of voluntary 501(c)3 social welfare organizations throughout the United States. The Yonkers agency is affiliated with Big Brothers/Big Sisters of America (BB/BSA), a private, voluntary organization that for more than 90 years has matched volunteer adult mentors with youth living in single-parent households. Today BB/BSA maintains about 75,000 matches each year.

Big Brothers/Big Sisters seeks to provide support that will enable youth to grow into responsible adults. Through carefully matched adult Big Brothers and Big Sisters, the organization seeks to reduce the incidence of antisocial behavior such as drug and alcohol abuse; to improve self-concepts and relationships with peers and parents; and to improve motivation, attitude, and achievement related to school work.

Local affiliates such as the Yonkers agency recruit and carefully screen volunteer applicants for one-on-one matches; screen youth, who usually come from single-parent households and who, with their parents, must want a Big Brother or Sister match; and match the adults and youths based on backgrounds, stated preferences, and geographic proximity. On average, the pair meets 3 to 4 hours three times per month for at least a year.

The big question with many social welfare programs is "Does it work?" Recent research (Tierney et al., 1995) demonstrates definitively that the Big Brothers/Big Sisters program does make a difference.

Applicants to the program from agencies in eight cities—boys and girls, African American and white, many from low-income families with a history of family violence or substance abuse—were randomly assigned to treatment and control groups. Members of the treatment group were paired with Big Brothers or Sisters. Control group members simply stayed on the waiting list. Baseline data were collected, and members of both groups were reinterviewed 18 months later.

Little Brothers and Little Sisters were 46 percent less likely than controls to initiate drug use during the study period. They were 27 percent less likely to initiate alcohol use, one-third less likely to hit someone, skipped half as many days of school, felt more competent about doing their schoolwork, skipped fewer classes, and showed modest gains in grade-point averages.

The Yonkers agency has its own policy-making board of directors and raises funds from local contributions supplemented by support from outside organizations including the United Way of Westchester County (a voluntary fund-raising organization), the Yonkers Bureau of Youth Services (a municipal agency), and the New York State Division of Criminal Justice Services (a division of state government). All services are provided free of charge to clients.

Sources: Big Brothers/Big Sisters of Yonkers, Inc. "Big Brothers/Big Sisters of Yonkers" (pamphlet), Yonkers, NY, 1988. Joseph Tierney, Jean Baldwin Grossman, and Nancy Resch, "Making a Difference: An Impact Study of Big Brothers/Big Sisters," Philadelphia: Public/Private Ventures, 1995. Westchester Community Services Council, *Westchester Human Services Directory,* White Plains, NY, 1984.

501(c)3 organizations are tax-deductible by their donors. Because 501(c)4 organizations may lobby and participate in political action, contributions to them are not tax-deductible (Brilliant, 1995:2471).

In 1993, philanthropic gifts for human services totaled nearly $12.5 billion, constituting 9.9 percent of all voluntary giving in the United States. The Combined Federal Campaign and the United Way are two of the largest annual voluntary fund-raising efforts. Approximately 2,300 local United Way organizations raised $3.05 billion in 1993, down from a high of $3.17 billion in 1991. More than 50 percent of United Way funds were distributed to "affiliates of 17 national organizations, including . . . the Red Cross, YMCA and YWCA, Boy Scouts and Girl Scouts, family agencies, and the Salvation Army (Brilliant, 1995:2474–2475). Criticism of the United Way by those who believe its funds disproportionately benefit noncontroversial programs for the middle class has resulted in the development of a growing network of "alternative united ways" seeking funds for social action organizations and programs targeted to the poor.

FIVE PILLARS OF SOCIAL SECURITY: SWEDEN[6]

With a few exceptions such as means-tested family, housing, livelihood, and funeral grants to persons serving full-time in the military, Swedish social welfare programs consist of universal, non-means-tested entitlements.

Old Age, Disability, and Death Benefits

Swedish National Pension Insurance consists of *basic pensions, supplemental pensions,* and *partial pensions* intended to provide financial security for all elderly persons and certain categories of persons unable to support themselves. Any person who has lived in Sweden for at least 40 years, or who has worked in Sweden for at least 30 years, receives the same *basic pension,* which is adjusted annually according to the cost of living. Persons who have lived or worked in Sweden for shorter periods receive reduced basic pensions. In addition, *national supplementary pensions* are paid based on earned income above a base amount. *Partial pensions* are paid to enable workers to scale back to part-time work between the ages of 60 and 65.

Through the basic pension program, persons 65 or older receive the base amount[7] and husband and wife couples older than 65 receive 157 percent of the base amount. The full base amount is paid to persons older than 16 who are permanently disabled by illness, physical disability, or mental disability. Persons with partial disabilities receive reduced basic pensions. Surviving children under 18 receive benefits based on the accumulated pension rights of their deceased parent. *Adjustment benefits* are paid for 1 year to any survivor under the age of 65 who was living with a person at the time of death. Adjustment benefits also are paid to a surviving spouse caring for a child until the child is 12 years old. Pensioners who qualify for little or no supplementary pension receive a *supplementary benefit* of 55.5 percent of the basic pension. Persons with disabilities receive a supplementary benefit of 105.5 percent of the basic pension. Special *child-care allowances* are provided to parents caring for disabled children under 16 at home. Local governments often provide tax-exempt *housing allowances* that supplement pensions for the elderly, persons with disabilities, and survivors.

---

[6]Unless noted otherwise, the information about Sweden is drawn from the Swedish Institute, *Fact Sheets on Sweden: Social Insurance in Sweden* (FS 5). Stockholm, Sweden: The Sweden Institute, 1993; and U.S. Department of Health and Human Services (USDHHS), 1994. *Social Security Programs throughout the World 1993*. Washington, DC: U.S. Government Printing Office.

[7]In 1993, the pension base amount was 34,400 SEK (Swedish krona)(Swedish Institute, 1993:FS5). With one SEK worth about 17 cents U.S., the base amount equaled about $5,848. In 1990, Swedish blue-collar workers were paid about 100,000 SEK annually after taxes, and white-collar workers received approximately 125,000 SEK after taxes (Swedish Institute, 1992:FS3). It is important to take into account the provision of health care, housing, and other benefits when comparing pensions or after-tax wages and salaries between the United States and Sweden.

The Swedish pension insurance program is administered by the National Social Insurance Board and is delivered through a network of regional social insurance offices. Basic pensions are funded by a 6.69 percent payroll tax on employers (which provides about 75 percent of the cost), supplemented by national general tax revenues. Supplementary pensions are funded solely by payroll taxes. Benefits are paid monthly, and retirees must apply for the program. Once approved, they are eligible for the rest of their lives (USDHHS, 1994:310–311).

Health Care, Sickness, and Maternity Programs

Sweden has developed a comprehensive system of national health insurance, including allowances for medical and dental care, sick-pay benefits, and maternity and parental benefits. [See "Health Care in Sweden."]

Work-Injury Programs

All employed and self-employed residents in Sweden are protected by *work-injury insurance.* Cash benefits are intended to replace total normal pay when sickness or injury incurred at work or on the way to or from work results in illness, disability, or death. The program is funded by a 0.9 percent payroll tax paid by employers, and is administered by the National Social Insurance Board through regional and local social insurance offices (USDHHS, 1994:311–312).

Unemployment Benefit Programs

Sweden's system of unemployment insurance is operated through labor union-based unemployment benefit societies. To qualify for benefits, a worker must have been employed for 75 days during at least 4 months in the year before becoming unemployed, must register in a public unemployment office, and must be capable of work. Workers are disqualified if they quit their jobs, are fired for misconduct, or are on strike, and they are disqualified for 4 weeks if they refuse a suitable job offer. Benefits may be received for up to 300 days, extended to 450 days for workers ages 55–64. When workers are laid off temporarily because of lack of work, they continue to receive their full wages, with the employer partially compensated by the government. The Swedish unemployment insurance program is financed by a 2.14 percent payroll tax paid by employers, supplemented by government general tax revenues. It is administered by the National Labor Market Board in cooperation with labor union unemployment benefit societies (USDHHS, 1994:312–313; Swedish Institute, 1993).

Family Allowances and Other Social Benefits

Through child allowances and supplements, Sweden ensures that every family has the resources necessary for the special costs of raising children. Tax-exempt *child*

HEALTH CARE IN SWEDEN

People get sick in Sweden just as they do everywhere else. However, all Swedes are covered by national health insurance, which makes illness less problematic than it is in many other countries. The Swedish approach to health care treats people as citizens with rights of membership. It does not categorize people, but it does respond to different needs. Everyone needs basic health care, so it is available on an equal basis to all. However, children and parents receive special benefits which reflect their special needs.

The information that follows is excerpted from *Fact Sheets on Sweden: Social Insurance in Sweden* (FS-5), Stockholm: The Swedish Institute, 1993.

Allowances For Medical Care

The various forms of care provided by the *outpatient, hospital, and dental services,* etc., come under the national health insurance system. They are financed from taxation revenue and through contributions from the government social insurance budget. These contributions are made monthly to the county councils by the social insurance office. The patient pays a fee for services received. . . .

In most areas insured persons pay no charge for counseling on *birth control*. . . . To some extent contraceptives are to be provided free of charge in connection with the counselling. . . .

A prescription holder pays only a certain proportion of the cost of . . . officially registered drugs . . . a set amount for the first item on the prescription and a smaller amount for each further item. . . .

No charge is made for drugs needed to treat chronic and serious diseases.

Those persons whose expenses for medical treatment and/or pharmaceutical preparations exceed a certain limit in the course of a year are entitled to free treatment and/or preparations for the rest of that twelve-month period.

An insured person who has received medical treatment, dental treatment or in-patient care is also entitled to reimbursement . . . for related *travel expenses*. . . . Parents or other relatives taking a sick child under the age of 16 for out-patient care may also be eligible for this type of reimbursement, as may those who are visiting a child in hospital.

Dental Care

The health insurance system also covers *dental care,* both treatment and preventive care, provided by members of the public dental service as well as by most dentists in private practice. . . . Treatment is at present divided into three price categories, with the patient paying a percentage of the costs—70% up to a certain ceiling, then 50% and 25% for any one course of treatment. . . . Children and young people are entitled to free dental care from the public dental service until the age of 18.

Cash Benefits

Under the 1992 Sick Pay Act, employed persons receive *sick pay* from the employer for the first 14 days of a period of illness. This amounts to 75% of normal income for the second and third days of each sick-pay period, there being no entitlement to compensation for the first day of absence from work.

allowances are paid to families for one or two children under 16, for students under 20, and for students under 23 attending special schools for persons with developmental disabilities. *Child allowance supplements* increase child allowance benefits by 50 percent for a third child in a family, by 100 percent for a fourth child, and by 150 percent for a fifth. Total program costs are paid by the government. Swedish child allowances are administered by the National Social Insurance Board through regional and local social insurance offices.

Additional universal social benefits include ongoing *adoptive support* when a single person adopts a child, *lump-sum adoption grants* when parents adopt a child from another country, *advance payment of child support* from the government to a custodial parent when a noncustodial parent fails to make child support payments

For the remainder of the period sick pay is 90%. On the 15th day the social insurance office takes over from the employer and pays *sickness benefit.* . . .

Sick pay and sickness benefit are taxable, which means that they count towards future payments from the national supplementary pension scheme . . . in the same way as other earned income. . . .

A person taking part in vocational rehabilitation—measures needed to help him or her obtain or retain a job, e.g., work testing, work training or education—is entitled to a *rehabilitation allowance.* This is divided into two parts: rehabilitation benefit, to cover loss of earnings, and a special grant to cover certain kinds of expenditure connected with rehabilitation.

A person who has a functional impairment or a long-lasting illness can obtain a grant from the social insurance office towards the *cost of employment aids.* . . .

Parental Insurance

A family policy which protects the child and its rights has been one of the cornerstones of Swedish social policy. Important elements are free maternal and child health care and a system of parental insurance, all of which come under the auspices of the national health insurance scheme.

Most people come into contact with the parental insurance system in connection with the birth or adoption of a child. *Parental benefit* is paid for a period of 450 days and enables a parent to stay at home with a child with compensation for loss of income. For the first 360 days, the amount received is approximately 90% of the parent's normal income. For the final 90 days, a standard amount (SEK 60 per day) is paid. . . .

This benefit can be utilized in various ways. It can be used by one parent to stay home full-time, or it can be combined with part-time working. . . . Benefit may be claimed at any time from birth up to the child's eighth birthday.

Fathers are entitled to ten days' leave of absence with parental benefit when a child is born.

The parental insurance also provides *temporary parental benefit* for 60 days . . . per child per year if a parent has to stay at home with a child who is ill, if the education or visit the child's pre-school, leisure time centre or school.

If an expectant woman is not able to work at her usual capacity and cannot be assigned more suitable work, she is entitled to *maternity benefit* for a maximum of 50 days before the expected date of delivery.

As might be expected, the Swedish health-care system is generally regarded as one of the best in the world. Life expectancy in Sweden is 78 years, compared with 76 in the United States, 72 in Poland, and 70 in Mexico. The 1992 Swedish under-5 infant mortality rate (U5MR) is 6 per 1,000 births, in contrast to 9 for the United States, 16 for Poland, and 33 for Mexico. (See Chapter 1, Table 1.2.)

Such a comprehensive system is necessarily expensive, yet in 1991 Sweden spent a smaller proportion of its gross national product on health care than did the United States—8.6 percent versus 13.4 percent. Total health spending per person in Sweden in 1991 was $1,443, compared to $2,867 in the U.S. (U.S. Department of Commerce, 1994). These figures demonstrate the heavy reliance in the United States on the private sector for the provision of health care.

on time, *car allowances* for persons whose mobility problems prevent them from using public transportation, *training allowances* comparable to unemployment compensation during job training, *special adult study assistance grants and loans* to replace income when an adult takes a leave of absence from employment to study at compulsory comprehensive or upper secondary schools, and *military allowances* for persons taking part in compulsory military service or civil defense training. Finally, any person unable to provide for her- or himself "is entitled to a *social welfare allowance,* no matter how the need has arisen." The right to social welfare allowances is guaranteed by the national Social Services Act. Payments vary from place to place but must be above a nationally defined minimum subsistence level (Swedish Institute, 1994).

FIVE PILLARS OF SOCIAL SECURITY: POLAND[8]

Like Sweden, Poland offers a wide range of universal, non-means-tested social insurance programs. Poland operates three social insurance funds: a general fund, a fund for private agriculture, and a fund for priests. The funds are administered by the Polish Social Insurance Institute (ZUS). Polish old age, disability, and survivor benefits; health care, sickness, and maternity programs; work-injury compensation programs; and family allowances are funded by a 43 percent employer-paid payroll tax. Unemployment benefits are funded separately. In Poland, social security benefits are counted as taxable income. Workers pay graduated personal income taxes of 20, 30, and 40 percent of income above a tax threshold.

Old Age, Disability, and Death Benefits

Polish *old age, permanent disability, and survivor benefits* cover "employees, apprentices, collective farmers, members of cooperatives, self-employed artisans, home-workers, attorneys, and clergy." Military personnel, police, and independent farmers are covered by separate systems (USDHHS, 1994:262). *Old age pensions* pay a minimum of 35 percent of the average national salary to men at age 65 who have worked for at least 25 years, and to women at age 60 who have worked at least 20 years. Dancers, acrobats, underground miners, teachers, and aviation and maritime workers may retire earlier. Benefit levels depend on previous earnings and numbers of years of work and are adjusted for inflation. It is possible to work nearly full-time and still receive a full old age pension. *Disability pensions* are paid to (group 1) persons who cannot work under normal conditions and cannot look after themselves, to (group 2) persons who cannot work under normal conditions but can look after themselves, and to (group 3) persons with long-term medical problems who can work and persons with partial disabilities. When disabilities are not work-related, pensions for group 3 are 75 percent of old age pensions, for group 2 are equal to old age pensions, and for group 1 are 30 percent higher. Poland also has developed interesting sheltered workshop cooperatives for persons with disabilities. (See "Polish Cooperatives for Persons with Disabilities.") *Survivors' pensions* are paid to spouses, children, and sometimes to parents of a deceased worker. One survivor receives 55 percent of the average monthly wage; benefits increase with family size.

Health Care, Sickness, and Maternity Programs

Polish workers with at least 8 years of employment receive *sickness benefits* of 100 percent of their average earnings for up to 26 weeks when they are sick, for up to 39 weeks if they are likely to recover, for up to 60 days to care for a sick

---

[8]Except as noted otherwise, the information on the five pillars of social security in Poland is drawn from The World Bank, *Poland: Income Support and the Social Safety Net during the Transition.* Washington, DC: The World Bank, 1993; and U.S. Department of Health and Human Services, Social Security Administration, *Social Security Programs throughout the World 1993,* SSA Publication No. 13-11805, Research Report #63, Washington, DC: U.S. Government Printing Office, 1994.

POLISH COOPERATIVES FOR PERSONS WITH DISABILITIES

While it was a socialist society, Poland emphasized the right and responsibility of people to work if they were able. There was no official unemployment. Everyone who wanted a job was guaranteed one, although not necessarily in the occupation or location of their choice. This emphasis on work carried over to those with mental or physical limitations.

At the close of World War II, Poland was devastated. Approximately 6 million Poles (20 percent of the population) had been killed and large numbers of others injured during the war (Nelson, 1983:105). At a time when its economic capacity for doing so was severely limited, Poland was faced with the need to assist its many citizens with war injuries. In order to provide this assistance, Poland established cooperatives for the disabled.

Cooperatives for persons with disabilities are independent organizations, governed by their own members and economically self-sufficient. They are supported by membership fees and from income earned through the production and sale of consumer goods. They receive no government grants but are granted tax benefits and the exclusive right to produce certain products. At least 70 percent of the membership of the cooperatives must be disabled; other members assist the disabled in their rehabilitation, work, and training.

In 1984 there were 452 Polish Cooperatives of Disabled People, whose efforts were coordinated through the Central Union of Invalids' Cooperatives (Mikulski, 1987:22,16). The Union coordinated its activities with the Ministry of Health and Social Welfare and the Ministry of Labor, Wages, and Social Affairs, the government bodies responsible for most social welfare services. Of the 1.9 million people with mental or physical limitations in Poland in 1984, 395,000 were vocationally active, 174,000 of them through cooperatives for the disabled (Mikulski, 1987:9).

The cooperatives provide work and a setting for that work that reflects the needs and abilities of their members. Such work constitutes a regular form of employment, and persons with disabilities are paid salaries whose average level is about two-thirds of the national average (Mikulski, 1987:39). It is up to the management of the cooperatives to make sure that they remain economically competitive.

In addition to jobs, the cooperatives provide many other services for their members. These include rehabilitation, vocational training, counseling, protheses, medical care, social and recreational opportunities, and access to vacation resorts. These services are provided free. Members of cooperatives were eligible also for services provided through the regular Polish social welfare system.

Cooperatives for the disabled employ psychologists, physical education instructors, physiotherapists, social workers, nurses, and physicians to provide services for their members. They also run their own inpatient and outpatient facilities for work, training, rehabilitation, and recreation. The residential facility at Konstancin, outside of Warsaw, where disabled young adults are prepared for productive personal and professional lives is one example of such a facility (The Education and Rehabilitation Centre for Disabled People, 1986).

Poland's cooperatives for the disabled are an interesting demonstration of the way in which social welfare services are shaped by a society's prevailing values and practices. The centrality of work as an organizing force in Polish life helped Poland create an innovative service delivery structure for those with mental or physical limitations. Policy choices integrate persons with handicaps into the economic system while at the same time reducing the need for other social welfare services. A cooperative approach also makes efficient use of the available resources in a society whose resources are severely limited. Finally, the cooperative model provides a holistic approach to meeting the needs of those with limitations. It is an approach that could profitably be studied by the United States and other societies.

Source: Interviews and personal observations of Ron Federico, 1987.

child under 14 or in certain cases for a well child under 8, and for up to 14 days to care for a sick adult family member. Sick pay may be followed with up to 12 months of *rehabilitation benefit* at 75 percent of average earnings if the worker is expected to recover. Employed workers and their dependents receive unlimited free *medical services* including general and specialist care, inpatient hospital or sanitorium care, dental care, and maternity care. If the worker becomes unemployed, eligibility for medical care continues for 26 or 39 weeks. Basic medicines are subsidized by the government.

Maternity benefits of 100 percent of the mother's previous wage are paid for 16 weeks for a first child, 18 weeks for second and subsequent children, and 26 weeks for multiple births. A mother is guaranteed return to her previous job following maternity leave unless her employer goes bankrupt. When a child is born, its mother also receives a cash *birth grant* equal to 2 months of family allowance payments (see below).

Work-Injury Programs

Persons in disability groups 1 and 2 with work-related injury or illness receive 100 percent of the average monthly wage. Those in group 3 receive 55 percent. (See "Old Age, Disability, and Death Benefits," above.)

Unemployment Benefit Programs

Under the former communist regime there was, by official definition, no unemployment in Poland and, therefore, no need for unemployment insurance. However, between January 1990 and March 1992, unemployment grew from 56,000 to 2.2 million, about 12.2 percent of the labor force. An unemployment compensation program was developed protecting workers and persons capable of working and seeking but unable to find jobs. Workers are eligible for benefits if a suitable job or job training is unavailable and they have worked at least 180 days during the previous year, have completed studies, are newly released from military service, have completed maternity leave, or have been released from prison.

Benefits, based on a percentage of the national minimum wage (defined as 1.9 times the cost of a market basket of food for a household of four), last for up to 12 months. Persons laid off individually, those not in training, and those more than 5 years from retirement receive 36 percent of the minimum wage. Persons who lost their jobs in mass layoffs and are within 5 years of retirement receive 75 percent of the minimum wage. New entrants to the labor force and those who have just completed university or training programs receive between 95 and 125 percent of the minimum wage. Unemployed workers remain entitled to medical care. Polish unemployment compensation is funded by a 2 percent payroll tax paid by employers, supplemented with general tax revenues. The program is administered by the Ministry of Labor and Social Policy through a network of local labor bureaus. When a person applies for benefits at his or her local labor bureau, the office attempts first to find a suitable job, second to place the applicant in a suitable training program, and only as a last resort provides cash unemployment benefits.

Family Allowances and Other Social Benefits

In Poland, cash *family allowances* are paid monthly to all insured families with a child or children younger than 16, or, if the child is in school, younger than 20.

Family allowances are also paid for a dependent spouse who stays at home to bring up a child under 8, or who is an invalid, or is a woman older than 50 or a man older than 60. The family allowance benefit for each qualifying child or dependent is equal to 8 percent of the average state sector wage. If a dependent child has a chronic major medical problem, a *nursing allowance* of approximately 10 percent of the average wage is paid in addition to the family allowance. For low-income households, an additional *bringing-up allowance* equal to 25 percent of the average wage is paid for up to 2 years to a parent who leaves a job to remain at home to raise children.

Recognizing that economic structural adjustment will generate unemployment and poverty, and that existing social and unemployment insurance programs do not provide complete protection, in 1989, Poland initiated a national *social assistance program* as a benefit of last resort for individuals and families with total income below the poverty line. The social assistance program consists of "commissioned" cash benefits mandated and funded by the central government and "noncommissioned," usually in-kind, benefits provided by local government. The law recognizes "11 categories of problem: poverty; orphanhood; homelessness; unemployment; physical and mental disability; helplessness in running a household, especially in single-parent and large families; alcohol and drug abuse; adaptation problems after release from prison; need for motherhood protection; chronic illness; and natural or ecological disaster." Eligibility for social assistance is established by a social worker who, during a home visit, determines that the individual or family is in poverty caused by one of the 11 conditions (World Bank, 1993:35).

The Polish system of social security is both comprehensive and expensive. In 1995, Poland is under considerable pressure from the World Bank to reduce social welfare expenditures by enhancing unemployment and poverty relief while cutting what the bank perceives to be excessive spending on other programs. This, according to the bank, will result in "an affordable, effective, and adaptable safety net" during the Polish transition to market capitalism (World Bank, 1993:1).

FIVE PILLARS OF SOCIAL SECURITY: MEXICO[9]

Mexico operates two major systems of social security. The larger is the Mexican Institute of Social Security (IMSS), which in 1993 provided benefits to about 38 million insured salaried workers, retirees, and dependents. Since its inception in 1944, the IMSS has served primarily industrial workers in urban areas, but in recent years coverage has been expanded to certain workers in rural areas and to students. The Institute of Security and Social Services for State Workers (ISSSTE), initiated in 1960, provides benefits to about 9 million insured state civil service employees, retirees, and dependents. Together, IMSS and ISSSTE insure about 57 percent of the Mexican population (ISSSTE, 1991; Durán et al.,

[9]Unless noted otherwise, the information regarding the five pillars of social security in Mexico is derived from Durán et al. (1994), *Sistemas de Bienestar Social en Norteamerica Analisis Comparado;* and U.S. Department of Health and Human Services (1994), *Social Security Programs throughout the World 1993.*

1994). A third, smaller system, IMSS-Solidaridad, provides more limited benefits to low-income persons in rural areas (Rabasa-Gamboa, 1991). Finally, workers in certain industries such as the state-owned petroleum industry (PEMEX) are insured separately.

Old Age, Disability, and Death Benefits

In Mexico, *old age, permanent disability, and survivor benefits* are financed by payroll taxes paid by employers (5.18 percent of payroll), workers (1.85 percent of average earnings), and general tax revenues (.3 percent of payroll). Insurance is supplemented by a *savings program for retirement* (SAR) funded by voluntary employee contributions and mandatory employer contributions of 2 percent of payroll. Employers contribute an additional 5 percent to a fund to finance housing construction or improvement. At age 65, insured workers draw pensions of one to six times the minimum wage in the Federal District (DF), supplemented according to their average earnings and length of covered employment. Pensions are increased by 15 percent for a wife and by 10 percent for a dependent parent, but may not exceed 100 percent of the retiree's former average wage. A 1-month bonus is paid at Christmas. A widow who remarries receives a final lump-sum payment equal to 3 years of her survivor's pension.

SAR benefits also are payable as lump sums or annuities at 65, but 10 percent of SAR savings may be withdrawn when unemployed. SAR housing funds may be withdrawn at any time to buy housing, or unconditionally every 10 years. When a wage earner dies, a widow or dependent disabled widower receives a *funeral grant* equal to 2 months of the DF minimum wage, and *a survivor pension* of 90 percent of the pension for which the deceased worker was eligible. Widows requiring constant attendance receive a 20 percent supplement. Orphans younger than 16 receive 20 percent. Insured workers with disabilities causing a 50 percent or greater loss of earning capacity are eligible for *disability pensions* equivalent to old age pensions. Old age, permanent disability, and survivors insurance programs are administered by the Ministry of Labor and Social Welfare through IMSS and ISSSTE.

Health Care, Sickness, and Maternity Programs

IMSS and ISSSTE provide access to health care for insured workers, while rural and other persons with scanty resources may be able to gain access through IMSS-Solidaridad. Yet another health system provides for petroleum workers and members of the armed forces. Within each system there are three levels of care. ISSSTE, for example, operates 1,077 family health clinics providing primary and preventative health care and family planning services, 82 hospital-clinics providing specialized medicine and hospitalization, and 11 regional hospitals providing highly specialized medical care—all providing health care to government employees (ISSSTE, 1991). A similar system is operated by IMMS for insured, non-governmental workers. IMMS-Solidaridad emphasizes primary and preventative health care for the uninsured poor who are able to access its clinics. Unfortunately, there are not yet enough clinics to meet the needs of the poor. In addition, many Mexicans who can afford to do so seek medical care from private physicians instead of relying on IMSS and ISSSTE medical services. Thus, in Mexico, as in the United States, private medicine plays a significant role in health care.

Insured Mexican workers who are temporarily unable to work because of illness are eligible for up to 52 weeks of *sick pay* of between 60 percent of the DF minimum wage and 60 percent of their average salary. Insured pregnant women workers are eligible for *paid maternity leave,* during which they receive 100 percent of their average wage for 6 weeks before and 6 weeks after birth of a child.

Work-Injury Programs

Temporary disability benefits pay 100 percent of average earnings to insured Mexican workers until they are able to return to work or are declared permanently disabled. *Permanent disability benefits* pay 70 percent of average earnings and a 1-month Christmas bonus. *Partial disability benefits* are pro-rated based on total disability benefits. Injured insured workers are eligible for "full medical, surgical, and hospital care, medicines, and appliances" (USDHHS, 1994:211). Surviving widows or dependent disabled widowers receive 40 percent of the insured worker's disability pension; each orphan younger than age 16 receives 20 percent. Disability insurance is financed solely by employers. The payroll tax ranges from 0.875 to 8.75 percent according to risk. The Mexican workers' compensation programs are administered by the Ministry of Labor and Social welfare through IMSS and ISSSTE. (An account of one injured worker's experiences with Mexican work-injury programs is found in Chapter 3, "The Human Face of Social Welfare 5: Children Workers.")

Unemployment Benefit Programs

Mexican employers are required by law "to pay dismissed employees a lump sum equal to 3 months' pay plus 20 days' pay for each year of service" (USDHHS, 1994:222). The social security system provides *old-age severance pensions* of 95 percent of the old age pension to unemployed workers 60 to 64 years old (Rabasa-Gamboa, 1991:141).

Family Allowances and Other Social Benefits

Mexico, like the United States, has no universal family allowance program. Employers are required to pay a 1 percent payroll tax to finance *child care* for their insured employees. *Tortilla vouchers* provide 1 kg of tortillas daily to 2.5 million very-low-income families, and an additional 5 million families regularly purchase *subsidized tortillas.* The two programs serve about 16 percent of Mexican families. About 23 percent of Mexican children under 14 have access to *free milk.* Smaller numbers of children have access to *school breakfasts.*

Lack of adequate housing is a serious problem in Mexico. It is estimated that increasing population in Mexico creates a need for approximately 350,000 new homes and the replacement or renovation of 400,000 more housing units annually. Together, the *Institute of the National Fund for Housing for Workers* (INFON-AVIT), *ISSSTE's Fund for Housing* (FOVISSSTE), the *Fund for Housing Operation and Banking Discounts* (FOVI), and the banks produced an annual average of only 134,000 new homes between 1981 and 1990. In their quest for housing, many Mexicans have established squatter communities in which they construct homes out of whatever materials can be obtained. The houses are initially substandard and lack basic services such as water, sewers, electricity, and trash removal (Durán et al., 1994:67). Builders of the new homes improve them as their circumstances permit, and, eventually, utilities and basic public services are secured for the new communities.

Since 1989, *Solidaridad,* the Mexican National Program of Solidarity, has been funding the improvement of housing for the poor and the development of infrastructure in low-income areas. In 1992 alone, Solidaridad reported developing 3,091 water and sewer systems, undertaking 4,213 neighborhood or village electrification programs, and improving 48,110 units of housing, as well as extensive road building (6,158 km), repairing (2,478 km), and conservation (25,596 km) (Durán et al. 1994:65). These are essential social welfare activities in a developing nation. Critics, however, contend that *Solidaridad* has focused its efforts in areas in which challenges to the ruling Revolutionary Institutional Party (PRI) are strongest, rather than where need is greatest, and that Solidarity funds are frequently used to benefit the nonpoor.

INTEGRATION OF SERVICES

We have seen in earlier chapters that people often have more than one type of need simultaneously, and these needs are often interrelated. Job-related stress, for example, may lead to alcohol or drug abuse, which in turn may have an adverse effect on a marital relationship and parenting. From the user's point of view, it would be desirable to be able to obtain all the various types of help needed to address one's needs from a single source. Unfortunately, services are seldom organized in this way. Instead, they tend to be organized by problem area, with one program, or set of programs, dealing with one problem, another with another, and so on.

This sort of specialization occurs because formal organizations such as social welfare agencies find it easier to organize their activities around specific goals. Having done so, they almost inevitably find it easiest to hire professionals whose expertise matches those goals and to obtain funds for directly related services.

As a result, needs tend to be addressed in a sequential way. People seek help for one problem—perhaps alcohol abuse—and, in the course of responding to it, identify needs for additional services. The result is a referral to another agency or agencies that can provide the needed assistance. Such specialization frequently is not the most effective way to meet people's needs, but it is typical of the social welfare system in the United States. Other societies, especially Sweden and to a lesser degree Poland, adopt a more integrated approach. (See "On the Street in Sollentuna.")

ON THE STREET IN SOLLENTUNA, SWEDEN—A COMPREHENSIVE APPROACH TO CARE

Sollentuna is a suburban community on the outskirts of Stockholm. It has a population of 49,000, eight percent of whom are immigrants representing some seventy nations. As is typical of Swedish communities, its system of municipal governance is carefully planned.

All aspects of social welfare are centrally planned and then administered locally through four decentralized municipal offices. All housing, for example, must be approved by the municipal government, which owns most of the land in the community. The purpose of this policy is to ensure that the housing needs of all residents will be met in a fair and satisfactory manner. Approximately 450 apartments are built in Sollentuna each year, some by private developers and others by the government. Regardless of who builds them, their construction and their design must be approved by the municipality. This applies even to single-family homes.

In addition, housing prices are regulated and rents are controlled by the municipal government. An apartment containing two rooms (plus a kitchen) rents for an average of 2,500 krona per month—about 25 percent of the average monthly wage of 10,300 krona for workers in the public sector. Special housing assistance is provided for the elderly and the handicapped.

Health and social services in Sollentuna are provided in conformity with national Swedish policy, but services are actually delivered via four decentralized municipal offices. The professional staff is comprised of specialists, primarily doctors, social workers, and others with psychological training. Their offices, however, are clustered together, and they often collaborate in delivering services. Primary health care for local residents is delivered by a local team of physicians and nurses. When more specialized health care is needed, the patient is referred to a nearby hospital. (The service area of the average Swedish hospital contains about 100,000 residents.) When discharged, the patient again becomes the responsibility of the local health-care team.

Teams of nurses and social workers provide care to the elderly and the disabled in their place of residence,

as well as to others who may require home care. Medical personnel refer any nonmedical problems they identify to social workers, who handle medical problems they identify in a similar fashion. Because members of the local health team become involved before a newborn leaves the hospital, they have a close relationship with families and can identify problems in their early stages. Infants are monitored especially closely—weekly until they are 6 months of age, monthly until the age of 1 year, and as needed thereafter. The services provided to the families of infants include instruction in child care and parenting skills. Any family problems identified as a result of this contact are referred to social workers. These services, it is important to note, are provided to everyone, not just low-income, minority, or problem families.

Since Sweden has a well-developed system of financial aid to needy individuals and families, social workers can offer their clients a range of financial and personal development services. When this is combined with Sweden's comprehensive health care, the result is a nearly comprehensive system. Teams of nurses and social workers visit the homebound regularly, making sure that they have proper meals each day, are bathed as needed, and are adequately housed. The simple act of visitation provides welcome human contact and stimulation.

As impressive as the social welfare delivery system is in Sollentuna, local professionals note that there are some problems. There is limited contact between hospital staffs and local medical personnel, making posthospitalization care less efficient than it might otherwise be. Psychological problems tend to be referred to hospitals, where they are treated medically rather than being referred for psychological and social treatment within the community. This can lead to problems in providing continuity of care.

In spite of these problems, Sollentuna provides an interesting example of how people's needs can be met in a holistic manner via an integrated system of social welfare services.

Source: Interviews and personal observations of Ron Federico, 1987.

LET'S REVIEW

This chapter has sought to provide a practical understanding of major public social welfare programs in the United States, Sweden, Poland, and Mexico. Programs in each country were described within a general framework outlining their purposes, eligibility requirements, benefits, administrative structure, the method of benefit delivery, and shortcomings. We hope you will find this simple framework helpful in analyzing any social welfare program.

This chapter concludes the first major section of our book. Thus far we have been focusing on social welfare as a concept, as a response to human and social needs, and as the provision of resources to address those needs. You should now understand what social welfare is, why it is needed, how it developed, and the types of resources it provides. Beginning in Chapter 8, we examine the relationship of social welfare to other parts of society. As you learn more about this interaction, you will be preparing yourself to address the final question posed in this book: What might be the future role of social welfare?

STUDY QUESTIONS

1 List the five pillars of social security. Under each heading, think about the social welfare benefits that you have received or will receive during your life. Then attempt to identify the specific programs through which these benefits are provided, the agency responsible, and whether the agency is public or private. Finally, write a one-page summary of your impression of the service delivery system based on your own experience.

2 Find out if your community has a directory of social services. If so, obtain a copy and browse through it. If not, use your local phone book to identify as many social welfare agencies as you can. Then prepare a brief (one paragraph or so) statement identifying potential gaps in the social welfare resources available in your community.

3 Select a specific social welfare program that interests you (a program for abused spouses, for example, or one for substance abusers). Visit the agency that administers the program and obtain all the information you need to apply the general program analysis framework described in this chapter. After doing so, identify at least one need you believe the program is not meeting.

4 Interview a classmate to discuss her or his experiences with any single social welfare program (e.g., a hospital, or a school program). Try to determine what led the person to seek help and how he or she found out about the program in question. Ask him or her to evaluate the effectiveness of the services received, and her or his personal feelings about the experience. (Was it easy or hard to find out about the program and actually obtain the service? Was he or she treated well? Did the services meet the original need?) Then write a one-paragraph statement describing what you learned from this exercise.

5 Two of the current major problems in the United States are homelessness and AIDS. Choose either problem, and list the services likely to be needed by those experiencing the problem. Within each service area, identify the programs and agencies in your own community that would be especially useful to those with the problem you have selected. (For example, people suffering from AIDS need health care. What health programs and facilities exist in your community that would be useful for AIDS victims?) Remember, though, that AIDS and homelessness are complex problems. In addition to health care, AIDS victims, for example, might need counseling, income maintenance assistance, recreation, help for a substance abuse problem, and so on.

KEY TERMS AND CONCEPTS

eligibility requirements
Old Age, Survivors, and Disability
  Insurance (OASDI)
Medicare
Medicaid
Special Supplemental Food Program for
  Women, Infants and Children (WIC)
Workers' Compensation
unemployment insurance
Supplemental Security Income (SSI)

Aid to Families with Dependent
  Children (AFDC)
standard of need
Food Stamps
Earned Income Tax Credit (EITC)
General assistance (GA)
Low-Income Home Energy
  Assistance (LIHEAP)
public housing
501(c)3 and 501(c)4 organizations

SUGGESTED READINGS

Encyclopedia of Social Work, 19th ed. 1995. Washington, DC: National Association of Social Workers. A basic reference for studying the social welfare system in the United States. The encyclopedia utilizes a social work perspective and includes useful information about the history, organization, and variety of U.S. social welfare programs.

U.S. Department of Commerce. Bureau of the Census. 1994. *Statistical Abstract of the United States.* Washington, DC: U.S. Government Printing Office. A compendium of data about the United States, including public social welfare programs (benefit levels, number of users, breakdown by geographic area, characteristics of users, and so on).

U.S. Department of Health and Human Services. Social Security Administration. 1993. *Social Security Programs in the United States.* SSA Publication No. 13–11758. Washington, DC: U.S. Government Printing Office. Describes clearly U.S. public social insurance and assistance programs, as well as programs for special groups such as veterans and railroad workers. A basic reference for anyone wanting to understand these programs—their history, benefits, and eligibility criteria.

REFERENCES

Abramowitz, Mimi. 1983. Everyone is on welfare: The "role of redistribution in social policy" revisited. *Social Work,* 28(6):440–445.

Barker, Robert. 1991. *The Social Work Dictionary,* 2nd ed. Washington, DC: National Association of Social Workers.

Brilliant, Eleanor L. 1995. Voluntarism. In *Encyclopedia of Social Work,* 19th ed. Washington, DC: National Association of Social Workers, pp. 2469–2482.

Center on Budget and Policy Priorities. 1995. The distribution of the Senate child tax credit and the EITC cuts. Washington, DC: Center on Budget and Policy Priorities.

Durán, Clemente Ruiz, Rosalba Carrasco, Licea, and Enrique Provencio Durazo, 1994. *Sistemas de Bienestar Social en Norteamerica: Analisis Comparado.* México, DF, México: SEDESOL (Secretaria de Desarrollo Social).

Educational and Rehabilitation Centre for Disabled People. 1986. Mimeographed pamphlet, Warsaw, Poland, December 14.

FRAC. 1995. *Community Childhood Hunger Identification Project: A Survey of Child-hood Hunger in the United States.* Washington, DC: Food Research and Action Center.

ISSSTE. 1991. *ISSSTE: Changing with Modern Mexico.* México, DF: ISSSTE.

Mikulski, Jerzy. 1987. *Rehabilitation Services in the Polish Cooperatives of Disabled Persons.* Warsaw: Research Center of Central Union of Invalids' Cooperatives.

Mulroy, Elizabeth A. 1995. Housing. In *Encyclopedia of Social Work,* 19th ed. Washington, DC: National Association of Social Workers, pp. 1377–1384.

Nelson, Harold. 1983. *Poland: A Country Study.* Washington, DC: U.S. Government Printing Office.

Pear, Robert. 1995. Another set of dire warnings on Social Security and Medicare trust funds. *The New York Times,* April 4, p. D23.

Rabasa-Gamboa. 1991. Mexico. In Martin B. Tracey and Fred C. Pampel, eds., *International Handbook on Old-Age Insurance.* New York: Greenwood Press, pp. 139–146.

Rein, Mildred. 1995. General assistance. In *Encyclopedia of Social Work,* 19th ed. Washington, DC: National Association of Social Workers, pp. 1095–1100.

Swedish Institute. 1992. *Fact Sheets on Sweden: Labor Relations in Sweden* (FS 3). Stockholm, Sweden: The Swedish Institute.

———. 1993. *Fact sheets on Sweden: Social Insurance in Sweden* (FS 5). Stockholm, Sweden: The Swedish Institute.

Tierney, Joseph, Jean Baldwin Grossman, and Nancy Resch. 1995. *Making a Difference: An Impact Study of Big Brothers/Big Sisters.* Philadelphia: Public/Private Ventures.

U.S. Department of Commerce. 1994. *Statistical Abstract of the United States 1994.* Washington, DC: U.S. Government Printing Office.

U.S. Department of Health and Human Services. Social Security Administration. 1993. *Social Security Programs in the United States.* SSA Publication No. 13–11758. Washington, DC: U.S. Government Printing Office.

———. 1994. *Social Security Programs throughout the World 1993.* SSA Publication No. 13–11805, Research Report #63. Washington, DC: U.S. Government Printing Office.

U.S. Office of Management and Budget. 1993. *1993 Catalog of Federal Domestic Assistance.* Washington, DC: U.S. Government Printing Office.

U.S. Department of Veterans Affairs. 1995. *Federal Benefits for Veterans and Dependents, 1995 ed.* Washington, DC: U.S. Government Printing Office.

Whitaker, William H. 1993. *Maine Community Childhood Hunger Identification Project Report.* Orono: University of Maine School of Social Work.

World Bank. 1993. *Poland: Income Support and the Social Safety Net during the Transition.* Washington, DC: The World Book.

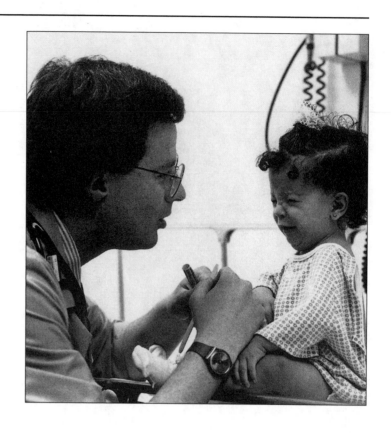

8

HOW DOES SOCIAL WELFARE RELATE TO SOCIETY?

WHAT TO EXPECT FROM THIS CHAPTER

This chapter explores the relationship between social welfare and the other major social institutions: the family, education, religion, government, and the economy. Each of these institutions performs one or more important functions. The family, for example, provides an environment for the birth and rearing of children who will become the adults of the future, enabling society to perpetuate itself. People's ability to perform their various roles within any given social institution depends to a large degree on the availability of certain basic resources. Parents, for example, need housing in which to raise their children, and workers need jobs.

Social welfare is itself a social institution. Its primary function is to help the other social institutions perform more effectively. It performs this function in two major ways. First, social welfare provides resources that enable people to carry out

261

their societal responsibilities. The provision of counseling services designed to improve parenting skills is an example. Second, it acts as a buffer between people and social changes that impair or alter the functioning of the other major social institutions—functioning, in effect, as the mechanism by which we respond to major social change. An example is social welfare's attempt to respond to the increasing need for adequate child care to enable more women to participate in the workforce—part of the economic institution.

This chapter examines the relationship between social welfare and each of the other major social institutions. The emphasis is on how social welfare supports the functioning of each, and how each institution in turn affects social welfare.

The chapter also addresses the question of who benefits from social welfare. Analyzing the impact of social welfare on each of the major social institutions helps us to see how pervasive it is in daily life. The wealthy, the middle class, and the poor all receive social welfare benefits. Collectively, society benefits when social welfare emphasizes prevention rather than amelioration of social problems. Most important, the connection between society and each of its members is reinforced by social welfare's efforts to demonstrate that individual persons matter. This strengthens the sense of community and provides the "glue" that helps hold society together.

LEARNING OBJECTIVES

When you have finished studying this chapter, you should be able to:

1 List six major social institutions of society, and define their functions within a constantly changing web of social relationships.

2 Identify resources provided by social welfare that help families to function more effectively.

3 List social welfare resources that help education function more effectively, and describe how education reduces the need for certain kinds of social welfare services.

4 Briefly describe the relationship between religion and social welfare.

5 Identify ways that social welfare increases the ability of people to participate in politics and how social welfare is affected by political decision making.

6 Describe examples of social welfare programs that address economic problems and of ways in which the economy affects social welfare.

7 Discuss how social welfare responds to the needs of all members of society and contributes to societal cohesion.

SOCIAL WELFARE AND OTHER SOCIETAL INSTITUTIONS

Recall that we defined social welfare in Chapter 1 as "a nation's system of programs, benefits, and services that help people meet those social, educational, and health needs that are fundamental to the maintenance of society" (Barker, 1991:221). As a social institution, social welfare shares certain characteristics that are common to all social institutions. It has been approved by society, it helps individuals and society to function more effectively, it distributes resources, and it organizes activities.

Social institutions perform their tasks most effectively when there is basic agreement about the importance of their tasks, and when the resources needed to perform those tasks are available. As an example of the importance of societal consensus and resource allocation, consider the current controversy over the role of the family in sex education.

The family is a socially approved structure that is intended to promote intimacy, reproduction, economic well-being, and successful child rearing. At one time, responsibility for all types of education—including sex education—rested with the family. With the growth of free public education, however, the family's responsibilities in this area gradually decreased. In due course, responsibility for basic and technical education was largely transferred to the schools. This was not necessarily true for sex education, where the absence of consensus on whether the school or the family should be responsible has resulted in extensive debate.

Sex education remains a controversial area. It used to be that children learned about sexuality from their parents, siblings, and friends, supplemented by whatever they could learn on their own or from experimentation. Many now argue, however, that this is insufficient, given the high cost to society of inadequate education in this area. While some have continued to defend the family's right to control the information made available to its members—and especially those members who are children—in this highly personal area, critics have pointed to the rising incidence of teen pregnancy and out-of-wedlock births. More recently, a continuing increase in the incidence of sexually transmitted diseases, especially AIDS, has added fuel to the critic's arguments.

In 1991, 12.9 percent of all births in the United States were to mothers younger than 20 years of age. Of the 532,000 births to women younger than 20, 69 percent were to unmarried mothers. About 2 percent (11,000) were to unmarried mothers younger than 15. Children born to teenage mothers are more likely to be born with low birth weights than are children born to older mothers. This is important because low-birth-weight babies are more likely to die as infants or to experience health problems with long-term consequences. Probably because of benefits of participating in the WIC program, the rate of low-birth-weight births to teenage mothers fell from 15.6 percent in 1980 to 12.9 percent in 1991. Many of the 22 percent of all white children and the 68 percent of all African American children born out of wedlock are raised in poverty (U.S. Department of Commerce, 1994, Tables 92 and 100).

Such children are exposed to increased risk of intravenous drug use, which is associated with poverty, and thus to one of the primary sources of **acquired immune deficiency syndrome (AIDS)** infection in the United States: the sharing of contaminated needles. AIDS is caused by the **human immunodeficiency virus (HIV),** *"a sexually-transmitted and blood-borne retrovirus that undermines and ultimately destroys the immune system"* (Lloyd, 1995:1257). The high incidence of teen pregnancy suggests that many teenagers are practicing sex without

THE HUMAN FACE OF SOCIAL WELFARE 16

A NEW APPROACH IN SEX EDUCATION

Most teen-age mothers are unmarried high-school dropouts. But as a student at the New Futures School, an Albuquerque public school for girls who are pregnant or have babies, Angela can keep up with her eighth-grade classes while her daughter, Crystal plays in the New Futures nursery. . . .

One of every eight babies born in the United States has a teen-age mother, and more than a fifth of the 478,000 teenagers giving birth every year have already had at least one child.

One expert in teen-age pregnancy said the idea of day care in schools was slowly taking hold because it helps the young parents and because other pupils who work in child care can get a lesson in how hard it can be.

"It used to be that a lot of people opposed day care in the school, saying it would make it too attractive for girls to get pregnant," said Karen Pittman, of the Children's Defense Fund, an advocacy group in Washington. "On-site day care may actually be a deterrent to teen pregnancy, and it certainly helps teenagers learn about parenting."

Such programs are aimed at helping the infants as well, particularly those like the one at New Futures that add counseling and care for girls while they are pregnant. The babies of teen-age parents face a greater likelihood of low birth weight and other medical problems and are more likely to grow up in poverty, drop out of school and become teen-age parents themselves.

Breaking the cycle is difficult. . . .

Nationally, 23 percent of all teen-age mothers have another baby within two years of their first,

and 43 percent have another baby within three years. But at New Futures School the repeat pregnancy rates are lower. . . .

"Preventing that second child is what it's all about," said Marian Wright Edelman, president of the Children's Defense Fund. "If you can delay that next baby, you can stop that teenager from messing up her whole life". . . .

Students are required to spend time working in the school's three nurseries, getting practical experience in diapering, feeding and bathing babies even before their own child is born. There are childbirth classes, and courses in child health, infant development, the care and raising of toddlers and children's literature. . . .

Mary, who got a part-time secretarial job at a construction company through the school's job-training programs, says she has become scrupulous about birth control since coming to New Futures. "Now, I will not miss a pill," she said. "I will not, I will not. I'm going to graduate and I'm going to work."

The New Futures School in Albuquerque, New Mexico, helps its students to become more responsible parents and to understand better the relationship among sexuality, personal aspirations, and economic success. The school's holistic approach goes well beyond the biology of sex to approximate the ideal of sex education as it might, but does not always, take place within the family. This innovative program illustrates how social welfare services can substitute for, or supplement the functioning of other social institutions.

adequate safeguards to avoid either pregnancy or sexually transmitted diseases including AIDS.

Even without the risk posed by AIDS, the cost of caring for a poor, out-of-wedlock child is high in lost potential, family disorganization, and medical costs. When AIDS enters the picture, the toll in money, pain, and personal and family stress is multiplied. (See "The Human Face of Social Welfare: Choices," in the Introduction.)

Perhaps inevitably, society's response to these developments has been to seek to educate people about responsible sexuality through the media and the educational system. This, however, is a controversial development, particularly for those who believe that only within the family can a full appreciation of sexuality's role as part of the complex web of human aspirations and responsibility be communicated adequately.

Whatever your views on the proper place for sex education, the issue illustrates the relationship between societal consensus and provision of resources and the capacity of social institutions to function effectively. The current lack of consensus about sex education raises many difficult questions. Should parents teach their children about sex, or should they rely on the school to do it? Are parents adequately informed about issues such as AIDS, and, if not, how can they become informed? How fair is it to the children involved that some schools have sex education programs and others do not?

Given the current uncertainty as to who knows what about sex, and who ultimately should be responsible for sex education, it is difficult to develop effective strategies for reducing the incidence of teen pregnancy and sexually transmitted diseases. Consequently, the social welfare system is left to cope with increasing numbers of problems resulting from sexual activity.

Even as social welfare seeks to help other social institutions perform their functions, it may itself be changed in the process. Its own role, for example, may be expanded to include new responsibilities such as sex education. The societal consensus underlying such an expansion may also serve to strengthen society's commitment to social welfare. Let's turn our attention now to the interaction between social welfare and each of the other major social institutions. Doing so will help us understand social welfare's role, not only in the lives of individuals, but in the larger society.

SOCIAL WELFARE AND THE FAMILY

The family is one of the major institutions of society, one with which we are all familiar but do not often stop to define. There are, in fact, many definitions of the family (see Chapter 4). For our purposes, we have defined the *family* as any grouping of one or more adults sharing affection, resources, residence, and responsibility for any children that may be present. Its functions include regulating sexual behavior, child bearing and child rearing, providing for the economic and emotional needs of its members, and socializing children to become successful participants in society. These activities are basic to the healthy development of individuals, as well as to the survival of society.

One of the purposes of social welfare is to help members of families make appropriate choices and to live with them successfully. Among the personal social services provided by social welfare to help in this process are marital counseling, family planning, nonfamily support networks, personal counseling, preparation for independent living, training in parenting skills, and income maintenance programs. These services attempt to strengthen the ability of family members to function effectively, and to link with other structures that offer needed physical and emotional resources. In a sense, the social welfare system is constantly trying to put itself out of business by helping people and systems to function well on their own. Successful intervention at the family level is an important part of this strategy.

Industrialization has had a substantial impact on the structure of the family and the ways that families perform their social functions. The large extended families common in agricultural societies have generally become small nuclear units that are better adapted to urban life. Smaller families are also more suited to an economic environment in which wages are used to purchase goods and services. Relatives other than spouses or partners and their children are less likely to share the same household. Even elderly parents may be expected to live in their own homes.

The concept of family is changing in both industrialized nations and in emerging economies. The traditional basis of a family is the marriage bond and blood ties between married people and their children or other kin. However, the functions of the family may also be performed within households comprised of people who are not married or related or who live in single-person households. Women today are more likely to have children without being married than they were in the past (Kantrowitz et al., 1985). Modern birth control techniques and reproductive technology have given women an increased range of choices with respect to parenting and marriage.

These kinds of choices open up many new possibilities. People may choose to live alone, to live with someone in a nonmarital relationship, or to marry. In each case, children may or may not be present. What emerges is an array of family types, each of which offers a different solution for meeting the needs of its members.

Recent data in the United States indicate some important shifts in how and when people establish family units. Increasingly, the tendency is to defer marriage. For example, the marriage rates per 1,000 single women ages 15 to 44 declined from 140.2 in 1970 to 91.0 in 1988. In addition, between 1970 and 1988 the median age at which women first married increased by about 3 years (U.S. Department of Commerce, 1994, Tables 139 and 142). Although this suggests that at least some women may be deliberately choosing to marry later, it is also true that deferring marriage tends to decrease the probability that a woman will ever marry, a consequence that may or may not be intended (Greer, 1986).

One factor in these changes is the increased desire—often reinforced by necessity—on the part of women to work and have a career outside the home. Women who work outside the home have less time and energy to devote to families than those who do not. In 1993, 54.1 percent of U.S. working-age women were employed—up from 35.5 percent in 1960. Sixty percent of all U.S. women with children younger than 6 were in the labor force (U.S. Department of Commerce, 1994, Tables 616 and 626).

Consider the elderly. As married partners grow older, their children frequently marry and establish their own homes. If one of the elderly parents dies or has to enter a nursing home, the other is left alone. Under these circumstances, unrelated elderly people sometimes choose to live together to share costs and companionship, and to provide mutual support. Relationships with other family members usually continue—calls and visits to children and grandchildren, for example. But the fundamentals of daily life take place in a household that does not meet the traditional definition of family.

This kind of family life is also common among other groups. Gay and lesbian people who are neither married nor biologically related often live together in stable, long-term relationships. People with mental or physical limitations may spend much of their lives in group homes that can meet their specialized needs more effectively than can their biological families of origin. In such cases, the household provides daily physical and emotional care, although contact is often maintained with the biological family as well.

Family units are not always stable over time. Between 1970 and 1991, the married proportion of the U.S. population fell from 71.7 to 61.2 percent, the divorced and not remarried population increased from 3.2 to 8.9 percent, and the percentage of never married people rose from 16.2 to 21.5 (U.S. Department of Commerce, 1994, Table 59). Today people frequently remarry after divorce. Many also divorce again after remarrying. In 1990, 95.5 percent of all women ages 50 to 54 were or had been married, 29.5 percent were currently divorced following a first marriage, 63 percent had remarried following divorce, and 34.5 percent were redivorced. Only about half (54.1 percent) of the marriages in 1988 were first marriages for both bride and groom (U.S. Department of Commerce, 1994, Tables 140 and 145).

These changes have had a significant impact on the nature of family life. More than a million U.S. children younger than 18 (1.6 percent of all U.S. children) lived in families in the process of divorce in 1988. In 1993, about 11 percent of all children in the United States lived in families comprised of one step-parent and one birth parent, while 30 percent lived with only one parent. Twenty-five percent of all white children, 35 percent of Hispanic children, and 63 percent of African American children lived in one-parent families (U.S. Department of Commerce, 1994, Table 143).

The Impact of Family Dissolution

When families dissolve, members are affected in a variety of ways. Children often feel rejected and guilty, believing that they somehow caused the divorce. Spouses or unmarried partners may be angry and fearful about their future well-being. The economic consequences of divorce can be substantial, especially for women who even now generally are given the responsibility for child care, and most especially for women who are members of minority groups (Kamerman, 1985:9–11). Creating conditions that allow children to maintain contact with both biological parents is another concern. (See "The Human Face of Social Welfare 17: Flying U.S. Children between Two Sets of Parents.")

Social welfare provides a range of services to address the changing needs of dissolved families and households. A variety of child welfare services, including income maintenance programs, programs designed to prevent child abuse and neglect, foster care, adoption services, and parenting skills programs, are available to help people deal with the strains caused by divorce or single parenthood. So, too, are a range of family and personal counseling programs designed to help adults and children cope

THE HUMAN FACE OF SOCIAL WELFARE 17

FLYING U.S. CHILDREN BETWEEN TWO SETS OF PARENTS

It is 10 o'clock on a Saturday morning and the parade of the children is beginning at Houston Intercontinental Airport.

Here comes 12-year-old Scott Craiger, skateboard hung rakishly over knapsack, on his regular filial pilgrimage from Wilmington, Delaware, where he lives with his mother, to spend the summer with his father in San Angelo, Texas. "I've been flying alone since I was 5," he says with aplomb.

Next comes tousle-haired Alvin Devore, 11, bound from Cleveland to visit his father in Irving, Texas.

At airports all over the country young children, clutching favorite toys and dolls, are traveling alone in record numbers. . . .

The airlines say the surge in young frequent fliers is a product of two unrelated facts of modern American life: the growing number of divorced couples and several years of airline deregulation, which has brought fares down and made flying nearly as routine as taking the bus.

While the young passengers require much special attention, the airlines welcome the business. . . . "They are the passengers of the future, and we want them to have a good experience the first time they fly" [said a long-time flight attendant.]

[Several airlines] have set up special supervised lounges for children at major hubs [which may include] television, toys, games and snacks to keep children occupied while awaiting connections. . . . [One airline] deals with about 300 unaccompanied children each day [at Houston's airport], and at Denver's [airport] . . . about 450 to 500 children a day. . .

Industry officials say they expect about half a million unaccompanied children [during the summer of 1986], normally the heaviest period for such travel. Most of the children, they say, are shuttling between parents separated by divorce or jobs. The main such divorce routes are along the heavily traveled corridor between Boston and Washington, and between cities such as Houston and Dallas in Texas and San Francisco and Los Angeles in California. . . .

The Federal Government has no rules governing unaccompanied children. . .

Not all children relish flying alone. It often means a frightening separation from parents, and flight crews find themselves playing child psychologist. [A flight attendant] recalls a 6-year-old girl who was being sent to live with her father and who did not want to leave her mother. The girl began to cry hysterically in flight, and the attendant tried to assure her about the new family awaiting her. Ultimately, [the flight attendant], using a common maneuver, calmed the child by deputizing her to hand out the peanuts during beverage service.

There are many statistics to demonstrate the impact of divorce on children, but sometimes it is the little things that provide the most insight. A glimpse into the lives of children who commute by air between separated parents is such an experience. It also illustrates how external factors such as technology (the modern jet airplane) and economics (airline deregulation and the desire of the airlines to woo children who will be the travelers of the future) can shape people's lives—in this instance, enabling children to maintain contact with separated parents who live many miles apart.

with the feelings of loss, anger, and anxiety that often accompany divorce and remarriage (NASW, 1987). Finally, job training and placement services provide assistance to those who seek employment as a result of divorce or remarriage.

Care for Dependent Children and Adults

As increasing numbers of parents work outside the home, many families find it difficult to arrange suitable care for their children or elderly members. Because of the number of people affected, the need for child care is a highly visible issue, (Ruggie, 1984:182–294; Kamerman, 1985:10–11; Fernandez, 1986; Quinn, 1988). Access to quality child care that provides a healthy and safe environment for the child is critical. For some children, child-care programs provide opportunities for stimulation and growth and supplement the limited opportunities available through the family because of poverty, the demands of single parenthood, or other factors.

While the social welfare system in the United States does include a network of public and private child-care facilities, the number of spaces available is insufficient to meet current demand. In addition, the costs involved are beyond the reach of many families and households. Gradually, however, we are seeing an expansion in the availability of child care as a result of cooperation between social welfare agencies and the business community. Among the several strategies that have emerged as a result of this cooperation are company subsidies to reduce the cost of child care, the provision of child-care facilities within the workplace, and increased use of flexible work hours and job sharing to make it easier for parents to care for their children.

Programs to help families care for the elderly are less well developed. The needs of elderly family members are less visible than those of children. In the United States, where the elderly are largely responsible for their own care, little attention is paid to the number of grown children who are called on to aid their elderly parents. Yet the financial strain, time pressures, and emotional burdens imposed on both parties by the reversal of the parent–child relationship are considerable. Degenerative illnesses that impair older persons' ability to care for themselves only increase the difficulties, as does the limited availability of affordable and appealing long-term-care facilities for the elderly. Medicare and Medicaid provide some coverage when medical care or home-based health-care services are needed. A variety of social agencies provide counseling services to help families manage interpersonal stress, and to identify and plan for needed care (Tonti and Silverstone, 1985). The availability of an increasing range of residential facilities for the elderly may also reduce pressure on families whose adult members must work and have little time to care for elderly parents or grandparents. Finally, the increasing use of preretirement planning in the workplace also helps families and households plan for the care of their elderly members (Monk, 1985).

Housing and Poverty

Increasing numbers of families in the United States are becoming poor and homeless. As the cost of housing rises and the supply of low-cost housing decreases,

ON THE STREET IN WARSAW—IN A DAY CARE CENTER FOR THE ELDERLY

The Day Care Center for the Elderly located in the Mocatow neighborhood of Warsaw illustrates Poland's efforts to employ a comprehensive and integrated approach to the provision of social welfare services. Housed in the same building as the Mocatow Social Services Center, the Center for the Elderly provides its residents with access to social workers and other social welfare personnel.

Polish law requires that the elderly be cared for by their families. For this reason, most public facilities provide care and recreation only during the day, when family members are working. However, elderly who have no families or who are homebound are eligible for in-home or residential care. All of these services are free, as is medical care. The elderly also receive a pension sufficient to provide a minimal standard of living.

The Mocatow Center serves about fifty neighborhood residents and has a warm, personal feeling. There are many more women than men, a result of the demographic reality that women generally live longer than men as well as the heavy military casualties suffered by Poland during World War II. There are several rooms that accommodate a variety of activities. The largest is a living room with armchairs and sofas. Here the inhabitants chat, watch television, and participate in activities they enjoy, such as knit-ting, embroidery, or painting. Their handiwork is displayed, and much of it is quite beautiful. There is also a room where medical care is provided, and another for the preparation of simple meals and snacks. Finally, there is a quiet room with lounging chairs, where the residents can nap or rest.

Occasionally there are trips or guest speakers. These seem to be much appreciated and enjoyed by the inhabitants. The Mocatow Center has its own scrapbook that chronicles the activities and even the deaths of its members. Pictures, descriptions of events, and eulogies to the dead are included, and they are proudly displayed and discussed with visitors.

As with much of the Polish social welfare system, the day care center accomplishes much with very little. It is a simple but comfortable facility, characterized more by a warm sense of companionship than by extensive facilities. Its small size and neighborhood location help those who attend to feel welcome and integrated into the group. It reduces the burdens of employed family members (remember that in Poland most people work) by providing care during working hours. This center demonstrates how social welfare services can help the family perform its functions while at the same time encouraging familylike interactions among its clients.

Source: Personal observations of Ron Federico, 1987.

poverty is accompanied by homelessness. During the past decade, homelessness increased even in relatively affluent areas, with families making up the fastest growing segment of the homeless and constituting as much as one-third of the homeless population (First et al., 1995). For example, in November 1987 there were 871 homeless families with 1,749 children in relatively affluent Westchester County, New York. Of these families, 673—with 1,323 children—were being temporarily housed in motels until permanent housing could be found (Westchester County Department of Social Services, 1987). A study by the Urban Institute in 1989 estimated that there are between 567,000 and 600,000 homeless people in the United States. It is estimated, too, that the number of homeless persons is increasing by about 5 percent per year (Johnson, 1995:1338). Other estimates of the total number of homeless people nationwide range from 250,000 to 2 million (Iatrides, 1988:11).

Housing is central to the functioning of the family. Its absence is associated with many other needs. Studies show that the homeless, in addition to needing a place to live, are likely to need substantial medical and psychiatric care (Sauber et al., 1988:116). Homeless children face special problems in the areas of education,

ON THE STREET IN YONKERS, NEW YORK— THE REAPS COMMUNITY LAND TRUST

Faced with a growing need for good housing and improved neighborhoods, residents of a multiracial, low-income community in Yonkers, New York, organized a *community land trust* which they named REAPS, Residents for Equitable & Affordable Permanent Shelter. Assisted by an MSW social worker with training in community organization, after 6 years REAPS owns thirty apartments in several buildings and has successfully turned over ownership of an apartment building to nine families, eight with incomes of $20,000 or less per year. The nine families—three African American, four Spanish-speaking, and two white—now own shares of their own rehabilitated co-op building, which they manage together. The land is owned by the REAPS Community Land Trust and leased to the owner-occupant organization for 99 years.

Community land trusts are organizations that ensure that housing is affordable and remains affordable to persons with low and moderate incomes. Land in a land trust is owned permanently by a not-for-profit organization such as REAPS. Buildings on the land are owned by their occupants. Land trust housing remains affordable through restricted resale prices. Owners leaving land trust housing are required to sell their home or apartment for a price reflecting their actual investment plus a modest increase determined by a fair equity formula instead of what the open market might bring.

The National Housing Act of 1990 recognized community land trusts as models for community development by nonprofit organizations. At least one third of the board members of a community land trust must be residents of the community that needs the housing. The intent is to enable low-income families to participate in making decisions for their communities by ensuring that those who need or want affordable housing or already live in it are represented on the policy-making board.

REAPS members knew what they wanted for their homes and their neighborhood. They knew that—before REAPS—their rents were high and their apartments not what they wanted them to be. With assistance from a social worker trained in community organizing, they formed a self-governing organization with a democratically elected board of directors. It took 2 years of hard work and planning by members and the winning of governmental financial support for REAPS to buy its first building. Two years later a second building was purchased for the land trust. After 6 years, the land trust included more than thirty apartments in four buildings.

As REAPS rehabilitated the buildings, a resident corporation of nine low-income, working families was organized to rehabilitate and buy a nine-unit apartment building that had always been an anchor on a street beset by arson and drug dealing. Told by the New York Affordable Home Ownership Program and the City of Yonkers that members were too poor to qualify for help, REAPS persevered. Eventually, a lender was identified who agreed to provide financing, and Yonkers provided funds for rehabilitation. The financial package included money from six different sources. And the dream of affordable home ownership became reality. Each apartment cost its owner about $6,000. Monthly fees help pay down the mortgage and provide funds for building maintenance and heating.

REAPS has grown to sixty members—working together, arguing about decisions, facing community problems, and gaining strength. REAPS members have held training sessions on hot summer nights to learn how to make presentations to City Hall, have cleaned up their street, and have learned how to select residents for land trust buildings, how to collect rents and maintenance payments, how to keep financial accounts, and how to negotiate difficult legal situations.

And REAPS is testimony to the ability of people to work together across lines that too often divide our communities. One night, as the project committee reviewed city code requirements for a new boiler room in a land trust building, members realized that they had only a day and a half to replace a ceiling and rebuild a wall. After talking it over, committee members went downstairs, put on dust masks, got on ladders with their hammers, tore down the ceiling, and cleaned up the mess. Four women and three men: one person with a handicap, three racial/ethnic groups, two languages. All REAPS members.

Neighborhood development through community land trusts takes time and perseverance, cooperation and tolerance. REAPS has made a good beginning. If it remains strong, its members will own enough properties to provide real stability to their community. As the neighborhood becomes more desirable, and therefore more expensive, the community land trust will stabilize prices on its properties so that people will be able to continue to live in the neighborhood they have redeveloped.

Source: Personal communication from Grace Braley, MSW, REAPS organizer, November 1995.

self-image, physical safety, and socialization. In an effort to meet some of these needs, a variety of special programs have been developed. These include mobile medical vans, roving teams of medical and social work personnel who go into the community to provide assistance to people on the street, and efforts to resolve the often thorny territorial disputes between school districts over responsibility for educating children from homeless families. In some places social welfare efforts are directed toward providing affordable housing. The REAPS community land trust (see "On the Street in Yonkers, New York") is a good example.

The limited effectiveness of the social welfare system in meeting the needs of homeless families reflects the degree to which this issue is tied to more fundamental social problems. What Iatridis (1988:11–12) calls a policy of "underdevelopment" has contributed to such problems as high unemployment rates among the urban poor, inadequate health care, surprisingly high illiteracy rates, inadequate welfare payment levels, and a dwindling stock of decent low-cost housing. These factors combine to force many families into poverty and onto the streets. Attempts to meet the immediate needs of homeless and poor families are important, but an enduring solution to their problems will require more fundamental changes in federal employment, income maintenance, health and housing policies.

Contributions of the Family to Social Welfare

The centrality of the family in people's lives makes it vitally important to the social welfare system. There are two principal reasons for this. The first is the family's ability to prevent and resolve problems. People reared in strong healthy families are more likely to perform their social roles effectively and to possess a sense of personal well-being. They are more likely to avoid self-destructive behavior, to be productive members of the workforce, and to form strong healthy families themselves. In so doing, they tend to avoid problems such as substance abuse, family violence, inadequate performance in the workplace, and alienation. The intergenerational support of the family to the social welfare system includes help provided as caregivers to one's older generation as well as to one's children.

A second way in which the family assists the social welfare system is by strengthening commitment to social welfare. It is within the family that most people learn many of their values. As children grow into adulthood, they live in family units that also develop and transmit values. When the values taught in the family include the importance of helping others to function more effectively, people are more likely to support the allocation of resources to social welfare. Such reciprocity means that, to the degree that social welfare succeeds in strengthening the family as a major social institution, it strengthens itself and the other social institutions as well.

SOCIAL WELFARE AND EDUCATION

The educational institution performs three major functions in society: socialization, preparing people to participate in the workforce, and promoting racial and ethnic integration. Let's look at each in turn.

Socialization

Socialization is *the process of social learning through which culturally approved ways of thinking, feeling, and behaving are internalized.* In the United States, children receive a considerable amount of their socialization in educational settings. All children are required to attend school from age 5 or 6 until age 16 or 17. In addition, many children spend time in other educational settings such as nursery school, programs of religious or language instruction, or courses in music, dance, and arts and crafts.

The importance of schooling goes well beyond course content. It is in school that we learn much about how to get along with others, follow instructions, learn how to learn, and assess our own abilities in comparison to others and in relation to organizational expectations. All of this helps prepare for successful adult lives, by increasing our ability to work in cooperation with others.

Ideally, the skills and attitudes taught in school are consistent with those taught in the family, another highly significant socializing structure. Ideally, too, the family prepares its members for school and reinforces the values taught there, including the value of education. Unfortunately, sometimes this does not occur. Some families—those with visually or hearing-impaired children for example—may lack the training and experience necessary to socialize their children appropriately. Other families may teach their youngsters values and behaviors that are considered undesirable by society in general. The school system then faces the problem of reorienting the student toward socially desirable values and behavior. The types of tension that can result are illustrated by the case of James Diggs. (See "The Human Face of Social Welfare 18: The Battle for James Diggs.")

Preparing for Work

In addition to socializing students, schools also teach them knowledge and skills useful for the job market. Since a wage is essential for survival in industrial societies, preparation for meaningful and well-paying work is important. Some of this learning occurs in families, but increasingly it takes place in school.

There are several reasons for this. The first is the increasing complexity and specialization of knowledge and skills. Another is the fact that most adults work outside the home, where their children can neither observe what they do nor easily acquire their skills. A third factor is the increasing reliance on academic degrees and other credentials as a prerequisite for many jobs. James Diggs, for example, needs a high school diploma to become a police officer. It is increasingly difficult to qualify for many jobs in the absence of the appropriate educational degrees or credentials.

Promoting Racial and Ethnic Integration

The socializing and skill-building functions of education are especially important for members of oppressed groups. There are two reasons for this. Many come from cultures outside the United States. If their families are poorly prepared to

THE HUMAN FACE OF SOCIAL WELFARE 18

THE BATTLE FOR JAMES DIGGS—GROWING UP ALONE IN NEW YORK CITY

James Diggs . . . comes from a troubled and impoverished family, from a neighborhood where drugs offer the constant temptation of escape and quick money, and he has poor academic skills. . . .

Those who share James' background are at high risk of dropping out—a description that applies to about 75 percent of those who enter New York City's schools. . . .

"They come from communities where poverty is the norm," [said a school official] "where the presence of drug and alcohol abuse is commonplace and where the likelihood of living with a single parent and several brothers and sisters gives them more reasons not to go to school than to go. What is remarkable is that young people who come out of those circumstances get through. . . ."

James slouched low in his seat in class one day in November. He rarely took off his calf-length gray parka, and that day was no exception. He was depressed, he said, as he showed a visitor a newspaper article about a homeless, 20-year-old mother.

"It makes me feel bad," he said.

His reaction to the article was instructive. In the next three months, as James talked about his experience at school and home, he was jarred by homelessness, and ultimately, the fear of becoming like the people he read about, or who surrounded him. That fear kept him in school.

At 17, an age when many have graduated, James . . . was midway through his sophomore year. His support system was tenuous at best. His father died when James was 9 years old, and his mother died four years later. "When my father died the house just went down," he said.

Two of his older brothers are in prison, one for murder, the other for robbery. A twin brother is handicapped and lives with his grandmother and two sisters. . . . For the time being, James lives alone. His grandmother threw him out last year when he quit school, and a friend's parents have lent him a small apartment. . .

[James enrolled in an alternative school for dropouts]. James says he battles constantly to stay out of trouble and in school. . . . He sold food at concession stands at sporting events. . . ., but wanted a job that kept him occupied every night. . . . Part of the reason, he said, was that too much free time might lead him to involvement with drugs. . . .

[Speaking about classes at the school, James' teacher said] "Some socialization goes on. . . . The whole world is really enemy territory to them [the students]. Almost all of them have low skills and so they act out in class. . . . "

James [has] no trouble connecting the value of a diploma with his future. He wants to be a police officer and to do that, he needs to graduate.

As the fall term went on, however, it became clearer that there was a gap between James's desire to finish and his will to attend classes. From November to the end of January, he missed 18 days and finished the term by completing only one and a half credits out of five.

"I look out in the morning," when it is raining and cold, he said, "and I think I ain't going to go. You know, we don't have anyone behind us telling us to go."

James Diggs' experience clearly illustrates how both the family and the school serve as socializing agents. Ideally, the lessons the two impart will be complementary, but for many people this is not the case. James Diggs is such a person. What he has learned at home does not reinforce what the school is trying to teach him, and the family is ill-prepared to support his efforts to internalize the values and goals imparted in the classroom. The social welfare system has tried to respond to James' need by creating a modified school that can compensate for the family's weaknesses. However, the inherent difficulty of the task is apparent from James's ongoing struggle.

Excerpted from Lydia Chavez, "Crisis over Dropouts: A Look at Two Youths," The New York Times, February 16, 1988, p. B1ff, and is adapted from the plural as written to the singular. Copyright © 1988 by The New York Times Company. Reprinted by permission.

teach them how to succeed in the United States, it becomes the school's task to do so. In addition, many members of oppressed groups are poor. For them, education is a way to qualify for better-paying jobs so that they can escape poverty. Unfortunately, education alone is often insufficient to prevent them from facing discrimination. Nevertheless, educational credentials help members of oppressed groups succeed.

Education is an important way to integrate persons from different racial and cultural backgrounds into American society. Today, as in the past, the United States is a multicultural society, although today's immigrants are increasingly from non-Western societies. Although we often tend to lump ethnic groups together by using labels such as Hispanic or Asian, each individual group is unique. Each has distinctive language, distinctive cultural beliefs and behavior patterns, and distinctive attitudes toward life in their new country (Castex, 1988; Gould, 1988). Evidence of the multicultural nature of the U.S. population appears in Table 8-1, which gives a breakdown of the major ethnic groups in Los Angeles in 1990. The U.S. population in both rural and urban areas throughout the United States is continuing to become more diverse.

The multicultural nature of American society encompasses groups, such as Native Americans, African Americans, and Hispanics, which have been here for many years and still experience unusually high rates of poverty and discrimination. For members of these groups, education continues to be an important route out of poverty.

Some progress is being made. Between 1975 and 1992, for example, the percentage of African American high school graduates enrolling in college increased from 24.9 to 30.1, and the percentage of Hispanic high school graduates enrolling in college increased from 24.4 to 27.8. Nevertheless, both groups lag behind whites, for whom the percentage for high school graduates entering college increased from 34.6 to 45.3 during the same period (U.S. Department of Commerce, 1994, Table 262). As the case of James Diggs suggests, the effects of poverty and discrimination are felt early, often offsetting any potential benefits from education in the lives of those from poor or minority backgrounds.

One of education's functions is to promote social integration by teaching people from oppressed groups how to function successfully in the dominant cultural environment, and to help all members of the society understand and respect each other. It does so by teaching positive values, including the importance of respecting and celebrating cultural differences and living together peacefully with others. Schools provide knowledge about different cultures—what others do, why they do it, and the contribution each group makes to society. Finally, schools provide a setting in which people from different groups interact so that abstract learning is reinforced by day-to-day contact. This is one of the reasons why school integration has been such an important issue in the United States.

Social welfare assists the educational institution in many ways. Some of the efforts that take place within the schools include counseling services for students and their families; programs that provide information about drugs, alcohol, pregnancy, and crime; and educational programs designed to meet the needs of

TABLE 8-1   THE RICH ETHNIC MIX IN LOS ANGELES COUNTY, 1990[a]

Total population	8,863,000
Born in the United States	5,968,000
Foreign born	2,895,000
White	5,045,000
African American	990,000
Native American	43,000
Hispanic origin	3,306,000
Born in Mexico	1,167,000
Born in El Salvador	213,000
Born in the Philippines	161,000
Born in Korea	114,000
Born in Guatemala	108,000
Born in Vietnam	77,000
Born in Iran	68,000
Born in China	67,000
Born in the Soviet Union	52,000
Born in Taiwan	49,000
Born in Canada	44,000
Born in Japan	40,000
Born in the United Kingdom	40,000
Born in Cuba	34,000
Born in Nicaragua	29,000
Born in Germany	27,000
Born in Cambodia	25,000

[a]In addition, there were more than 10,000 but fewer than 25,000 persons living in Los Angeles County who were born in each of the following countries: India, Hong Kong, Honduras, Peru, Lebanon, Thailand, Columbia, Argentina, Italy, Israel, Ecuador, Poland, and Egypt.

Of all Los Angeles residents, 4,441,000 spoke only English in their homes. Another 2,565,000 spoke Spanish; 209,000 spoke Chinese; 124,000, Korean; 156,000, Tagalog. Arabic, German, Vietnamese, and Japanese were each spoken in between 29,000 and 63,000 homes.

Source: U.S. Department of Commerce, *1990 Census of Population. Social and Economic Characteristics. California. Section 1 of 4,* Washington, DC: U.S. Government Printing Office, 1993. Tables 1, 6, 138, 139.

exceptional students (the gifted, those with limitations, students with behavior problems, and others). Such programs entail a variety of educational approaches designed to engage and motivate students, such as bringing in guest speakers from the business world to talk about work opportunities, co-op programs in which students alternate between work and school, work-study programs that pay students while they study, and college and career placement programs. Finally, social welfare's basic message—that people matter—reinforces the efforts of schools to socialize people in such a way that they can lead more satisfying and productive lives.

Reciprocally, education strengthens social welfare. As we have seen, educated people are more likely to be successful in the workplace and thus less likely to need income support programs and related services. Ideally, as is the case with the family, the values fostered by the educational institution are supportive of social welfare. In many schools, teachers develop and try to implement lesson plans that emphasize values such as the importance of playing by the rules, sharing and collaboration, and positive regard for diversity. Understanding of common human aspirations and needs and recognition of the marvelous diversity of human life helps people value themselves and others. This sense of shared experience often leads people to help others and to believe that helping should be a normal part of social life. Finally, there are educational programs that prepare interested persons for social work and other helping professions.

SOCIAL WELFARE AND RELIGION

Religion, as a social institution, *helps people relate to the known and the unknown.* Through religion people grapple with questions about the fundamental nature of human existence, the meaning of life and death, and our individual and social responsibility for the world in which we live. For many, religious beliefs provide answers to these basic questions. In addition, organized religious life provides a sense of community to its members, as well as guidelines for behavior in everyday life.

In 1994, 69 percent of respondents to a national Gallup poll reported believing that religion is becoming less influential in American life today. Poll results indicate that religion continues to be an important part in the life of more than three out of five Americans. However, the percent reporting belief that religion can answer all or most of today's problems declined from 81 in 1957 to 61 in 1991. Similarly, the percent reporting that religion is very important in their own lives fell from 75 to 55 during the same period (Gallup, 1995:62–65). In addition, participation in formal religious services has declined for Protestants, Catholics, and Jews. Forty-two percent of the population 18 years old or older regularly attended church or synagogue in 1991, down from 47 percent in 1957 (U.S. Department of Commerce, 1994, Table 85).

What seems to have emerged is an increased tendency for individuals to challenge or reinterpret church doctrines with which they are uncomfortable. This appears to be especially true among Catholics, for whom formal church positions may not be as influential in guiding people's behavior as in the past, particularly with respect to issues such as premarital sex and the use of birth control devices. Nevertheless, many Americans continue to exhibit a strong belief in fundamental religious values.

Religion and religious values play a significant role in many aspects of society including politics. In the United States, for example, the fundamentalist Protestant minister, Pat Robertson, was a serious candidate for the Republican Presidential nomination in 1988. More recently, Robertson founded the Christ-

ian Coalition, which has played a major role in generating support for the
Republican Contract with America. Other religious organizations—the interde-
nominational Bread for the World and the Catholic Network, for example—
have worked to support social welfare programs designed to reduce hunger and
poverty.

In Poland, a predominately Catholic nation, the Catholic Church continues to
be a powerful institution. The church in Mexico, also a Catholic country, plays a
somewhat more traditional role, encouraging family life and discouraging birth
control. Ironically, religion plays the least significant role in Sweden, the only
country among the four discussed in this book that, until 1996, had a state religion—Lutheranism.

In contrast to the family and education, religion has more of an impact on social
welfare than vice versa. Since the earliest days of social welfare, many personal
social services have been delivered under religious auspices. This is still true today.
Among the services commonly provided by religious groups are informal care for
the poor and the homeless, counseling, and a variety of other helping services.

Of particular significance for social welfare is religion's emphasis on the value
of human life and the right of each person to be treated with love and respect.
Such values encourage a sense of a human community in which people have
responsibility for their neighbors. This sense of caring and of community responsibility is the bedrock on which social welfare is built. Religious teachings that
reinforce it are important, especially in the face of the continuing challenge from
more economically motivated views that seek to limit society's commitment to
social welfare.

As we noted in Chapter 6—see especially Table 6-1, "Roman Catholic Social
and Emergency Services in the United States, 1994," religious organizations provide extensive personal social services, contributing as much as $7.5 billion annu-
ally to social welfare programs (Ortiz, 1995).

The exchange between religion and social welfare is not all in one direction.
Social welfare does aid the religious institution in some ways. Public social welfare programs, for example, often contribute to the support of private church-run
programs by contracting with them, as we saw in the example of the New York
City foster-care program discussed in Chapter 6. Also, just as religion reinforces
social welfare values, so does social welfare strengthen religious values. The
social welfare system provides opportunities for people to operationalize their religious commitments by working as volunteers or as professionals. It is also common for religious groups to join social welfare activists in advocating for legislation that better meets human needs.

SOCIAL WELFARE AND GOVERNMENT

Politics, like social welfare, is a universal phenomenon. The major function of
government is to ensure an orderly process for societal decision making, and to
provide a workable structure for enforcing rules and laws. Political systems take a
variety of forms. More democratic forms of government provide for some degree
of citizen participation, usually in the form of elections in which citizens choose

leaders to represent their interests. Political systems differ greatly from society to society on a variety of dimensions, including (1) the extent to which governmental and economic planning is centralized, (2) the ability of powerful groups to control elections and dominate the policy process, and (3) the ability of citizens to vote in a free and informed manner.

Social welfare performs two major functions that affect the political system. First, it empowers citizens to participate in the political process so that they can express and advocate for their needs. While this generally occurs within the framework of the existing political structure, on occasion it is the structure itself that people want to change. Empowering citizens is a multifaceted effort that includes educating people about issues and the manner in which the political system works, and helping them develop the skills needed to seek social change through collective action.

A second way in which social welfare influences government is by seeking to monitor and protect human rights. One way in which it does so is by encouraging the enforcement of existing laws protecting rights and advocating the passage of laws needed to protect rights that have not yet received legal protection. Because legislation is often insufficient, litigation and direct action may be needed to encourage those violating people's rights to cease. To this end, social welfare employs a variety of tactics, including the negotiation of procedural and structural changes within businesses and other organizations, educating people about the effects of their discriminatory behavior, boycotting those who do discriminate, and organizing other forms of collective protest.

These efforts do not guarantee that all people will be treated fairly. Examples of continued inequity in the treatment of oppressed groups and others can be found in all of the countries discussed in this book, including the United States. Equal treatment for all is, nonetheless, a declared goal of the social welfare institution.

Social welfare seeks to achieve its goals in the political process in a number of ways. Personal counseling programs help people recognize their needs, develop the strength and skills to express and advocate for them, and identify opportunities to seek their goals. Community action agencies conduct voter registration drives, are involved in community education efforts, and promote collective action. Legal aid societies litigate to challenge discrimination or exclusion from the political process. Social welfare agencies and professions actively lobby, provide testimony during lawsuits, and participate in organizational and governmental policy making. Social workers such as Maryland Senator Barbara Mikulski and California Congressman Ron Dellums have run successfully for national office and are effective advocates of social change through their promotion of progressive legislation.

The Effects of Politics on Social Welfare

Government, of course, has powerful effects on social welfare. The availability of public-sector social services and income maintenance programs depends on decisions made in the political arena. Without legal authorization and the funding needed to support them, such services cannot exist. Choices made in the legislative and budgeting processes determine the extent to which human needs will be recognized and addressed through the social welfare system.

ON THE STREET IN CRACOW: POLISH INTELLECTUALS STRUGGLE FOR POLITICAL CHANGE

On the university campus in Cracow, Poland, there is a tremendously moving monument to eighty-five distinguished professors who were among the first residents of Cracow to be arrested and killed when the Nazis invaded the city during World War II. In addition to serving as a memorial to these scholars, it is testament to the power of social welfare in politics. The Nazis feared the power of knowledge and its ability to mobilize people to resist political oppression. They knew that eliminating Cracow's leaders would reduce the probability of organized resistance.

Today, Polish intellectuals continue to struggle with their proper role in the political system. The imposition of martial law in 1981, effectively suspending civil rights and opportunities for collective action, led to an exodus of Poles from their homeland. Although Poland is now an independent country with a democratically elected government, Poles continue to emigrate. It is estimated that about 100,000 Poles, most of them young, emigrate each year—this out of a total population of approximately 37 million. Among the emigrants are about 10 percent of all Polish university graduates (Tagliabue, 1988).

Many Polish intellectuals struggle continuously with the issue of whether to go or stay. As academics, they often have access to the resources and the connections outside Poland needed to leave. However, they also recognize the importance of their leadership role in efforts to improve the political system. A prominent Polish sociologist, for example, recently conducted research that demonstrated people did not believe the government-run health service, although

free, was meeting their needs. In addition, she studied the alternative health-care organizations that were created because of people's dissatisfaction with the existing national system. Her research led to an acknowledgement of the inadequacies in its health-care system by the government and governmental encouragement of the development of alternative systems (Diehl, 1988).

Others have exercised leadership outside of the government. Some intellectuals have chosen to work with citizen groups, providing them with information and helping them devise strategies to advocate for change. Polish university professors who teach social work, social welfare, and social policy, for example, recently banded together with social welfare practitioners to form an association of Polish social workers. This group provides an opportunity for social welfare professionals to develop self-help strategies, to build a network of colleagues able to work together to solve problems in the government-controlled social welfare system, and to have an organized voice for seeking improvements in social welfare services.

For many of these professionals, leaving the country would be the easier and more comfortable option. Their wages are relatively low, and daily living conditions in Poland can be difficult. That they choose not to do so is only in part because of their pride as Poles and their commitment to their culture. It is also because they realize that their departure would make political and social change all the more difficult for those who remain behind. In their decision, we can better appreciate social welfare's role in the political institution.

Source: Personal interviews and observations of Ron Federico, 1987.

It is through politics that a society establishes its priorities. When social welfare issues are on the whole ignored, as occurred during the Reagan administration, or when wholesale efforts, such as those initiated by the Republican-dominated Congress in the mid-1990s, are made to reduce funding for social welfare programs and to shift resources from the poor to the wealthy in the name of balancing the federal budget, society's commitment to meeting human needs is called into question.

Continuing ability to identify needs and to obtain access to the resources needed to address them is vital to the functioning of the social welfare system. A reduction in society's efforts to enhance the lives of its members is likely only to produce an increase in the extent of its members' human needs. Sadly, if the social environment is sufficiently uncaring, even an increase in such needs may not prompt an increase in the resources allocated to social welfare.

SOCIAL WELFARE AND THE ECONOMY

The economic institution is concerned with the production, distribution, and consumption of goods and services. At its heart are work, wages, and the class divisions that result from the unequal distribution of wealth. People's access to income and other economic resources is determined by at least five factors: (1) their family of origin; (2) their educational level; (3) their genetically endowed abilities; (4) the structural characteristics of the workplace that determine the type and quantity of available jobs; and (5) discriminatory social and organizational policies that channel particular groups of people in certain directions. Taken as a whole, the economy produces the resources available to achieve society's goals, as these are determined through politics.

Work is central to life in industrialized societies (Ran and Roncek, 1987:360). Work provides most people's primary source of income, as well as their sense of identity. One of the most frequently asked questions when we meet someone new is, "And what do you do?" Since wages are so important, workers seek to maximize them. Employers, however, try to keep their payroll costs as low as possible. In the United States, political intervention in this struggle between workers and employers is relatively rare. In social democracies such as Sweden, however, unions are active participants in the political system, where they advocate for the needs of workers (Esping-Andersen, 1985:10).

Wages are essential to production and consumption. In industrial societies, pay provides an important incentive for people to work. Their work makes the production of goods and services possible and rewards workers with wages that enable them to consume goods that have been produced. Consumption is possible because people have income to purchase the goods or services they need or want. While income most often comes from wages, it can also come from other sources such as investments, inheritances, or social welfare income maintenance benefits.

Most persons depend on work to provide income for meeting their needs. Both personal problems and social issues occur when people are unemployed. As unemployment increases, production is affected. Unemployed workers consume less unless they have replacement income from unemployment insurance or other sources. When consumption declines, fewer goods are produced for sale. Thus, high levels of unemployment become a corporate and societal problem. If society provides social welfare benefits to the unemployed so they can survive, another problem may be encountered. The money for such benefits is needed precisely when government income from individual and corporate income taxes is falling.

Full employment is an important goal of most industrialized societies. The achievement of this goal, however, is not totally within the control of any single society in today's world. All countries import and export goods and services. The balance between the money spent to purchase imports and the income earned from the sale of exported goods greatly affects levels of employment. The automobile industry in the United States is an excellent example. When U.S. consumers buy imported cars, domestic manufacturers reduce their production so they are not producing more cars than they can sell. Building fewer cars requires fewer workers.

Unemployment increases. This would not happen if foreign autos were not imported, or if the value of American cars being exported roughly equaled the value of those being imported.

The relationship between the economic values of a nation's imports and exports is called the **balance of trade.** *When a country's imports exceed its exports,* the result is a **trade deficit.** This is currently a serious problem in the United States. Many developing countries have a similar problem, but the effects are more severe because of the more fragile condition of their economies (Sheahan, 1987).

There are several employment-related problems in the United States at the present time. In 1993, unemployment stood at 6.8 percent of the workforce, down from a peak of 7.4 percent a year earlier. However, with 8.7 million people unemployed, unemployment is still a substantial issue (U.S. Department of Commerce, 1994, Table 614). These figures hide some troubling additional concerns. Data indicate that about 6 million people, called "discouraged workers," have given up even trying to find work because they have been chronically unsuccessful. An additional 18 million people work less than half the year (Uchitelle, 1987).

Another issue is the increasing use of temporary rather than permanent workers. Workers hired on a full-time but temporary basis are usually paid less and receive fewer benefits than permanent full-time workers (Uchitelle, 1988). Even permanent workers suffer because of the inadequate level of the U.S. minimum wage. In 1995, the minimum wage of $4.25 an hour provided a weekly income of only $170 and an annual income of $8,840 for a full-time worker, well under the poverty level of $15,150 for a family of four or even the $12,590 needed to bring a family of three out of poverty.

As we can see, in the United States there are a number of problems facing both unemployed workers and those who are working under poorly paid or uncertain conditions.

Finally, there is the problem of discrimination. As we have noted, one of the goals of the social welfare institution is to eliminate discrimination in the larger society. Despite many years of public attention, the problem of discrimination continues to affect many American workers. That African Americans and Hispanics continue to face discrimination is documented by the data in Table 8-2. As the data in the table indicate, whites continue to earn more than African Americans or Hispanics. Between 1983 and 1993, wages of African American men and women increased slightly faster than those of white men and women, but a major disparity persists—much of which may be attributed to discrimination.

Women in each of the three racial groups continue to earn substantially less than do men, and the rate of increase of both white and African American women's wages is considerably less than that of men in their groups. It is difficult to say, however, how much of the male–female differences is caused by discrimination. Women in the United States work shorter work weeks than do men and, because of taking time out from employment to bear and raise children, often have fewer years of workplace experience. This is reflected in a wider wage and salary gap for persons 55–64 years old ($0.67 for women for every $1.00 for men) than for persons 25–34 years old ($0.82 for women for every $1.00 for men). In 1987,

TABLE 8-2   COMPARATIVE MEDIAN WEEKLY EARNINGS IN THE UNITED STATES

Category	1983	1993	Percent increase, 1983 to 1993	Percent of 1993 white male earnings
White males	$387	$531	72.9	100.0
White females	$254	$403	63.0	75.9
Black males	$293	$392	74.7	73.8
Black females	$231	$349	66.2	65.7
Hispanic males	NA	$352	NA	66.3
Hispanic females	NA	$314	NA	59.1

Source: U.S. Department of Commerce, *Statistical Abstract of the United States 1994,* Washington, DC: U.S. Government Printing Office, 1994, Table 665.

childless female white workers ages 20–44 earned hourly wages of 86–91 percent of those earned by their male counterparts. When women's shorter work weeks and fewer years of work experience are taken into account, the wage differential between men and women narrows considerably (Sommers, 1994:238–241).

The reliance of the United States on a market economy makes unemployment or underemployment likely. The determination of the number of workers needed at any given time is left to the marketplace, so the workforce expands or contracts in response to market conditions.

Not all societies take this approach. National policy in Sweden calls for full employment. In 1984, when unemployment in the United States was 7.4 percent, it was only 3.1 percent in Sweden (Zimbalist, 1987:23). By late 1992, however, the official U.S. unemployment rate was 6.8 percent, while 5.4 percent of the Swedish labor force was out of work. As a socialist nation, Poland had no official unemployment. Everyone who wanted to work was guaranteed a job. In Sweden and Poland, economic planning is used to regulate the labor market so that jobs are created as necessary and people are kept employed. These countries attempt to manage the labor market in such a way as to control the level of employment rather than allowing the workforce to be controlled predominantly by the market.

Whatever the type of economic system, the economy is assisted by the social welfare institution. In the United States, Poland, and Sweden, the social welfare system provides income maintenance programs to help support those who are unemployed or who do not earn an income adequate to meet their needs. Job training and job placement programs provided by the social welfare system also seek to reduce employment-related problems. By actively preparing people for employment, the educational system helps to minimize unemployment, especially in Sweden (Ruggie, 1884:143–181). Certain other social welfare services, notably those related to child welfare, health care, and housing, are useful in dealing with the unhealthful emotional and physical conditions associated with low income that may accompany unemployment (Wyers, 1988).

Finally, personal counseling programs can help those who have become discouraged and have dropped out of the workforce. As we have already noted, stress increases the probability of dysfunctional behavior. In a modern wage-based economy, unemployment can breed feelings of panic and humiliation, feelings that personal counseling can help counteract while a person is seeking a new job. Counseling, however, cannot substitute for adequate income.

The practice of linking many benefits, such as health care, to full-time, permanent employment—a common pattern in the United States, Mexico, and Poland—contributes to the vulnerability of workers in the societies involved. When this is the case, part-time and temporary workers often fail to qualify for benefits. A further complication is that, even when workers are eligible for benefits, the value of benefits may decline as employers attempt to lower costs by reducing benefits or by requiring workers to share in the cost of benefits provided (Freudenheim, 1985). In the first instance, the workers' benefits and the protection they provide are reduced. In the second, workers' disposable income is reduced. In either case, workers are worse off.

The tools available to social welfare for addressing these problems include political action and litigation. Unions and other groups have filed suits to obtain increased protection for workers. In addition, social welfare advocates have sought such legislative changes as increases in the minimum wage and the establishment of universal national health insurance so that people do not have to rely on the workplace for health protection.

Consumer protection is another concern of social welfare that is related to the economy. In a market economy in which people are free to buy whatever they want and can afford, there is often a staggering proliferation of products. Some products may be dangerous (e.g., firearms) or unhealthful (e.g., tobacco or excessive alcohol, sugar, salt, or fat). Others do not work well, or do not perform as advertised. Unethical sales and advertising practices are sometimes employed to trick people into purchasing items they do not really want or need, or into purchasing needed goods at artificially high prices.

Social welfare attempts to prevent such problems through consumer education programs and by seeking consumer protection legislation. In addition, legal aid programs help consumers seek redress when they have been exploited by producers, distributors, advertisers, or salespeople.

The Impact of the Economy on Social Welfare

The economy has very powerful effects on social welfare. The rise of the modern welfare state has been linked with the productivity made possible by industrialization. The extensive social welfare programs we take for granted are costly. In 1991, for example, Sweden spent 56.4 percent of its central government budget on public housing, social security, and welfare, and the United States spent 28.7 percent for the same purposes (see Chapter 1, Table 1-1). Mexico is a good example of a nation whose struggling economy is unable to support such an extensive public social welfare institution. Even Poland, which has a comprehensive public

A WORKER STUMBLES, IN SWEDEN AND IN THE UNITED STATES

The difference between benefits that are work-related and those that are not is illustrated in the following realistic account of the resources provided to two workers, and their respective families, confronting similar situations in Sweden and the United States.

The situation is the following. A 45-year-old researcher with two teenage children and a spouse who is employed by a consulting company becomes permanently disabled because of alcoholism and related medical problems. The spouse, like the worker, is also employed outside the home in a full-time professional-level position. The strains on the family result in a nervous breakdown for one of the two teenage children. Both the worker and the teenager have to be hospitalized, the worker several times for serious medical complications related to alcoholism. In such a situation, what resources are available to this family?

As we shall see, the resources available in Sweden and the United States are quite different. In Sweden, government disability, pension, and health programs provide nearly comprehensive protection for workers and their families. Benefits in the United States are much less comprehensive and tied to employment, leaving workers much more vulnerable.

Sweden

In Sweden, the researcher, once diagnosed as suffering from chronic alcoholism, is declared disabled and begins receiving a monthly government disability payment. This money, along with the spouse's income, ensures the family's continued economic security. Hospital care for both the researcher and the teenage child is free, while the cost of longer-term medical and psychiatric care and prescriptions is minimal. The family's only medically related expenses are a very small, set fee for each of the first ten visits to the doctor and the first ten prescriptions. Thereafter, all medical care and prescriptions are free. The researcher's spouse makes use of the 5-week annual vacation to which all Swedes are entitled by law to help care for the researcher and the teenage child. In addition, the spouse is able to use

paid sick leave as needed to deal with any additional family crises.

As a result of the benefits available to Swedish workers, the family's life style is preserved while its disabled members struggle to reestablish themselves. Should the researcher's disability become permanent, both spouses, upon reaching retirement age, will still receive their individual government pension based on their own work history. Thus the researcher's interrupted earnings will not reduce the spouse's pension.

United States

As in Sweden, the researcher is diagnosed as suffering from chronic alcoholism and determined to be eligible for disability benefits from the government. This, along with the spouse's income, protects the family's economic security to some degree. The disabled worker qualifies for health insurance through the employer's private plan. Under this plan, the family is reimbursed for 80 percent of the cost of all medical and hospital care, but receives no reimbursement for prescription costs. Fifty percent of the cost of the teenager's psychiatric care is covered by the spouse's health insurance plan provided by the spouse's employer. This plan, however, limits hospitalization coverage to 30 days and outpatient treatment to 1 year. The spouse's employer also provides 2 weeks' paid vacation and 12 days of sick leave that the spouse is able to use during the course of dealing with the family's medical crises. The Family Leave Act provides an option of additional unpaid leave.

As a result of its circumstances, the family amasses large medical and drug bills, which force severe economies in its lifestyle. A second mortgage is used to help pay the medical bills, and the second child has postponed graduate school to work and help support the family.

Should the researcher's disability become permanent, the family's retirement income will be reduced because the working spouse's pension will be tied to the worker's now interrupted work history.

Source: Personal interviews and observations of Ron Federico, 1987.

social welfare system, finds it difficult to provide the resources necessary to house its citizens adequately.

In the United States, where there are fewer public programs than in many other societies, private philanthropy is important. Many people contribute voluntarily to various private social welfare programs, providing a valuable supplement to the public social welfare system and, to a very limited degree, voluntarily redistribut-ing wealth. Such charitable giving is made possible by the productivity of the eco-nomic system. Unlike planned universal systems of social welfare in Sweden or Poland, however, voluntary giving is often inconsistent and unpredictable. It almost always falls far short of meeting total need. Reliance on private philan-thropy characterized by lack of planning and coordination may contribute to frag-mentation and maldistribution of services.

SOCIAL WELFARE FOR ALL

An examination of the relationships between social welfare and each of the other major social institutions helps us understand how social welfare touches the lives of everyone. This can happen in a very personal way, as when a middle-class, middle-age gay man becomes ill with AIDS and requires medical care and emo-tional counseling. If he is fortunate, his work-based health insurance plan will pay for much of the necessary care. Or consider the wealthy industrialist who develops a drinking problem, or discovers that his daughter-in-law is being battered by her husband. A variety of social welfare agencies stand ready to help in these situa-tions, even though those needing help are not poor. Social welfare serves every-one, those who are economically secure as well as the homeless family or the unwed teenage mother with no income.

Social welfare is a pervasive part of our society, indeed of all societies. It helps families develop parenting skills, students obtain financial aid, communities resolve conflicts, and workers find employment. By touching everyone in a soci-ety, social welfare also has a larger cumulative effect. When problems arise, the social welfare system provides channels for people to express their needs, to seek help, and to advocate for change in an orderly way. Destructive social conflict is frequently avoided when people believe that their basic needs are being met.

Social welfare's impact on all members of society takes at least three forms.

1 **Preventing problems.** Social welfare services complement the efforts of other social institutions to prevent problems. One of the clearest examples of this is education, where social welfare programs increase the likelihood that people will be able and willing to attend school and thus increase their prospects for becoming self-reliant adults. By preventing problems, social welfare reduces expenditures otherwise needed to ameliorate them, reduces the pain experienced by people, and makes life more pleasant for everyone. For example, many people find it troubling and unpleasant to encounter homeless, alcoholic, or mentally ill people on the street. Programs that provide housing and rehabilitation for those who are in need not only help the homeless and potentially homeless; they also make life more pleasant for the average citizen.

2 **Reinforcing the link between people and society.** Social welfare is tangi-ble evidence that society cares for its members. When we pay our taxes, we some-times question the value of doing so. But when we see that our money improves life in tangible ways, our commitment to society itself is likely to increase. Most of us feel good when we see a child with disabilities helped to obtain schooling,

or a battered child receiving the physical and emotional care that he or she needs. Such incidents affirm our collective responsibility to aid those in need. Social welfare helps us carry out that responsibility.

3 Asserting that people matter. A fundamental principle of social welfare is that each individual deserves a decent, satisfying life. Each life is precious, and each is to be nurtured. The needs of organizations or even society itself must never be allowed to crush individuals. This goal is sometimes elusive in daily life, but social welfare's commitment is a firm one. It is important that there be a clear, steady, insistent voice in society with this message. Everyone benefits as a result.

Linking people and society, preventing problems, and asserting that people matter depend on interplay between social welfare and the other institutions of society. It is through these institutional structures that helping is made possible on a daily basis. It is also through them that social welfare seeks to influence the decisions that will shape the future.

LET'S REVIEW

This chapter began by discussing the concept of social institutions. Social institutions are socially approved, perform identifiable social functions, distribute resources, and organize activities. The major social institutions are social welfare, the family, education, religion, government, and the economy.

The main focus of the chapter was on how social welfare relates to each of the other social institutions. Particular attention was paid to how social welfare helps each institution perform its major social functions. Ways in which social welfare is itself influenced by the other social institutions were also explored. It was noted too, that changes in the other major social institutions often create new needs to which social welfare attempts to respond.

The chapter concluded with a brief examination of how everyone benefits from social welfare. Rich and poor, men and women, no matter what race or ethnicity, everyone's life is touched—usually in positive ways—by the social welfare institution. Improved personal functioning and strengthened social cohesion are the goals of social welfare's efforts to make society more responsive to the needs of its citizens.

Now only two chapters remain. The next chapter discusses the activities of social welfare professionals, a topic of particular interest if you are considering such a career, but helpful also to anyone who makes use of the services the social welfare system provides—which is to say, virtually everyone. The final chapter examines the future of social welfare, with emphasis on likely developments during the next few years.

STUDY QUESTIONS

1 Write your own definition of social welfare as a social institution. Be sure that your definition takes account of all of the major characteristics exhibited by all social institutions. Then provide a specific example of each of these characteristics as exhibited by social welfare.

2 Interview and record the answers of at least three people to the following two questions: *(a)* What do you believe are the most pressing needs of the contemporary American family? *(b)* What do you believe society should do to meet these needs? Compile a list of the needs mentioned and briefly indicate what you believe society should do about each.

3 This chapter discussed the positive aspects of religion and social welfare. Can you think of any negative interactions? For example, some believe that social welfare programs that promote birth control undermine religious beliefs. Others believe that fundamentalist religious beliefs increase problems by oppressing certain groups, especially gay men and lesbians, children, and racial minorities. What are your thoughts about these issues, and any others you can identify?

4 Research the current literature on technology and the workplace. What kinds of changes are predicted concerning the number and types of workers who will be needed in the future? What kinds of problems can you foresee if these predictions prove accurate? How do you believe the social welfare institution should respond to these problems?

5 This chapter makes the point that everyone benefits from social welfare, both at the personal level and in terms of a better-functioning society. Do you agree with this? Can you identify aspects of your own life that have been improved because of social welfare? Can you think of people you know whose lives have not been improved? Prepare a summary of your personal views on the value of social welfare to society as a whole.

KEY TERMS AND CONCEPTS

acquired immune deficiency syndrome (AIDS)
human immunodeficiency virus (HIV)
socialization

religion
balance of trade
trade deficit

SUGGESTED READINGS

Clarke-Stewart, Alison. 1977. *Child Care in the Family.* New York: Academic Press. A study of the needs of children in families and the factors that determine whether those needs are met. The author discusses and recommends several policies designed to strengthen families, and argues on behalf of her view of the proper role of social welfare in improving child care.

Esping-Andersen, Gosta. 1985. *Politics against Markets.* Princeton, NJ: Princeton University Press. Analyzes the development of social democracy in Sweden, Norway, and Denmark, and explains why it has been a crucial factor in the development (or decline) of social welfare programs in those countries. A historical work that clearly illustrates the relationship among the political, economic, and social welfare institutions.

Gutmann, Amy, ed. 1988. *Democracy and the Welfare State.* Princeton, NJ: Princeton University Press. An edited work that explores current issues in the relationship of social welfare to the other institutions of society. It thoughtfully examines the influence of social institutions on the value base of social welfare in democracies.

Kozol, Jonathan. 1995. *Amazing Grace: The Lives of Children and the Conscience of a Nation.* New York: Crown Publishers. The author of many books of incisive social commentary (including *Death at an Early Age, Rachael and Her Children,* and *Savage Inequalities*), Kozol describes the violence of pediatric AIDS, gang rivalries, and arson in the South Bronx. Through the words of children, parents, and priests in the poorest congressional district in the United States, we learn how the ghetto "is created and sustained by greed, neglect, racism, and expediency."

Social Work. 1987. Vol. 32, No. 1. This issue of the major journal published by the National Association of Social Workers addresses ways of helping families adjust to divorce and related problems.

REFERENCES

Barker, Robert L. 1991. *The Social Work Dictionary,* 2d ed. Silver Spring, MD: National Association of Social Workers.

Castex, Graciela. 1988. *The Creation of "Hispanic": Social Myths and Objective Realities.* Paper presented at the annual program meeting of the Council on Social Work Education, March 8, Atlanta, GA.

Diehl, Jackson. 1988. Poles plan capitalist cure for health system. *Washington Post,* June 6, p. A1.

Esping-Andersen, Gosta. 1985. *Politics against Markets.* Princeton, NJ: Princeton University Press.

Fernandez, John. 1986. *Child Care and Corporate Productivity.* Lexington, MA: Lexington Books.

First, Richard, John Rife, and Beverly Toomey. 1995. Homeless families. In *Encyclopedia of Social Work,* 19th ed. Washington, DC: National Association of Social Workers, pp. 1330–1337.

Freudenheim, Milt. 1985. Company expenses for retirees soar. *The New York Times,* September 9, p. A1.

Gallup, George, Jr. 1995. *The Gallup Poll: Public Opinion 1994.* Wilmington, DE: Scholarly Resources, Inc.

Gould, Ketayun. 1988. Asian and Pacific islanders: Myth and reality. *Social Work,* 33(2):142–148.

Greer, William. 1986. The changing women's marriage market. *The New York Times,* February 22, p. 48.

Iatridis, Demetrius. 1988. New social deficit: Neoconservatism's policy of social underdevelopment. *Social Work,* 33(1):11–15.

Johnson, Alice. 1995. Homelessness. In *Encyclopedia of Social Work,* 19th ed. Washington, DC: National Association of Social Workers, pp. 1338–1346.

Kamerman, Sheila. 1985. *Children and Their Families: The Impact of the Reagan Administration and the Choices for Social Work.* Proceedings of the Werner and Bernice Boehm Distinguished Lectureship in Social Work. New Brunswick, NJ: School of Social Work of Rutgers University.

Kantrowitz, Barbara, Renee Michael, Lori Rotenberg, Elisa Williams, and Nikki Finke Greenberg. 1985. Mothers on their own. *Newsweek,* December 23, pp. 66–67.

Lloyd, Gary A. 1995. HIV/AIDS overview. In *Encyclopedia of Social Work,* 19th ed. Washington, DC: National Association of Social Workers, pp. 1257–1290.

Monk, Abraham. 1985. Preretirement planning programs. In Abraham Monk, ed., *Handbook of Gerontological Services,* New York: Van Nostrand Reinhold, pp. 322–340.

NASW. 1987. *Social Work,* 31(1).

Ortiz, Larry P. 1995. Sectarian agencies. In *Encyclopedia of Social Work,* 19th ed. Washington, DC: National Association of Social Workers, pp. 2109–2116.

Quinn, Jane. 1988. A crisis in child care. *Newsweek,* February 15, p. 57.

Ran, William, and Dennis Roncek. 1987. Industrialization and world inequality: The transformation of the division of labor in 59 nations. *American Sociological Review,* 52(6):359–369.

Ruggie, Mary. 1984. *The State and Working Women.* Princeton, NJ: Princeton University Press.

Sauber, Robert, Eleanor Dwyer, Katherine Ryan, Stephen Goldfinger, and John Kelly. 1988. Medical and psychiatric needs of the homeless—A preliminary response. *Social Work,* 33(2):116–119.

Sheahan, John. 1987. *Patterns of Development in Latin America.* Princeton, NJ: Princeton University Press.

Sommers, Christina. 1994. *Who Stole Feminism? How Women Have Betrayed Women.* New York: Simon & Schuster.

Tagliabue, John. 1988. Emigrant flow from Poland worries regime and church. *The New York Times,* February 14, p. 18.

Tonti, Mario, and Barbara Silverstone. 1985. Services to families of the elderly. In Abraham Monk, ed., *Handbook of Gerontological Services,* New York: Van Nostrand Reinhold, pp. 211–239.

Uchitelle, Louis. 1987. America's army of non-workers. *The New York Times,* September 27, p. 3-1.

———. 1988. Reliance on temporary jobs hints at economic fragility. *The New York Times,* March 16, p. 1.

U.S. Department of Commerce. 1994. *Statistical Abstract of the United States 1994.* Washington, DC: U.S. Government Printing Office.

Westchester County (NY) Department of Social Services. 1987. Number of homeless families, children and singles: November 1987. Mimeographed, December 1.

Wyers, Norman. 1988. Economic insecurity: Notes for social workers. *Social Work,* 33(1):18–22.

Zimbalist, Sidney. 1987. A welfare state against the economic current: Sweden and the United States as contrasting cases. *International Social Work,* 30(1):15–29.

9

HOW DO THE
SOCIAL WELFARE
PROFESSIONS FUNCTION?

WHAT TO EXPECT FROM THIS CHAPTER

This chapter discusses the social welfare professions and their role in delivering helping services to people. It also examines the relationship between these professions and the informal helping network, which, as we have seen, is also an important source of social welfare services. The chapter concludes with a look at the opportunities for helping that are available to all of us.

An understanding of the structure and function of the social welfare professions is useful in several ways. First, it completes our picture of social welfare as a social institution. An examination of how helping professions have developed can help us better understand how society operationalizes its helping role and how closely linked social welfare is to the other institutions of society. We will see that there is competition and overlap among the social welfare professions, a situation we might expect in a market-oriented society that limits centralized government planning and control. Finally, if you are considering a helping career, you will find this overview of the helping professions particularly useful.

This chapter increases your understanding of the institutional components of social welfare by bringing together many of the issues discussed earlier. The next chapter, which is the last, moves in a different direction. Rather than examining the past or the present, it looks to the future. What is the role of social welfare likely to be in the years ahead? For now though, let's focus on the people and the professions who deliver helping services today.

LEARNING OBJECTIVES

When you have finished studying this chapter, you should be able to:

1 List four major characteristics of a profession, and apply them to a social welfare profession of your choice.

2 Discuss the roles of licensing, certification, and registration as they are used in social welfare.

3 List at least five social welfare professions, and briefly describe the function of each.

4 Give an example of a generalist role and a specialist role in one of the social welfare professions.

5 Distinguish between professional and volunteer roles in social welfare, and discuss how they interact.

6 Discuss ways in which ordinary people can become involved in societal helping efforts.

THE FUNCTIONS OF THE HELPING PROFESSIONS

All the helping professions share the goal of helping people and institutions function more effectively so that people's lives are enhanced and social cohesion is strengthened. Each profession approaches this task from its own particular vantage point. We will see that each profession trains its members to be skillful and effective providers of particular kinds of services. However, they also work together so that the distinctive services provided by each type of professional fit together into a holistic helping effort.

The Generalist Approach

The **generalist approach** involves *professional, comprehensive use of a broad spectrum of knowledge and skills in responding to human needs or problem situations* (Barker, 1991:91). Some professions, such as social work, are by their very nature generalist. Social work adopts a holistic view of the interaction between people and their environment, seeking to improve this relationship by strengthening the individual's ability to function independently, modifying the environment, or both. Social workers, therefore, provide a variety of services, including personal counseling, political advocacy, organizing community groups, family therapy, counseling in personal financial management, and so on. A generalist approach involves using a variety of skills to intervene at all the levels required to ensure that all elements of a problem are addressed.

Consider the example of a social worker, employed in a senior citizen center, who one day observes that one of the women who attends regularly has bruises. Through skillful counseling, the worker discovers that the elderly woman lives with her son and his family, and that she is subject to emotional and physical abuse. Furthermore, her son has forced her to sign over most of her assets to him, limiting her ability to move out. Employing a generalist approach, the worker might well define the types of assistance needed to solve the problem as including each of the following:

1 Legal help to protect the elderly woman's assets and rights

2 Medical care to treat her injuries

3 Psychological help to address her emotional trauma

4 Counseling to help her plan a safe and secure future for herself

5 Housing assistance to help her locate an affordable place to live that will be appropriate for her physical abilities and social needs

6 Contact with other community social agencies and professional groups to explore the problem of elder abuse as a social problem, and to plan appropriate community and legislative action

7 Counseling with the family to help members participate in finding solutions to the problem.

One professional working alone obviously cannot provide all the services listed in this example. The generalist approach facilitates focusing on the whole problem while breaking it down into its component parts so that each can be addressed by professionals with specialized expertise. This assures that the users of services receive help in ways that address all relevant aspects of their needs and contribute to an overall sense of well-being. A generalist often becomes a **case manager,** *a professional who coordinates the efforts of staff in an agency or several agencies to meet the needs of a given client through professional teamwork* (Barker, 1991:29).

The Specialist Approach

Specialization is an alternative but complementary approach to that of the generalist. The **specialist approach** *utilizes professionals with specialized training to solve particular problems.* We are all familiar with medical specialists to whom our family practitioner refers patients with problems that require specialized treatment, such as kidney disease, hearing loss, or cancer. Specialists have extensive training in a particular area that makes them highly qualified to respond to needs within that area.

Some professions utilize both generalists and specialists. Physicians are an excellent example. All physicians are specialists in the sense that they treat problems involving people's physical health. However, some doctors specialize much more than others. Family practitioners concern themselves with their patient's overall health, referring problems that lie outside their immediate competence to other physicians who specialize in a particular branch of medicine or type of disease. For example, a referral might be made to an oncologist for the treatment of cancer. In such cases, responsibility for all aspects of the patient's care other than the need that led to the referral usually is left to the generalist family practitioner. Medicine is an example of a profession in which we find both generalists and specialists.

Both generalist and specialist approaches are employed in social work. All social workers are trained as generalists, and many function in this capacity. Many others, however, particularly those with graduate-level training, also develop specialties that become their primary mode of practice. A **clinical social worker,** for example, *uses counseling and related services to treat and prevent emotional and mental disorders. The term is sometimes used interchangeably with social caseworker or psychiatric social worker* (Barker, 1991:38–39). Clinical social workers often work in mental health agencies or in private practice. Other MSW social workers specialize in research, administration, or public policy development and analysis, in social work with families and children, in school social work, public child welfare, or in social work in a wide variety of other specialized settings. Since the social work role almost always includes some case management responsibilities, even highly specialized social workers are likely to provide a mix of generalist and specialist services.

Generalists and specialists serve complementary functions. People need help with their particular problems, help the specialist is uniquely qualified to provide. However, to be effective, help must be integrated into their daily lives so that the fabric of their existence is maintained.

Future Prospects

There will be a continuing need for social welfare professionals during the foreseeable future. The increasing complexity of modern society poses problems for those whose education, age, or physical or mental capacities limit their ability to function independently. Families continue to struggle with consequences of social change, such as increasing numbers of working and single parents, high divorce rates, and high levels of stress that damage marital and parent–child relationships. Long-standing problems of racism and sexism continue to disadvantage large numbers of people. Continued growth of the elderly population will require increased services to maintain and enhance the quality of their lives. In addition, there is growing concern about environmental and economic problems. All of these trends and more suggest a continued need for social welfare and its professions.

The resurgence in the number of applications to schools of social work which began during the mid-1980s in the United States (Wilkerson, 1987) may indicate that society is recognizing this need. Perhaps, as some feel, a growing awareness of social problems such as AIDS and homelessness has increased people's interest in helping careers. Another factor may be disappointment with jobs that provide little human contact, seem to make little difference in people's lives, or that are financially rewarding but not personally enriching. For all of these societal and personal reasons, it is likely that the social welfare professions will continue to grow.

THE NATURE OF PROFESSIONS

Professions are vocational fields with very special characteristics. Professionals, like other workers, have jobs; they may work for an organization, or they may be self-employed. However, the professional's primary commitment is to professional practice itself rather than to an employer.

Professions share four important characteristics. However, as has been noted by Khinduka (1987:682), "professionalism is not an either-or phenomenon. Instead, the attributes of a profession constitute a continuum, and professionalism should thus be viewed as a scale." With that caution in mind, let's examine the four characteristics of a profession.

1 Professions have specialized knowledge and skills. Most professions involve mastery of a large body of specialized knowledge that requires extensive education. Lawyers, for example, undergo 3 years of graduate-level training in legal precedent, existing law, and legal procedures. Most professional training involves *practica*—field placements—in which students apply their knowledge in an effort to refine practice skills. Only those who master the required specialized knowledge and skills qualify for professional membership.

Consider the example of social work. Many people believe that social work is just common sense. Those who call social workers "do-gooders" are, in effect, suggesting that social workers are guided primarily by good intentions rather than specialized knowledge or skills. Those who hold to this view believe that social work consists simply of sympathizing with others, filling out forms, and giving advice.

In reality, professionally trained social workers must master a large body of knowledge about all aspects of human and social functioning. Among other things, social workers must know about the life cycle, theories of personality development, elements of intergroup dynamics, political processes, and existing social welfare programs. In addition, they require very specific problem-solving skills. Of special importance are the skills required to relate effectively to others, to understand and build on the strengths of members of various ethnic and life-style groups, to identify problems and the resources needed to solve them, to help people implement changes in behavior, and to evaluate the results of helping efforts. Training in these areas distinguishes professional social workers from other professionals and from "natural" helpers.

Like social work, each of the helping professions has a distinctive knowledge base, values, and set of skills that make its members uniquely capable of performing helping activities.

2 Professions operate within a **code of ethics,** *an explicit statement "of the values, principles, and rules of a profession, regulating the conduct of its members"*

(Barker, 1991:39). Each profession has its own code, but all are grounded in similar beliefs: the value of human life, a respect for the right of people to control their own lives, and a commitment to strive to help others rather than to enrich or promote oneself. Professional codes of ethics place the value of human life and human dignity ahead of the profit motive. Because they address situations in which human rights, physical and emotional well-being, fundamental human relationships, and even life itself are at stake, codes of ethics take great care to protect users of services.

The professional code of ethics protects users from exploitation by professionals or the agencies for which they work. The code also extends protection in the form of guaranteeing that information will be kept confidential, that people will be treated with respect, fairness, and equality, and that they will retain control over decision making about their own lives. Finally, the code of ethics protects the user's right to receive competent services. Social work's code of ethics is illustrative. (See "The NASW Code of Ethics.")

3 Professions practice self-regulation and are relatively autonomous. Professions claim the right and responsibility to monitor the behavior of their members. This makes them self-regulating and autonomous, meaning that control over the behavior of their members occurs primarily within the profession rather than from outside.

Professions accept the responsibility to monitor the behavior of their members to ensure ethical and competent behavior. They establish structures through which the behavior of their members is monitored. The National Association of Social Workers (NASW), for example, has established committees of inquiry at the national and state chapter levels. A **committee of inquiry** is *a group of professionals assembled "to determine if any wrong-doing has been committed by or to a peer"* (Barker, 1991:42). The NASW committees of inquiry monitor violations of the NASW Code of Ethics and personnel standards. NASW members found to have violated the code are sanctioned. The strongest sanction involves revocation of membership in the professional association. Agencies which violate NASW personnel standards are publicized, with the expectation that members of the association will refuse to work there while sanctions are in effect. Professions operate with relatively little external control because, they argue, society can trust them to regulate themselves.

Of course, society does not grant professions complete autonomy. There are laws and procedures regulating certain aspects of professional behavior (King, 1988). Society regulates professions through *licensing, certification,* and *registration.*

Licensing involves *formal governmental authorization of the use of a title and the practice of a profession.* For example, only people licensed as physicians may call themselves by that title and practice as physicians. Anyone who does either without the proper license is subject to legal sanctions. Licensing may exist at multiple levels of practice. In the state of Maine, for example, in 1996, persons who have earned a bachelor's degree in social work may take a test to be licensed as "licensed social workers" and use the initials LSW following their names. Those who have completed master's-level studies in social work and who pass an

THE NASW CODE OF ETHICS

Overview

[Every 3 years the National Association of Social Workers (NASW) Delegate Assembly is convened to set organizational policy. In 1996, the Delegate Assembly approved a new NASW Code of Ethics. The first three sections of the draft of the new code—Preamble, Purpose, and Ethical Principles—are reproduced here. The complete code is available from the NASW chapter in your state.]

The National Association of Social Workers Code of Ethics is intended to serve as a guide to the everyday professional conduct of social workers. This code includes four sections. Section one, "Preamble," summarizes the social work profession's mission and core values. Section two, "Purpose of the Code of Ethics," provides an overview of the Code's main functions and a brief guide for dealing with ethical issues or dilemmas in social work practice. Section three, "Ethical Principles," presents broad ethical principles, based on social work's core values, that inform social work practice. The final section, "Ethical Standards," includes specific ethical standards to guide social workers' conduct and to provide a basis for adjudication.

Preamble

The primary mission of the social work profession is to enhance human well-being and help meet basic human needs, with particular attention to the needs of people who are vulnerable, oppressed, and living in poverty. An historic and defining feature of social work is the profession's focus on individual well-being in a social context and the well-being of society. Fundamental to social work is attention to the environmental forces that create, contribute to, and address problems in living.

Social workers promote social justice and social change with and on behalf of clients. 'Clients' is used inclusively to refer to individuals, families, groups, organizations, and communities. Social workers are sensitive to cultural and ethnic diversity and strive to alleviate discrimination, oppression, poverty, and other forms of social injustice. These activities may be in the form of direct practice, community organizing, supervision, consultation, administration, advocacy, social and political action, policy development and implementation, education, and research and evaluation. Social workers seek to enhance the capacity of people to address their own needs. Social workers also seek to promote the responsiveness of organizations, communities, and other social institutions to individuals' needs and social problems.

The mission of the social work profession is rooted in a set of core values. These core values, embraced by social workers throughout the profession's history, are the foundation of social work's unique purpose and perspective:

- Service
- Social justice
- Dignity and worth of the person
- Importance of human relationships
- Integrity
- Competence

The constellation of these core values reflects what is unique to the social work profession. Core values, and the principles which flow from them, must be balanced within the context and complexity of the human experience.

Purpose of the code of ethics

Professional ethics are at the core of social work. The profession has an obligation to articulate its basic values, ethical principles, and ethical standards. The NASW Code of Ethics sets forth these values, principles, and standards to guide social workers' conduct. The code of ethics is relevant to all social workers, regardless of their professional functions, the settings in which they work, or the populations they serve.

This NASW Code of Ethics serves six purposes:

- The code identifies core values on which social work's mission is based.
- The code summarizes broad ethical principles that reflect the profession's core values and establishes a set of specific ethical standards that should be used to guide social work practice.
- The code of ethics is designed to help social workers identify relevant considerations when professional obligations conflict or ethical uncertainties arise.
- The code provides ethical standards to which the general public can hold the social work profession accountable.
- The code socializes practitioners new to the field to social work's mission, values, ethical principles, and ethical standards.
- The code articulates standards that the social work profession itself can use to assess whether social workers have engaged in unethical conduct. NASW has formal procedures to adjudicate ethics complaints filed against its members.[1] In subscribing to

[1] For information on NASW adjudication procedures, see *NASW Procedures for the Adjudication of Grievances.*

(continued)

this code social workers are required to cooperate in its implementation, participate in NASW adjudication proceedings, and abide by any NASW disciplinary rulings or sanctions based on it.

This code offers a set of values, principles, and standards to guide decision making and conduct when ethical issues arise. It does not provide an unambiguous set of rules that prescribe how social workers should act in all situations. Specific applications of the code must take into account the context in which it is being considered and the possibility of conflicts among the code's values, principles, and standards. Ethical responsibilities flow from all human relationships, from the personal and familial to the social and professional.

Further, the code of ethics does not specify which values, principles, and standards are most important and ought to outweigh others in instances when they conflict. Reasonable differences of opinion can and do exist among social workers with respect to the ways in which values, ethical principles, and ethical standards should be rank-ordered when they conflict. Ethical decision making in a given situation must apply the informed judgment of the individual social worker and should also consider how the issues would be judged in a peer review process where the ethical standards of the profession would be applied.

Ethical decision making is a process. There are many instances in social work where simple answers are not available to resolve complex ethical issues. Social workers should take into consideration all the values, principles, and standards in this code that are relevant to any situation in which ethical judgment is warranted. Social workers' decisions and actions should be consistent with the spirit as well as the letter of this code.

In addition to this code, there are many other sources of information about ethical thinking that may be useful. Social workers should consider ethical theory and principles generally, social work theory and research, laws, regulations, agency policies, and other relevant codes of ethics, recognizing that among codes of ethics social workers should consider the NASW Code of Ethics as their primary source. Social workers also should be aware of the impact on ethical decision-making of their clients' and their own personal values, cultural and religious beliefs, and practices. They should be aware of any conflicts between personal and professional values and deal with them responsibly. For additional guidance social workers should consult relevant literature on professional ethics and ethical decision

making, and seek appropriate consultation when faced with ethical dilemmas. This may involve consultation with an agency-based or social work organization's ethics committee, regulatory body, knowledgeable colleagues, supervisors, or legal counsel.

Instances may arise where social workers' ethical obligations conflict with agency policies, relevant laws or regulations. When such conflicts occur, social workers must make a responsible effort to resolve the conflict in a manner that is consistent with the values, principles, and standards expressed in this code. If a reasonable resolution of the conflict does not appear possible, social workers should seek proper consultation before making a decision.

This code of ethics is to be used by NASW and by other individuals, agencies, organizations, and bodies (such as licensing and regulatory boards, professional liability insurance providers, courts of law, agency boards of directors, government agencies, and other professional groups) that choose to adopt it or use it as a frame of reference. Alleged violation of standards in this code does not automatically imply legal liability or violation of the law. Such determination can only be made in the context of legal and judicial proceedings. Alleged violations of the Code would be subject to a peer review process. Such processes are generally separate from legal or administrative procedures and insulated from legal review or proceedings in order to allow the profession to counsel and/or discipline its own members.

A code of ethics cannot guarantee ethical behavior. Moreover, a code of ethics cannot resolve all ethical issues or disputes, or capture the richness and complexity involved in striving to make responsible choices within a moral community. Rather a code of ethics sets forth values, ethical principles and ethical standards to which professionals aspire and by which their actions can be judged. Social workers' ethical behavior should result from their personal commitment to engage in ethical practice. This code reflects the commitment of all social workers to uphold the profession's values and to act ethically. Principles and standards must be applied by individuals of good character who discern moral questions and, in good faith, seek to make reliable ethical judgments.

Ethical principles

The following broad ethical principles are based on social work's core values of service, social justice, dignity and worth of the person, importance of human relationships, integrity, and competence. These principles set forth ideals to which all social workers should aspire.

VALUE: *Service*

Ethical Principle: *Social workers' primary goal is to help people in need and to address social problems.*

Social workers elevate service to others above self-interest. Social workers draw on their knowledge, values, and skills to help people in need and to address social problems. Social workers are encouraged to volunteer some portion of their professional skills with no expectation of significant financial return (pro bono service).

VALUE: *Social Justice*

Ethical Principle: *Social workers challenge social injustice.*

Social workers pursue social change, particularly with and on behalf of vulnerable and oppressed individuals and groups of people. Social workers' social change efforts are focused primarily on issues of poverty, unemployment, discrimination, and other forms of social injustice. These activities seek to promote sensitivity to and knowledge about oppression, and cultural and ethnic diversity. Social workers strive to ensure equality of opportunity, access to needed information, services, resources, and meaningful participation in decision making for all people.

VALUE: *Dignity and Worth of the Person*

Ethical Principle: *Social workers respect the inherent dignity and worth of the person.*

Social workers treat each person in a caring and respectful fashion, mindful of individual differences and cultural and ethnic diversity. Social workers promote clients' socially responsible self-determination. Social workers seek to enhance clients' capacity and opportunity to change and to address their own needs. Social workers are cognizant of their dual responsibility to clients and to the broader society. They seek to resolve conflicts between clients' and the broader society's interests in a socially responsible manner consistent with the values, ethical principles, and ethical standards of the profession.

VALUE: *Importance of Human Relationships*

Ethical Principle: *Social workers recognize the central importance of human relationships.*

Social workers understand that relationships between and among people are an important vehicle for change. Social workers engage people as partners in the helping process. Social workers seek to strengthen relationships among people in a purposeful effort to promote, restore, maintain, and enhance the well-being of individuals, families, social groups, organizations, and communities.

VALUE: *Integrity*

Ethical Principle: *Social workers behave in a trustworthy manner.*

Social workers are continually aware of the profession's mission, values, ethical principles, and ethical standards, and practice in a manner consistent with them. Social workers act honestly and responsibly and promote ethical practices on the part of the organizations with which they are affiliated.

VALUE: *Competence*

Ethical Principle: *Social workers practice within their areas of competence and develop and enhance their professional expertise.*

Social workers continually strive to increase their professional knowledge and skills and to apply them in practice. Social workers should aspire to contribute to the knowledge base of the profession.

Source: Frederick Reamer, Rhode Island College. Draft for submission to NASW 1996 Delegate Assembly.

examination are designated "licensed master social workers" (LMSWs). LMSWs who complete 2 years of supervised clinical practice and pass an additional test are designated "licensed clinical social workers" (LCSWs).

Certification is *an official assurance by government or a professional association that a person has attained a specified level of knowledge and skill.* Certification does not usually prevent uncertified persons from practicing specific behavior, but does prevent them from using the title and the designation "certified" (Barker, 1991:32). In states in which psychologists are certified, for example, persons without certification may not use the title "psychologist" or "certified psychologist." However, since only the title is protected, anyone can do what psychologists do, as long as they do not call themselves psychologists. Similarly, the National Association of Social Workers provides certification through the Academy of Certified Social Workers (ACSW). Social workers who have earned a masters degree (MSW), have completed at least 2 years of post-MSW employment supervised by an ACSW social worker, have passed the ACSW examination, are members of the National Association of Social Workers, and pay an annual fee may use the letters ACSW after their names.

Registration, the least stringent form of regulation, involves *listing in a professional registry those persons who have met qualifying criteria such as level of education and duration of supervised practice* (Barker, 1991:198).

By 1993, social work licensing, certification, or registration laws were in effect in every state and the District of Columbia (U.S. Department of Labor, 1994).

Society grants professions considerable autonomy, in part because of their commitment to helping and to high standards of competence and ethical behavior. However, as we all know, professionals are not perfect. They, too, sometimes make mistakes. When this occurs, they may be sued, providing clients with a type of protection and society with a limited form of control. For the most part, though, professions regulate their own behavior.

4 Professions have their own associations. Professional associations provide their members with a source of professional identity. They do so by providing a variety of services aimed at promoting professional growth and strengthening a sense of professionalism among their members. Most professional associations publish journals to disseminate research findings, set standards for professional education programs, lobby on behalf of the profession's interests in the political arena, and develop and implement a code of ethics. In addition, they may offer professional liability insurance, publish newsletters or other informal publications that focus on professional issues and news of the profession, and even offer study trips designed to contribute to professional enrichment.

Professional associations promote and protect the interests of their members and their clients. Association activities include political action, legislative lobbying, influencing administrative regulations, and developing internal procedures for regulating professional practice.

To summarize briefly, we have seen that a profession has four distinctive characteristics: a specialized knowledge and skill base, a code of ethics that includes a commitment to service, a considerable degree of autonomy that includes self-regulation, and a professional association. Now let's look at some of the major helping professions. Each has all of the characteristics of a profession as described above, and each provides particular kinds of social welfare services.

MAJOR HELPING PROFESSIONS

There are many helping professions and many possible ways to classify them. We examine the following professions: social work, physical health, mental health, education, and law. Together these groups provide the majority of the workers involved in the delivery of social welfare services.

Although they are highly diverse in function and make up, these professions share the common goal of improving the functioning of individuals and social institutions. While each group performs a particular specialized function or set of functions, their members are often called on to work together in order to help people effectively. Similarly, they often cooperate in efforts to improve the social welfare institution through the political process. Nevertheless, disputes sometimes arise over territorial boundaries, especially those concerning which profession should provide certain kinds of services to particular groups of people.

Social Work

The profession that is most closely identified with social welfare is social work. Social workers attempt to enhance human well-being and to alleviate personal distress, interpersonal conflicts, poverty, and oppression. According to the Council on Social Work Education (1992), social work has four related purposes:

1 "The promotion, restoration, maintenance, and enhancement of the social functioning of individuals, families, groups, organizations, and communities by helping them to accomplish tasks, prevent and alleviate distress, and use resources."

2 "The planning, formulation, and implementation of social policies, services, resources, and programs needed to meet basic human needs and support the development of human capacities."

3 "The pursuit of policies, services, resources, and programs through organizational or administrative advocacy and social or political action, so as to empower groups at risk and promote social and economic justice."

4 "The development and testing of professional knowledge and skills related to these purposes."

Thus, social workers help people ameliorate and prevent social problems and human suffering, enhance personal satisfaction and well-being, and change social conditions that adversely affect individuals, groups, organizations, and communities. Social workers respond to human needs and problems from birth to death. (See "The Human Face of Social Welfare 19: Keeping Families Intact.")

Social workers practice in a wide range of settings—in preschools, homes for the elderly, schools, legislatures, hospitals and clinics, group homes and halfway houses, settlement houses and community centers, private agencies such as Big Brothers and Big Sisters, public departments of human services, prisons and reformatories, grass-roots social change organizations and social policy think-tanks, trade unions and employee assistance programs, and many more. Some social workers are self-employed, preferring to set up their own private practice in a manner similar to many physicians and lawyers.

Within these settings social workers carry out a wide range of activities, roles, and responsibilities. Baccalaureate social work (BSW) education provides preparation for generalist practice. Master's-level (MSW) education prepares graduates "for advanced social work practice in an area of concentration." BSW and MSW education differ in their depth, breadth, and specificity of knowledge and skill

THE HUMAN FACE OF SOCIAL WELFARE 19

KEEPING FAMILIES INTACT

This account describes a day in the life of an African American social worker employed by a private, nonprofit agency in New York City. It portrays the mixture of challenge, frustration, and satisfaction experienced by social workers everywhere.

He cannot console the girl whose mother is dying of AIDS, or promise the frightened young woman that her boyfriend will not hit her again. He cannot replace the father who was murdered, or comfort a child late at night, when the gunfire starts.

But on a good day, Carlos Scott can offer a family hope.

Mr. Scott is a social worker at the Children's Aid Society, one of the largest social welfare agencies in New York. . . . Although his field is preventive services, he fights problems that have plagued poor families for centuries: domestic violence, drug abuse, illness and emotional distress.

For some, he fills in for an absent relative, offering guidance and support. . . . His goal is unchanging: keeping families intact in the face of poverty and despair.

He visits schools, courtrooms, hospitals and homes. . . . Crises are common, and he sometimes works into the night, finding a battered woman a space in a shelter or taking a child to the emergency room.

This article chronicles a typical day in Mr. Scott's career.

9 A.M. Mr. Scott leaves his Brooklyn apartment and travels by subway and bus to Manhattan Children's Psychiatric Center. . . . En route, he studies a tattered set of index cards with information about his clients. . . .

10:15 A.M. Mr. Scott is ready to see a 12-year-old boy he has counseled since 1990. But the therapist is running late. . . . He pulls out the worn notebook where he records the details of every meeting and phone call. Later, he will copy his daily notes onto legal paper and file them as official records.

11 A.M. The therapist and client arrive and meet with Mr. Scott for 30 minutes. He placed the boy in the psychiatric hospital because of violent behavior. . . .

"I wanted to get him into a stable environment and on medication, then continue to act as an authority figure," Mr. Scott said. "The idea is to help him become a productive member of society."

Soon, the boy will leave the center for a group home, and Mr. Scott visits weekly to monitor his behavior and prepare him for the transition. . . .

1 P.M. After wolfing down a granola bar and updating his supervisor, Mr. Scott supervises a visitation between a woman and her teenage son. The woman has maintained a relationship with an abusive boyfriend. . . .

One recent night, after the man attacked the mother, Mr. Scott insisted that she enter a domestic violence shelter. Meanwhile, he placed her three children in foster care. . . .

(Council on Social Work Education, 1992). BSW social workers usually function as brokers, enablers, educators, mediators, and advocates (Compton and Galaway, 1989), but they may work also as community organizers, case managers, researchers, and policy analysts. MSW social workers carry out these roles, too, but often are more specialized, functioning in addition as clinicians, consultants, supervisors, and administrators.

Social workers view people and their environment as integrally intertwined and interactive. Therefore, social workers not only work with individuals toward personal change, they also share a commitment to working for changes in institutions and society. The underlying purpose of all social work practice is to release human

2:15 P.M. The visitation is interrupted by a phone call. A city caseworker wants Mr. Scott to make an emergency visit to one of his families. . . . He arranges to meet the mother at [a school] where he has an office. "When you're dealing with volatile issues, it's best to meet on neutral ground," he says. He cancels his next appointment. . . . And then he is off.

3 P.M. On the express train . . . Mr. Scott concocts a strategy for the intervention. Caution is a must: in four years on the job, he has suffered many threats and often found himself in harrowing situations. . . .

4:45 P.M. Mr. Scott has talked with the mother, who swears that her children are safe. He walks her home to check on the children and make sure the boyfriend leaves. Today he is lucky—the man departs without incident. . . .

5:30 P.M. For his last appointment, Mr. Scott makes a home visit. . . . He has counseled the mother, a Dominican immigrant, since her husband developed a genetic disease and had to be placed in a nursing home. . . .

When Mr. Scott arrives, the youngest girl leaps into his arms. The brothers hover nearby, treating him like a beloved uncle. Home visits give social workers a chance to examine the family up close. And they also offer a rare opportunity for laughter and relaxed conversation.

He asks about the children's grades and compliments the older girl's braids. The boy beckons him to another room for a private chat about shaving. . . .

7 P.M. As the A train rockets from Washington Heights to Brooklyn, Mr. Scott mulls over the day's events. His last meal was 12 hours ago, but food is far from his mind. This is the best time to reflect on each family's problems and contemplate solutions.

If there are no urgent messages waiting, he can look forward to a quiet evening with his notebook. But after keeping a professional composure all day, nights are often wrought with emotion.

"Sometimes when you get home, your feelings come rushing in," he said. "But you have to put them away before you face another day."

Mr. Scott is a dedicated social worker, deeply concerned about the well-being of the families with whom he works. Nevertheless, he runs the risk of "burnout" by apparently devoting his life exclusively to his social work. In order to maintain their ability to work over the long run, social workers and other social welfare professionals need consciously to develop interests, activities, and associations that are not related to their jobs. Celebration of the strengths and successes of their clients, as reflected in Mr. Scott's final visit of the day, is another important way in which social workers can "keep their batteries charged" and avoid burnout.

power in individuals for personal fulfillment and social good, and to release social power for the creation of the kinds of society, social institutions, and social policies which make self-realization most possible for all individuals. Two values which are primary in such purposes are respect for the worth and dignity of every individual and concern that all individuals have the opportunity to realize their potential as individually fulfilled, socially contributing persons (paraphrased from Khinduka, 1987).

Thus, the profession of social work requires practitioners who are flexible, socially and politically aware, self-motivated, eager to learn over a lifetime, desirous of personal growth, altruistic, comfortable with ambiguity, and interested in changing social conditions that are adverse to healthy human development, self-determination, and social justice (University of Maine School of Social Work, 1995).

Social work's generalist approach to the delivery of helping services has three distinctive characteristics.

1 An emphasis on problem solving. Social workers employ a systematic problem-solving process in carrying out their work. Consisting of a series of steps, problem solving begins by involving the prospective user in the helping process, moves on to an assessment of needs and resources, and then to the development of a plan—based on the person's strengths—for resolving the problem. The plan is then implemented and the results evaluated, after which the helping relationship either ends or new plans are developed as necessary.

2 A systems focus. People participate in groups of many kinds and sizes—families, friendship groups, communities, organizations, bureaucracies, and social institutions—all of which may be viewed as systems. All of these systems affect the conditions under which people live and their responses to the social and physical environment. Social workers consider these various systems in their assessment, planning, and intervention-related activities, so that the problem-solving process takes into account all relevant resources and obstacles. This *focus on the many groups in which people participate, and the ways in which these groups affect people's lives,* is called a **systems approach.**

3 An awareness of human diversity. Social workers work with many kinds of people, who differ with regard to gender, age, race, ethnicity, culture, sexual orientation, physical and mental abilities, socioeconomic status, education, religion, and so on. Social workers are trained to respect, understand, and make use of these distinctive characteristics in the problem-solving process. Because social workers work with all kinds of people, they are themselves sometimes stigmatized because of the low status of many of the people to whom they provide services—a group that includes the poor, substance abusers, unwed mothers, abusive adults, and members of oppressed groups.

According to government figures, there were approximately 484,000 social workers employed in the United States in 1992. Through the year 2005, social work jobs are projected to increase more rapidly than the average for all occupations. Social work salaries vary widely. According to a 1992 NASW membership survey, the median income for social workers with BSW degrees was $20,000, and the median income for those with MSW degrees was $30,000. A 1993 study of hospital social workers reported salaries ranging from $25,600 to $38,700. In the same year, federal government social workers averaged $41,400 (U.S. Department of Labor, 1994:136–137).

Physical Health

There are many kinds of physical health professionals. In 1992, the largest such groups in the United States were registered nurses (1,835,000), licensed practical nurses (659,000), and physicians (556,000) (U.S. Department of Labor, 1994).

**THE STATUS OF SOCIAL WORK:
A FOUR-COUNTRY COMPARISON**

The four nations that we have been using for comparative purposes in this book—the United States, Mexico,
Poland, and Sweden—share some interesting similarities in the status of social workers.

Most social workers in the four countries are
women. Relative to the standards of their respective
societies, they receive modest salaries, and many feel
that they are relatively powerless to influence social policy. In spite of varying degrees of formal commitment to
equality for women within their societies, many also feel
that their low pay and lack of power reflects lingering
sexism. Many social workers in all four societies also
believe that human values are considered less important than economic issues by those in power.

There are, however, also differences in the beliefs of
social workers in these four countries as to why members of their profession are not more highly valued and
better rewarded. In general, professions which serve
impoverished, politically weak, and disenfranchised
people tend to be devalued. Social workers in Mexico
and Poland tend to cite the presence of a certain
degree of political repression as the likely explanation.
Social workers in the United States are more likely to
blame their profession's lack of status on the conflict

between capitalist and humanitarian values. Sweden
seems to suffer from an ambiguous stance toward
social work. On one hand, the value of social work to
individuals and the society as a whole is widely recognized. On the other hand, there is a certain resentment
of the high cost of the social welfare system. This
ambivalence seems to translate into relatively low pres-
tige and income for social workers. Also, when poor and
oppressed people with whom they work and identify are
"kicked," social workers also feel the pain.

The United States offers both baccalaureate and
graduate-level training for social workers. Social work
training in Sweden and Mexico is carried out primarily
at the baccalaureate level, although a few graduate programs also exist. Most social work practitioners in
Poland receive their training through 2-year technical
programs, equivalent to the U.S. associate degree.
Compared to the U.S. curriculum, social work programs
in Mexico, Poland, and Sweden include more time in
agency-based field practica and more classroom
emphasis on the impact of political and economic
systems on social welfare. Private practice by social
workers is virtually unknown in these three countries.

Sources: Personal interviews and observations of Ron
Federico, 1987, and of Bill Whitaker, 1994 and 1995.

Other important groups of health professionals include physician assistants, para-
medics, audiologists and speech pathologists, nutritionists and dieticians, physical
and occupational therapists, dentists, optometrists, and podiatrists.

Registered Nurses   *Registered nurses* (RNs) "care for the sick and the injured
and help people stay well." They "observe, assess, and record symptoms, reactions, and progress; assist physicians during treatments and examinations; administer medications; and assist in convalescence and rehabilitation." RNs may be
hospital nurses, nursing-home nurses, public-health nurses, private-duty nurses,
office nurses, occupational-health nurses, and supervisory nurses. There are three
educational routes terminating in the RN credential: 2-year associate degree programs, 4- or 5-year bachelor of science programs, and 2- or 3-year hospital-based
diploma programs (U.S. Department of Labor, 1994:175–177).

Full-time salaried RNs earned median incomes of $34,424 in 1992. The median
income of staff nurses was $33,278, of supervisory nurses $47,335, and of nurse
anesthetists $66,622. Job opportunities for RNs are projected to increase much
faster than the average of all occupations through 2005 (U.S. Department of
Labor, 1994:175–177).

Licensed Practical Nurses *Licensed practical nurses* (LPNs) provide nursing care under the direction of physicians and RNs. LPNs provide basic bedside care, observe patients and report adverse reactions to medications or treatments, help deliver and care for infants, develop care plans, supervise nurses aides, and carry out clerical duties. LPNs must pass an examination after completing a 1-year, state-approved practical nursing program (U.S. Department of Labor, 1994:211–112).

Full-time, salaried LPNs earned median incomes of $21,476 in 1992. Average salaries ranged from less than $15,392 to more than $31,668. Long-term health-care needs of increasing numbers of very old people are expected to generate expanding job opportunities for LPNs through 2005 (U.S. Department of Labor, 1994:211–112).

Physicians There are two basic types of physicians, MDs or *allopathic physicians* and DOs or *osteopathic physicians.* Both MDs and DOs function as primary-care physicians, the first health professionals usually consulted by patients. Primary-care physicians include pediatricians, general and family practitioners, and general internists. DOs emphasize the contribution to good health of the alignment of bones, muscles, ligaments, and nerves. MDs often specialize in fields such as cardiology, oncology, neurology, ophthalmology, gynecology, pediatrics, and surgery (U.S. Department of Labor, 1994:161–163).

Physicians are the highest-paid health professionals. According to the American Medical Association, in 1991 MDs earned median net salaries of $139,000 and averaged $170,600 each. General and family practice physicians averaged $98,000, obstetricians $200,000, and radiologists $223,000 per year. Employment opportunities for physicians are expected to increase faster than the average for all occupations through the year 2005 (U.S. Department of Labor, 1994:161–163).

One result of specialization in the medical profession is that nurses and family practitioners often function as case managers. In some cases, however, this function is performed by social workers who cooperate with medical professionals to oversee the delivery of a comprehensive physical health care plan.

The increase in **health maintenance organizations (HMOs),** *organizations that provide comprehensive medical care for a set, prepaid fee,* has tended to bring large numbers of medical personnel under corporate umbrellas, where their salaries are generally less than in private practice.

Poland and Sweden provide free or low-cost medical care to their citizens. This is true, too, in Mexico, although a much smaller proportion of the Mexican population receives such benefits. Medical professionals in these societies are generally less well paid than in the United States, where most medical care is provided on a for-profit basis. In societies that offer free or low-cost medical care, there is often a two-tier health-care system consisting of the public system and a much more costly private system. In such cases, medical professionals in private practice are likely to earn far more, and the quality of private care is thought to be better. Generally speaking, although medicine tends everywhere to be a highly regarded

TABLE 9-1   ACTIVITIES OF MENTAL HEALTH PROFESSIONALS

Diagnosis and evaluation of mental illness	Supervision of mental health aides
Individual and group therapy	Behavior modification
Testing and measurement of psychological functioning	Case management
Care in mental hospitals and mental health clinics	Community mental health education
Family and marital therapy	Consultation
Predischarge planning and postrelease follow-up	In-service training
Counseling	Life-long learning

profession, its status is less high in those societies where the public health-care system predominates than in those with a primarily private system of health care.

Mental Health

Four professions specialize in providing help to people with psychological needs: *psychology, psychiatry, psychiatric/mental health nursing,* and *clinical social work. Psychiatric/mental health nursing* and *clinical social work* are specialties within the larger nursing and social work professions discussed previously. *Psychiatry* is a branch of medicine, and psychiatrists have medical as well as mental health training. As a result, they can prescribe medicine, whereas other mental-health professionals cannot. In 1992, there were in the United States about 144,000 psychologists, 31,000 psychiatrists, and 12,500 psychiatric/mental health nurses. There were about 20,000 clinical social workers holding Diplomate certificates recognizing "clinical experience and advanced training and supervision beyond the master's level" (U.S. Department of Labor, 1994; American Psychological Association, 1995; Swenson, 1995). The wide range of activities carried out by mental health professionals is outlined in Table 9-1.

Psychologists   Psychologists are scientist/practitioners who study human behavior and apply their research findings to attempts to reduce individual psychological suffering and to improve overall societal conditions. Roles played by psychologists include "researcher, educator, diagnostician, therapist, supervisor, consultant, administrator, social interventionist, and expert witness." Graduate training typically consists of 5 years beyond completion of undergraduate education and culminates in the PhD degree. Major skills of practicing psychologists include psychodiagnosis, psychological assessment, and psychological intervention. Although some psychologists practice in hospital settings, most work on an outpatient basis. The practice of psychology is regulated in each state and the District of Columbia (American Psychological Association, 1995:14–23).

In 1991, psychologists with PhD degrees earned median salaries ranging from $48,000 in counseling psychology to $76,000 in industrial psychology. Median salaries for psychologists with master's degrees ranged from $37,000 in counseling psychology to $53,000 in school psychology. Starting salaries for bachelor's-level psychologists averaged about $18,300 in 1993. Job opportunities through 2005 are expected to grow strongly for PhD psychologists, to be highly competitive for master's-level psychologists, and minimal for bachelor's-level psychologists (U.S. Department of Labor, 1994:124–126).

Psychologists, psychiatrists, psychiatric/mental health nurses, and clinical social workers often work collaboratively. Although many mental health professionals are employed in mental hospitals and mental health centers, many others are employed in private practice. Psychologists or social workers who have private practices may have a professional relationship with a psychiatrist, who helps with diagnoses, prescribes medication when needed, and provides consultation.

Education

Teachers are by far the largest professional group in the field of education. In 1992, there were more than 4 million kindergarten, primary, secondary, and post-secondary teachers in the United States. They included about 358,000 special education teachers trained to work with students with disabilities and special learning needs. There were also about 351,000 education administrators and nearly 108,000 educational and vocational counselors. In addition, a large number of paraprofessionals work as teacher's aides and child-care workers (U.S. Department of Labor, 1994).

Some teachers specialize in a particular subject area or the learning needs of particular students. At the secondary and higher levels, teachers usually have specialized training in their subject areas. Other teachers are trained to work with special populations, such as children with developmental disabilities, emotional disturbances, or autism.

Schools today are paying increasing attention to students' emotional well-being as well as their academic achievement. Schools are responding to growing numbers of two-income, single-parent, and teen-parent families by providing services such as child care, family resource centers, parenting classes, and social service referrals. They are collaborating with other organizations to counter increases in crime, drug and alcohol abuse, and sexually transmitted disease among students (U.S. Department of Labor, 1994).

Teachers generally have to have state or local certification to hold regular teaching positions. Pay scales vary tremendously, in part because most teachers are employed by local school districts. In 1992–1993, earnings of public secondary school teachers averaged about $36,000 a year, while public elementary school teachers averaged about $34,800. Special education teachers earned comparable salaries. In general, teachers in higher education earn more than their elementary or secondary-level counterparts, but this is not always true. The job outlook for kindergarten, elementary, and secondary school teachers is good through 2005. Dramatic growth is projected in the number of jobs in special education (U.S. Department of Labor, 1994).

Education provides a good example of the continuum of professionalism. Many of those who teach are not trained as teachers. For example, many in-service, community education, and art courses are taught by people who are experts or practitioners in the subject area but have not been trained as teachers. The need for professional qualifications and certification is, in fact, sometimes challenged by those who lack such credentials but are employed in a teaching capacity. This can pose a problem for the profession.

This is particularly likely to occur when nonprofessionals employed in a teaching capacity perform poorly. In such cases, the public at large may fail to recognize that the individual involved is not a trained teacher, with the result that his or her poor performance has an adverse effect on people's opinion of the education profession. It is the desire to prevent situations of this sort that explains why professions are often so protective of their title, functions, and training procedures.

Law

Many people would probably not consider the law a helping profession. Certainly the commercial transactions that account for a significant proportion of the profession's activities are often largely unrelated to social welfare. Nonetheless, the law helps people to meet their needs in a variety of important ways. Lawyers and judges make important contributions to social well-being in such areas as civil rights, consumer protection, child welfare, and the enforcement of legal contracts affecting families and individuals.

Lawyers and *judges* dominate the legal profession. In 1992, there were about 626,000 lawyers and 90,000 judges in the United States (U.S. Department of Labor, 1994:114–117). Attorneys work in a variety of settings, including government agencies, private practice, and legal aid offices that provide free or low-cost legal help to those unable to afford a lawyer. Judges apply the law as they preside over the public and administrative court systems. As such, they are invariably public officials, but the majority are appointed rather than elected to office.

The salary of attorneys employed in the private sector is likely to be much higher than that of their counterparts in government or legal aid work. Starting salaries for attorneys in private industry averaged about $36,600 in 1992, while their most experienced colleagues averaged more than $134,000 and senior partners in top law firms received over $1 million annually. Those employed in the public sector earn much less. (See "The Human Face of Social Welfare 20: A Do-Gooder Lawyer.") In 1993, salaries of state-level judges ranged from about $62,500 to $121,000, averaging about $89,500. Full-time federal administrative judges averaged $94,800. It is projected that numbers of trained lawyers in excess of the available jobs will result in stiff competition for jobs through 2005 (U.S. Department of Labor, 1994:117).

The wide range of activities open to lawyers means that involvement in helping people is very much a matter of individual choice. Attorneys are generally free to choose an area of practice, with available choices ranging from work in a legal aid

THE HUMAN FACE OF SOCIAL WELFARE 20

A DO-GOODER LAWYER

The following account is by a father who is reminiscing about his son's career as an attorney. It captures the social welfare dimensions of the law profession, as well as some of the societal ambivalence about doing good versus being economically successful.

[Talking about his son, this father begins] Frankly, I despaired when he turned down a $66,000 job with a Wall Street law firm—that's what they were paying highly ranked law-school graduates in June of 1986. Chris chose instead to work for the Legal Aid Society's Office for the Aging. . . .

I suppose other fathers of sons who have chosen to do good instead of well can understand my concern. I paid $80,000 for his undergraduate and graduate education (he still has $10,000 in student loans to repay). And the rejection of a high-salaried job seemed to me, a man born in the Depression year of 1934, an affront to common sense. Add to that my dislike of the idea of government helping community groups sue the government. . . .

Chris spends an enormous amount of his time in . . . housing court, a place a reporter once described as seething with anger, potential violence and marginally ill people. . . . It is hardly a place where his clients would stand a chance without a smart, dedicated and well-trained advocate. . . .

[The father then describes a typical work situation encountered by his son.] Back at his office, Chris found a message to call another client, who told the secretary she couldn't remember her own phone number. At that moment, my son says, he envied a female acquaintance who took a job like the one he turned down. It wasn't the work she described; she hates it. And it wasn't the money; he says he gets along just fine on $29,749. But he figured that her clients . . . know their own phone numbers. That flash of regret passed and he looked up his new client's phone number. . . .

I have always admired the dedication of people who stand at the edge, where society's fabric is in constant danger of unraveling. I understood them to be big-city policemen. I now know them to be Legal Aid attorneys as well.

Excerpted from James Lamb, Jr., "My Son, the Do-Gooder," *Newsweek,* November 16, 1987, pp. 14–15. Copyright © 1987, Newsweek, Inc. All rights reserved. Reprinted by permission.

agency through corporate law. Whatever their area of practice, attorneys are subject to professional standards. However, whereas the legal aid attorney clearly contributes to social welfare, the corporate attorney generally does not.

Similar choices exist in the other professions. In selecting an area of practice, doctors can choose to serve those with low and moderate incomes or to enter an area of practice such as cosmetic surgery, where their primary clientele is the very wealthy. The medical profession, like the law, encompasses a range of activities, some of which are related directly to social welfare goals and others of which are not. For members of most of the professions we have described, involvement with the social welfare institution is a matter of individual choice rather than professional mandate.

THE ROLE OF THE PARAPROFESSIONAL

Not all of the people who work in social welfare are professionals. Many are paraprofessionals. A **paraprofessional** is *a person with specialized knowledge and technical training who works under the supervision of a professional and* *carries out tasks formerly performed by the professional* (Barker, 1991:167). Among the types of paraprofessionals in social welfare are mental health technicians, health aides, social work aides, substance abuse counselors, recreational therapists, and teacher's aides. Paraprofessionals perform important service-delivery activities, but usually have not had the training required for professional certification or licensing.

The manner in which paraprofessionals are sometimes used in social welfare has raised issues of sexism and racism. Many paraprofessionals are minority women, for whom professional education has been an unrealistic goal given their economic resources and life situation. Lacking professional status, they are less well paid. Often their positions are among the first to be eliminated during budgetary cutbacks. In addition, the pattern of generally white, often male, professionals supervising minority women has seemed all too representative of discriminatory social patterns in the larger society.

As a result, some schools have developed programs designed to help talented paraprofessionals obtain additional training. The most common such programs are the 2-year Human Service Programs that offer an associate's degree. For many workers, these programs have served as a stepping stone to baccalaureate and graduate-level training in one of the social welfare professions.

Declassification

The availability of a growing workforce of skilled paraprofessionals has presented a temptation to declassify positions in social agencies suffering from budget cutbacks. **Declassification** is *the practice of reducing the amount of education and experience required for performing a job* (Barker, 1991:57). By declassifying positions that had heretofore been held by professionals, and then hiring paraprofessionals to fill these positions, public agencies could both respond to political pressure from paraprofessional groups and save on salaries.

Declassification itself is not necessarily undesirable. It becomes so when the qualifications required for a particular position are determined by the desire to save money or respond to political pressure rather than by a careful analysis of the tasks to be accomplished. Some tasks are appropriate for paraprofessionals, some for entry-level professionals, and others for more experienced professionals. Ensuring that the qualifications established for each position within a given agency or organization are appropriate to the tasks to be performed is an important goal in social work and education.

OTHER PEOPLE WHO DELIVER SOCIAL WELFARE SERVICES

Having looked at the structure of several major helping professions, let's turn to others who are involved in helping people. We have seen at many points in this book that not all social welfare services are provided by professionals. Among the nonprofessionals who are important to the delivery of helping services are those involved in natural helping networks and volunteers.

Natural Helping Networks

As you already know, natural helping networks are comprised of people who help others in the course of their day-to-day activities. Family members, friends, colleagues at work, and neighbors are often part of such networks. Sometimes the help provided is purely spontaneous, as when a neighbor offers to babysit so that you can respond to an unexpected situation. Other such helping efforts are more planned. Neighbors may form a carpool to transport children to and from school, or people who work together may form a support group to discuss work- or family-related stresses.

Natural helping networks result from the interpersonal bonds formed among small groups of people due to common family ties, shared interests, or a sense of community. The efforts of those involved are frequently not viewed as part of a helping network but rather as simply part of being a good neighbor or a good friend. The desire to help in such cases arises from a personal commitment to people one likes and cares about, not necessarily from a larger sense of societal obligation. Within such networks there is often a sense of mutual responsibility; those providing help often believe that others would in turn help them if the need arose.

As countries modernize and urbanize, there is a tendency to replace reliance on natural helping networks with reliance on more formal social welfare activities. Some persons in the United States decry the loss of community that seems to be occurring as a consequence. Sweden and Poland appear to be doing a better job of balancing the relationship between formal social welfare activities and informal helping networks. In Mexico, as is the case in many emerging economies in which formal social welfare structures are in early stages of development, natural helping networks continue to play a major role for large parts of the population. In both industrialized and industrializing nations, natural helping networks are vital to successful daily living for many people and help maintain a sense of societal cohesion and mutual responsibility.

Volunteers

Volunteerism is *"the mobilization and utilization of unpaid individuals and groups to provide human services outside the auspices of government agencies"* (Barker, 1991:249). Volunteers perform a more formal helping role than that of natural helping networks, because they usually work within some type of organized social welfare program. The program itself can be fairly loosely structured, such as a church-run soup kitchen. But inherent in the volunteer role is a formal commitment to perform certain functions at certain times within some organized structure.

Some social welfare agencies rely very heavily on volunteers. The Red Cross, for example, uses more than 1.4 million volunteers nationwide in such settings as community health clinics, child-care centers, and hospitals, during blood drives, in disaster situations, and others (American Red Cross, 1984:9). The volunteers are trained and perform under the supervision of social welfare professionals. Their contribution is an important one. Without the help of volunteers, the Red Cross could not provide the services it does.

Volunteering, then, is a second level of personal helping. It is more formal than the helping in natural helping networks. It is also linked more directly to a larger sense of responsibility for the well-being of others than is participation in a natural helping network, since volunteers often help people they are unlikely to know on a personal basis.

Cooperation between Professionals and Others

Professionals and nonprofessionals work together in many social welfare programs. An excellent example of such a program is Elderplan, a nonprofit experimental program to help the elderly remain independent as long as possible (Freudenheim, 1986). Similar in function to a health maintenance organization, Elderplan provides both social and medical services. Its purpose is to provide health, mental health, and personal-care services that supplement those provided by the elderly person's natural helping network of family and friends. The program is designed to work in conjunction with the natural helping network, stepping in only to assist with needs that exceed the network's resources.

Ideally, the Elderplan pattern would be the norm in social welfare programs; the efforts of professionals would be designed to complement the natural helping network and the work of volunteers (Miller, 1985). This is not always easy. In some cases, it can be difficult for professionals to identify the members of the client's natural helping network. Some natural helpers may be reluctant to become involved with professionals. Professionals may frighten them, and they may not think of their own activity as "helping." The amount of time and effort required to identify and make contact with these people may strain the resources of often overworked professionals.

Volunteers are generally more accessible and the results of working with them more predictable than reliance on natural helping networks. Even so, issues can arise. Unless they are adequately trained by the agency, volunteers may make mistakes that take time and effort to correct. Further, the task of figuring out how to help volunteers function effectively and make the best use of their skills is itself a time-consuming task.

In spite of these problems, the contributions to social welfare of each of the groups we have discussed—natural helping networks, volunteers, paraprofessionals, and professionals—are significant. Each has a special role to play. Natural helping networks are best suited to providing relatively limited types of help needed in daily situations. Volunteers provide a personal touch and valuable extra hands in often hard-pressed social welfare agencies. Paraprofessionals bring a special combination of skill, motivation, and life experience to the helping situation. Professionals have the special knowledge, skill, and commitment required to plan and deliver the services that make large-scale helping possible. Working together, each group strengthens society's commitment to interpersonal caring and helping activities.

FINDING A PLACE FOR YOURSELF IN SOCIAL WELFARE

The Responsibility for Helping

The extent of our responsibility for helping others is something each of us must decide for ourselves. That decision will, in turn, determine much of our behavior toward others. If we believe that we are responsible for others, we will be far more likely to attempt to help than we will if we believe other people should care for themselves. The choice is ours. Although it was clearly written from the point of view that people should feel a sense of responsibility for others, this book also reflects another basic social welfare value: People have the right to make their own decisions.

Opportunities to Help

If you are one of those who feel a responsibility to help others, you may wonder how you can act on your belief. People sometimes do not know how to go about helping others. Actually, opportunities to help surround us. They range from involvement with our own natural helping networks through the decision to enter a social welfare profession. Let's look a little more closely at this spectrum of opportunities.

Day-to-day situations in which we can be helpful abound. Remember that helping is not always written with a capital "H" and does not always involve a dramatic or life-threatening event. There are countless small opportunities to help others. Giving directions to a stranger, taking a moment to listen to someone who is momentarily frightened by the loss of her or his money, smiling at a friend who seems glum, or touching a family member to let him or her know you care are all examples of helping. To be sure, you may someday happen upon an automobile accident where you can aid someone who is seriously injured, but you are more likely to spend most of your days with people who are buffeted by the stresses of daily life. Reaching out to others in small ways is very much a part of helping.

We should also not overlook the fact that helping can be done by contributing money or other needed goods. Sometimes people believe that they are too busy, under too much pressure, or too shy to reach out to others personally. For such people, contributing to programs run by others is a useful and legitimate alternative to personal involvement. Community fund-raising efforts such as those of the United Way provide excellent opportunities to help in this way. Although the satisfactions involved are different from those provided by more personal helping, giving is a significant expression of one's commitment to the well-being of others. This sort of helping is exemplified by the establishment of the Olga Tamayo House in Cuernavaca, Mexico. (See "On the Street in Cuernavaca.")

Many people prefer to focus their helping activities on those to whom they feel a special commitment. Family members may devote extraordinary time and energy to the care of a child with physical or mental limitations, for example. These efforts may include involvement with support groups run for parents of children with special problems, fund-raising activities to support research or expanded services, and activities run by social agencies for children like theirs.

ON THE STREET IN CUERNAVACA— THE OLGA TAMAYO NURSING HOME

Tucked in the shadow of a large hospital in a busy section of Cuernavaca, Mexico, is a one-story, modern, white building. The Olga Tamayo Nursing Home is an interesting example of how one person can contribute to the well-being of others through a financial contribution.

The nursing home was built with money donated by Mexican artist Rufino Tamayo, famous for his public murals depicting historical themes connected with the country's Indigenous heritage and its Revolution. Tamayo's money created the facility, which is named in honor of his wife, and the government now runs it. It is part of the social welfare structure available to government workers or, in the case of the Olga Tamayo Nursing Home, retired government employees.

What the artist's donation made possible is a lovely facility serving 55 residential elderly people and 16 day

users. It has a staff of 125, and provides comprehensive services to meet the needs of its residents—housing, medical care, therapy, recreation, and so on. Residents share double rooms, each with its own patio and small garden. The public areas include a spacious and airy dining room, lounges, and a large auditorium. In addition, there are facilities for medical care and therapy. The Olga Tamayo Nursing Home is located in an area where the elderly can walk to shopping if they wish.

Mexico's economic difficulties have limited the public sector's ability to meet the nation's social welfare needs. In such an environment, initiatives by private citizens, such as Rufino Tamayo, provide resources that would otherwise be unavailable. Although the needs of many Mexicans remain unmet, such contributions are nonetheless beneficial to the social welfare system.

Source: Personal interviews and observations of Ron Federico, 1987.

A similar pattern of involvement is often found among groups whose members share a characteristic that makes them a target of discrimination. Some African Americans are particularly active in efforts to help other blacks, while gay and lesbian people may be especially attracted to activities designed to help members of their own group. This kind of group cohesiveness has historically been an important impetus for the development of social welfare services.

Another possible avenue for involvement with social welfare is to advocate for people's rights. Often this begins with increased self-awareness and greater personal strength. For example, it has been difficult to get men and women to understand how sexism affects their own lives. Once understood, it is not easy for many people to develop the strength to refuse being treated in a sexist manner. However, it is the cumulative effect of people standing up for their rights that increases the likelihood of social change. The civil rights movement illustrated this in a powerful way. Since respecting people's rights is so basic to social welfare, any progress in this area strengthens the entire social welfare institution.

In a democracy, being an informed participant in debates and decision making about social welfare is another way to help. In order to do so effectively, you must first have a basic understanding of social welfare issues. As we have seen, these often involve sensitive and sometimes painful value-related questions that many people would rather not examine closely.

In dealing with such questions, the natural tendency is to fall back on one's assumptions and reject relevant factual information. This, however, only tends to perpetuate stereotypes that prevent the adoption of more effective solutions to social welfare problems. Progress in the area of social welfare requires an informed population that plays an active role in societal decision making. When we do not participate in such decision making, we permit others to determine social welfare policy (and many other aspects of social life).

Beyond informal helping and participation in social welfare decision making, one can volunteer. As we have seen, becoming a volunteer involves a commitment to work within a particular social welfare agency or program. Aside from the satisfaction that comes from knowing you are improving the delivery of services, you will benefit from learning new skills and meeting new people. Volunteering can be a very rewarding experience.

Finally, you may choose to become a social welfare professional. If so, you will devote much of your time and energy to assisting people to improve and better manage their own lives. The social welfare professions offer you many opportunities to work with others in whatever ways are most appealing. The opportunities to help are boundless. No matter what kind of life you choose for yourself, you can include helping activities. Whether and how you wish to do so is your choice.

LET'S REVIEW

This chapter has focused on the helping professions. We began by looking at the common goal of helping professions: improving social functioning and individual well-being. This goal can be met most effectively through the combined efforts of professional generalists and specialists. The chapter then explored the meaning of a profession. The profession's specialized knowledge and skill base, its code of ethics, self-regulation and autonomy, and its reliance on a professional association were shown to be major defining characteristics.

Five social welfare professions were discussed briefly, so that you have a sense of the activities and rewards of each. They are social work, physical health, mental health, education, and law. Some of the issues noted in passing included ways in which professions overlap and relate to each other, and the use of professional credentialing to protect title and function. The role of paraprofessionals and issues related to declassification were also addressed. The interaction of natural helping networks, volunteers, paraprofessionals, and professionals was shown to be of great importance for the creation of an effective, comprehensive service-delivery system.

The chapter concluded with an effort to personalize involvement in social welfare activities. For people who believe that we all share responsibility for the well-being of others, there is a broad spectrum of possible helping activities. These vary in scope in terms of whom we choose to help and the degree of formality involved in how we help. Nevertheless, all provide an opportunity to act out one's personal sense of commitment to others.

Where do we go from here? This chapter has perhaps given you some ideas where your own life might go in relationship to social welfare. In the next chapter we will try to take a broader look: Where should society go?

STUDY QUESTIONS

1 Select one of the social welfare professions discussed in this chapter. Go to the library and research it, getting information about the training and education needed, the kinds of jobs available, the specific tasks involved, and salary levels. Then write a short paper describing your reactions to the information you have obtained. Focus on whether the profession is what you thought it would be, and how you now feel about it.

2 Visit an agency in your community that uses volunteers. Find out what volunteers do, and what kind of training and supervision they receive. Then make arrangements to interview a volunteer or two to find out what they like and dislike about their work. Also try to find out their motivations for volunteering. To what degree is their motivation personal, and to what degree do they see their work as a contribution to the well-being of others?

3 Select a profession that interests you and contact its professional association (the reference librarian can help you locate its name and address). Ask the association to send you the profession's code of ethics and a description of the services available to members. Compare this information with the information obtained by your classmates from at least one other professional association. What are the similarities and differences in this material? What do you think these similarities and differences tell you about the professions involved?

4 Write a one-paragraph statement explaining your current thinking about the responsibility you feel for helping others. If you feel such a responsibility, select one of the opportunities to help discussed in the chapter and write a short essay on how you could implement it in your own life.

5 Based on your personal experiences, do you think that professions regulate the activities of their members effectively? Give specific examples to support your position. Do you think that licensing of professionals is necessary and effective? Could you suggest additional or alternative strategies to regulate professional behavior?

KEY TERMS AND CONCEPTS

generalist approach	certification
case manager	registration
specialist approach	systems approach
clinical social worker	health maintenance organizations (HMO)
code of ethics	paraprofessional
committee of inquiry	declassification
licensing	volunteerism

SUGGESTED READINGS

Davies, Martin. 1981. *The Essential Social Worker.* London: Heinemann. Although it was published in England, this book provides a realistic sense of what it is like to be a social worker in any society. It presents a good balance between personal, organizational, and structural issues that social workers face in their work.

Guzzetta, Charles, with Arthur Katz and Richard English, eds. 1984. *Education for Social Work Practice: Selected International Models.* Washington, DC: Council on Social Work Education. The articles in this book explore different approaches to educating and deploying social work professionals. They raise stimulating issues about the most effective strategies for training social welfare professionals and about the most effective uses of such people in society.

Lubove, Roy. 1969. *The Professional Altruist.* New York: Atheneum. This classic study of the development of the profession of social work provides insight into the political, economic, and interpersonal factors that influence professions. It explores in some detail how professions support their claim to specialized knowledge and self-regulation.

U.S. Department of Labor, Bureau of Labor Statistics, 1994. *Occupational Outlook Handbook.* Washington, DC: U.S. Government Printing Office. This government publication provides detailed information about all social welfare occupations, including tasks performed, training required, salaries, and employment projections. It is an excellent reference for those interested in exploring specific social welfare careers.

REFERENCES

American Red Cross. 1984. What you should know about your Red Cross. Pamphlet.

American Psychological Association Office of Rural Health. 1995. *Caring for the Rural Community: An Interdisciplinary Curriculum.* Washington, DC: American Psychological Association.

Barker, Robert L. 1991. *Social Work Dictionary,* 2d ed. Washington, DC: National Association of Social Workers.

Compton, Buelah R., and Galaway, Burt. 1989. *Social Work Processes.* Belmont, CA: Wadsworth.

Council on Social Work Education. 1992. Curriculum policy statement for baccalaureate degree programs in social work education. Washington, DC: Council on Social Work Education.

Freudenheim, Milt. 1986. Health plan helps elderly to stay at home. *The New York Times,* December 27, p. 17.

Khinduka, S. K. 1987. Social work and the human services. In *Encyclopedia of Social Work,* 18th ed. Silver Spring, MD: National Association of Social Workers, pp. 681–695.

King, Lisa. 1988. Certification, licensure, and legitimacy. *Footnotes,* 16(1):11.

Miller, Pamela. 1985. Professional use of lay resources. *Social Work,* 30(5):409–416.

Swenson, Carol R. 1995. Clinical social work. In *Encyclopedia of Social Work,* 19th ed. Washington, DC: National Association of Social Workers, pp. 502–512.

University of Maine School of Social Work. 1995. *BASW Program Guide: 1995–1996.* Orono, ME: University of Maine School of Social Work.

U.S. Department of Labor, Bureau of Labor Statistics. 1994. *Occupational Outlook Handbook, (1994–1995 ed.)* Bulletin 2450. Washington, DC: U.S. Government Printing Office.

Wilkerson, Isabel. 1987. Schools of social work swamped by applicants. *The New York Times,* November 9, p. A17.

10

WHAT IS THE FUTURE OF SOCIAL WELFARE?

> "I can't believe *that!*" said Alice.
>
> "Can't you?" the Queen said in a pitying tone. "Try again: draw a long breath and shut your eyes."
>
> Alice laughed. "There's no use trying," she said. "One *can't* believe impossible things."
>
> "I daresay you haven't had much practice," said the Queen. "When I was your age, I always did it for half an hour a day. Why sometimes I believed as many as six impossible things before breakfast."
>
> *Through the Looking Glass* by Lewis Carroll.
> *Complete Works.* New York: Modern Library, p. 200.

INTRODUCTION

This chapter has a different purpose and structure than those that you have already completed. Its purpose is to share with you our thinking about the future of social welfare in the United States. In previous chapters we have generally tried to be neutral about issues, seeking instead to provide an overview of the basic facts about social welfare in the United States in comparison with Sweden, Poland, and

Mexico. Now you are ready to begin formulating your own positions about social welfare and its future. Remember that social welfare is about choices. With your new knowledge, you are ready to make informed choices.

To help you think about these choices, in this chapter we discuss a variety of issues and concerns that seem to us to be important to the future of social welfare. This involves identifying ongoing and emerging social concerns, exploring how the social welfare system itself can be strengthened, and developing a vision about what social welfare's future role should be.

In talking about his life as a runaway on the streets of San Francisco, a teenager said, "That's what street life is like. You learn to survive. But you also learn not to care if you don't" (Axthelm, 1988:66). This comment captures the essence of why we must continue the struggle to solve social problems. As social welfare professionals, we deeply respect the strengths that people possess. Even when they face terrible living conditions and little hope, most people continue to seek better lives. However, underlying such efforts is often a desperation and a feeling of worthlessness that translates into dangerous alienation. Under such conditions, conventional rules may seem irrelevant. What reason is there not to commit suicide, or even awful crimes against others? What does it matter?

Social problems take a toll in human life and suffering, a dreadful and unnecessary toll. People's lives are diminished or destroyed. Society is disrupted by the behavior of those who no longer care, or who are so damaged that they cannot function in acceptable ways. Our society continues to suffer from serious problems, some of them longstanding and others more recent. As I write, policymakers in Washington are enacting legislation that, under the rubric of "reform," seems to me to be mean-spirited, punitive, and short-sighted. Social welfare programs reflecting our painfully slow progress from the old paradigm to the new—progress won through decades of mobilization by persons and groups seeking a more equitable society—are being threatened with catastrophic reductions in funding and with wholesale dismantling. Times like these call, more than ever, for the very best thinking and analysis from every caring person. In this section, we discuss briefly those issues that we believe most require serious attention in the years ahead.

Because this chapter is based on personal perspectives rather than commonly accepted theory and data, it takes the form of a dialogue. Unfortunately, the limitations of a book format make the dialogue one-way. It is therefore up to you to identify and sort out your own reactions as you go along. If, upon conclusion, you'd like to write and engage in a real dialogue, I[1] (Bill Whitaker) would be delighted to hear from you. You can write to me at the University of Maine School of Social Work, 5770 Annex C, Orono, Maine 04469-5770 or contact me by e-mail (Whitaker@Maine.Maine.EDU). In any case, we hope the following discussion stimulates you to develop your own ideas and your own plans for action.

---

[1]In this chapter the first-person singular pronoun "I" refers to Bill Whitaker. Ron Federico initiated the process of dialogue in the first edition of our book and believed strongly in it. So do I. Many of the words and ideas expressed in this chapter were first written by Ron. His thoughts and ideas provide an essential foundation for our discussion.

To imagine how social welfare should be shaped in the future can be daunting. As we have stressed throughout this book, the lives of real people will be affected in many ways by the choices that you, we, and many others will make among the options and possibilities that lie ahead. We encourage you to consider seriously the Queen's advice to Alice: We encourage you to practice believing what at first blush may even seem impossible.

ENDURING SOCIAL CONCERNS IN UNCERTAIN TIMES

The Need for a Revised Social Compact

A **social compact** is *"the set of assumptions about what citizens and the government owe each other"* (Schorr, 1995). The social compact under which we have been operating in the United States—forged in response to the Great Depression and World War II—is under increasing attack by reactionary ideologues. Alvin Schorr (1995) argues convincingly that, even without the conservative challenge, fundamental demographic and economic changes in the United States have generated significant issues which must be addressed vis à vis the five pillars of U.S. social security. Schorr's analysis is summarized in Table 10-1, which outlines assumptions on which contemporary public social welfare programs are grounded, describes demographic and economic changes that call many of these assumptions into question, and discusses implications of the changes.

Reduced benefits in a time of increasing need, the potential for serious intergenerational conflict over allocation of societal resources, and pressure to rely more heavily on work-based benefits in an economy in which well-paying jobs are becoming harder to find pose significant challenges that must be addressed by social welfare advocates.

Addressing Poverty and Income Distribution

The paradox of entrenched poverty amidst plenty in the United States continues to haunt the lives of millions of people. Government figures reveal that, in 1992, 36.9 million people, or 14.5 percent of the U.S. population (up from 14 percent in 1985), were living in poverty (U.S. Department of Commerce, 1994: Table 727). These same figures also show a widening gap between the incomes of the rich and the poor, as Table 10-2 demonstrates.

The data in Table 10-2 show that the wealthy were receiving an increasing share of the income of the United States even before the impact of the 1995–1996 legislation, which cut funding for programs for the poor and at the same time increased benefits for the rich. In 1994, the poorest 40 percent of the U.S. population received the smallest share of total income and the richest 40 percent, the largest share of income since 1967, when such data were first gathered by the Bureau of the Census. The richest 20 percent of U.S. households received four times as much income as the poorest 40 percent. In 1994, the middle-class 60 percent of households received 47.3 percent of household income—a record low—

TABLE 10-1   ASSUMPTIONS AND CURRENT REALITIES OF THE U.S. SOCIAL COMPACT

Assumptions	Fundamental changes	Meaning
1. Support for families is provided normally by men working full-time, following traditional career paths.	More than half of all women—with or without children or husbands—work outside the home. Opportunity for full-time work is being replaced by part-time and occasional work.	It is becoming less and less clear why spouses should receive benefits they have not earned themselves. Current rules about Social Security, unemployment insurance, and private benefits will provide lower or no benefits for many people.
2. Men earn a so-called family wage.	Most employers no longer intend to pay a family wage. The job market is splitting between well-paying jobs and low-paying service sector jobs. Full-time, year-round work at the minimum wage formerly brought a family of four above poverty. Now the wage is sufficient only for a family of two.	Low-paid, occasional, or part-time workers will be economically vulnerable, unable to save money or to accumulate equity in a home, in need of protection, but less protected based on their earnings.
3. Women are assured income, if not from their husbands, then through benefits to which men's work has entitled them.	Women increasingly are seen as being responsible for their own incomes.	Benefits based on spouses' earnings are likely to erode. Higher-income persons, unconcerned because they can protect themselves with IRAs and other tax benefits, will no longer support the compact.
4. A normal family consists of two parents and a child or children. Single-parent families arise largely because of the death of a husband and are assured income through the deceased husband's work-related entitlement.	Family composition has changed dramatically. Almost one-fourth of families with children are headed by a single parent. One-fourth of never-married women have had a child. Single-parent families typically have lowest incomes of all families.	Social insurance programs provide the weakest protection for families with children. Reduced disability, unemployment, and survivors' insurance benefits are an increasingly serious problem.

while the richest 5 percent of the U.S. population received 21.2 percent—a record high, more than 1.5 times that received by the poorest 40 percent. Inequality of income is increasing dramatically in the United States (Rosen et al., 1987; U.S. Department of Commerce, 1994; Center on Budget and Policy Priorities, 1995).

Other indicators confirm the disparity between rich and poor. In 1986, for example, "the top 10 percent of [U.S.] income receivers owned 85 percent of publicly traded stock, 92 percent of mutual bonds, 72 percent of all other bonds, [and] 80 percent of mutual funds. . . . Families in the top 1 percent of the income distribution held 19 percent of all assets and 34 percent of financial assets" (Rosen et al., 1987:13). In 1989, 1,260 U.S. millionaires shared a total net worth of about $3.5 trillion. Thirty-six wealthholders shared a total net worth of $890 billion (U.S. Department of Commerce, 1994: Table 743).

A 1995 study of income in eighteen industrialized nations found that poor children in the United States were worse off than poor children in every other country except Israel and Ireland. The United States had the second highest level

TABLE 10-1   ASSUMPTIONS AND CURRENT REALITIES OF THE U.S. SOCIAL COMPACT   *(Continued)*

Assumptions	Fundamental changes	Meaning
5. The population includes many children and declining numbers of adults in successive age groups, . . . a relatively small percentage of aged people.	The number of people over 65, i.e., those needing some degree of social supports, has increased from 10 per 100 working people in 1930, to 20 per 100 in 1990, and will go to 30 per 100 by 2025. This trend is partially offset by decreasing numbers of dependent children per worker.	Working-age people will bear heavier tax burdens. If tax burden is defined as an issue of intergenerational equity, severe difficulties in financing social security may result.
6. The shared experiences of the Great Depression and World War II have generated a preponderant sense of communal responsibility for those who are in trouble.	Preponderant sense of communal responsibility has faded in recent years.	Safety-net programs are likely to become increasingly inadequate, especially if wage levels with which they are compared remain low.
7. Individuals and governments share responsibility for social welfare and human well-being.	Individual responsibility is being asserted as if it were a new element in the social contract, focusing mainly on work and representing a deep sense of public frustration.	The drive to induce or force applicants to work will persist.
8. Increasing affluence and government revenues permit implementation of the social compact.	For two decades, real incomes have declined for between 25 and 50% of the working population. This has generated pressure for caps on taxation and government spending, and for balanced governmental budgets.	Prospects for liberalizing social welfare programs, as now conceived, are limited.

Source: Alvin Schorr. Long-term issues. Concept paper distributed by Odyssey Forum, McLean, VA, 1995.

of economic output per person and the most prosperous affluent children, but the widest gap between the rich and the poor, and the least generous social welfare programs of any of the eighteen nations studied (Bradsher, 1995).

Further, poverty continues to afflict certain groups much more than others. African Americans, some Hispanic groups, and female-headed families comprise a disproportionate share of those living in poverty. So too do rural residents, who are also more frequent victims of poverty than the population as a whole (McCormick, 1988). Poverty among women has become so serious that it even has a name: the feminization of poverty (Pearce, 1978; Bane, 1988). Of all the groups that have traditionally suffered from poverty, only the elderly have made substantial progress in improving their economic situation over the past few decades. Table 10-3 documents the differential incidence of poverty.

The effects of poverty are well known. Individual effects include stunted physical growth, psychological stress, social isolation, alienation, feelings of help-lessness and hopelessness, and increased risk of disease, alcohol and drug abuse,

TABLE 10-2   DISTRIBUTION OF FAMILY INCOME IN THE UNITED STATES

Income group by quintile	Percent of total money income			
	1960	1970	1980	1994
Poorest fifth	4.8	5.4	5.2	3.6
Second fifth	12.2	12.2	11.5	8.9
Third fifth	17.8	17.6	17.5	15.0
Fourth fifth	23.7	23.6	24.3	23.4
Richest fifth	40.7	40.5	41.5	49.1
Richest 5%	15.7	15.5	15.3	21.2

Sources: Sumner, Rosen, David Fanshel, and Mary Lutz, eds., *Face of the Nation 1987: Statistical Supplement to the 18th Edition of the Encyclopedia of Social Work,* Silver Spring, MD: National Association of Social Workers, 1987, p. 16. U.S. Department of Commerce, *Statistical Abstract of the United States 1994,* Washington, DC: U.S. Government Printing Office, 1994, Table 716. Center on Budget and Policy Priorities, "Only High-Income Households Have Recovered Fully from the Recession," Washington, DC: Center on Budget and Policy Priorities, October 24, 1995.

and violent death. Poverty also contributes to a host of social problems: domestic violence, family disintegration, teen pregnancies, prostitution, juvenile delinquency, crime, and welfare dependency.

We know that poverty can become entrenched in communities and families, and that the costs of current programs that maintain the poor represent a continuing

TABLE 10-3   POVERTY IN THE UNITED STATES, 1960–1993[a]

Group	Percent of group in poverty				
	1960	1970	1980	1990	1993
Total population	22.2	12.6	13.0	13.5	15.1
People age 65 and over	NA	24.6	15.7	12.2	12.2
African American people	55.1*	33.5	32.5	31.9	33.1
African American people in families headed by women	70.6*	58.7	53.4	50.6	53.0
Hispanic-origin people	NA	21.9**	25.7	28.1	30.6
Hispanic-origin people in families headed by women	NA	57.4**	54.5	53.0	53.2
White people	17.8	9.9	10.2	10.7	12.2
White people in families headed by women	39.0	28.4	28.0	29.8	31.0

[a]NA, data not available for this group for this year; *data are for the year 1959 instead of 1960; **data are for the year 1973 instead of 1970.

Source: U.S. Department of Commerce. Bureau of the Census. 1993. *Current population reports. Consumer income.* Series P60–188. *Income, poverty, and valuation of noncash benefits: 1993.* Washington, DC: U.S. Government Printing Office.

drain on society's financial resources. Yet as great as the cost of these programs may be, the social costs of our failure to end poverty—the wasted lives and the foregone contributions to society—are far greater still. Only if we are prepared to address seriously its systemic causes will we be able to help people break out of the patterns of oppression that perpetuate poverty.

I believe it is increasingly important that we make this effort. As we have seen, the distance between the poor and the wealthy in the United States is increasing. We are becoming a polarized society with an increasing number of very rich, an increasing number of very poor, and a shrinking middle class.

This polarization is perilous. We know from observing other societies throughout the world that common results of polarization include corruption, alienation, crime, and even social upheaval. When poverty is seen as inevitable and unchangeable, those who are poor have little incentive to respect societal norms. Instead, they must attempt to survive in whatever ways they can, giving little concern to a future that may or may not exist for them.

In response, societies often become increasingly repressive and uncaring, seeking only to stop crime by whatever means are available and to separate those who are well off from the unpleasant realities of life as experienced by the poor.

In the United States today we imprison a higher percentage of our total population than any other nation in the world. We attempt to separate ourselves from the realities of poor people in ways that seem little changed since Michael Harrington's *The Other America* (1971) focused attention on our "invisible poor." As you may recall, Harrington's book was a wake-up call that helped trigger the Johnson administration's War on Poverty. Today, concern about ending poverty seems to be diminishing.

Jonathan Kozol, in *Amazing Grace: The Lives of Children and the Conscience of a Nation* (1995), provides many chilling examples of the ways in which the affluent and modestly well off attempt to ignore the existence of the poor. He describes, for example, how along I-95 in the South Bronx in New York City, "pictures of flowers, window shades and curtains, and interiors of pretty-looking rooms . . . have been painted on the sides" of abandoned apartment buildings. Facing away from the neighborhood, the paintings are seen primarily by tourists and commuters driving the interstate highway. The words of Gizelle Luke, an African American community organizer, illustrate the pent-up frustration and anger generated by glossing over the problems of poverty. The painting project, she says, is "far beyond racism. It's just—'In your face! Take that! We don't clean up your neighborhood, don't fix your buildings, or give you decent hospitals or banks. Instead, we paint the back sides of the buildings so that people driving to the suburbs will have something nice to look at'" (Kozol, 1995:31). Such insensitivities polarize the nation, widen the psychological and emotional gulf between socioeconomic classes, and erode society's commitment to human life and social justice (Butterfield, 1988).

Efforts to reduce or eliminate poverty must be linked with changes in all the institutions of society. This is a large and politically sensitive task. History has shown that those who benefit from the existing social system are often reluctant to change it (Weir et al., 1988). This certainly seems to be true in the United States, where, for example, it has been extremely difficult to obtain the cooperation of groups such as unions and corporations, whose assistance is needed to open up meaningful employment opportunities for the poor.

Poverty continues because we allow it to. The unequal way in which it affects different groups is also something we allow. There is no doubt that the perpetuation of these patterns weakens society. Indeed, in my opinion, our society's economic vitality and productivity is increasingly being impaired by poverty and discrimination. People who are ill, alienated, uneducated, or addicts are rarely effective participants in an urbanized, high-tech society.

Solving such problems requires a new compact affirming the importance of human life and social justice. The redistribution of resources and opportunities from those who are most privileged in our society to those who are at its fringes is controversial. Eliminating poverty and increasing social justice will require very different choices than those that are being made by our elected representatives in Congress in 1996. Much work and mobilization by caring persons will be required to motivate elected officials to embark boldly on such a new path.

Responding to Immigration and Racism

Immigration is an important factor in the changing demographic face of the United States. Although the United States has always been a multicultural society, the great diversity in the racial and ethnic backgrounds of today's immigrants— together with the fact that many contemporary immigrants are from non-Western cultures about which most U.S. citizens know little—are creating new challenges. Many of us, for example, assume that all Spanish-speaking people are alike, and, similarly, lump together people from many different Southeast Asian cultures.

These stereotypes make it easy to ignore the richness of the cultural diversity and the different needs of each immigrant group. If the United States is to maintain its tradition as a haven for oppressed people, we must develop more sensitivity to cultural differences so that more appropriate responses to varying needs can be developed.

Today's immigrants face increasing hostility from citizens who feel that the newcomers threaten their jobs and economic security. Such concerns become fertile soil for state-level anti-immigrant initiatives such as Proposition 187, which passed in California in 1994, and for the federal legislation enacted by Congress in 1996 restricting both legal and illegal immigration.

Anti-immigrant fears are heightened by anxiety over the decline in the domestic manufacturing industry resulting in part from a great increase in low-cost imports from developing nations. Together, the influx of immigrants and imports are leading many to question the extent to which America's borders should be open. To resolve this issue, we must strike a balance between meeting the economic needs of our current residents and responding to those of new immigrants and refugees. The economic pressures fueling immigration to the United States from the Mexican state of Michoacán are described on pages 332 and 333 in "The Human Face of Social Welfare 21: They've Gone to the Other Side."

Immigration by and relatively high birth rates among people of color are contributing to a "browning" of the U.S. population, which has important implications for the social welfare institution. In response to changes in the racial and ethnic composition of the United States, racism is likely increasingly to influence the future willingness of "haves" to respond to needs of "have-nots," who disproportionately are people of color (see Table 10-3).

Between 1970 and 1980, U.S. residents of Hispanic origin increased by 61 percent, compared with a 9 percent increase in the population as a whole (Kincannon, 1983:4). Between 1980 and 1992, the U.S. Hispanic population increased by 63 percent, compared with 13 percent for the population as a whole (see Table 10-4). Given the relative youth of the Hispanic population and its higher-than-average birth rate, this trend is likely to continue (Rendon, 1985:13). In 1992, Hispanics made up 9.5 percent of the U.S. population. Government projections predict that Hispanics will comprise about 13.5 percent of the population in the year 2010, and 22.5 percent in 2050.

The percentage of the U.S. population that is black was 11.9 in 1992. African Americans are projected to increase to 12.6 percent of the population in 2010 and 14.4 percent in 2050. By 2010, however, Hispanics will have surpassed African Americans as the largest U.S. minority group of color. As Table 10-4 indicates, if current immigration patterns continue, other racial groups are likely to grow in size and importance as well. By 2050, a year in which many persons now reading this book can expect to be alive, albeit retired, whites will constitute a bare majority of 52.5 percent in the United States (U.S. Department of Commerce, 1994: Table 18). Not many years later, whites will make up less than half of the people of the United States.

If the growing minority proportion of the population is to be successfully integrated into American life, new and different types of social welfare services will have to be developed. If members of oppressed groups are not to continue to be disadvantaged in terms of employment, income, and educational opportunities, they must have access to employment that pays a livable wage and to culturally appropriate, publicly funded, personal social services that make effective use of natural helping networks and other sources of voluntary assistance. Such services must be accompanied by changes in societal values so that people of color are viewed as valuable contributors to society rather than as potential threats to an entrenched social order.

Strengthening Families

Perhaps this would be a good time to revisit the social welfare report cards in Chapter 1. Revisit, too, the Chapter 1 sidebar, "Moments in America for Children." How does the United States measure up? In what regards are we doing well? What needs are not being met? Remember that statistics are not just numbers: They represent the daily struggles of real people to earn a living, to raise their children, to survive.

As the social welfare report card indicates, by some measures of family well-being the United States is doing well. Life expectancy at birth is high;

THE HUMAN FACE OF SOCIAL WELFARE 21

THEY'VE GONE TO THE OTHER SIDE

With a sweep of her hand, Rosa Guzmán Alverez gestures beyond the produce displayed on her fruit and vegetable stand to the rest of the open-air market in this central Mexican town.

"As you can see, the majority of us are women and children here," she says, pointing to the other vendors and customers. "As for the men, they've gone to the other side; they've gone to the United States."

While her husband works the harvest in Illinois, Rosa keeps up the small business the two of them started three years ago. It's a common arrangement here in Michoacán, a poor, rural state that has sent more migrants to the United States than has any other region.

Today experts estimate that slightly more Michoacános harvest strawberries in California, pick apples in Oregon, and work construction in Illinois—about 2 million—than the 1.9 million adults who still permanently call the state home.

Despite common knowledge about crossing the northern border becoming more difficult, a grapevine that says jobs in the US are becoming harder for undocumented immigrants to find, and California's anti-immigrant Proposition 187 becoming a household term, the urge to travel north to work is as strong as ever.

"It took my husband a month and four tries before he finally got across, but he kept trying because he didn't have a choice," says Rosa. "When you're from Michoacán, you know its pretty much the only way to survive or ever think of getting ahead."

Michoacán has been sending immigrants north for decades. . . . But recent years have produced some changes in the pattern of migration. . . . First, the US amnesty program that offered legalization to millions of illegal immigrants in the late 1980s, plus the more recent stepped-up policing of the US side of the border, have meant that visits back to Michoacán are less frequent. . . .

And second, the heightened difficulty in crossing, plus the fact that most families here now have relatives established on the US side to take them in, have led more young people to marry and then go north together, with no intention of moving back. . . . Families are going north to stay.

Recognizing the important impact immigration has on its people, Michoacán [in 1992 established] an office to offer legal and administrative services to migrant workers. The original idea was to help the migrant who had lost important papers in transit or who had suffered a work injury in the US and was back in Mexico for care.

While the office still handles those tasks, officials say their focus has shifted to rights-

low-birth-weight births, infant mortality, and under-5 mortality for the population as a whole have fallen substantially. We have a high rate of enrollment in education beyond high school. Most of our population has access to safe drinking water and sanitation. Food costs are low compared to average household incomes.

There are other measures of well-being, however, of which we should be less proud. Our under-5 mortality rate is far too high compared to our economic ability; an unconscionably high percentage of our children are not fully immunized; we can end but have not ended childhood hunger; far too many of our brothers and sisters are poor. Our country has earned the dubious distinction as the worst among industrialized nations in achievement scores for children, school dropout rates, percentage of population in prison, homicide, cocaine junkies, crack babies, ghettos, and homelessness.

abuse problems as the mood toward illegal immigrants in the US has toughened and as crossing the border has become riskier.

"We're seeing more beatings and other rights violations of our people with the anti-Mexican turn taken in the US," says Jesús Vargas Alejos, director of the migrant services office in Morelia, the state capital.

"The 15 cadavers we've received from the border or the US interior this year are already double last year's number."

Mr. Vargas, nine of whose 11 siblings now live in the US, says part of the increased violence stems from the fact that younger Michoacános with no crossing experience and more women are going north. And out in the towns, many people say that much of the violence they hear about occurs on the Mexican side of the border. . . .

Another hardship for Michoacán's first-time migrants is the rising cost of contracting a *pollero,* the person paid to guarantee passage across the line. Help getting to a city like Los Angeles used to cost $400, but now costs $1200 or more.

"The bigger money has drawn new *polleros* who aren't always as scrupulous as the old-timers," says [a] Villa Morelos priest. "That's where we get a lot of the robberies and rapes."

To cut down on the violence and uncertainty Michoacános face in crossing the border, while guaranteeing California farms the cheap labor he says they will always need, Vargas recommends creating a guest-worker program something like the Bracero program the US had in the 1950s.

But neither the US nor the Mexican government seems eager to go in that direction, Vargas adds. So in the meantime his office is [encouraging] Michoacános who have settled in the US . . . to help create small businesses back home.

With Michoacános in the US sending home about $1 billion a year, Vargas figures just a small fraction of that could be turned into an important stimulus for development in the state. . . .

This excerpt illustrates the economic pressures fueling immigration which result when a very rich nation and a very poor nation share a common border. U.S. policy makers who wish to limit immigration into the United States from Mexico are building steel barriers in an attempt to wall out people driven by poverty to seek work in the United States to support their families. Such attempts are destined to fail. Only improved economic opportunities in Michoacán are likely to stem the flow of immigration. The article demonstrates how Mexico and the United States live in an increasingly interdependent world.

Excerpted from Howard LaFranchi, "The Michoacán Story: Mexican State Sends More Workers to US Than It Has at Home," *Christian Science Monitor,* November 8, 1995, pp. 1ff. Copyright © 1995 by The Christian Science Publishing Society. Reprinted by permission.

Even positive national averages frequently conceal a Third World population of oppressed racial and other minority groups for whom life is more grueling. This Third World population within the United States—in our nation's capital, in every major city, in many remote rural communities—consists of people whose daily struggles to make ends meet differ outrageously from our national averages.

Infants born at low birth weight into poverty; teenage mothers; children arrested for violent crimes, doing drugs, being murdered, committing suicide, contracting AIDS—all are real people. Each of us is affected directly or indirectly by social welfare policy choices that have been made and are yet to be made. With this as our context, let's think some more about the family.

The family occupies a place in United States mythology that does not reflect its current reality. We expect families to perform in ways that are not always realistic in today's world. Families are expected to be effective economic units, generating

TABLE 10-4   RACIAL COMPOSITION OF THE U.S. POPULATION, 1980–2050

Group	1980 Population	1992 Population	Percent Increase, 1980–1992	Percent U.S. Population, 1992	Projected Percent U.S. Population, 2010	Projected Percent U.S. Population, 2050
Total	226,546,000	255,082,000	13	100	100	100
White	180,906,000	190,802,000	5	74.8	67.7	52.5
African American	26,215,000	30,316,000	16	11.9	12.6	14.4
Hispanic	14,869,000	24,238,000	63	9.5	13.5	22.5
Asian, Pacific Islander	3,563,000	7,867,000	121	3.1	5.4	9.7
Native American, Eskimo, Aleut	1,326,000	1,850,000	40	0.7	0.8	0.9

Source: U.S. Department of Commerce, *Statistical Abstract of the United States,* (table 18). Washington, DC: U.S. Government Printing Office, 1994, Table 18. Projections report a "middle series" projection. There are also "lowest" and "highest" series projections in this source.

the income their members need to survive and thrive. Families are expected to be first-class social units, nurturing and supporting, socializing and disciplining their children, and, increasingly, caring for their elderly.

Families tend to fragment as members pursue their own individual goals. Adults who work outside the home have less time for each other and for traditional parenting roles. Children have more freedom to select their own activities, and to conceal their activities from their parents. An increasing number of American adolescents hold part-time jobs while attending high school, leaving them with reduced time for family life. Increasingly, the elderly also live independently, often far from other family members. And, should they need to enter a residential treatment facility, their contact with other family members and with young people is often restricted.

If families are to have a reasonable chance of meeting our expectations, we need to develop a coherent set of family policies at the national, state, and community levels. At a minimum, family policy should include access to jobs that pay a livable wage; enforcement of child support from absent parents; health insurance independent of one's employment; affordable, good-quality child care available to everyone who needs it; and maternal and parental leave policies that allow women time away from employment to bear children and enable both men and women to devote time to their children during illness or critical periods of development.

Attention must be paid, too, to the needs of the increasing proportion of elderly in our society (see Table 10-5). As people live longer, they have increased needs for health, housing, financial, and personal-care services. Increased longevity affects directly the costs of Social Security retirement and survivors' pensions, Medicare, and the nursing-home care provided through Medicaid.

Finally, much of the future need for social welfare services will be determined by society's response to the needs of women. As we have seen, an increasing number of women are single parents, divorced, or unmarried. We have also seen

TABLE 10-5 CARING FOR THE ELDERLY: A FOUR-COUNTRY COMPARISON

	Mexico	Poland	Sweden	United States
Percent of population 60 or older in 1990	6	15	23	17
Primary responsibility for the elderly	Family	Family	Society	Self/society
Elderly covered by public retirement insurance	Some	Most	All	Nearly all
Appropriate housing available for elderly	Little	Limited	Extensive	Some
Value of elderly in society	Respect	Respect	Respect	Tolerance

Source: World Bank, *World Development Report 1993: Investing in Health—World Development Indicators,* New York: Oxford University Press, 1993, Table A.3.

that female-headed families are more likely to be poor, and that women are disadvantaged in terms of employment opportunities and income. Yet women continue to bear the primary responsibility for child rearing and are increasingly important in a gradually shrinking workforce. The role of women in society is too important to continue institutional patterns that impede their ability to function. Social welfare must continue to play an important role in advocating for women's needs.

Rebuilding Moral Commitments

Large industrial nations find it difficult to maintain a sense of common purpose and destiny. As work and leisure activities become increasingly specialized, societies tend to fragment into groups whose members know little about each other and who find it difficult to perceive shared interests. The resulting sense of social isolation is often reinforced by special-interest talk shows and print media designed to appeal to the immediate self-interest of different groups and too often to pit one group against another.

Capitalism itself is often alienating and fragmenting. Its common goal of individual economic success is not always compatible with community needs. The increasing centralization of economic power through mergers and buyouts has made workers and consumers more vulnerable to the policies and decisions of a shrinking number of large corporations. At the same time, people have less input into the formulation of policies that have a real impact on their lives. The stresses that result affect many people in negative ways. Exhausted by worry and overwork, they may want to go home and simply watch television rather than participate in family activities. Others seek a sense of well-being and purpose by pursuing self-gratification regardless of its effects on others. Still others withdraw into self-protective emotional shells, or strike out against those who are more vulnerable.

The alienating tendencies within modern society are strengthened by unethical activities by governmental and corporate leaders. Scandals in the government, on

Wall Street, in corporate board rooms, and among evangelists all undermine the belief that individual sacrifice and interpersonal cooperation are necessary for societal well-being. It can easily seem that the only way to succeed is to cheat, and that power is to be used for one's own purposes. Observing the self-enriching activities of many influential people, ordinary citizens can easily conclude that it is foolish to allow ethical principles to stand in the way of personal gain.

The government's role as overseer of other major social institutions is being eroded. Deregulation, privatization, and a markedly less vigorous level of enforcement of civil rights legislation mark a significant reduction in government's traditional role as protector of human rights. As government retreats, the market's sphere of influence grows and public scrutiny is reduced. As the social domain of the market expands, the most vulnerable members of society tend to be ignored or excluded because of their economic and social powerlessness.

While not all problems can be solved by government, government as a moral force is essential. Public officials must model ethical behavior and demand it from leaders in the corporate, financial, and religious fields. In a modern society, only government can ensure the overall quality of the conditions under which its people live and work, regulate the relationship between consumers and the market in order to protect the weak, and fund the educational infrastructure required to create an informed and skilled workforce.

Government must also take leadership in reaffirming the value of people. This can occur only if "human impact" becomes a factor in all policy decisions, including decisions that affect the relationship between the public and private sectors. The conditions under which people live must allow and encourage them to act out the values that nurture human life. What are needed are policies that strengthen family life rather than divide family members, and that strike a better balance between short-term economic gains and the long-term development of our most valuable resource, people. In the long run, it is a society's sense of moral commitment and common purpose that either holds it together or allows it to disintegrate.

Reassessing Universal and Selective Approaches

As we have seen, the social welfare system in the United States is atypical in its extensive use of selective, residual programs. As in Poland and Sweden, most industrialized societies employ more comprehensive or universal approaches. The intent of the Contract with America is to replace the major universal entitlements that do exist with inadequately funded block grants to the states, together with few mandated standards for program eligibility or operation. This threatens to result in the proliferation of inconsistently available selective programs characterized by gaps in service, fragmentation, inequity, and inaccessibility.

Selective programs not only complicate service delivery and pose difficulties for recipients of services, they also undermine public support for social welfare itself. They tend to stigmatize social welfare as an activity that serves only the poor and others who are "failures."

By contrast, universal programs make it easier for people to perceive social welfare as a positive influence that enhances everyone's life. Rather than being seen as a drain on societal resources, universal social welfare programs are more likely to be seen as improving productivity and the overall quality of social life.

Universal services can also be funded in more acceptable ways. In Sweden, all cash benefits received from social welfare programs are treated as taxable income, thus helping to fund the programs involved while simultaneously diminishing the perception that participants are receiving handouts.

When everyone pays and everyone benefits, social welfare is more likely to be accepted as a natural part of daily life for all. It is less likely to be seen as an irritant by those who believe they pay to support "deadbeats," while never themselves receiving any benefit from their payments—perceptions that, however inaccurate, nevertheless influence behavior. Under a more universal system, it is easier to justify progressive taxes that transfer a larger proportion of program costs to the wealthy.

Providing multiple levels of benefits is another means by which universal systems can be strengthened. In Sweden, as we have seen, many programs provide two levels of benefits: basic and supplemental. Basic benefits are provided to everyone, supplemental benefits to those with special needs. All elderly people, for example, receive a basic pension, while those with special physical or economic needs also are given special housing allowances to supplement their pensions.

Such an arrangement has at least two advantages. Providing basic benefits to everyone attests to society's interest in the well-being of all citizens and contributes to a stable, productive societal structure. By making supplemental benefits available to those with special needs, society acknowledges both the needs and its obligation to help those who are more vulnerable. When everyone receives some benefits while those with special needs receive special help, society's sense of community is strengthened.

Whatever the specific strategies involved, the move from a selective to a universal system of social welfare would strengthen the U.S. social welfare system. The stigma associated with a selective approach would be greatly reduced, thereby lessening resentment against social welfare professionals and those they serve. Such a move would provide social welfare personnel and consumers with more opportunities to participate in societal decision making and reduce their need to defend social welfare programs and those they serve from critics fixated on inefficiencies. While inefficiencies should be corrected, they are not the most important issue we must face. More important, as I see it, is the need to craft social welfare programs that ensure adequate levels of income maintenance as well as providing high-quality personal services for those who need them.

Improving Social Welfare Services

Two kinds of improvements are needed in social welfare services. First, services must be made more "user friendly." Second, they must be staffed with competent, appropriately rewarded staff.

If services are to be used, they must be accessible. Unfortunately, social welfare services are sometimes located where they are physically inaccessible to people, especially those who must rely on public transportation. Lengthy, confusing, or complicated application procedures can also reduce access. So, too, can the way in which applicants are treated. If people are made to feel uncomfortable, unwanted, or misunderstood, or if they perceive that they are being treated disrespectfully, incompetently, or in a discriminatory or culturally insensitive manner, they are far less likely to make use of the services involved. User-friendly services are physically, emotionally, culturally, and financially accessible. The Swedish example of provision of social services to immigrants is an example of what can be done. (See "Maximizing Access to Social Welfare for Immigrants in Sweden.")

Effective services depend heavily on the people who provide them. Personnel should be properly trained, their workloads realistic, and their working conditions conducive to maintaining their motivation and sense of professional purpose.

This is not always the case. Sometimes, in an attempt to save money, agencies hire inadequately trained paraprofessionals rather than hiring more expensive professionals. Too often, workers struggle with unrealistic workloads that frustrate their attempts to provide adequate services. Sometimes social welfare personnel work in environments in which their privacy and even physical safety is compromised, or earn salaries far below the level appropriate for their education and work responsibilities.

It is sometimes difficult to gain recognition for the fact that effective helping requires education and training. Seeing helping as "natural" or "instinctive," some people believe social work requires goodheartedness but little intellect. Such attitudes display little awareness of the training, ability to analyze problems, and

---

MAXIMIZING ACCESS TO SOCIAL WELFARE FOR IMMIGRANTS LIVING IN SWEDEN

Sweden has taken a number of unusual steps to ensure that social welfare services are accessible to immigrants. A concerted effort is made to reduce the economic, cultural, emotional, and geographic barriers to participation in Swedish society, including the social welfare system. Among the major elements of that effort are:

1 Free Swedish language instruction
2 700 hours of leave from work to study Swedish
3 Several hours of native language instruction per week in their own community for all children from preschool through the secondary level
4 Grants to fund the publication of Swedish literature in immigrants' languages and the purchase of foreign literature by local libraries

5 Funding to assist the ethnic press
6 Grants to fund national immigration organizations to help members maintain their ethnic identity and provide a vehicle for the public expression of that identity
7 A policy that all aliens who have resided in Sweden for at least 3 years may vote and run for local and regional office (but not for the national Parliament)
8 A policy that all applicants have the right to receive help from social welfare agencies in their native language, and a program of courses to train interpreters for this task
9 An ombudsman to counteract ethnic discrimination at work and in other areas of community life.

Source: The Swedish Institute, *Fact Sheets on Sweden: Immigrants in Sweden,* FS 63. Stockholm: The Swedish Institute, 1993.

intellectual demands required of professional helpers. In reality, social workers and other social welfare professionals need *both* hearts and heads in good working order.

All social welfare personnel should be educated and trained to be competent practitioners. Competence must, of course, be defined in terms of the tasks to be performed. Volunteers, paraprofessionals, and professionals perform different tasks requiring different levels of knowledge and skill. Their training should reflect these differences, although all should be thoroughly schooled in the meaning and application of the values that guide social welfare practice.

Once they are educated, the different types of professional helpers should be assigned tasks appropriate to their levels of competence. The inappropriate use of personnel is illogical, counterproductive, and wasteful.

At the organizational level, agency and program administrators should resist the tendency to base personnel requirements on cost rather than competence. They must be willing to advocate for additional funds when needed, and to create ways to use personnel with different competencies. The current tendency for social welfare administrators to have business backgrounds, but little or no social work training or practice experience, limits their ability to understand the importance of competence and related issues.

Recruiting and retaining competent personnel requires providing rewarding and meaningful careers. People considering a social welfare career usually find intrinsic satisfaction in helping others, and this motivation is a powerful incentive. However, one's occupation is also a source of self-esteem as well as the income needed to obtain the resources necessary for daily life, for personal or family needs, and so on. Improving salary levels and enhancing the value attached to careers in social welfare are both essential if social welfare professions are to attract sufficient numbers of competent people.

Working conditions are also important. Social welfare personnel who feel overworked and underappreciated are likely to become alienated, discouraged, and ineffective (Simpkin, 1983:45–112). When stress and disappointment become intolerable, people change jobs. Many nurses, for example, have abandoned their profession in recent years because of poor working conditions and inadequate salaries. Teachers too sometimes find the stresses involved in public school teaching too difficult and unrewarding. These stresses include fears for personal safety, inadequate instructional materials, and unmotivated or unprepared students. And all social welfare personnel find it tiresome and discouraging to have to continually justify the value of their work in response to attacks in the media and expressions of doubt from friends and acquaintances (Wells, 1989:169–178).

Working for Environmental Change

Helping individuals solve their personal and collective problems is a major function of social welfare. However, it cannot be the only one. The environment in which people live affects their behavior in powerful ways. It serves either to support or impede people's efforts to live healthy, satisfying lives. Therefore, part of the task of social welfare is to help create an environment that is conducive to healthy living.

That effort must concern itself with both the physical and social environments. Factors in the physical environment, such as the quality of water, air, and farm land, affect people's physical health. Similarly, people's lives are influenced by a variety of factors in the social environment. The physical and organizational features of the workplace, discrimination, economic pressures, adequacy of neighborhood services, housing quality, family or community violence, and respect for human rights all are important facets of the human environment. In the absence of a healthy environment, social welfare must continually address problems that could be prevented through environmental change.

Bringing about such changes often involves politics. Governmental decision making has a major effect on the conditions under which people live. It is through government that we determine how resources will be used, create legislation that affects people's rights, reaffirm values and behaviors that respect human life, and ensure safe working conditions.

One way for social welfare organizations and professionals to influence that process is through their own direct participation. This is reasonable and legitimate. However, it is also important for them to involve the network of social agencies and users of services in such efforts. This is especially important at the state and local levels, where many decisions are made that affect daily life.

In addition to governmental decisions, the physical and social environment is also deeply affected by the decisions of many other large organizations. These decisions, too, need to be monitored. Large corporations, for example, make many decisions that affect working conditions, resources available for charitable purposes, and levels of economic investment in the community and the larger society. The decisions of transnational corporations affect people and living conditions here and in other nations. Social agencies themselves make policies that influence the services delivered and their effectiveness.

Participation in politics and monitoring the decisions of large organizations are only two of the possible ways to influence the environment. Boycotts of organizations that exploit people, and protests such as sit-ins, rent strikes, and letter-writing campaigns also can be effective tools for change.

Mobilizing people for social action is an important tactic for bringing about environmental change. Mobilization is essential and requires hard work, but it is possible. Some social welfare workers may not recognize the importance of this part of their work or may be uncomfortable with social action. In addition, users of social welfare services often feel disenfranchised because of their limited education, minority status, or fear that political or social action will lead to the loss of their benefits. They may also feel hopeless about the potential for change, or intimidated by feelings of powerlessness and confusion about systems that are strange to them. Helping people empower themselves and become effective change agents is an important social work responsibility.

Social welfare professionals must continue to promote social change that enhances human functioning. Playing an active role in such efforts promotes feelings of hope and empowerment, and strengthens social welfare's role in society.

The ultimate goal is for social welfare professionals and consumers to be allied as active participants in social planning so that the environment of the future is one that promotes healthy and satisfying human life. This is most likely to occur if helping professionals actively seek such a role and are tireless in their monitoring of decision making that affects social welfare. Understanding the importance of solidarity with those they serve is also essential for developing coalitions powerful enough to bring about change.

WHY WE CAN'T AFFORD TO FAIL: NATIONAL AND INTERNATIONAL PERSPECTIVES

The success of social welfare is important for the world's future. From a national perspective, the costs of social problems are unacceptably high. We need to stop spending billions of dollars on prisons in which inmates spend years of idleness. We must stop losing people to AIDS and other preventable diseases. We must help people avoid becoming so mired in poverty that they are unable to be productive citizens. We must stop losing young people to drugs and to lives of ignorance because they drop out of school. We must stop wasting the abilities of women and members of other oppressed groups. We must stop losing the contributions of our elders whose productive lives are prematurely ended by poor-quality health and personal care.

Instead, social welfare resources should be used to prevent problems and to enhance human functioning. Does it really make sense to focus our energies and resources on short-term solutions to problems, knowing that they will reoccur again and again? Doesn't it make more sense to see human development as a long-term investment, much as we see economic development? Unless we do so, costs will continue to escalate and conditions under which people live will worsen. Investing in human development is expensive. Over the long run, however, the result will be a healthier and more productive society.

If we fail to invest in people, we may come to regret our failure to do so. A stratified society in which the very wealthy coexist with those who live in poverty with little hope of escape is a bomb waiting to explode. When affluence is flaunted in the media, and when new accounts of white-collar crime in business and government are reported almost daily, we can expect that those who are poor and alienated will become increasing restless. If having money and the things money can buy is seen as the way to achieve social acceptance, poor and alienated people will take steps to be part of the mainstream. Ultimately, those who feel alienated may come to believe that they have little to lose by simply taking what they want.

We need to learn from the negative experiences of other countries in which there are vast socioeconomic differences between classes. In societies with large numbers of poor and uneducated people, crime and harshly repressive efforts to control crime are common. These are the conditions under which military rule and dictatorships flourish. Once these patterns are established, it is very difficult to break them or to establish democracy. While this may not yet be a likely scenario in the United

States, we must realize that the decisions we make about social welfare today have implications for the polarization of social classes in the future. This, in turn, will affect the future of democracy and capitalism in the United States.

These issues also have international implications. As a multicultural society, the United States is host to large numbers of immigrants from societies where poverty and dictatorships are common. An effective social welfare system is critical to their integration into our society. If we fail to help immigrants—whether they have entered the country legally or illegally—become productive citizens, they may require costly long-term assistance or resort to crime in order to survive.

Increasingly, our ability to remain a world economic leader depends on an educated and flexible workforce. Unless the social welfare and business communities work together more effectively in the future, the United States will fall further behind in its ability to compete in the international marketplace. Devising policies that key social welfare services to conditions in the workplace and governmental fiscal practices will require creative thinking and close cooperation among the major social institutions of American society. For a model of how such cooperation can be achieved, we can look to Sweden.

ON THE STREET IN GOTHENBURG— EDUCATION FOR EMPLOYMENT

When I entered a gift shop in Gothenburg, Sweden, I was greeted and offered assistance by a young woman. Her knowledge of the store's merchandise turned out to be limited, but she was able to obtain any needed information from the other clerk, an older woman.

As I paid for my purchases, I asked the more experienced woman if the other was her daughter. She laughed and said no. She then explained that the clerk who had waited on me was a high school student who, as part of her studies, spent several weeks in the workplace to learn about different types of jobs and the work skills required. All Swedish young people do this during their schooling.

This is one example of Swedish coordination of education and labor policies. Sweden believes that education is essential if its workers are going to participate effectively in a rapidly changing and increasingly complex workplace. Skilled workers will in turn enable Swedish businesses to be efficient and effective competitors in the world economy. The goal is to maintain a high level of productivity so that Sweden can continue to fund its impressive network of social welfare services.

Education in Sweden prepares students for the world of work in other ways as well. In addition to the usual academic curricula, there are well-developed vocational and continuing education programs. All Swedish students learn English as well as Swedish in school, and they are encouraged to study other languages as well. The public radio stations even have instructional programs to teach listeners popular languages such as French and German.

Even child-care centers are designed to contribute to the productivity of the workforce. These programs, which provide day care for all children of preschool age, are intended to give women equal access to the job market. This not only helps provide women with equal opportunity in the workplace, it also results in a larger workforce of higher quality.

And the children themselves are not ignored. Child-care centers do not attempt to teach children to read and write. This takes place when the children go to school. Instead, they are taught social skills—how to get along with others, follow instructions, and be patient. These are skills that come in handy in the workplace, and are useful in many daily living situations as well.

We can see, then, how Sweden coordinates social welfare policy (education, in this case) with labor policy. This type of integrated planning helps to ensure that social institutions work together to achieve societal goals.

Source: Personal observations of Ron Federico, 1987.

Finally, we need to recognize that the United State's continued ability to provide leadership in the world community will depend on its commitment to human values. We have long been vulnerable to accusations that we allow and perpetrate at home the very human rights abuses we sometimes seek to prevent abroad. Our international economic policies and the practices of U.S.-based transnational corporations routinely contribute to the underdevelopment of other nations and to the maintenance of dictatorships.

The scandal of widespread homelessness amid affluence in the United States leads others to question our commitment to social justice and human well-being. The success of our social welfare system's efforts on behalf of the most vulnerable and oppressed among us is vital to the legitimacy of our claim to moral leadership in the world community.

The United States is a major player in the world economic system. It is a major participant in international lending; U.S.-controlled transnational corporations are active throughout the world. The economic power of the United States can be used to help other societies solve their economic problems and to encourage the realization of social justice and individual freedom.

U.S. corporations, however, have been ambivalent about assuming this role, either at home or abroad. Government policy has done little to encourage or to require good corporate citizenship. Choices need to be made between maximizing profit and fostering democratic social development; the two are often incompatible. In the long run, helping other nations develop in a way that minimizes social problems will, we believe, prove the least expensive alternative, reducing the probability of having to deal with large numbers of refugees, dictatorships that become hostile toward the United States, and requests for financial aid.

One difficulty is figuring out how to wean free-market capitalists from their preference for short-term profits regardless of social costs. The earth's resources are finite. How to develop and enforce sustained-use policies which are fair to all the people of Planet Earth while still permitting free enterprise to flourish is a question of critical importance.

Of the four countries we have been studying, the United States seems the most reluctant to develop and implement plans that would regulate the use of nonrenewable resources. Indeed, the trend in the United States in recent years has been in favor of deregulation accompanied by accelerating exploitation of finite resources. Change will have to occur if we are to share resources more equitably with others, to live harmoniously with other nations in which longer-range planning is a way of life, and to avoid the extinction of countless species which play important ecological roles in the biosphere upon which all life depends.

CONCLUSION

Social welfare has a role to play that is central to the future of our society and our role in world affairs. We must improve the linkages between social welfare and the other institutions of society if we are to move toward a future with fewer problems and more opportunities for all.

As you finish reading this book, we hope that you feel a sense of accomplishment about what you have learned. The facts you have acquired will be useful in your own life, and in the lives of those you love. For some of you, this knowledge will also be useful in your work. You have a better understanding, too, of how society works and social welfare's role in the larger social fabric. Finally, you are aware of some of the issues that will shape our future.

As you think further about what you have learned, we hope you will realize how many opportunities you have to affect the future. Knowledge is power. Our final hope is that you will use your knowledge to make the world of today and tomorrow better for everyone.

STUDY QUESTIONS

1 What do you consider to be the most serious issue facing the United States in the years ahead? How can the social welfare institution help to resolve it?

2 Go to the library and locate the most recent census data for your community. (The reference librarian can assist you.) Look at the data from 1960 to the present and identify as many demographic changes as you can—the number of elderly people, for example, or the population of racial group members. Briefly discuss the impact on the social welfare system in your community of each change you identify.

3 Interview a social welfare professional in your community. Learn as much as you can about the aspects of the position involved and the working conditions that your respondent finds most frustrating. Find out how your respondent handles these frustrations.

4 Interview one of your local legislators concerning the problems facing your community that he or she views as most pressing. Ask your respondent to discuss how the social welfare system can help solve these problems.

5 Research the current employment, education, and housing situation in Mexico. Compare your findings with similar data from the United States. Then discuss briefly how the two countries can help each other solve these problems.

KEY TERMS AND CONCEPTS

social compact

REFERENCES

Axthelm, Pete. 1988. Somebody else's kids. *Newsweek,* April 25, pp. 64–68.

Bane, Mary Jo. 1988. Politics and policies of the feminization of poverty. In Margaret Weir, Ann Skola Orloff, and Theda Skorpol, eds., *The Politics of Social Policy in the United States.* Princeton, NJ: Princeton University Press, pp. 381–396.

Barker, Robert L. 1991. *The Social Work Dictionary,* 2d ed. Washington, DC: National Association of Social Workers.

Bradsher, Keith. 1995. Low ranking for poor American children. U.S. youth among worst off in study of 18 industrialized nations. *The New York Times,* August 14, A1.

Butterfield, Fox. 1988. New Yorkers grow angry over aggressive panhandlers. *The New York Times,* July 28, p. A1.

Center on Budget and Policy Priorities. 1995. Only high-income households have recovered fully from the recession. Washington, DC: Center on Budget and Policy Priorities, October 24.

Harrington, Michael. 1971. *The Other America: Poverty in the United States.* Baltimore: Penguin Books.

Kincannon, C. Lewis. 1983. *Condition of Hispanics in America Today.* Washington, DC: U.S. Government Printing Office.

Kozol, Jonathan. 1995. *Amazing Grace: The Lives of Children and the Conscience of a Nation.* New York: Crown.

McCormick, John. 1988. America's third world. *Newsweek,* August 8, pp. 20–24.

Pearce, Diana. 1978. The feminization of poverty: Women, work, and welfare. *Urban and Social Change Review,* 1:28–36.

Rendon, Armando. 1985. *Nosotros. . . . We.* Washington, D.C.: U.S. Government Printing Office.

Rosen, Sumner, with David Fanshel and Mary Lutz, eds. 1987. *Face of the Nation 1987. Statistical Supplement to the 18th Edition of the Encyclopedia of Social Work.* Silver Spring, MD: National Association of Social Workers.

Schorr, Alvin. 1995. Long-term issues. Concept paper circulated by Odyssey Forum, McLean, VA.

Simpkin, Michael. 1983. *Trapped within Welfare,* 2d ed. London: Macmillan.

U.S. Department of Commerce. 1994. *Statistical Abstract of the United States, 1994.* Washington, DC: U.S. Government Printing Office.

Weir, Margaret. 1988. Understanding American social politics. In Margaret Weir, Ann Skola Orloff, and Theda Skorpol, eds., *The Politics of Social Policy in the United States,* Princeton, NJ: Princeton University Press, pp. 3–35.

Wells, Carolyn Cressy. 1989. *Social Work Day to Day,* 2d ed. White Plains, NY: Longman.

ADDENDUM: WELFARE REFORM AND OTHER 1996 SOCIAL WELFARE LEGISLATION[1]

On August 22, 1996, President Clinton signed into law H.R. 3734, the "Personal Responsibility and Work Opportunity Reconciliation Act of 1996." Although he had vetoed two earlier versions of welfare reform legislation, and expressed "strong objections" to the depth of cuts in the Food Stamp Program and to the denial of Federal assistance to legal immigrants and their children in the bill he signed, he was intent upon defusing welfare as an issue which could be used against him and other Democrats by Senator Bob Dole and the Republicans in the 1996 presidential election campaign.

The welfare reform act of 1996 was touted by some supporters as creating work opportunities in inner cities, reducing the rising numbers of out-of-wedlock births, and stemming the flow of immigrants into the United States. Its latent functions included forcing the poor to seek employment in competition with existing low-wage workers, helping to balance the Federal budget by 2002, and providing savings which could be used to finance additional tax cuts for the wealthy. The legislation calls for increased personal responsibility on the part of welfare recipients for moving to self-reliance through work, but provides only minimal supports and work opportunities while making major reductions in food stamps and financial assistance.

The new law is extremely complicated, with local, state, and federal policymakers struggling to interpret it (Englehardt, 1996). Among its major effects, the welfare reform law of 1996:

---

[1]Except as otherwise noted, the information in this addendum is drawn from David Super, Sharon Parrott, Susan Steinmetz, and Cindy Mann. 1996. *The New Welfare Law*. Washington DC: Center on Budget and Policy Priorities.

- cuts $55 billion from Federal expenditures for low-income programs over six years and permits states to divert an additional $40 billion in state funding during the same period;
- abolishes the entitlement, established in the Social Security Act of 1935, of poor women with children to public assistance by replacing Aid to Families With Dependent Children (AFDC) with a block grant program, Temporary Assistance to Needy Families (TANF); requires families receiving TANF to find paid employment within two years, limits them to a lifetime maximum of five years of assistance or work program benefits, and permits states to set time limits as short as states wish, but also permits states to waive the five year limit for up to 20 percent of their caseloads on the basis of hardship;
- reduces food stamp benefits for families with children, the working poor, the elderly, and persons with handicaps by $28 billion, lowering the average food stamp benefit from 80 cents per person per meal in 1996 to 66 cents per person per meal in 1998;
- generally limits poor, unemployed persons between 18 and 50 who are not raising minor children, to 3 months of food stamp benefits while unemployed during any 3 year period;
- denies safety net protection including Supplemental Security Income, Medicaid, and food stamps to most *legal* immigrants (illegal immigrants were already ineligible for these programs);
- pushes 2.6 million people including 1.1 million children—largely from the working poor since nearly all welfare recipients were already below the poverty line—into poverty;
- deepens and intensifies child poverty by increasing the "poverty gap"—the total amount of income needed to bring all families above the poverty line—by 20 percent (more than $4 billion); and
- decreases the incomes of 8.2 million families—1 in 5 U.S. families with children—by an average of $1300 per year.

Most of the $55 billion in Federal savings comes from areas other than AFDC, $28 billion from cuts in food stamps and $22 billion from cuts in safety-net programs for legal immigrants.

Historically, the Federal social safety-net was created in response to states failing to meet the needs of the poor. In the early 1970s, for example, when the states were allowed to set eligibility levels, food assistance reached fewer than one-fifth of the people living in poverty (Englehardt, 1996). Nevertheless, the new law returns much public responsibility for responding to basic survival needs of the poor from the Federal level to the states.

There is serious question about whether the states have sufficient resources to meet the mandates of the new Federal law. Under the essentially fixed funding available through TANF, states will receive Federal support equal to what they received for AFDC in 1994 regardless of changes in their level of need. Because welfare caseloads in general declined between 1994 and 1996, many states will at first receive more than enough funds to maintain services to families eligible for

TANF. However, in event of a nationwide recession, states are likely to exhaust their Federal block grants and their share of the $2 billion "contingency fund" provided by the legislation.

Funding for mandated work programs also is inadequate. According to the Congressional Budget Office (CBO), the legislation falls $12 billion short of meeting the costs of its work requirements other than child care from 1996 through 2002. And, by 2002, child care funding is projected to fall short an additional $1.8 billion.

In spite of the loss of the Federal AFDC safety-net, 1996 saw improvements won by advocates in some other important aspects of social welfare. Funding for Head Start and the Child Care and Development Block Grant was increased. The Health Insurance Portability and Accountability Act of 1996 will make it more difficult for insurance companies to deny coverage to persons with health problems. The Newborns' and Mothers' Health Protection Act of 1996 protects infant and maternal health by requiring insurance companies to pay for at least 48 hours of hospitalization following normal births and 96 hours of hospitalization following Caesarean births. The Mental Health Parity Act of 1996 requires insurers to treat mental health problems like any other illness when limiting benefits. And, perhaps most important, the Federal minimum wage was increased by 90 cents to $5.15 per hour effective September 1, 1997 (Children's Defense Fund, 1996:1, 14-15).

Many congressional proposals which would have further weakened the social welfare institution were defeated in 1996. They included a balanced budget amendment to the U.S. Constitution which, if enacted, would require additional draconian cuts in public welfare expenditures; proposals to "block-grant" Medicaid, food stamps, school lunches, foster care, adoption assistance, and to drastically cut Supplemental Security Income; amendments allowing states to bar children of illegal immigrants from attending public schools and to deport children of legal immigrants who received any benefits for 12 months; and the Istook amendment which would have severely limited the ability of nonprofit organizations to use their *nongovernmental* funds to advocate or lobby (Children's Defense Fund, 1996:15).

With the re-election of a Democrat as President and continued Republican control of Congress, the future of social welfare programs in the United States will continue to be contested. Whether states choose to reduce costs by adopting ever shorter periods of eligibility and ever lower rates of benefits in a "race to the bottom," or whether they opt for programs which genuinely make work pay and remove barriers to increased self-reliance, will depend both on available resources and on the ability of advocates to generate political will.

Throughout the United States anti-hunger advocates have agreed to work together in 1997 to try to reverse some of the setbacks of 1996. Second Harvest, Bread for the World, the Food Research and Action Center and other organizations have launched a campaign to reduce domestic hunger under the banner "Hunger Has a Cure." The advocates are 1) seeking national legislation to improve and expand the federal nutrition programs, 2) strengthening state-level anti-hunger advocacy work, 3) encouraging increased charitable efforts, and 4) promoting policies that improve job prospects for low-income people and address other causes of poverty (Englehardt, 1996).

With the devolution of considerable responsibility for social welfare to the states likely to continue, advocates are increasing their state level efforts. In Maine, for example, the Maine Coalition for Food Security is working to implement the recommendations of the State of Maine Blue Ribbon Commission on Hunger and Food Security. Among them: increasing the state minimum wage; creating a state earned income credit; establishing an "out of poverty wage" which would bring a family of three with a full-time, year-round breadwinner above the poverty line; eliminating state income tax liabilities for low-income workers; and making affordable, good quality child care and health care available to families of working poor people (Benson and Whitaker, 1996). As the full impact of the welfare reform legislation is felt, increased mobilization of low-income persons and their conscience constituency allies seems likely.

Bill Whitaker
(December 1996)

REFERENCES

Children's Defense Fund. 1996. *CDF Reports,* 17(12).
Englehardt, Lynette. 1996. *The 1996 Welfare Law.* Silver Spring, MD: Bread for the World.
Super, David, Sharon Parrott, Susan Steinmetz, and Cindy Mann. 1996. *The New Welfare Law.* Washington, DC: Center on Budget and Policy Priorities.
Benson, Joyce, and William Whitaker. 1996. *Food for Life and Work Through Normal Channels: Ending Hunger in Maine. Report of the Maine Blue Ribbon Commission on Hunger and Food Security.* Augusta, ME: Maine State Planning Office.

GLOSSARY

active choice Social welfare systems result from choices made by individuals, families, communities, agencies, legislatures, courts, and others about what the functions and structure of social welfare ought to be. Such choices reflect prevailing values, needs, resources, power relationships, and decision-making structures and processes. The social welfare system is neither inevitable nor unchangeable, but rather is the product of thousands of human choices which are constantly being made.

acquired immune deficiency syndrome (AIDS) A deadly infection caused by the human immunodeficiency virus (HIV), a sexually transmitted and blood-borne retrovirus that undermines and ultimately destroys the immune system. AIDS is transmitted through the exchange of body fluids during sex, transfusions of contaminated blood, and sharing needles when injecting drugs.

Aid to Families with Dependent Children (AFDC) The federal/state funded assistance program in the United States that provides support for children in families in need because of the incapacity, death, continued absence, or unemployment of a parent. AFDC is the largest, most costly U.S. public assistance program and is commonly referred to as "welfare."

almshouses Institutional shelters in which a bed, food, and minimal physical care were provided for worthy destitute individuals and families who could not care for themselves in their own homes.

anemia A condition in which lack of dietary iron causes deficiency in red blood cells or hemoglobin in the blood. Anemia affects both men and women, and has major consequences for women during pregnancy and lactation. Anemia results in impaired work performance, body temperature regulation, behavior, and intellectual performance; decreased resistance to infections; and increased susceptibility to lead poisoning.

balance of trade   The relationship between the economic values of a nation's imports and exports. When a country's imports exceed its exports, the result is a trade deficit.

beneficiary constituencies   Persons who stand to benefit directly if a social reform effort is successful.

blaming the victim   The process by which middle-class liberals and others justify inequality by finding defects in the victims of inequality. The process enables victim blamers to reconcile their class interests with their humanitarian impulses. By focusing on the defects of the individual, victim blamers overlook personal strengths and environmental factors such as unequal distribution of income, social stratification, political struggle, ethnic and racial group conflict, and inequality of power.

block grants   Federal grants to states that are earmarked for a specific social welfare purpose and are accompanied by relatively few guidelines regarding program design and implementation. Block grants for local health, education, and welfare needs marked a major shift from federal to state responsibility for social welfare.

case manager   A person who coordinates the efforts of staff in an agency or several agencies to meet the needs of a given client through professional teamwork.

case services   Remedial, selectively provided personal social services intended to help those with personal maladjustments, problems, illness, or other difficulties. Psychotherapy, marriage counseling, job counseling, medical care, and nursing-home care are examples.

cash benefits   Social welfare resources provided in the form of money. Cash benefits foster maximum freedom of choice for those who receive them.

certification   Official assurance by government or a professional association that a person has attained a specified level of knowledge and skill. See *licensing, registration.*

charity organization society   Social welfare agencies established in the latter part of the 1800s that utilized a "scientific charity" approach to studying the needs of individuals and families, and attempted to reduce duplication of helping efforts by compiling directories of social agencies and registries of families being assisted. The social work method of social casework originated in the charity organization societies.

citizen   A person who, in exchange for allegiance, is entitled to certain rights, privileges and protection from the government. A citizen has rights of membership to a healthy life and human fellowship. Citizens are included in community life, and are provided resources to earn a living or to thrive even if they cannot work.

classical liberalism   The political and economic philosophy that traces its roots to seventeenth- and eighteenth-century thinkers such as Thomas Hobbes, John Locke, and Jeremy Bentham. Classical liberals stressed limited government, free markets, and inalienable human rights.

clinical social worker   An MSW social worker who uses counseling and related services to treat and prevent emotional and mental disorders. The term is sometimes used interchangeably with social caseworker or psychiatric social worker. Clinical social workers often work in mental health agencies or in private practice.

code of ethics   A statement of the values, principles, and rules of a profession, regulating the conduct of its members.

committee of inquiry   A group of professionals assembled under the auspices of a professional association to determine if any wrongdoing has been committed by or against a peer.

common human needs   Needs shared by all human beings that are basic to human survival and development.

Communist Manifesto   A document, published in 1848 by Karl Marx and Friedrich Engels, which claimed to demonstrate through "scientific socialism" the historical inevitability of working-class victory over capitalists.

compassion   Sympathetic consciousness of other's distress, together with a desire to alleviate it. See *empathy*.

conflict   A condition in which there exists an opposition of alternatives; a situation in which more than one choice is possible.

conscience constituencies   Supporters of a reform effort who do not themselves stand to benefit directly from its success.

Contract with America   The 1994 Republican campaign platform which appealed simplistically and effectively to mainstream values and fears, helped elect Republican majorities in the House of Representatives and the Senate, and initiated major changes in social welfare.

contracting   The practice of hiring private agencies to carry out specified public social welfare activities—such as delivering social services—in return for payment from public funds.

cross-cultural comparative perspective   The approach to learning taken in this book, in which varying national responses to common human needs are contrasted.

culture   The rules concerning what are perceived to be the most significant aspects of everyday life and which are followed by members of groups and organizations within a social environment.

declassification   The practice of reducing the amount of education and experience required for performing a job.

deinstitutionalization   The practice of releasing people from residential institutions and placing them in the community, where help can be provided in less restrictive ways through the use of community support systems.

democratic socialism   The belief that the transition to socialism can be achieved peacefully, through legislated reforms, without resorting to revolutionary violence. Democratic socialists stress that civil rights must be safeguarded and contend that without freedom there cannot be socialism.

Earned Income Tax Credit   A means-tested, refundable federal tax credit in the United States that supplements the wages primarily of low-income working families with children.

economic depression   A socioeconomic condition in which business activity is lowered for a prolonged time, unemployment rates are high, and purchasing power is greatly diminished.

Economic Opportunity Act of 1964   The centerpiece of President Johnson's War on Poverty, which provided services through which it was hoped the poor would escape poverty and which, for a time, also attempted to shift the balance of political power in favor of the poor.

economic recession   A milder or shorter version of economic depression.

eligibility requirements   Conditions which must be met in order to receive a social welfare benefit.

Elizabethan Poor Law of 1601   Codified a system of national standards for social welfare providing for categorizing the poor, for local parish-level administration, and for a land tax to generate public funds for social welfare services when private charity was insufficient for this purpose. This was the first such use of public funds and the first formal acknowledgment in England of governmental responsibility for the well-being of citizens.

empathy   The act of perceiving, experiencing, and responding to the emotional state, ideas, and circumstances of another person.

entitlement   The principle that government should be responsible for guaranteeing to all eligible persons, as a right of membership, benefits necessary to meet their common needs.

entitlement programs   Government-funded benefits of cash, goods, or services that are guaranteed to all people who meet eligibility requirements. Examples include Medicare in the United States and health services in Sweden.

family   Any grouping of one or more adults sharing affection, resources, residence, and responsibility for any children which may be present. Family functions include regulating sex behavior, child bearing and child rearing, providing for the economic and emotional needs of its members, and socializing children to become successful participants in society. Traditional conceptualization distinguished nuclear families, consisting of married pairs of adults and their children, and extended families of one or more nuclear families and a network of persons related by blood or marriage. Extended families often included representatives of more than two generations.

family allowances   Benefits, also known as child allowances, in which every eligible family, regardless of financial need, is allocated a specified sum of money for the benefit of its children.

fertility rates   Total fertility rates report the number of children that would be born per woman, if she were to live to the end of her child-bearing years and bear children at each age in accordance with prevailing age-specific fertility rates.

501(c)3 and 501(c)4 organizations   U.S. Internal Revenue Service designation for charitable nonprofit public benefit organizations. 501(c)3 and 501(c)4 agencies and associations are exempt from paying federal and many local and state taxes. In addition, contributions to 501(c)3 organizations are tax deductible by their donors. Because 501(c)4 organizations may lobby and participate in political action, contributions to them are not tax deductible.

formal social welfare programs   Programs which are organized, structured responses to need.

Freedmen's Bureau   The first federally funded and operated welfare agency. Founded to assist former slaves, the agency distributed food and medical supplies to both blacks and whites, and established schools and orphanages for black children.

friendly visitors   The workers (initially untrained) who did investigations for the charity organization societies. Together with settlement house workers, friendly visitors were predecessors of social workers.

general assistance (GA)   Means-tested financial and other aid provided from state and/or local funds to persons in the United States who are ineligible for federally subsidized assistance programs such as SSI or AFDC. GA, sometimes called "general relief" or "town assistance," is often a highly stigmatized assistance of last resort.

generalist approach   An approach to problem solving that attempts to address all of the needs being experienced by the people experiencing the problem.

goiter   Enlargement of the thyroid gland, visible as swelling of the throat, which results from iodine deficiency. May be accompanied by severe mental retardation.

Great Society   The Economic Opportunity Act of 1964 and other programs, which constituted President Lyndon Baines Johnson's "War on Poverty."

halfway houses   Small residential facilities that provide treatment and supervision while at the same time allowing residents to be at least partially integrated into community life.

health maintenance organization (HMO)   Health-care organization that provides comprehensive medical care for a set, prepaid fee.

holistic approach   An attempt to understand and treat the whole person or phenomenon by taking into account and integrating all the relevant social, cultural, psychological, and physical influences. This way of thinking recognizes that, as biological, psychological, and social beings, people seek to meet their needs through interpersonal relationships and the social structures in their environment. This unity of the biological, psychological, and social components of humans has come to be called the biopsychosocial whole.

houses of correction   Residential institutions similar to prisons established under the Elizabethan Poor Law. With major stigma and severe degrees of social control, they housed criminals, vagrants, workhouse residents who violated the rules, and other persons deemed unworthy.

human diversity   The biological, psychological, social, and cultural differences among people that affect the ways their needs are expressed and satisfied. Some of the most significant types of diversity are gender, age, race, ethnicity, physical and mental health, sexual orientation, and socioeconomic class.

human immunodeficiency virus (HIV)   A sexually transmitted and blood-borne retrovirus that undermines and ultimately destroys the immune system. See *acquired immune deficiency syndrome (AIDS).*

humanism   An intellectual reaction against Roman Catholicism. Humanist philosophers disputed the literal interpretation of the Bible and advocated a more just and equal world based on reason rather than church teachings.

hunger   In the United States, hunger is defined as the mental and physical condition that comes from not eating enough food due to insufficient economic, family, or community resources. In 1995, an estimated 4 million U.S. children under 12 experienced hunger sometime during the year, and another 9.6 million children under 12 lived in households at risk of hunger. See *stunting, underweight, wasting.*

income maintenance programs   Social welfare programs that attempt to ensure adequate financial resources for people.

indenture   A type of child welfare service formalized by the Elizabethan Poor Law in which orphans and children who had been removed from needy, therefore "unsuitable," families were placed in the homes of "proper" people who agreed to provide care in return for the child's labor.

indoor relief   Social welfare support provided within residential institutions rather than to a person living in his or her own home.

Industrial Revolution   The era in which machine power replaced human and animal power in the production process, generally said to have first begun on a large scale in England during the 1600s.

infant mortality rate (IMR)   The number of deaths of infants under 1 year of age per 1,000 live births. More specifically, the probability of dying between birth and exactly 1 year of age.

informal (or natural) helping networks Family, friends, neighbors, local churches, synagogues, and mosques, service organizations, and others who provide either spontaneous charity or mutual support in times of need.

in-kind services Social welfare resources provided as needed commodities themselves rather than in cash. Food assistance and medical care are examples.

institutional approach to social welfare An approach that emphasizes the preventive role of social welfare in modern industrial societies. From an institutional perspective, social welfare is a "mainline" social institution—on equal footing with the family, religion, the economy, and government—in which programs are permanent and provide for the overall security and emotional support of people. From the institutional perspective, social welfare should play a normative, ongoing role in modern industrial societies.

institutional discrimination Discrimination which, in the hands of people with power, raises to the level of social structure the tendency to use superiority as a solution to discomfort about difference.

laissez faire economics The doctrine attributed to Adam Smith that an efficient and productive economy is best achieved by minimizing governmental intervention in economic activities.

latent functions of social welfare The less visible, and sometimes unintentional, effects of social welfare programs that often serve the special needs of powerful groups in society.

less eligibility The Elizabethan Poor Law principle that no unemployed person receiving public assistance should be better off than the lowest-paid self-supporting worker.

licensing Formal governmental authorization of the use of a title and the practice of a profession. See *certification, registration.*

life expectancy at birth The number of years newborn children would live if subject to the mortality risks prevailing for a cross section of the population at the time of their birth.

life span The period from conception to death, usually discussed as chronological stages, each associated with a distinctive set of social expectations about how needs will be met.

literacy rates Adult literacy rates report the percentage of people aged 15 and over who can read and write. Persons are considered functionally illiterate if their reading and writing skills are inadequate for use in normal socioeconomic relationships.

low birth weight Birth weights less than 2,500 grams (about 5.5 pounds). Infants with low birth weights are commonly referred to as being born prematurely. Such infants are at greater risk of disability, disease, and death than are those born at normal birth weight.

Low-Income Home Energy Assistance (LIHEAP) U.S. federally funded block grants to states and other jurisdictions to help low-income households meet the costs of home heating and/or cooling.

manifest functions of social welfare The intended and recognized consequences of social welfare programs.

Marxism The ideology based on the works of Marx and Engels which inspired revolutionary movements in Russia, China, and many parts of the developing world. Marxists argued that, in order to make a profit, capitalist employers had to extract "surplus value" from their employees, exploiting and reducing them to "wage slavery." According to Marxists, the modern state exists to meet the needs of the capitalist class. Capitalism, they contended, would be overthrown when increasing worker "class consciousness" resulted in revolution.

maternal mortality rate The number of deaths of women from pregnancy-related causes per 100,000 live births.

means-tested programs Programs in which benefits are granted to people if their assessed income does not exceed a given—usually fairly low—threshold.

Medicaid A federal/state matching grant program in the United States through which medical services are provided to recipients of Aid to Families with Dependent Children, low-income elderly persons, and other low-income persons with minimal assets.

Medicare An entitlement program in the United States providing access to health care for the elderly and disabled through a combination of payroll taxes, premiums paid by participants, and government subsidies.

micronutrient malnutrition Malnutrition which results from a lack of micronutrients such as vitamin A or iodine. Lack of vitamin A results in permanent blindness for 250,000 children every year and leaves tens of millions more susceptible to the three leading causes of child death: diarrheal disease, measles, and pneumonia. Iodine deficiency disorders including goiter and cretinism affect 200 million people throughout the developing world.

needs Physical, psychological, economic, cultural, and social requirements for survival, well-being, and fulfillment.

neo-liberalism Contemporary political and economic philosophy in which the free-market tenets of classical liberalism are modified only to the extent necessary to give them a more "human face." Under neo-liberalism, workers' protections and benefits that were won through extended social mobilization are being dismantled.

New Deal The Social Security Act of 1935, and other programs of President Franklin Delano Roosevelt, that were intended to bring the United States out of the Great Depression and to provide basic economic and social welfare for U.S. citizens.

not-for-profit agencies Voluntary social welfare organizations established for social purposes other than making money for investors. Examples include organizations such as Catholic Charities USA, the Child Welfare League of America, Big Brothers/Big Sisters, and settlement houses.

Old Age, Survivors, and Disability Insurance (OASDI) A social security program in the United States that partially replaces income lost to a worker or to the worker's family when the worker retires, becomes severely disabled, or dies. Commonly referred to as Social Security.

oral rehydration therapy Oral rehydration therapy (ORT) is an inexpensive, effective remedy which uses salt solutions, rice water, or weak tea to counter the affects of dehydration accompanying diarrhea. Although ORT saves a million lives every year, throughout the world 2 million children under 5 die needlessly each year from such dehydration.

outdoor relief social welfare support provided to persons in their own homes—not in institutions.

paraprofessional A person with specialized knowledge and technical training who works under the supervision of a professional and carries out tasks formerly performed by the professional.

per-capita gross national product The share of the financial value of a country's total output of goods and services theoretically available to each resident if everyone received equal shares.

personal social services   Nonfinancial social welfare programs that enhance people's personal development and functioning. Education, protection from physical and emotional harm, health care, and personal counseling to help people solve problems, manage interpersonal relationships, and participate more effectively in society are examples.

personal troubles   Private matters which occur when an individual feels that his or her cherished values are threatened. Troubles are found within the character of individuals and within the range of their immediate relations with others. See *social problem* or *social issue*.

philosophy   The set of values, ethics, and principles by which one attempts to understand the world, to develop one's perspective on social and economic justice, and to behave.

poverty   Absolute poverty exists when people are unable to afford the least costly satisfaction of a minimum nutritionally adequate diet plus a few other essential nonfood requirements. Relative poverty exists when people are able to satisfy minimum socially accepted needs, but are deprived compared to nonpoor members of their society. Relative poverty lines are generally set at 40 to 50 percent of a nation's median income.

private social welfare programs   Programs funded by voluntary charitable contributions of individuals and private organizations, by fees people pay for the services they receive, or by funds spent by corporations to provide social welfare services to their employees. The public–private distinction in the United States has become increasingly blurred as government grants are used to purchase services from "private" agencies, and government tax breaks are made available to corporations to offset the costs of their "private" welfare expenditures.

privatization   The shift from meeting social needs through public and voluntary not-for-profit social welfare programs to for-profit corporations, partnerships, private practice, and proprietary social services within the private sector.

progressivism   A multifaceted middle-class movement that emphasized parks and beautification, education, the "Americanization" of new citizens, and professionalization, as well as social insurance and regulatory controls. Progressivism popularized the idea that charity is demeaning to both giver and receiver and that collective responses to normal life risks through social insurance are superior to charity. Progressivism put poverty, immigration, slums, child welfare, mental health, public health, and gender and race on the social policy and political agendas.

proprietary social agencies   Businesses which attempt to make a profit for their investors by selling personal social services. For-profit nursing homes and halfway houses, and social workers in private practice, are examples.

Protestant ethic   The belief, based on Protestant religious values, that work fulfills God's will and that those who do not work are sinners.

Protestant Reformation   The social movement of persons who objected to the Roman Catholic doctrine that placed the clergy in the role of intermediary between God and humankind. Protestants argued for a direct relationship between the individual and God, thus eliminating the need for much of the ritual and structure of the Roman Catholic Church. Protestants also placed great emphasis on the value of work and, in at least some instances, tended to view economic success as an indication of personal salvation.

public health approach to social welfare   A strategy emphasizing preventing rather than repairing social problems. The strategy assumes that all persons experience a series of predictable risks during the course of their lives. Since risks are predictable and universal, it is reasonable to develop universal programs in response.

public housing   Residences that are built, maintained, and administered by government to provide low- or no-rent homes for needy people.

public social utilities   Social services that are seen as part of the normal system of response to needs that most people experience at various times during their lives and are made available to all members of society who have a need for them. Public schools, police and fire protection, public parks, public water and sewer systems, and highways are examples. Universally available personal social services also are public social utilities.

public social welfare programs   Programs funded by tax monies.

recession   A milder, shorter form of economic depression.

registration   Listing in a professional registry those persons who have met qualifying criteria such as level of education and duration of supervised practice. See *certification, licensing.*

religion   The social institution that helps people relate to the known and the unknown.

residence requirement   A form of social control in which assistance is provided only to persons who have lived in a community for at least a prescribed time.

residual approach to social welfare   An approach in which the proper role of social welfare is seen as that of limited response to breakdowns in the normal functioning of the economy, the family, or the individual.

revenue sharing   Federal grants provided to the states with nearly complete freedom in how the monies can be used.

safety nets   Systems of public and private social welfare programs which aim to prevent the massive impoverishment of the population.

scientific method   Principles and procedures for the systematic pursuit of knowledge, involving the recognition and formulation of a problem, the collection of data through observation and experiment, and the formulation and testing of hypotheses.

scientific philanthropy   An attempt in the United States during the late 1800s to coordinate the help provided by different social agencies within communities by collecting empirical data about individuals or families receiving assistance. See *charity organization society, friendly visitors.*

selective approach to social welfare   The policy that benefits should be focused on the "truly needy," and relatively little assistance provided to those believed able to care for themselves on their own. Consistent with the residual view that social welfare programs should respond only to breakdowns in the normal functioning of the marketplace, the family, or the individual, selective social welfare programs are usually remedial rather than preventative.

settlement houses   Social welfare agencies established in the late 1800s, primarily to serve immigrants, which used community-oriented approaches to serving people. Settlements were attempts to reduce the distance between socioeconomic classes by moving formally educated, middle- and upper-class volunteers into working-class neighborhoods. The ministers, educators, and college students "settled in" (hence the term "settlement house" or "social settlement") to exchange ideas and information with their new neighbors. The social work methods of social group work and community organization originated in the settlement houses.

social assistance programs   Government-financed, means-tested public transfers provided to people in need who meet certain eligibility conditions for regular or occasional income support. Social assistance is commonly referred to "welfare." Examples include General Assistance and Aid to Families with Dependent Children.

social compact The set of assumptions about what citizens and the government owe each other.

social Darwinism The belief popularized by Herbert Spencer that Darwin's principle of the survival of the fittest applied to humans as well as other species. Social Darwinists argued against help for the needy on the premise that it was right, and natural, that the weak should perish while the strong survived. See *survival of the fittest.*

social environment The social arrangements created by people that serve to structure their daily behavior. Other individuals, families, small groups, organizations and communities, social welfare and other social institutions, our values and beliefs, the norms which guide our behavior, and the roles we play as we interact with others are all part of the human social environment.

social inequality A condition in which some members of a society receive fewer opportunities or benefits than other members.

social insurance Pension, health care, unemployment compensation and similar programs financed by a combination of worker, employer, and/or government payments. Participation depends on previous employment history and, in general, is not means-tested. Old Age, Survivors', and Disability Insurance and Medicare are examples.

social justice A condition in which all members of a society have the same basic rights, protection, opportunities, obligations, and social benefits.

social order Predictable patterns of behavior which enable people to live together. When agreement to follow such patterns breaks down, organized behavior becomes impossible and society disintegrates into a series of unplanned interactions among individuals and groups, making it far more difficult for most people to meet their needs.

social policy A set of decisions intended to achieve a certain level of social welfare or security, either for the whole population or for certain population groups.

social problem or social issue A social condition that is perceived by significant numbers of the population, powerful groups, or charismatic individuals to be a threat to society that could be resolved or remedied. In contrast to personal troubles, social issues involve large numbers of persons and generally stem from environmental conditions rather than from personal shortcomings. See *personal troubles.*

social reform Activity designed to rearrange social institutions or the way they are managed in order to achieve greater social justice or other desired change.

social security As the term is used in most countries, social security consists of programs of social insurance and social assistance aimed at providing existential security to the population. There are five "pillars" of social security: (1) old age, disability, and death benefits; (2) health-care, sickness, and maternity benefits; (3) work-injury compensation; (4) unemployment support; and (5) family allowances.

Social Security Act of 1935 The New Deal legislation that established insurance-based protection of income for retirement, for disabled workers, and dependent survivors of a deceased breadwinner, and means-tested assistance for the elderly, blind, and disabled, and dependent children.

social services Activities of social workers and other professionals in promoting the health and well-being of people and in helping people to become more self-sufficient; preventing dependency; strengthening family relationships; and restoring individuals, families, groups, or communities to successful social functioning.

social welfare A nation's system of programs, benefits, and services that help people meet those social, economic, educational, and health needs that are fundamental to the maintenance of society.

social welfare agency A formal organization whose manifest function is to administer social welfare programs so that they effectively and efficiently meet people's needs.

social worker Term coined by Simon Patten in 1900 to include friendly visitors and residents of settlement houses. Today the term refers to professionally trained persons who help individuals, groups, and communities function optimally and create societal conditions which contribute to that goal.

socialism An economic philosophy which advocates a system of social organization in which private property and the distribution of income are subject to social control, rather than solely to determination of individuals pursuing their own interests or to the market forces of capitalism.

socialization The process through which individuals learn to think, feel, and behave willingly in accordance with the prevailing standards of their culture. Most socialization occurs during infancy and childhood, when behavior patterns and social expectations are learned at home and in school. Socialization continues throughout the life span, although less intensively than during early childhood.

Special Supplemental Food Program for Women, Infants, and Children (WIC) A popular and highly successful preventative health program in the United States that provides nutrition education and a monthly package of nutritious foods tailored to the dietary needs of low-income infants, children under 5, and pregnant, postpartum, and breast-feeding women. Studies indicate that each dollar spent on WIC prenatal benefits saves up to $3 in Medicaid expenditures during the first 6 months of a child's life.

specialist approach An approach to problem solving that utilizes professionals with specialized training to solve particular problems.

standard of need The amount of money—taking into account costs of food, clothing, shelter, utilities, and other necessities—that a state determines is necessary to provide a minimum standard of living in that state for a family of a given size.

strengths-based approach to social work Celebrates the ability of people to survive and to overcome enormous barriers in their social environment and asks how the natural abilities of all persons can be nurtured to enable them to realize their maximum potential.

stunting A measure of height for age against a reference population. Stunting is frequently the outcome of persistent long-term malnutrition. UNICEF defines a child as moderately or severely stunted whose height for age is "below minus two standard deviations" from the median for children in a reference group.

Supplemental Security Income (SSI) The federally funded (frequently state-supplemented) assistance program in the United States that provides a minimum monthly income to low-income persons who are blind, disabled, or older than 65.

supplicant A person without rights, who must earnestly and humbly beg that his or her needs be met. Meeting the needs of supplicants depends on acts of charity, benevolence, or kindness to which they have no entitlement.

supply-side economics The theory, popular under President Ronald Reagan, that lower taxes for the wealthy would result in more money in the economy that would "trickle down" to benefit low-income persons. Belief in supply-side economics influenced Reagan to advocate a combination of reduced government spending for social programs, increased military expenditures, tax cuts for the wealthy, and a balanced federal budget. Opponents characterized supply-side economics as "feeding the sparrows by feeding the horses."

survival of the fittest Charles Darwin's term for the mechanism by which the strongest members of a species are the ones most likely to survive, to breed, and to pass on their genetic traits to future generations. See *social Darwinism.*

systems approach An approach to problem solving that focuses on the many groups in which people live, and the ways in which these groups affect the lives of their members.

tetanus An acute, infectious bacterial disease that is often introduced through an open wound. An early symptom of tetanus is muscle spasms and inability to open the jaws, hence its colloquial name, "lockjaw." Throughout the world, an estimated 50,000 women giving birth and 600,000 newborn children die of tetanus each year.

Thrifty Food Plan The least expensive of four food budgets developed by the U.S. Department of Agriculture. Assuming that most families spend one-third of their household budgets on food, the cost of the Thrifty Food Plan is multiplied by 3 to calculate the poverty line.

trade deficit The result when the value of a country's imports exceeds the value of its exports.

under-five mortality rate (U5MR) The number of deaths each year of children under 5 years of age per 1,000 live births. The U5MR reflects the probability of a child dying before his or her fifth birthday.

U5MR performance gap The difference between the level of U5MR which a country could reasonably be expected to achieve given its per-capita gross national product and its actual level of U5MR.

underweight A measure of weight for age against a reference population.

unemployment insurance The social security program that temporarily replaces part of the wages of most regularly employed U.S. workers who become involuntarily unemployed and are able and willing to work.

universal approach to social welfare A policy in which benefits are made available to all people as needed, independent of their employment records or income. The universal approach is consistent with the institutional view that social welfare programs should be a normal aspect of daily living. Such programs are intended to prevent problems rather than trying to remedy them after they occur.

universal benefits Social resources made available to a nation's citizens or residents as rights of membership, independent of employment record or income. They may be provided in cash, such as Sweden's child allowances, or in kind, such as public education in the United States.

unworthy poor An Elizabethan Poor Law category consisting of able-bodied unemployed—considered irresponsible, lacking in ambition, and potentially dangerous to society. Even today, poor persons deemed unworthy tend to receive lower social welfare benefits than those deemed worthy.

values Customs, standards of conduct, and principles considered desirable by a culture, a group of people, or an individual. Behavior consistent with values is considered ethical behavior.

volunteerism The mobilization and utilization of unpaid individuals and groups to provide human services outside the auspices of government agencies.

War on Poverty   The Economic Opportunity Act of 1964 and related programs, which constituted President Lyndon Baines Johnson's Great Society. Although the War on Poverty was never fully funded, Great Society programs resulted in a major decrease in poverty in the United States.

wasting   A measure of weight for height against a reference population. Wasting is a possible consequence of severe short-term malnutrition.

witch hunts and **red baiting**   Attempts to discredit the ideas and proposals of reformers and to destroy their careers by accusing them of being communists.

worthy poor   Persons with a socially acceptable work history or those who could not be expected to work because of age or infirmity. The poor considered worthy are treated better than the unworthy poor, who because they are considered more to blame for their plight, are subjected to harsher forms of social control.

Workers' Compensation   The U.S. social security program that provides cash benefits and medical care to workers injured on the job and to surviving dependents of workers who are killed in work-related accidents.

workfare   A policy which requires people who receive public assistance to work in return for their benefits.

workhouses   Residential institutions established under the Elizabethan Poor Law, by which government contracted with private individuals to feed and clothe the involuntarily unemployed in exchange for their work. Workhouses sheltered infants, children, older and disabled people, and diseased as well as able-bodied adults.

INDEX